Simply Delicious
COOKING

Editor   Angela Rahaniotis

Graphic Design and Layout   Zapp

Cuisine
Coordinator   Chef Yvan Bélisle

Photography   Michel Bodson

Stylist   Murielle Bodson

© 1991 by Tormont Publications Inc.
338 Saint-Antoine St. East
Montreal, Quebec, Canada H2Y 1A3
Tel. (514) 954-1441
Fax (514) 954-1443

ISBN 2-921171-61-9

Printed in Canada

RON KALENUIK

Simply Delicious COOKING

TORMONT

Foreword

If you are one of those people who simply loves wonderful food, but doesn't want to spend hours in the kitchen preparing it, then *Simply Delicious Cooking* is exactly the cookbook you have been waiting for.

Even if you already own dozens of cookbooks, you probably find yourself relying on the same two or three cherished and well-worn volumes when you are looking for inspiration.

My hope is that *Simply Delicious Cooking* will join that special group of cookbooks. I have carefully selected the recipes to make sure this will be a book you automatically turn to, whether you are planning a quick meal or a gourmet extravaganza.

My own love affair with good food goes back to my boyhood, when I spent hours studying a display on chocolate-making in my home town of Niagara Falls. Since then, I have spent more than 15 years as a professional chef at some of the finest restaurants and hotels in North America.

In those years, I learned first-hand what kinds of foods brought customers back again and again. And those are exactly the kinds of foods I have included in *Simply Delicious Cooking*.

You will find recipes for some of the great classic dishes, as well as for some old standbys, like rice pudding, that never really go out of fashion. You'll find out how to fill your home with the aromas of fresh-baking bread, and how to make some of the wonderful international and regional dishes that are becoming so popular.

In fact, I think you'll find years and years of useful information and tantalizing recipes, recipes that will inspire you even on days when you feel like taking it easy in the kitchen. So welcome to the world of *Simply Delicious Cooking*!

Ron Kalenuik

CONTENTS

Appetizers
p. 8

Pâtés
p. 24

Soups
p. 30

Salads and Dressings
p. 48

Eggs
p. 66

Beef
p. 80

Poultry
p. 98

Pork
p. 122

Veal, Lamb and other Meats
p. 140

Fish and Seafood
p. 158

International Cooking
p. 190

Vegetables
p. 222

Pasta
p. 258

Rice
p. 284

Sauces
p. 294

Cheese
p. 310

Sandwiches
p. 322

Breads
p. 344

Desserts
p. 360

Beverages
p. 410

Microwave
p. 420

Index
p. 440

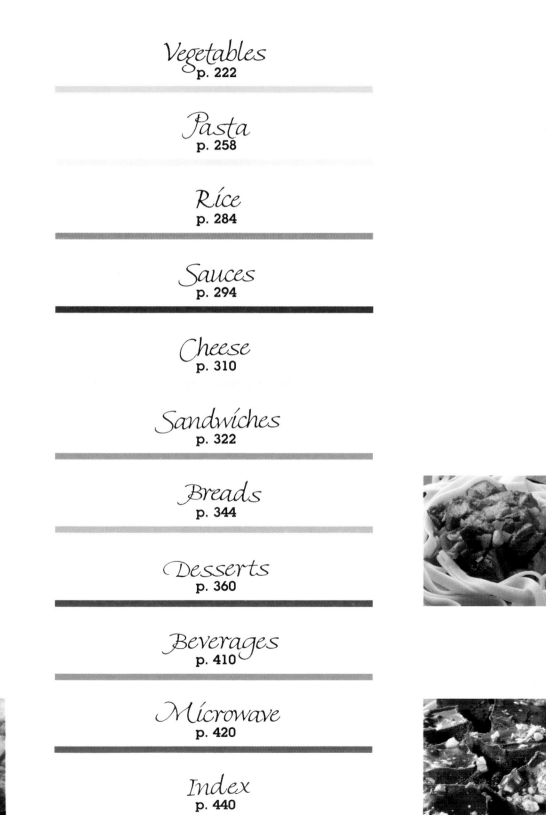

Appetizers

Not so long ago, French chefs avoided the very idea of an appetizer or "starter" course, on the theory that it would destroy the diner's appetite. The Italians had their antipasto and the Russians their famous *zakuska* table, but a fine French meal began with little more than a simple soup, so that everyone would have room for the *pièce de résistance*.

Today, fortunately, good cooks everywhere know that a well selected appetizer or an interesting selection of hors d'oeuvres will pique the appetite for further delights and set the tone for the rest of the meal.

We hope the selection of appetizers in this chapter will whet your appetite and stimulate your interest for further chapters.

You'll find a selection of first courses both hot and cold, ranging from the traditional to the nouveau. We've even included some terrific party dips.

Just remember that you should choose your starter course with the idea of providing a balanced menu, in terms of nutrition, texture and flavor. Play off a rich course against a light one, or an exotic first course against a more simple main course.

Or you can take a slightly different approach, and build a complete meal or party around a selection of recipes from this chapter alone. So here's to great beginnings!

Ham and Cheese Boat

4 servings

1	sheet puff pastry (frozen type)
1	egg yolk
1 tbsp	(*15 mL*) milk
6 oz	(*170 g*) Black Forest ham, thinly sliced
2 tbsp	(*30 mL*) peach jam
2 tbsp	(*30 mL*) prepared mustard
¾ cup	(*180 mL*) grated Havarti cheese

Preheat oven to 350°F (*180°C*).

Thaw the pastry. Mix the egg yolk with the milk.

Brush the ends of the pastry with the egg.

Fold the pastry in half lengthwise. Seal the ends.

Open the center to shape a boat. Layer the bottom and sides with ham.

Mix the peach jam with the mustard. Brush onto ham. Sprinkle with cheese. Brush sides of pastry with egg.

Bake in oven 10 to 12 minutes, or until golden brown.

Ham and Cheese Boat

Mangos in Prosciutto

6 servings

2	medium mangos
12	slices prosciutto
3	limes

Peel and slice mangos into 12 even pieces.

Wrap each piece with a thin slice of prosciutto.

Cut limes in quarters.

Place mangos on a platter and surround with limes.

Almond Cheese Slices

22-24 slices

1 cup	(*250 mL*) blanched almonds
3 tbsp	(*45 mL*) butter
4 oz	(*115 g*) cream cheese
4 oz	(*115 g*) Havarti cheese, grated
2 tbsp	(*30 mL*) finely diced pimiento
2 tsp	(*10 mL*) lemon juice
1 tsp	(*5 mL*) salt
1 tsp	(*5 mL*) Worcestershire sauce
½ tsp	(*3 mL*) paprika

Sauté the almonds in the butter, then chop fine.

In a food processor, blend the cheeses with the remaining ingredients.

Shape into a roll. Place almonds on a piece of wax paper. Roll cheese roll in almonds to coat, wrapping with wax paper.

Refrigerate 2 hours. Remove wax paper and cut into even slices.

Angels on Horseback

24 appetizers

24	oysters
4 tbsp	(*60 mL*) lemon juice
1 tsp	(*5 mL*) salt
½ tsp	(*3 mL*) pepper
1 tsp	(*5 mL*) chopped parsley
12	slices bacon

Shuck the oysters; remove the meat and discard shells.

Mix lemon juice and seasonings together.

Pour lemon juice over oysters. Marinate 15 minutes.

Wrap one oyster with a half slice of bacon. Fasten with a toothpick.

Broil in oven until bacon is crisp.

Pineapple Sausage Tidbits

8 servings

16	sausages, cut in half and cooked
32	pineapple chunks, fresh or canned
2 tsp	(*10 mL*) cornstarch
½ cup	(*125 mL*) pineapple juice

Using toothpicks, skewer sausage halves with pineapple chunks. Set aside.

Mix the cornstarch with the pineapple juice.

Heat in a saucepan and simmer until thick.

Place tidbits in a chafing dish.

Pour sauce over tidbits.

Almond Cheese Slices and Pineapple Sausage Tidbits

Cornish Pasty

24 appetizers

1½ tsp	(*8 mL*) salt
4 cups	(*1 L*) flour, sifted
¾ cup	(*180 mL*) butter
1 cup	(*250 mL*) water
1 lb	(*450 g*) lean ground beef
3	potatoes, thinly sliced
1	onion, thinly sliced
¼ tsp	(*1 mL*) black pepper
1 tbsp	(*15 mL*) water

Preheat oven to 350°F (*180°C*).

Mix ½ tsp (*3 mL*) salt with the flour. Add the butter and blend. Add 1 cup (*250 mL*) water and knead into a stiff dough.

Roll out dough to ⅛ in. (*0,3 cm*) thickness. Cut dough into 6-in. (*15 cm*) rounds.

Mix ground beef, potatoes, onion, remaining salt, pepper and 1 tbsp (*15 mL*) water together.

Divide mixture into equal portions. Top each pasty round with meat mixture.

Fold each round over or in half. Seal the edges with a fork.

Bake in oven for 1¼ hours.

1

Roll out dough and cut into 6-inch (*15 cm*) rounds.

2

Top each round with meat mixture.

3

Fold each round over or in half and seal edges with a fork.

4

Bake in oven for 1¼ hours.

Ham and Cheese Wontons

24 appetizers

6 oz	(*170 g*) ham, chopped
6 oz	(*170 g*) Cheddar, diced
24	wonton wrappers
1	egg, beaten
4 cups	(*1 L*) oil

Mix the ham with the cheese. Place ½ tbsp (*8 mL*) on each wonton wrapper. Brush sides with egg.

Fold wrappers over into triangle shapes. Seal the edges.

Heat oil to 375°F (*190°C*). Fry wontons in oil until golden brown. Serve hot with savory sauce of your choice.

Curry Chicken Wontons

24 appetizers

½ lb	(*225 g*) chicken, cooked and diced
3 tbsp	(*45 mL*) minced onion
3 tbsp	(*45 mL*) minced celery
2 tsp	(*10 mL*) curry powder
¼ cup	(*60 mL*) mayonnaise
24	wonton wrappers
1	egg, beaten
4 cups	(*1 L*) oil

Mix the cooked chicken with the onion and celery. Blend together the curry powder and mayonnaise.

Blend the chicken and vegetables together with the curry powder and mayonnaise.

Place ¾ tbsp (*12 mL*) of filling in the center of each wonton.

Brush with egg. Fold over in triangles and seal the edges.

Heat oil to 375°F (*190°C*).

Fry wontons until golden brown.

Serve hot with your choice of savory sauces.

Curry Chicken Wontons

Herb and Spice Shrimp

8 servings

2¼ lbs	(*1 kg*) raw shrimp, peeled and deveined
1	recipe court bouillon (see *Soups*)
¼ cup	(*60 mL*) butter
1 tsp	(*5 mL*) garlic powder
¼ cup	(*60 mL*) tomato purée
1 cup	(*250 mL*) tomato juice
¾ cup	(*180 mL*) water
¼ tsp	(*1 mL*) basil
¼ tsp	(*1 mL*) oregano
¼ tsp	(*1 mL*) thyme
1 tsp	(*5 mL*) salt
½ tsp	(*3 mL*) black pepper
¼ tsp	(*1 mL*) cayenne pepper
½ tsp	(*3 mL*) paprika
½ cup	(*125 mL*) sherry

Cook the shrimp in court bouillon. Remove from liquid and cool completely.

Melt the butter in a saucepan. Add the garlic powder, tomato purée, tomato juice and water.

Simmer for 5 minutes; add the remaining ingredients.

Simmer 5 more minutes. Pour into a bowl. Arrange shrimp around bowl.

Use sauce as a dip.

Oysters Rockefeller

6 servings

1½ doz	oysters
¼ cup	(*60 mL*) butter
10 oz	(*284 g*) spinach, cleaned and chopped
2 tbsp	(*30 mL*) parsley flakes
3 tbsp	(*45 mL*) minced green onion
2 tbsp	(*30 mL*) lemon juice
2	garlic cloves, minced
1 tsp	(*5 mL*) salt
2 tsp	(*10 mL*) black pepper
1 cup	(*250 mL*) breadcrumbs

Preheat oven to 350°F (*180°C*).

Shuck oysters. Loosen meat from shell, but do not remove.

Heat butter in a saucepan. Gently sauté the spinach. Remove from heat.

Add remaining ingredients; mix thoroughly. Place oysters in a baking dish. Place 1 tbsp (*15 mL*) of mixture on top of each oyster.

Bake in oven for 35 minutes.

Serve hot.

Chilled Shrimp with Mustard Mayonnaise

6 servings

1	egg
3 tbsp	(*45mL*) lemon juice
3 tbsp	(*45mL*) Dijon mustard
1 tsp	(*5 mL*) sugar
pinch	pepper
¼ tsp	(*1 mL*) salt
1 cup	(*250 mL*) olive oil
2¼ lbs	(*1 kg*) shrimp, peeled, deveined, cooked and chilled

In a blender, blend the egg together with the lemon juice, mustard and seasonings.

Slowly pour in the oil with machine running.

Place in a serving bowl and surround with shrimp.

Stuffed Mushroom Caps

Deep-Fried Frog Legs

6 servings

24	pairs frog legs
2	eggs, well beaten
¼ tsp	(*1 mL*) salt
¼ tsp	(*1 mL*) cayenne pepper
¼ cup	(*60 mL*) heavy cream
½ cup	(*125 mL*) flour
1 cup	(*250 mL*) fine breadcrumbs
4 cups	(*1 L*) oil
½ cup	(*125 mL*) Honey-Mustard Sauce (see *Sauces*)

Split the frog legs.

In a mixing bowl, blend together the eggs, salt, cayenne pepper and cream.

Place flour and breadcrumbs in separate bowls.

Dust frog legs with flour. Dip in egg mixture and roll in breadcrumbs.

Heat oil to 375°F (*190°C*).

Fry frog legs in oil for about 5 minutes or until golden brown.

Place on a serving tray and serve with sauce.

Stuffed Mushroom Caps

36 appetizers

36	large mushroom caps
¼ cup	(*60 mL*) butter
¼ cup	(*60 mL*) cream cheese, at room temperature
¼ cup	(*60 mL*) chopped crab meat
¼ cup	(60 ml) chopped, cooked baby shrimp
pinch	nutmeg
	salt and pepper

Sauté mushrooms in butter over high heat, about 3 minutes.

Beat cream cheese until smooth. Stir in crab, shrimp, nutmeg, and seasonings.

Stuff each cap with a little of the seafood mixture; arrange on a baking sheet.

Place under a heated broiler until bubbling.

Cocktail Meatballs

36-48 pieces

½ lb	(225 g) lean ground beef
¼ lb	(115 g) ground pork
¼ lb	(115 g) ground lamb
½ cup	(125 mL) breadcrumbs
½ cup	(125 mL) sherry
1	small onion, minced
1	egg, beaten
1	garlic clove, minced
1 tbsp	(15 mL) parsley flakes
½ tsp	(3 mL) salt
½ tsp	(3 mL) pepper
½ tsp	(3 mL) oregano
½ tsp	(3 mL) basil
½ tsp	(3 mL) thyme

Sauce

1 cup	(250 mL) chili sauce
½ cup	(125 mL) apple jelly
1 tsp	(5 mL) paprika
1 tsp	(5 mL) basil

Preheat oven to 350°F (180°C).

Mix the ground meats together thoroughly. Blend in all remaining ingredients.

Shape into small balls. Bake in oven for 12 minutes or until done.

Mix the chili sauce, jelly and seasonings together in a saucepan.

Heat slowly until hot; do not boil.

Place meatballs in serving dish, pour sauce over meatballs and serve.

Clams Casino

24 appetizers

2 doz	littleneck clams, cleaned
1	hard-boiled egg
¼ cup	(60 mL) butter
3	onions, finely diced
½ tsp	(3 mL) oregano
½ tsp	(3 mL) salt
½ tsp	(3 mL) pepper
½ cup	(125 mL) breadcrumbs
4	bacon strips, diced

Preheat oven to 400°F (200°C).

Remove meat from clam shells. Reserve the shells.

Coarsely chop clam meat and egg in food processor.

Melt the butter in a saucepan and add clam mixture and onions. Sauté until tender.

Mix the seasonings with the breadcrumbs. Mix into clam mixture.

Scoop the filling into the shells. Top with the diced bacon.

Bake in oven for 20 minutes, or until golden brown on top.

Serve with a spicy tomato sauce.

Prosciutto Escargots

24 appetizers

24	large snails, canned
1	recipe court bouillon (see *Soups*)
6	slices prosciutto
¼ cup	(*60 mL*) butter
1 tsp	(*5 mL*) minced garlic
½ tsp	(*3 mL*) parsley
½ tsp	(*3 mL*) lemon juice

Preheat oven to 500°F (*260°C*).

Drain and wash the snails. Simmer for 10 minutes in court bouillon. Drain and cool.

While snails are simmering, slice prosciutto into strips of 4.

Soften butter and blend in the garlic, parsley and lemon juice.

Wrap each snail with a strip of prosciutto. Skewer with a toothpick.

Place one skewer in each cavity of an escargot dish.

Drop a little garlic butter on each snail.

Bake for 5 minutes in oven. Serve with Garlic Cheese Bread, (see *Cheese*).

Mini Pizzas

Mini Pizzas

6 servings

6	English muffins
¼ tsp	(*1 mL*) oregano
¼ tsp	(*1 mL*) thyme
¼ tsp	(*1 mL*) basil
¼ tsp	(*1 mL*) salt
¼ tsp	(*1 mL*) pepper
1 cup	(*250 mL*) tomato sauce (see *Sauces*)
12	slices salami
1 cup	(*250 mL*) grated mozzarella cheese
12	tomato slices
½	green pepper, diced
24	pineapple chunks

Preheat oven to 400°F (*200°C*).

Cut muffins in half.

Blend the seasonings in the tomato sauce.

Spread 2 tsp (*10 mL*) of sauce on each muffin half. Top the sauce with 1 slice of salami. Sprinkle with cheese.

Cover cheese with one slice of tomato, a sprinkle of green pepper and 2 pineapple chunks per half muffin.

Bake in oven 5 to 7 minutes or until cheese is melted.

Seafood Kabobs

6 servings

6	slices bacon
12	large scallops
12	large shrimp, peeled and deveined
12	medium mushrooms, whole
12	cherry tomatoes
1 cup	(*250 mL*) teriyaki sauce (see *Sauces*)

Slice bacon in half. Wrap each scallop with a piece of bacon.

On each skewer, place 2 each of : shrimp, scallop, mushroom and tomato.

Broil 5 minutes per side, brushing with teriyaki sauce.

Serve hot.

Shrimp in Blueberry Sauce

6 servings

1½ lbs	(*675 g*)	shrimp, peeled and deveined
1		recipe court bouillon (see *Soups*)
1 tbsp	(*15 mL*)	cornstarch
⅛ tsp	(*0,5 mL*)	salt
1 tsp	(*5 mL*)	lemon juice
¾ cup	(*180 mL*)	sugar
1 cup	(*250 mL*)	water
2 cups	(*500 mL*)	blueberries

Cook shrimp in court bouillon. Drain and chill.

Blend cornstarch, salt, lemon juice and sugar in the water.

Bring to a boil.

Add the blueberries and simmer 10 minutes. Chill.

Pour sauce in serving dish and arrange shrimp on top.

Escargots

4 servings

24		mushroom caps
2 tbsp	(*30 mL*)	garlic butter
24		escargots
1		(*125 g*) pkg. cream cheese
2 tbsp	(*30 mL*)	garlic butter
1 cup		(*250 mL*) grated mozzarella cheese
1 cup		(*250 mL*) grated Swiss cheese
1 cup		(*250 mL*) grated old Cheddar cheese
		Garlic Cheese Bread (see *Cheese*)

Sauté mushroom caps in first quantity of butter over high heat.

Place one escargot in each cavity of escargot dishes. Top with 1 tsp (*5 mL*) cream cheese and a mushroom cap.

Spoon ¼ tsp (*1 mL*) garlic butter over each escargot.

Place dishes under heated broiler until bubbling.

Combine grated cheeses and sprinkle over each dish. Return to broiler just until cheese melt.

Serve very hot with Garlic Cheese Bread.

Oyster Remique

6 servings

½ cup	(*125 mL*) chili sauce
½ cup	(*125 mL*) hot horseradish
1 cup	(*250 mL*) grated old Cheddar cheese
1 cup	(*250 mL*) grated mozzarella cheese
1 cup	(*250 mL*) grated Brick cheese
36	oysters
2 cups	(*500 mL*) fine dry breadcrumbs

Preheat oven to 450°F (*230°C*).

Combine the chili sauce and horseradish. Combine the grated cheeses.

Shuck oysters; drain. Discard flat upper shell and detach flesh.

Over each oyster in shell, spoon 1 tsp (*5 mL*) chili sauce mixture and sprinkle with cheese.

Top with breadcrumbs and bake in oven until cheese has browned.

1

Shuck oysters and drain.

2

Discard flat upper shell and detach flesh.

3

Over each oyster in shell, spoon 1 tsp (*5 mL*) chili sauce mixture and sprinkle with cheese.

4

Top with breadcrumbs and bake in oven until cheese has browned.

Steamed Mussels Mike Smith

8-10 servings

2¼ lbs	(*1 kg*) mussels
1	onion, minced
1	carrot, sliced
1	celery stalk, sliced
1 cup	(*250 mL*) white wine
2 cups	(*500 mL*) water
8	peppercorns
1	bay leaf
1 tsp	(*5 mL*) salt
2	parsley sprigs
1 cup	(*250 mL*) liquid honey
1 tbsp	(*15 mL*) garlic powder

Scrub the mussels and remove beards.

In a large pot, place the onion, carrot, celery, wine, water, seasonings and parsley. Bring to a boil.

Add the mussels and cover. Steam for 5 minutes or until mussels open; discard any that do not open.

While mussels are steaming, heat the honey in a saucepan. Whisk in the garlic powder. Make sure there are no lumps.

Drain mussels well. Place in a large bowl.

Pour honey over mussels and stir well.

Serve with French bread, or Garlic Cheese Bread (see *Cheese*).

Steamed Mussels Mike Smith

Tea Eggs

12 servings

12	large eggs
½ cup	(*125 mL*) soya sauce
4 oz	(*115 g*) loose tea
2 tsp	(*10 mL*) salt
¼ tsp	(*1 mL*) nutmeg
¼ tsp	(*1 mL*) ground cloves
¼ tsp	(*1 mL*) cinnamon

Boil eggs, in enough water to cover, for 10 minutes.

Mix soya sauce with tea, salt, nutmeg, cloves and cinnamon.

Remove eggs. Crack shells all over by lightly tapping with a teaspoon, and replace in water.

Pour the soya mixture into water. Cover and simmer 45 to 60 minutes.

Allow to cool in the liquid. Place in refrigerator for two days.

Shell the eggs. Cut in half and serve.

Avocado Dip

2¼ cups (560 mL)

1	ripe avocado
1	250 g pkg. ricotta or cream cheese
½ cup	(125 mL) mayonnaise
1 tbsp	(15 mL) lemon juice
1 tsp	(5 mL) chervil
1 tsp	(5 mL) basil
1 tsp	(5 mL) chives
½ tsp	(3 mL) salt

Peel the avocado, slice and mash it. Cream together the avocado with the cheese.

Blend in the remaining ingredients. Serve with vegetables, chips, shrimp, etc.

Curry Dip

1½ cups (375 mL)

1 cup	(250 mL) mayonnaise
3 tbsp	(45 mL) chili sauce
1 tbsp	(15 mL) curry powder
1 tbsp	(15 mL) Worcestershire sauce
1 tbsp	(15 mL) minced onion
¼ tsp	(1 mL) salt
¼ tsp	(1 mL) pepper

Blend all the ingredients thoroughly.

Use with chilled seafood, chips, vegetables or fried foods.

Roquefort Dip and Curry Dip

Roquefort Dip

2 cups (500 mL)

3 oz	(90 g) Roquefort or blue cheese
1	250 g pkg. cream cheese
½ cup	(125 mL) sour cream
¼ tsp	(1 mL) onion powder

Crumble the cheese.

Blend all the ingredients together.

Use for vegetables when serving buffalo chicken wings or any other fried food.

French Onion Dip

2 cups (500 mL)

1	250 g pkg. cream cheese, at room temperature
1 cup	(250 mL) sour cream
1	pkg. dry onion soup mix
2 tbsp	(30 mL) chopped chives
1 tsp	(5 mL) dried chervil
1 tsp	(5 mL) paprika
1 tsp	(5 mL) Worcestershire sauce

Combine all ingredients; beat until smooth.

Serve with fresh vegetables or potato chips.

Mexicali Salad Dip

7 cups (1,75 L)

2 cups	(500 mL) sour cream
1 cup	(250 mL) cream cheese
1 tsp	(5 mL) chili powder
¼ tsp	(1 mL) thyme
¼ tsp	(1 mL) basil
¼ tsp	(1 mL) pepper
1 tsp	(5 mL) salt
2	green onions, chopped
2 cups	(500 mL) chili sauce
1½ cups	(375 mL) grated medium Cheddar
1	onion, diced
1	green pepper, diced

Cream together the sour cream and cream cheese.

Mix the seasonings and the green onions into chili sauce and blend with the sour cream.

Sprinkle Cheddar cheese on top.

Top by sprinkling with onions and green peppers. Serve with nacho chips.

Optional : Fry 4 oz (115 g) diced bacon to crisp; drain. Sprinkle on top of the Cheddar cheese.

Vegetable Dip

2 cups (500 mL)

¼ cup	(60 mL) heavy cream
1	250 g pkg. cream cheese
¼ cup	(60 mL) sherry
2 tbsp	(30 mL) minced onion
¼ tsp	(1 mL) salt
¼ tsp	(1 mL) dry mustard
¼ tsp	(1 mL) chervil
¼ tsp	(1 mL) basil
¼ tsp	(1 mL) chives
¼ tsp	(1 mL) paprika

Blend together the cream, cheese and sherry. Add the onion and seasonings. Mix well.

Use for dipping raw vegetables.

Mexicali Salad Dip, French Onion Dip and Vegetable Dip

Pâtés

Pâtés and terrines are, basically, a combination of ground meat, seasonings and binding agents cooked in some type of mold.

Mousses are similar to but more delicate than pâtés, and usually involve fish or vegetables, and include gelatine.

Pâtés can range from the simple to the complex, but the more you experiment with them, the more you will want to try others. Don't back away from what may appear to be a complicated recipe, just take your time, and you'll have a result worthy of your efforts.

Tips for Successful Pâtés

A) When the recipe calls for bacon, place it between two sheets of wax paper and roll it thin, being careful not to break it. Blanch to remove smoky flavor.

B) When using a food processor, chill the bowl, blades, and ingredients, and process small quantities at a time.

C) If the recipe calls for cooking in a water bath, set the mold in a larger container of water and keep the water level ⅔ of the way up the side of the mold.

D) Weighting a terrine after cooking produces a denser texture. Apply the weight 30 minutes after removal from the oven.

E) Pâtés must be covered with a layer of fat, preferably fat back, before cooking.

F) Remove all membranes and vessels from liver of any kind before using in a pâté.

Shrimp and Salmon Mousse

10 servings

1 tbsp	(*15 mL*)	unflavored gelatine
¼ cup	(*60 mL*)	white wine
1½ cups	(*375 mL*)	fish or chicken broth
½ cup	(*125 mL*)	mayonnaise
1 tsp	(*5 mL*)	salt
¼ tsp	(*1 mL*)	nutmeg
1 tsp	(*5 mL*)	paprika
½ tsp	(*3 mL*)	pepper
1 tbsp	(*15 mL*)	grated lemon peel
1 tbsp	(*15 mL*)	minced onion
½ cup	(*125 mL*)	minced celery
1½ cups	(*375 mL*)	cooked shrimp, minced
½ cup	(*125 mL*)	saltine crackers, finely ground
1 cup	(*250 mL*)	heavy cream
2 cups	(*500 mL*)	cooked salmon, flaked

Shrimp and Salmon Mousse

Soften the gelatine in the wine. Add the broth and bring to boil. Measure ¾ cup (*180 mL*) of broth.

Pour into a lightly greased 9 x 5-in. (*22 X 12 cm*) loaf pan. Chill to set.

In a large mixing bowl, combine mayonnaise, salt, nutmeg, paprika, pepper, lemon peel, onion and celery.

Fold in ¾ cup (*180 mL*) of broth.

Mix in the shrimp, crackers and cream.

In a second bowl, mix salmon with the remaining broth.

Pour half the shrimp mixture into the loaf pan, spread the salmon on top.

Then pour the remaining shrimp mixture on top of the salmon.

Chill 5 to 6 hours or overnight. Unmold and serve.

Pistachio and Chicken Terrine

20 servings

⅓ lb	(*150 g*) asparagus spears
2¼ lbs	(*1 kg*) boneless, skinless chicken
2	eggs
2 cups	(*500 mL*) heavy cream
1 tsp	(*5 mL*) salt
½ tsp	(*3 mL*) pepper
1 cup	(*250 mL*) unsalted pistachio nuts, shelled

Preheat oven to 325°F (*160°C*).

Blanch the asparagus. Drain and dry them.

Process the chicken in a food processor until very smooth.

Add the eggs, cream, salt and pepper. Blend well. Stir in the nuts by hand.

Line a 9 x 5-in. (*22 x 12 cm*) loaf pan with foil. Leave a little over the edges. Butter the foil.

Pour half the chicken mixture in the pan. Lay the asparagus on top. Pour in the remaining mixture.

Butter a piece of wax paper and place it, buttered side down, on the mousseline. Place in a large pan with 1½ in. (*4 cm*) water.

Bake in oven for 40 minutes. Remove. Weigh lightly for 2 hours.

Chill. Unmold and serve.

Pâté de Champagne

20 servings

2¼ lbs	(*1 kg*) chicken livers
1 lb	(*450 g*) sausage meat
1 lb	(*450 g*) lean veal
1	garlic clove, minced
1 tsp	(*5 mL*) marjoram
1 tsp	(*5 mL*) thyme
1 tsp	(*5 mL*) salt
1 tsp	(*5 mL*) paprika
3	eggs, slightly beaten
½ cup	(*125 mL*) champagne

Preheat oven to 375°F (*190°C*).

Process meats in a food processor until finely ground.

Mix meats together with garlic and seasonings. Add the eggs and champagne. Lightly grease a 9 x 5-in. (*22 x 12 cm*) loaf pan and fill with mixture.

Bake in oven for 2 hours. Remove pâté; weigh it down (2 bricks are great). Cool. Chill and serve.

Orange-Flavored Duck Terrine

20 servings

2¼ lbs	(*1 kg*) duck meat
½ lb	(*225 g*) chicken breast, cut into 1-in. (*2,5-cm*) strips
½ lb	(*225 g*) lean pork, cut into 1-in. (*2,5 cm*) strips
¾ lb	(*340 g*) bacon
1	duck liver
2	green onions, minced
1¼ cups	(*310 mL*) orange juice
⅔ cup	(*160 mL*) orange liqueur
2 tsp	(*10 mL*) salt
1 tbsp	(*15 mL*) green peppercorns
⅓ cup	(*80 mL*) fine breadcrumbs
3	eggs, beaten
2 cups	(*500 mL*) finely chopped apricots
½ cup	(*125 mL*) pistachio nuts (optional)

Preheat oven to 350°F (*180°C*).

Process the duck, chicken, and pork in food processor until very smooth. (Process a little at a time).

Then process half the bacon and the duck liver until smooth.

In a large mixing bowl, mix the meats, green onions, juice, liqueur, salt, peppercorns, breadcrumbs and eggs thoroughly. Add the apricots and nuts.

Line a large loaf pan with the remaining bacon. Spoon in mousseline mixture.

Butter a piece of wax paper. Place it on top, buttered side down.

Bake in a water bath for 1½ hours. Remove and allow to rest 30 minutes. Weigh it down overnight.

Chill for 5 days.

Unmold; remove bacon. Wipe away excess fat.

Slice and serve.

Cheese Vegetable Pâté

16-20 servings

2 cups	(*500 mL*) broccoli
2 cups	(*500 mL*) carrots, peeled and diced
3 tbsp	(*45 mL*) butter
1	onion, minced
4 oz	(*115 g*) mushrooms
2 tbsp	(*30 mL*) unflavored gelatine
1 cup	(*250 mL*) sherry
1 cup	(*250 mL*) chicken broth
2 cups	(*500 mL*) grated Havarti cheese
½ cup	(*125 mL*) mayonnaise
1 cup	(*250 mL*) heavy cream
1 tbsp	(*15 mL*) lemon zest
½ cup	(*125 mL*) breadcrumbs
1 tsp	(*5 mL*) salt
½ tsp	(*3 mL*) pepper
1 tsp	(*5 mL*) paprika

Boil the broccoli and carrots until tender. Place in food processor and finely chop.

Heat the butter; sauté the onion and sliced mushrooms. Pour into a large mixing bowl. Add the carrots and broccoli.

Dissolve the gelatine in the sherry. Add to chicken broth; bring to boil. Cool, do not chill.

Mix in remaining ingredients. Add vegetables. Pour into a lightly buttered loaf pan.

Chill 4 to 6 hours or overnight. Unmold and serve.

1 Sauté the onion and mushrooms in butter and pour into a large mixing bowl with carrots and broccoli.

2 Dissolve the gelatine in the sherry and add to chicken broth.

3 Pour mixture into a lightly buttered loaf pan.

4 Chill 4 to 6 hours, or overnight, then unmold and serve.

Smoked Salmon Timbali with Lobster Cream

4 servings

½ lb	(*225 g*) smoked salmon filet
¾ cup	(*180 mL*) cream, whipped
1 tsp	(*5 mL*) butter
2 tbsp	(*30 mL*) diced shallots
¼ cup	(*60 mL*) heavy cream
6 oz	(*170 g*) cooked lobster meat, chopped
½ tsp	(*3 mL*) salt
¼ tsp	(*1 mL*) pepper
	green peppercorns

Preheat oven to 275°F (*140°C*).

Finely dice the salmon; chill thoroughly and process in a food processor.

Beat in the whipped cream. Keep cool.

Heat the butter in a saucepan. Add the shallots and cook until soft.

Add the cream and reduce until thick. Strain through a sieve.

Add the lobster, salt and pepper. Leave to cool. Generously grease 4 timbali molds. Cover the bottom and the sides with some of the salmon mixture.

Fill with lobster mixture and top with the remaining salmon.

Bake in water bath for 15 minutes.

Serve with a Mornay sauce (see *Sauces*) and garnish with green peppercorns.

Apple and Chicken Liver Terrine

16-20 servings

2¼ lbs	(*1 kg*) chicken livers
½ lb	(*225 g*) ground pork
1 tsp	(*5 mL*) salt
¼ tsp	(*1 mL*) pepper
1 lb	(*450 g*) apples, pared and diced fine
¼ cup	(*60 mL*) Calvados
1 cup	(*250 mL*) heavy cream
3	eggs, beaten
½ cup	(*125 mL*) fine breadcrumbs
8	slices bacon

Preheat oven to 350°F (*180°C*).

Process the chicken livers, pork, salt and pepper in food processor until very smooth.

In large bowl, mix the apples, Calvados, cream, eggs and breadcrumbs together.

Blend in the meat.

Line a 9 x 5-in. (*22 x 12-cm*) loaf pan with tin foil. Grease the foil.

Layer the bacon on the foil and add the mousseline mixture.

Butter a piece of wax paper and place on top, buttered side down.

Bake in a water bath for 2 hours. Remove and weigh down.

Chill overnight with weights in place. Remove weights.

Chill 3 to 4 days. Unmold. Remove bacon and wipe away excess fat.

Slice and serve.

Cognac Black Peppercorn Pâté

Preheat oven to 350°F (*180°C*).

Trim the livers thoroughly (remove any blood vessels, skin, etc.).

Grind or process the livers and bacon to a fine grind. Grind or process the onion.

Whip the eggs, fold in the seasonings.

Heat butter, add flour and stir into a roux. Cook 2 minutes, do not brown.

Add the cream, cognac and chicken stock. Simmer until thick.

Allow cream mixture to cool; fold in eggs.

Add the puréed liver and beat until completely incorporated.

Line a loaf pan with half the fatback.

Pour the mixture into the pan. Place remaining fatback on top. Cover with foil.

Bake in a water bath for 1½ hours. Remove foil and cool.

When completely chilled, unmold.

Remove fatback and wipe away excess fat. Coat sides, top, bottom and ends with peppercorns.

Slice and serve.

Cognac Black Peppercorn Pâté

10 servings

10 oz	(*280 g*)	pork liver
10 oz	(*280 g*)	calf liver
¾ lb	(*340 g*)	bacon
1		small onion, minced
2		eggs
1 tsp	(*5 mL*)	salt
½ tsp	(*3 mL*)	allspice
¼ tsp	(*1 mL*)	cinnamon
¼ tsp	(*1 mL*)	ginger
2 tbsp	(*30 mL*)	butter
2 tbsp	(*30 mL*)	flour
1 cup	(*250 mL*)	heavy cream
¼ cup	(*60 mL*)	cognac
½ cup	(*125 mL*)	chicken stock
¾ lb	(*340 g*)	fatback, thinly sliced
2 cups	(*500 mL*)	black peppercorns, crushed

Soups

Nothing adds a homey, loving touch to a meal quite as much as a bowl of hearty homemade soup. There is something about it that makes us feel the cook really cares.

Soup is magical in another way, too. We now know there is some truth to the old wives' tale that soup is the ideal food for someone who is sick. That is because, in the process of simmering the stock, the vitamins and nutrients are dissolved out of the food, and become easier to digest.

Stocks for Soups and Sauces

The stock is the essence of a good soup or sauce. If the stock is weak, the final product will be weak and flat as well. Good stocks are derived from the freshest ingredients, simmered slowly.

This chapter includes recipes for beef, chicken, fish and vegetable stocks, all of which will be useful to add to your basic cooking repertory.

Basic Soup Types

Cream soups can be made with any number of ingredients, including vegetables, fish, or meat, which are thickened with starch and finished with milk or cream. Most cream soups are served puréed to a smooth consistency.

Bisque usually refers to a cream soup made with a shellfish base and generally finished with wine or sherry.

Chowder is similar to a cream soup, but the ingredients are not puréed.

Purées are usually made with legumes (such as beans, lentils or peas) as the base. The legumes also serve as the thickening agent, are often cooked in a strongly flavored stock (ham, mutton) and are sometimes finished with cream.

Bouillons are strongly flavored broths, sometimes served plain, but more often used as a base for other soups. The most common are beef, chicken, fish, tomato and vegetable.

Consommés are strong, richly flavored bouillons which have been filtered so that they are completely clear. They are sometimes served garnished with pasta, vegetables, meat, or whatever else the imagination suggests.

Cream of Tomato Rice

8 servings

½ cup	(*125 mL*) butter
1	small onion, minced
1	large carrot, minced
2	celery stalks, minced
4 cups	(*1 L*) chicken broth
3 cups	(*750 mL*) tomato purée
1 cup	(*250 mL*) chopped tomatoes
1 cup	(*250 mL*) flour

4 cups	(*1 L*) heavy cream
1 cup	(*250 mL*) cooked rice
¼ tsp	(*1 mL*) pepper
1 tsp	(*5 mL*) salt

In a pot, heat the butter.

Add the vegetables and sauté until tender.

In saucepan, heat the broth, tomato purée and tomatoes.

Add the flour to the sautéed vegetables. Cook for 2 minutes.

Add the cream and simmer until very thick. Slowly whip tomato broth into the cream.

Add the rice and seasonings.

Serve at once.

Cream of Tomato Rice

Beef or Chicken Stock

6-7 cups (1,5 L)

2¼ lbs	(1 kg) meaty beef bones or chicken bones
¼ cup	(60 mL) margarine (for beef stock only)
10 cups	(2,5 L) cold water
2	celery stalks, coarsely chopped
2	carrots, coarsely chopped
1	onion, coarsely chopped
½ tsp	(3 mL) salt
¼ tsp	(1 mL) pepper
pinch	rubbed thyme
pinch	dried oregano leaves
pinch	rubbed sage

In a heavy Dutch oven, brown beef bones slowly in margarine over low heat, about 30 minutes, stirring occasionally. (Chicken bones do not need to be browned.)

Add water and remaining ingredients; bring to a simmer. Simmer, uncovered, for 3 to 4 hours, skimming off any grease or scum that rises to the top.

Remove meat, bones, and vegetables. Strain through a sieve.

Chill stock and remove fat from surface.

Both stocks have best flavor after standing 24 hours. Use as required.

Fish Stock

8 cups (2 L)

5 lbs	(2,2 kg) fish, trimmings and bones
1	onion, diced
3	carrots, diced
3	celery stalks, diced
2	bay leaves
3	parsley sprigs
1	garlic clove
1 tbsp	(15 mL) salt
10	peppercorns
12 cups	(3 L) water

Cut the fish into small pieces. Place in a large pot. Add the vegetables and seasonings. Cover with water.

Heat gently without boiling. Simmer gently for 2 hours. While simmering, remove any scum which may rise to the top.

Drain through a sieve, then through a cheesecloth.

Use as required.

Vegetable Stock

6-8 cups (1,5-2 L)

¼ cup	(60 mL) butter
2	onions, diced
6	carrots, diced
4	celery stalks, diced
1	garlic clove, crushed
1 lb	(450 g) tomatoes, diced
2 tbsp	(30 mL) parsley
10	peppercorns
1 tsp	(5 mL) thyme
2	bay leaves
2 tsp	(10 mL) salt
12 cups	(3 L) water

In a pot, heat the butter.

Sauté the onions, carrots, celery and garlic until tender.

Add the tomatoes, seasonings and water.

Simmer gently until water is reduced by half.

Strain and use as required.

Court Bouillon

16 cups (4 L)

16 cups	(4 L) water
1 tbsp	(15 mL) green peppercorns
1 tbsp	(15 mL) salt
1	onion, sliced
2	carrots, chopped
1	celery stalk, chopped
1	lemon, cut in half
1 cup	(250 mL) white wine
1	bouquet garni*

Combine all the ingredients.

Bring to a boil. Boil 10 minutes.

Strain through a cheesecloth. Reserve the liquid.

Use liquid for cooking fish and shellfish.

*A bouquet garni is : thyme, marjoram, peppercorns, bay leaf and parsley, tied together in a cheesecloth.

Garden Pea Soup

8 servings

⅓ cup	(*80 mL*) butter
¼ cup	(*60 mL*) minced onions
¼ cup	(*60 mL*) minced celery
¼ cup	(*60 mL*) minced carrots
⅓ cup	(*80 mL*) flour
4 cups	(*1 L*) chicken stock
¼ lb	(*115 g*) cooked ham, diced
2 cups	(*500 mL*) frozen peas
2 cups	(*500 mL*) light cream

In a pot, heat the butter.

Sauté the onions, celery and carrots until tender.

Add the flour and cook for 2 minutes.

Add chicken stock, ham and peas.

Simmer for 10 minutes.

Add the cream; simmer for an additional 10 minutes.

Serve hot.

Purée Mongole

8 servings

1 cup	(*250 mL*) yellow split peas
2 tbsp	(*30 mL*) butter
1	onion, minced
1	carrot, minced
2	celery stalks, minced
1	ham bone
4 cups	(*1 L*) chicken stock
2 cups	(*500 mL*) water
4 cups	(*1 L*) chopped tomatoes
¼ tsp	(*1 mL*) pepper
1 cup	(*250 mL*) heavy cream

Soak peas overnight.

Melt the butter in a pot.

Sauté the onion, carrot and celery.

Add the ham bone, chicken stock, water and peas. Simmer until peas are tender.

Remove ham bone. Add the tomatoes and pepper.

Simmer for 10 minutes longer.

Add the cream and simmer for 2 more minutes.

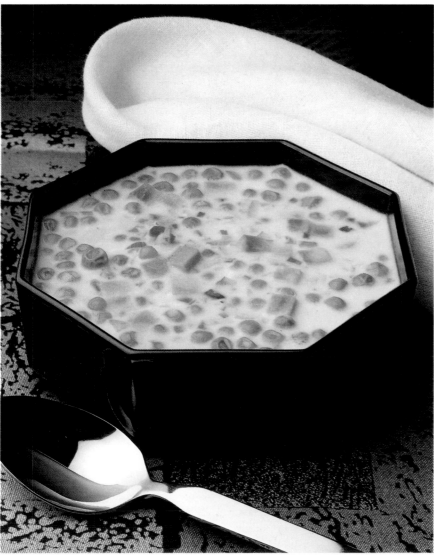

Garden Pea Soup

Vichyssoise

6 servings

4	leeks
¼ cup	(60 mL) butter
1½ cups	(375 mL) potatoes, pared and thinly sliced
4 cups	(1 L) chicken stock
1 cup	(250 mL) heavy cream
½ tsp	(3 mL) salt
¼ tsp	(1 mL) pepper
1 tbsp	(15 mL) minced chives

Trim the leeks. Discard the root and the stem ends except 2 in. (5 cm) above the white portion.

Slice and wash the leeks. Dice.

Heat the butter in an 8-cup (2 L) saucepan.

Sauté the leeks for 5 minutes. Do not brown. Add the potatoes and chicken stock.

Cover and simmer until potatoes are very tender. Press through a sieve or food mill.

Reheat and add the cream, salt and pepper. Serve garnished with chives.

Vichyssoise is usually served chilled.

Blueberry and Banana Soup

6 servings

4	bananas
3 tbsp	(45 mL) lemon juice
6 cups	(1,5 L) apple juice
¼ cup	(60 mL) sugar
1½ tbsp	(20 mL) cornstarch
½ tsp	(3 mL) cinnamon
2½ cups	(625 mL) heavy cream
2 cups	(500 mL) blueberries

In a food processor, purée bananas with lemon juice.

Place in a pot and bring to a boil with 3 ½ cups (875 mL) apple juice. Add the sugar; set aside.

Blend the cornstarch into the remaining apple juice.

Add to the soup. Simmer for 2 minutes. Remove and chill.

Add the cinnamon to the cream. Whip into soup. Stir in the blueberries.

Serve in chilled soup bowls.

Gazpacho

6 servings

2	garlic cloves, minced
2	green peppers, diced fine
3	celery stalks, diced fine
1	onion, diced fine
3 cups	(750 mL) tomatoes, peeled, seeded and chopped
3 cups	(750 mL) chicken broth
1 tbsp	(15 mL) salt
1 tsp	(5 mL) paprika
½ tsp	(3 mL) cracked black pepper
1 tbsp	(15 mL) Worcestershire sauce
1	cucumber, diced fine
3 tbsp	(45 mL) lemon juice
3 tbsp	(45 mL) olive oil
½	cucumber, sliced

In a food processor, blend the garlic, half the green peppers, half the celery, and half the onions with the tomatoes.

Pour into a large bowl. Blend in the chicken broth, seasonings, diced cucumber lemon juice and the oil.

Add the remaining green peppers, celery, and onions.

Chill 24 hours. Pour into chilled soup cups.

Garnish with sliced cucumber.

Vichyssoise; Blueberry and Banana Soup

Oyster Stew

8 servings

¼ lb	(*115 g*) bacon, diced
3 tbsp	(*45 mL*) butter
4	potatoes, peeled and diced
1	onion, diced
2	carrots, diced
2	celery stalks, diced
3 tbsp	(*45 mL*) flour
4 cups	(*1 L*) fish stock
2 cups	(*500 mL*) heavy cream
2 cups	(*500 mL*) shucked oysters

In a saucepan, sauté the bacon and pour off the grease.

Melt the butter and sauté the vegetables.

Add the flour and stir into a paste (roux).

Add the fish stock and cream. Stir and bring to a simmer.

Add the oysters and simmer for 30 minutes.

Old-Fashioned Chicken and Rice

8 servings

2 tbsp	(*30 mL*) butter
1	onion, minced
2	celery stalks, minced
2	large carrots, minced
3 cups	(*750 mL*) chicken, cooked and diced
8 cups	(*2 L*) chicken broth
1½ cups	(*375 mL*) cooked rice
2 tbsp	(*30 mL*) chopped parsley

In a pot, heat the butter, add the onion, celery and carrots. Sauté until tender.

Add the chicken and broth. Simmer for 15 minutes.

Add the rice and parsley. Simmer 5 more minutes.

Serve very hot.

Tomato Soup

6 servings

1 tbsp	(*15 mL*) oil
¼ cup	(*60 mL*) minced onions
¼ cup	(*60 mL*) minced celery
¼ cup	(*60 mL*) minced green pepper
4 cups	(*1 L*) chopped tomatoes
1	bay leaf
¼ tsp	(*1 mL*) thyme
¼ tsp	(*1 mL*) marjoram
¼ tsp	(*1 mL*) cracked pepper
1 tsp	(*5 mL*) salt
1 tsp	(*5 mL*) chopped parsley
4 cups	(*1 L*) chicken stock

Heat the oil in a saucepan. Add the onions, celery, green pepper and sauté until tender.

Add tomatoes, seasonings and chicken stock.

Bring to a boil; reduce and simmer 5 minutes.

Remove bay leaf and serve.

Onion Soup au Gratin

8 servings

1	French baguette stick, about 3 in. (*7 cm*) in diameter
3 tbsp	(*45 mL*) butter
2 cups	(*500 mL*) thinly sliced onions
¼ cup	(*60 mL*) all-purpose flour
5 cups	(*1,25 L*) mild beef stock
	salt and pepper
¾ cup	(*180 mL*) grated medium Cheddar
¾ cup	(*180 mL*) grated Swiss cheese
¼ cup	(*60 mL*) grated Parmesan cheese

Preheat oven to 325°F (*160°C*). Cut French bread into slices about ½ in. (*1,5 cm*) thick.

Bake in oven for 25 to 30 minutes or until bread is dry and lightly browned. Set aside.

Melt butter in a saucepan; cook onions over low heat, stirring occasionally until onions are a rich golden brown, about 30 minutes.

Sprinkle flour over onions and cook, stirring, for 2 minutes.

Add the stock, salt and pepper; simmer for about 30 minutes.

Transfer soup to serving bowls and top each with a slice of toasted bread. Combine cheeses and sprinkle over bread.

Place under heated broiler until bubbly and lightly browned.

1

Melt butter in a saucepan and cook onions over low heat until golden brown, about 30 minutes.

2

Add the beef stock, salt and pepper and simmer for about 30 minutes.

3

Transfer soup to serving bowls, top each with a slice of toasted bread and sprinkle with cheeses.

4

Place under heated broiler until bubbly and lightly browned.

Cock-a-Leekie Soup

Cream of Chicken and Mushrooms

8 servings

⅓ cup	(80 mL) butter
4 oz	(115 g) mushrooms, sliced
⅓ cup	(80 mL) flour
1½ cups	(375 mL) chicken, cooked and diced
3 cups	(750 mL) chicken broth
2 cups	(500 mL) heavy cream
¼ tsp	(1 mL) pepper
1 tsp	(5 mL) salt
2 tbsp	(30 mL) chopped parsley

In a pot, heat the butter. Add the mushrooms and sauté until tender.

Add the flour and cook for 2 minutes.

Add the chicken, broth, cream, seasonings and parsley.

Simmer for 15 minutes.

Serve hot.

Cock-a-Leekie Soup

8 servings

2¼ lb	(1 kg) stewing chicken
8 cups	(2 L) chicken stock
6-7	leeks, whites only
2 tbsp	(30 mL) butter

Gently simmer the chicken in the chicken stock for 2 ½ hours.

Add water to maintain liquid level. Remove chicken and strain liquid.

Bone chicken. Dice the meat. Cut the leeks into julienne strips.

Heat the butter in a pot. Sauté the leeks in the butter until tender.

Add the meat and broth. Reheat to a boil.

Serve very hot.

Bouillabaisse (Provençale Fish Soup)

Bouillabaisse (Provençale Fish Soup)

8 servings

⅔ cup	(160 mL) oil
1	carrot, minced
2	onions, minced
1 lb	(450 g) boneless whitefish
1 lb	(450 g) boneless pike
1 lb	(450 g) boneless ocean perch
Or 3 lbs	(1,4 kg) any firm fish
1	bay leaf
1½ cups	(375 mL) tomatoes, peeled, seeded and chopped
¼ cup	(60 mL) sherry
4 cups	(1 L) fish or chicken stock
1 doz	clams
1 doz	mussels
2 doz	shrimp, peeled and deveined
1 cup	(250 mL) lobster or crab meat
2	pimientos, diced
2 tsp	(10 mL) salt
½ tsp	(3 mL) paprika
½ tsp	(3 mL) saffron

Heat the oil in a large pot or Dutch oven. Add the carrots and onions. Sauté until tender.

Cut the fish into 1-in. (2,5 cm) strips. Add to pot and cook 5 minutes.

Add the bay leaf, tomatoes, sherry and fish stock. Cover and simmer for 20 minutes. Do not boil.

Add the shellfish, pimientos and seasonings.

Simmer for 10 more minutes.

Salmagundi

8 servings

½ cup	(125 mL) butter
1	carrot, diced
2	celery stalks, diced
1	onion, diced
3	large potatoes, pared and diced
⅓ cup	(80 mL) flour
1 cup	(250 mL) chopped tomatoes
8 cups	(2 L) fish stock
½ cup	(125 mL) white wine
1 tsp	(5 mL) salt
½ tsp	(3 mL) pepper
1 tsp	(5 mL) curry powder
1 lb	(450 g) whitefish, cooked and flaked

In a pot or Dutch oven, heat the butter.

Add the carrot, celery, onion and potatoes and sauté until tender.

Add flour and stir into a paste (roux). Do not brown.

Add the tomatoes, stock, wine, and seasonings.

Bring to a boil 5 minutes. Add the fish. Simmer 5 more minutes.

Pepper and Cream Cheese Soup

8-10 servings

2	large green peppers, diced
1	Spanish onion, finely chopped
3	celery stalks, thinly sliced
3 cups	(750 mL) sliced mushrooms
¼ cup	(60 mL) butter
¼ cup	(60 mL) all-purpose flour
6 cups	(1,5 L) beef stock
1	250 g pkg. cream cheese
2 cups	(500 mL) sliced cooked roast beef
1 cup	(250 mL) cooked fettuccine noodles, coarsely chopped
	salt and pepper

Sauté the vegetables in butter over medium heat until tender.

Sprinkle with flour and cook, stirring, for 2 minutes.

Gradually stir in stock and simmer until soup has thickened slightly. Stir in cheese until melted.

Add the beef slices; simmer over low heat 5 minutes, stirring constantly. Stir in the noodles.

Season to taste and serve immediately.

My Mulligatawny

8-10 servings

1	medium onion, finely chopped
2	medium carrots, coarsely grated
2	celery stalks, thinly sliced
1½ cups	(375 mL) sliced mushrooms
3	medium potatoes, coarsely grated
¼ cup	(60 mL) butter
½ cup	(125 mL) all-purpose flour
6 cups	(1,5 L) chicken stock
2 cups	(500 mL) milk
1	250 g pkg. cream cheese
2 tbsp	(30 mL) curry powder
2 cups	(500 mL) diced cooked chicken
	salt and pepper

Sauté the vegetables in butter over medium heat, stirring often, until tender but not browned.

Sprinkle with flour and cook, stirring, for 2 minutes. Gradually stir in stock and milk. Heat to simmering.

Stir in the cheese until melted. Add the curry powder and chicken; simmer 5 minutes.

Season to taste.

Marsala and Scallop Soup

8 servings

¼ cup	*(60 mL)* butter
1	small onion, minced
2	carrots, minced
2	celery stalks, minced
1 lb	*(450 g)* small scallops
½ cup	*(125 mL)* flour
3 cups	*(750 mL)* chicken broth
3 cups	*(750 mL)* light cream
1 cup	*(250 mL)* Marsala wine

In a pot, heat the butter. Sauté the onion, carrots and celery until tender.

Add the scallops and sauté 3 minutes.

Sprinkle with flour and cook 2 minutes.

Add the broth, cream and wine.

Simmer for 15 minutes. Serve hot.

Marsala and Scallop Soup

Nelusko (Cream of Chicken Almond Soup)

8 servings

3 tbsp	*(45 mL)* butter
½ cup	*(125 mL)* minced celery
1	small onion, minced
3 tbsp	*(45 mL)* flour
4 cups	*(1 L)* chicken stock
1 cup	*(250 mL)* light cream
¼ cup	*(60 mL)* ground almonds
1 cup	*(250 mL)* chicken meat, cooked and diced
⅓ cup	*(80 mL)* heavy cream
¼ tsp	*(1 mL)* paprika

In a 2-quart *(2 L)* saucepan, heat the butter.

Sauté the celery and onion until tender.

Add the flour and stir into a paste (roux). Do not brown.

Add the chicken stock, light cream and simmer for 15 minutes.

Add the almonds, chicken meat and heavy cream. Simmer for another 5 minutes.

Garnish with paprika.

New England Clam Chowder

10-12 servings

¼ lb	(115 g) bacon, diced
½ cup	(125 mL) butter
1 cup	(250 mL) diced onion
1 cup	(250 mL) diced celery
1 cup	(250 mL) diced carrots
3 cups	(750 mL) diced potatoes
1 cup	(250 mL) flour
4 cups	(1 L) fish stock or clam broth
3 cups	(750 mL) chopped clams
3 cups	(750 mL) heavy cream
¼ tsp	(1 mL) pepper
½ tsp	(3 mL) thyme
1 tsp	(5 mL) salt

In a large pot, fry the bacon until crisp. Drain the grease.

Add the butter and vegetables. Sauté until tender.

Stir in the flour. Cook for 2 minutes. Add all remaining ingredients. Bring to a boil.

Reduce to a simmer. Simmer until thick, 15 to 20 minutes. Stir frequently.

Harry Hatch's Lobster Bisque

8 servings

¼ cup	(60 mL) butter
½ cup	(125 mL) minced celery
½ cup	(125 mL) minced onions
¼ cup	(60 mL) flour
2 cups	(500 mL) fish stock
3 cups	(750 mL) heavy cream
1 tsp	(5 mL) salt
¼ tsp	(1 mL) white pepper
¼ cup	(60 mL) cream-style sherry
1 lb	(450 g) lobster meat, cooked
8	lobster meat claws, cooked

Heat the butter in a saucepan. Add the celery and onions. Sauté until tender. Add the flour and stir into a paste. Do not brown.

Add the fish stock and cream. Simmer for 15 minutes. Add the salt, pepper, sherry and lobster meat. Simmer for 5 more minutes.

Press through a sieve or process in a food processor until smooth.

Garnish with the lobster claws.

Corn and Chicken Chowder

8 servings

¼ cup	(60 mL) butter
1	onion, diced
4	potatoes, peeled and diced
2	carrots, diced
2	celery stalks, diced
1 cup	(250 mL) corn kernels, frozen
¼ cup	(60 mL) flour
4 cups	(1 L) chicken stock
2 cups	(500 mL) heavy cream
2 cups	(500 mL) chicken, cooked and diced
1 tbsp	(15 mL) parsley flakes

Melt the butter in a saucepan. Sauté the vegetables until tender.

Add the flour and stir into a paste (roux).

Add the stock and cream. Simmer 20 minutes. Add chicken and simmer 5 more minutes.

Sprinkle with parsley and serve.

NOTE : for crab or shrimp bisque change to preferred meat. Omit lobster.

Chive Cheese Soup

4 servings

¼ cup	(*60 mL*) butter
¼ cup	(*60 mL*) minced chives
2 tbsp	(*30 mL*) chopped parsley
¼ cup	(*60 mL*) flour
2 cups	(*500 mL*) chicken broth
2 cups	(*500 mL*) heavy cream
½ cup	(*125 mL*) blue cheese, crumbled

In a saucepan, heat the butter, add the chives and parsley. Cook gently for 2 minutes.

Stir in the flour. Continue to cook another 2 minutes.

Add the broth and cream. Bring to a boil. Reduce to a simmer. Simmer for 10 minutes.

Crumble in the cheese. Simmer 5 more minutes.

Chive Cheese Soup

Old-Fashioned Beef Vegetable Soup

Old-Fashioned Beef Vegetable Soup

8 servings

1 lb	(450 g)	diced beef
2 tbsp	(30 mL)	barley
8 cups	(2 L)	beef stock
3 tbsp	(45 mL)	butter
1		onion, diced
2		carrots, sliced
3		celery stalks, diced
2 cups	(500 mL)	tomatoes, seeded and chopped
1 tsp	(5 mL)	salt
½ tsp	(3 mL)	pepper
1 tsp	(5 mL)	basil
3 tbsp	(45 mL)	soya sauce
1 tbsp	(15 mL)	Worcestershire sauce
1 tsp	(5 mL)	paprika

Gently boil the beef and barley in the stock for 30 minutes. Remove any scum that floats to the top.

In a saucepan, melt the butter and sauté the vegetables.

Add the tomatoes and seasonings.

Pour this mixture into the stock and simmer ½ hour longer.

Consommé

8 servings

2 cups	(500 mL)	beef stock
2 cups	(500 mL)	chicken stock
2 cups	(500 mL)	tomatoes, seeded and chopped
1		onion, diced
2		carrots, diced
3		celery stalks, diced
1		bouquet garni
1		egg white, with shell

Combine all ingredients, except egg white, and simmer. Do not boil.

Cover for one hour. Strain through muslin or cheesecloth.

Whip the egg white and whisk into soup. Add egg shell and simmer another 10 minutes.

Strain a second time through muslin or cheesecloth. Serve.

Chicken Florentine and Rice

Chicken Florentine and Rice

8 servings

1½ tbsp	(*22 mL*) butter
6 oz	(*170 g*) spinach, chopped
8 cups	(*2 L*) chicken broth
2 cups	(*500 mL*) chicken meat, diced
1½ cups	(*375 mL*) cooked rice

Heat the butter in a pot. Sauté the spinach for 2 minutes.

Add the chicken broth and chicken meat. Simmer for 10 minutes.

Add the rice, simmer 5 more minutes.

Serve hot.

Broccoli and Cheddar Soup

6-8 servings

4 cups	(1 L)	diced broccoli
3 tbsp	(45 mL)	butter
¼ cup	(60 mL)	all-purpose flour
5 cups	(1,25 L)	chicken stock
1 cup	(250 mL)	milk
1 cup	(250 mL)	whipping cream
1 cup	(250 mL)	grated medium Cheddar cheese
		salt and pepper

Sauté the broccoli in butter over medium heat until tender.

Sprinkle with flour and cook, stirring, for 2 minutes. Gradually stir in stock and milk; heat just to simmering.

Stir in cream and cheese. Allow cheese to melt in soup; season to taste and serve sprinkled with croutons.

FOR BROCCOLI AND MUSHROOM SOUP : Add 3 cups (750 mL) sliced mushrooms and replace Cheddar with grated Parmesan.

Egg Drop Soup

8 servings

6 cups	(1,5 L)	chicken stock
2		eggs
2 tbsp	(30 mL)	water
⅓ cup	(80 mL)	frozen peas

Bring chicken stock to a boil. Whip the eggs in the water. Add the peas to the soup. Pour in the eggs in a fine stream. Cook for 2 minutes. Serve.

Cream of Carrot and Pumpkin

10-12 servings

⅓ cup	(80 mL)	butter
2 cups	(500 mL)	grated carrots
⅓ cup	(80 mL)	flour
4 cups	(1 L)	chicken stock
1 tbsp	(15 mL)	lemon juice
2 cups	(500 mL)	pumpkin purée
¼ tsp	(1 mL)	ginger
¼ tsp	(1 mL)	nutmeg
3 cups	(750 mL)	heavy cream

In a pot, heat the butter.

Sauté the carrots until tender.

Add the flour and cook for 2 minutes.

Add the stock, lemon juice, pumpkin purée, and seasonings.

Simmer for 10 minutes. Add the cream; simmer for an additional 15 minutes.

Serve at once.

Cranberry and Raspberry Soup

8 servings

4 cups	(1 L)	cranberries
4 cups	(1 L)	apple juice
2 cups	(500 mL)	raspberries
¼ cup	(60 mL)	sugar
2 tbsp	(30 mL)	lemon juice
½ tsp	(3 mL)	cinnamon
2 cups	(500 mL)	light cream
2 tbsp	(30 mL)	cornstarch

Wash the cranberries. Heat the cranberries in the apple juice; simmer for 10 minutes. Press through a sieve.

Press the raspberries through the same sieve. Discard what remains in the sieve and return to a boil.

Blend in the sugar, lemon juice and cinnamon. Add 1½ cups (375 mL) cream. Mix the cornstarch with the remaining cream.

Add to soup; simmer for 5 minutes. Serve hot or cold.

Cranberry and Raspberry Soup

Blackberry Soup

6 servings

4 cups	(1 L)	blackberries
4		apples, pared, cored and diced
4 cups	(1 L)	apple juice
3 tbsp	(45 mL)	sugar
¼ tsp	(1 mL)	cinnamon
1 tbsp	(15 mL)	cornstarch
3 tbsp	(45 mL)	water

Pick over the berries — discard stems, and bruised berries.

Place berries and apples in a pot. Pour in the apple juice. Simmer for 20 minutes.

Mash with a potato masher. Strain through a sieve.

Add the sugar and cinnamon. Mix the cornstarch in the water. Add to soup. Bring to a boil. Remove and serve hot or chilled.

If served cold, you may wish to serve whipping cream with the soup.

Salads and Dressings

Salads are a great opportunity to express your creativity. You can seek out the freshest greens and vegetables, including some of the more exotic varieties becoming available in most markets, and combine them in a variety of ways so that every salad you make is a new taste experience. You can experiment with fresh herbs and even some of the increasingly popular edible flowers.

Whatever ingredients you choose, though, there are some simple rules you should follow. Choose salad greens and vegetables that are as young and as fresh as possible. Pay attention to color, form and texture, as well as flavor.

As soon as you bring your salad greens home, wash them and store them loosely wrapped in the salad crisper of your refrigerator. Assemble salads at the last possible moment, using cold ingredients and add dressing only when ready to serve. Only add enough dressing to make the salad moist.

The basic dressings for salads are mayonnaise and vinaigrette — most others are a variation of one of these. The oil should be light and flavorful, and combined with your choice of lemon juice, raspberry vinegar, or flavored vinegar. Herbs and spices should be fresh, and chosen so that their flavors enhance the final product.

Serve salads on well-chilled plates. Simply place them in the freezer 30 minutes before serving time.

Salads can fall into four basic categories:

Appetizer salads should be light and just big enough to whet the appetite. Select ingredients that will set the stage for the remaining courses.

Salad accompaniments are served with the main entrée. They should not be so sweet or tart that they overwhelm the flavors of the main dish. They can also be served after the main course, European-style, to clear the palate for the next course.

Main course salads should be hearty and flavorful. These salads should contain more than just salad greens, with enough variety to satisfy appetites as well as nutritional requirements.

Dessert salads are designed to end the meal on a sweet note, and usually involve fruit or molded gelatine.

Salade Niçoise

Salade Niçoise

4 servings

¾ cup	(*180 mL*) oil
¼ cup	(*60 mL*) vinegar
1 tsp	(*5 mL*) salt
½ tsp	(*3 mL*) pepper
½ tsp	(*3 mL*) dry mustard
2 tbsp	(*30 mL*) lemon juice
8	potatoes, peeled, cooked and diced
1	small onion, finely diced
½ lb	(*225 g*) green beans, blanched
4	lettuce leaves
4	tomatoes, peeled and quartered
4	hard-boiled eggs, quartered
10	black olives, pitted
8	anchovy filets
1 tbsp	(*15 mL*) chopped basil

Combine the oil, vinegar, salt, pepper, mustard and lemon juice.

Pour ¼ of the dressing over potatoes. Chill for 1 hour.

Toss the onion with the green beans.

Pour ¼ of the dressing over the beans and chill for 1 hour.

Toss the beans with the potatoes.

Place the lettuce leaves on plates. Top with equal portions of salad.

Arrange the tomatoes, eggs, olives and anchovies on the salad.

Drizzle more dressing over these. Sprinkle with basil and serve.

Hot Chicken & Tomato Salad

4 servings

¼ cup	(*60 mL*) lemon juice
½ cup	(*125 mL*) oil
2 tbsp	(*30 mL*) chopped parsley
1 tsp	(*5 mL*) salt
¼ tsp	(*1 mL*) thyme
¼ tsp	(*1 mL*) oregano
¼ tsp	(*1 mL*) pepper
3 tbsp	(*45 mL*) olive oil
2	garlic cloves, minced
1 lb	(*450 g*) boneless chicken, in strips
24	cherry tomatoes, halved
6 oz	(*170 g*) feta cheese, diced
1	head romaine lettuce, chopped

Blend the lemon juice, oil, parsley, salt, thyme, oregano and pepper together.

Heat the olive oil in a skillet. Add the garlic and sauté 2 minutes.

Add the chicken and brown. Pour in the dressing and heat for 1 minute.

Add the tomatoes and cheese. Heat 1 more minute.

Place lettuce on plate. Spoon chicken, tomatoes and cheese with dressing over the lettuce.

Serve at once.

Sweet and Sour Shredded Vegetable Salad

6 servings

2 cups	(500 mL)	shredded cabbage
1 cup	(250 mL)	shredded carrots
2 cups	(500 mL)	shredded zucchini
4 cups	(1 L)	bamboo shoots
½ cup	(125 mL)	chopped green onions
½ cup	(125 mL)	mayonnaise
3 tbsp	(45 mL)	cider vinegar
1 tsp	(5 mL)	salt
1 tsp	(5 mL)	sugar
¼ tsp	(1 mL)	pepper

Mix the vegetables together in a mixing or serving bowl.

Blend the mayonnaise, vinegar and seasonings together.

Pour over vegetables.

Sweet and Sour Shredded Vegetable Salad

Herb-Marinated Baby Mushrooms

6 servings

2		garlic cloves, crushed
1 tbsp	(15 mL)	oil
⅓ cup	(80 mL)	oil
1 tbsp	(15 mL)	lemon juice
2 tbsp	(30 mL)	chopped parsley
1 tbsp	(15 mL)	oregano
1 tbsp	(15 mL)	sweet basil
2¼ lbs	(1 kg)	button mushrooms

Heat garlic in 1 tbsp (15 mL) oil. Sauté 1 minute.

Add remaining ingredients and pour over mushrooms.

Refrigerate 6 hours or overnight.

Curried Seafood Salad

6 servings

1 cup	(*250 mL*) mayonnaise
2 tbsp	(*30 mL*) lemon juice
2 tsp	(*10 mL*) curry powder
½ tsp	(*3 mL*) salt
½ cup	(*125 mL*) minced celery
½ cup	(*125 mL*) tomatoes, seeded and chopped
½ cup	(*125 mL*) green pepper, minced
4 cups	(*1 L*) vermicelli, broken, cooked
1 cup	(*250 mL*) salmon, cooked and flaked
1 cup	(*250 mL*) scallops (very small)
1 cup	(*250 mL*) baby shrimp

Blend the mayonnaise, lemon juice and seasonings together.

Mix together the celery, tomatoes, green pepper and vermicelli. Combine with the dressing.

Place on a platter. Layer with salmon, scallops and shrimp.

Smoked Cheese Potato Salad

6 servings

2 cups	(*500 mL*) smoked cheese, diced
3 cups	(*750 mL*) potatoes, cooked and diced
2	celery stalks, diced fine
3	green onions, minced
2	hard-boiled eggs, grated
1 cup	(*250 mL*) ham, cooked and diced
2 tbsp	(*30 mL*) lemon juice
1 cup	(*250 mL*) mayonnaise
½ tsp	(*3 mL*) salt
¼ tsp	(*1 mL*) pepper

Blend the cheese, potatoes, celery, onions, eggs and ham together.

Mix the lemon juice and mayonnaise with the seasonings.

Pour into the salad and toss.

Chill for 1 hour. Serve.

Dandelion Salad

6-8 servings

8 cups	(*2 L*) dandelion leaves, washed and trimmed
1½ cups	(*375 mL*) sliced mushrooms
2	tomatoes, cut in wedges
¼ cup	(*60 mL*) croutons
¼ cup	(*60 mL*) slivered almonds, toasted
½ cup	(*125 mL*) golden Italian salad dressing
½ cup	(*125 mL*) coarsely grated Havarti cheese

Combine dandelion leaves, mushrooms, tomatoes, croutons and almonds.

Toss with Italian dressing and sprinkle with cheese.

Spiced Lime Fruit Salad

6 servings

1	fresh pineapple
¼ cup	(*60 mL*) fresh lime juice
¾ cup	(*180 mL*) oil
2 tsp	(*10 mL*) grated lime peel
1 tsp	(*5 mL*) salt
1 tsp	(*5 mL*) cracked pepper
2 tbsp	(*30 mL*) chopped parsley
2	oranges
1 lb	(*450 g*) fresh seedless grapes
1	cantaloupe
6	romaine lettuce leaves

Peel, core and dice the pineapple.

Blend together the lime juice, oil, lime peel and seasonings.

Mix the diced pineapple into the dressing.

Cut the oranges into sections. Halve the grapes. Use a melon baller and scoop out the cantaloupe.

Mix the remaining fruit in with the pineapple. Marinate 30 minutes.

Place romaine lettuce leaves on plates.

Divide the salad equally over the lettuce.

 1

Peel, core and dice the pineapple.

2

Cut the oranges into sections.

3

Using a melon baller, scoop out the cantaloupe.

4

Place romaine lettuce leaves on plates and divide salad equally over the lettuce.

Jennifer's Pear Salad

8 servings

Dressing

1 cup	*(250 mL)*	mayonnaise
½ cup	*(125 mL)*	sour cream
¼ cup	*(60 mL)*	icing sugar

Salad

10		unpeeled pears, cored and diced
½ cup	*(125 mL)*	sliced almonds, lightly toasted
1 cup	*(250 mL)*	diced mild Cheddar cheese
2 cups	*(500 mL)*	diced seeded tomatoes
		shredded lettuce

Combine dressing ingredients; mix well and chill.

Combine pears, almonds, cheese, and tomatoes; gently toss with dressing.

Serve in nests of shredded lettuce.

Jennifer's Pear Salad

Sweet and Sour Pasta Salad

6 servings

½ lb	*(225 g)*	multicolored rotini
3		green onions, diced
½ cup	*(125 mL)*	sliced mushrooms
1		green pepper, diced
¼ cup	*(60 mL)*	almonds, toasted
4		slices bacon, diced
2 tbsp	*(30 mL)*	minced onion
3 tbsp	*(45 mL)*	sugar
3 tbsp	*(45 mL)*	vinegar
½ cup	*(125 mL)*	water
1⅓ cups	*(330 mL)*	mayonnaise

Boil rotini al dente; run under cold water until cool. Drain thoroughly.

Mix in the green onions, mushrooms, green pepper and almonds.

Fry bacon in a skillet. Add the onion and cook until tender.

Blend in the sugar, vinegar and water. Bring to a boil and reduce liquid by half.

Whip in the mayonnaise and remove from heat. Cool.

Pour dressing over salad. Blend well. Serve.

Pasta Seafood Salad

6 servings

6	tiger shrimp, butterflied
½ lb	(225 g) multicolored rotini pasta
6	artichoke hearts, marinated
2 tbsp	(30 mL) capers
1 tsp	(5 mL) celery seeds
3 tbsp	(45 mL) pimiento
1	red pepper, finely diced
½ lb	(225 g) baby shrimp, cooked
7.5 oz	(213 g) canned salmon, drained
8 oz	(227 mL) canned mini-corn, drained
2 oz	(60 g) cashews

Preheat over to 350°F (*180°C*).

Bake tiger shrimp in oven for 10 minutes. Cool.

Boil rotini in salted water al dente.

Run under cold water until cool. Drain well.

Place in a large mixing bowl.

Add the artichoke hearts, capers, celery seeds, pimiento and red pepper; toss well.

Blend in the dressing, (see above right).

Arrange baby shrimp, salmon, mini-corn, cashews and tiger shrimp on top.

Dressing

¼ cup	(60 mL) raspberry coulis (see *Sauces*)
½ cup	(125 mL) mayonnaise
½ cup	(125 mL) heavy cream
2 tbsp	(30 mL) icing sugar
1 tsp	(5 mL) black pepper

Combine all ingredients thoroughly.

Use as required.

Pasta Seafood Salad

Monte Cristo Salad

6 servings

Dressing

1 cup	(*250 mL*) mayonnaise
1 tsp	(*5 mL*) Dijon mustard
½ tsp	(*3 mL*) chopped, fresh tarragon or ¼ tsp (*1 mL*) dried tarragon

Salad

1 cup	(*250 mL*) cooked, cubed lobster meat
1 cup	(*250 mL*) diced cooked potatoes
1 cup	(*250 mL*) sliced mushrooms
1 cup	(*250 mL*) coarsely grated Swiss cheese
4	hard-boiled eggs, coarsely chopped
	romaine lettuce
1	tomato, cut in wedges

Combine the dressing ingredients; mix well and chill.

Combine the lobster, potatoes, mushrooms, cheese and eggs.

Toss gently with the dressing and arrange neatly on leaves of romaine.

Garnish with tomato wedges.

Swedish Cucumber Sour Cream Salad

6 servings

1 tbsp	(*15 mL*) sugar
1 tsp	(*5 mL*) salt
1 cup	(*250 mL*) sour cream
3 tbsp	(*45 mL*) minced green onion
2 tbsp	(*30 mL*) vinegar
6	cucumbers, peeled and thinly sliced
1	small lettuce

Blend the sugar, salt, sour cream, green onion, and vinegar together.

Combine into the cucumbers.

Chill for several hours.

Serve in a bowl ringed with lettuce leaves.

Honeyed Carrot Salad

6 servings

4 cups	(*1 L*) shredded carrots
2	apples, pared and diced
½ cup	(*125 mL*) raisins
½ cup	(*125 mL*) pine nuts
¼ cup	(*60 mL*) lemon juice
¼ cup	(*60 mL*) honey
¼ tsp	(*1 mL*) cinnamon

In a mixing bowl, combine the carrots, apples, raisins and pine nuts.

Blend the lemon juice, honey and cinnamon together.

Pour over salad.

Serve cold.

Smoked Chicken Veronique

Smoked Chicken Veronique

6 servings

3 cups	(750 mL)	diced smoked chicken
1 cup	(250 mL)	seedless green grapes
½ cup	(125 mL)	cashews
⅓ cup	(80 mL)	mayonnaise
⅓ cup	(80 mL)	lemon-flavored yogurt
3 tbsp	(45 mL)	honey
2 tsp	(10 mL)	cracked black pepper
6		romaine lettuce leaves
6		grape clusters

Mix the chicken, grapes and cashews together.

Blend together the mayonnaise, yogurt, honey and pepper.

Combine the chicken mixture with the dressing.

Arrange the lettuce leaves on plates.

Divide the salad equally on leaves.

Garnish with grape clusters.

Hearts of Palm Salad

2 servings

8 oz	(227 mL)	hearts of palm, drained
		butter lettuce leaves
¼ cup	(60 mL)	oil
2 tbsp	(30 mL)	lemon juice
2 tsp	(10 mL)	minced green onion
2 tsp	(10 mL)	minced pimiento
1 tsp	(5 mL)	fresh cracked pepper
1 tsp	(5 mL)	raw sugar

Arrange the hearts of palm on the lettuce leaves.

Combine the oil, lemon juice, green onion, pimiento and pepper.

Pour over hearts.

Sprinkle with sugar. Serve.

Spinach Scallop Salad

4 servings

8	slices bacon, diced
½ lb	(*225 g*) very small scallops
¼ cup	(*60 mL*) oil
3 tbsp	(*45 mL*) red wine vinegar
2 tsp	(*10 mL*) Dijon mustard
1 tsp	(*5 mL*) anchovy paste
¼ tsp	(*1 mL*) cracked black pepper
3 oz	(*90 g*) mushrooms, sliced
10 oz	(*284 g*) spinach

Sauté the bacon. Add the scallops and cook until tender.

Add the oil, vinegar, mustard, anchovy paste and pepper. Swirl and heat.

Mix the mushrooms in the spinach. Pour sauce over spinach.

Allow leaves to wilt and serve at once.

Caesar Salad

6-8 servings

3	large cloves garlic
3	anchovy filets, drained
1 tsp	(*5 mL*) seasoned salt
¼ tsp	(*1 mL*) dry mustard
1	drop hot pepper sauce
1 tbsp	(*15 mL*) Worcestershire sauce
4 tsp	(*20 mL*) red wine
2 tbsp	(*30 mL*) lemon juice
⅓ cup	(*80 mL*) white vinegar
2	egg yolks
1 cup	(*250 mL*) vegetable oil
2	heads romaine lettuce
1 lb	(*450 g*) bacon, cooked and crumbled
1 cup	(*250 mL*) croutons
¾ cup	(*180 mL*) grated Romano cheese

In food processor with steel blade, mince garlic and anchovy filets.

With machine running, add salt, mustard, hot pepper sauce, Worcestershire sauce, red wine, lemon juice and vinegar.

Add egg yolks and process until blended. With machine running, slowly add oil.

Tear lettuce and combine with bacon and croutons. Toss with dressing. Add cheese and toss again.

Shrimp & Crab Tomato Vinaigrette

6 servings

½ lb	(*225 g*) large shrimp, cooked
½ lb	(*225 g*) crab meat, cooked
4	tomatoes, peeled, seeded and chopped
1	small onion, minced
1	garlic clove, minced
½ tsp	(*3 mL*) salt
½ tsp	(*3 mL*) pepper
½ tsp	(*3 mL*) marjoram
½ tsp	(*3 mL*) basil leaves
½ tsp	(*3 mL*) dry mustard
3 tbsp	(*45 mL*) lemon juice
¼ cup	(*60 mL*) vinegar
¾ cup	(*180 mL*) oil
6	Bibb lettuce leaves
2 tbsp	(*30 mL*) chopped parsley

Mix together the shrimp, crab, tomatoes, onion and garlic.

Blend the herbs and spices together with the lemon juice, vinegar and oil.

Pour the vinaigrette over the seafood salad. Cover and refrigerate 2 hours.

Place the lettuce leaves on chilled plates, spoon the salad over the leaves.

Sprinkle with parsley and serve.

Salmon Salad Mold

6 servings

1 tbsp	(*15 mL*) unflavored gelatine
¼ cup	(*60 mL*) cold water
¾ cup	(*180 mL*) mayonnaise
3 tbsp	(*45 mL*) lemon juice
2 tsp	(*10 mL*) salt
1 tsp	(*5 mL*) white pepper
1	small onion, minced
1	carrot, minced
1	celery stalk, minced
1¼ cups	(*310 mL*) cooked, flaked salmon
2 tbsp	(*30 mL*) butter
12	jumbo shrimp, peeled deveined and cooked

Soften the gelatine in the water 10 minutes.

Blend together with the mayonnaise, lemon juice and seasonings.

Fold in the vegetables and salmon. Turn into a buttered mold.

Chill 3½ to 4 hours. Unmold and garnish with shrimp. Serve.

Salmon Salad Mold

Five Bean Salad

8 servings

1 lb	(*450 g*) canned kidney beans
1 lb	(*450 g*) canned broad beans
½ lb	(*225 g*) white beans, soaked overnight
1 lb	(*450 g*) fresh green beans
1 lb	(*450 g*) fresh yellow beans
½ cup	(*125 mL*) sour cream
¼ cup	(*60 mL*) chopped parsley
½ cup	(*125 mL*) oil
⅓ cup	(*80 mL*) lemon juice
1 tsp	(*5 mL*) salt
pinch	pepper

Drain and rinse the canned beans. Drain the white beans.

Blanch the green and yellow beans for 5 minutes.

Mix the sour cream, parsley, oil, lemon juice, salt and pepper together.

Toss the beans with the dressing and refrigerate for 3 hours.

Warm Spinach Salad

8 servings

Salad

1 lb	(*450 g*) bacon
2	10 oz (*284 g*) bags spinach
4 ½ cups	(*1,1 L*) sliced mushrooms
¾ cup	(*180 mL*) grated Parmesan cheese
3	hard-boiled eggs, coarsely chopped

Dressing

3 tbsp	(*45 mL*) Dijon mustard
4 tsp	(*20 mL*) granulated sugar
½ cup	(*125 mL*) white wine vinegar
2 tbsp	(*30 mL*) Worcestershire sauce
1 tbsp	(*15 mL*) seasoned salt
1 cup	(*250 mL*) olive oil
6	green onions, chopped

Warm Spinach Salad

Cut bacon into ½ in. (*1 cm*) pieces and fry until crisp, reserving ¼ cup (*60 mL*) drippings.

Wash the spinach, remove stems, and tear into bite-size pieces.

Toss with bacon pieces, sliced mushrooms, cheese and eggs.

To prepare the dressing, combine reserved bacon drippings, mustard and sugar in a small saucepan. Whisking constantly, bring to a boil.

Whisk in the vinegar, Worcestershire sauce, and salt.

Very slowly, add the oil, whisking constantly. Stir in the green onions and pour hot mixture over salad.

Toss and serve immediately.

Romaine Salad with Oranges

8 servings

Dressing

1 cup	*(250 mL)* salad dressing or mayonnaise
¼ cup	*(60 mL)* orange juice concentrate
¼ cup	*(60 mL)* peach or apple juice concentrate
¼ tsp	*(1 mL)* cinnamon

Salad

1	large head romaine lettuce
8	mushrooms, sliced
2 cups	*(500 mL)* grated Swiss cheese
1 cup	*(250 mL)* seedless red grapes
1 cup	*(250 mL)* fresh orange sections
½ cup	*(125 mL)* sliced almonds, toasted

Combine dressing ingredients; mix well and chill.

Wash romaine lettuce, remove stems, and tear into bite-size pieces.

Toss with sliced mushrooms, cheese, grapes and oranges.

Sprinkle almonds on top.

Serve the dressing separately.

Mayonnaise

2 cups (500 mL)

2	egg yolks
1 tsp	*(5 mL)* dry mustard
1 tsp	*(5 mL)* salt
2 tsp	*(10 mL)* sugar
⅛ tsp	*(0,5 mL)* cayenne pepper
1½ cups	*(375 mL)* oil
3 tbsp	*(45 mL)* lemon juice
1 tbsp	*(15 mL)* water

Place egg yolks in a blender. Add the mustard and the seasonings.

With the machine running, slowly pour in the oil.

Mix the lemon juice with water.

Slowly pour the lemon juice into the sauce in a steady stream while the machine runs.

Use as required. Will keep 7 days refrigerated.

Garlic & Herb Dressing

1½ cups (375 mL)

1 cup	*(250 mL)* olive oil
2	garlic cloves, minced
1 tbsp	*(15 mL)* minced parsley
¼ tsp	*(1 mL)* basil
¼ tsp	*(1 mL)* oregano
¼ tsp	*(1 mL)* thyme
¼ tsp	*(1 mL)* salt
¼ tsp	*(1 mL)* pepper
⅓ cup	*(80 mL)* vinegar

Blend together the oil, the garlic and seasonings in a blender.

With the machine running, slowly add the vinegar.

Use as salad or vegetable marinade.

French Dressing

2 cups (500 mL)

1 tsp	*(5 mL)* salt
¼ tsp	*(1 mL)* pepper
1 tsp	*(5 mL)* sugar
1 tsp	*(5 mL)* paprika
1	garlic clove, minced
1½ cups	*(375 mL)* oil
½ cup	*(125 mL)* vinegar

Mix the seasonings and garlic into the oil. Slowly whisk in the vinegar.

Fresh Tomato Dressing

2 cups (500 mL)

1 cup	(*250 mL*) tomatoes, peeled, seeded and chopped
¼ cup	(*60 mL*) honey
1 tsp	(*5 mL*) Worcestershire sauce
½ tsp	(*3 mL*) dry mustard
1 tsp	(*5 mL*) salt
2 tsp	(*10 mL*) oregano
½ tsp	(*3 mL*) fresh cracked black pepper
3 tbsp	(*45 mL*) lemon juice
¼ cup	(*60 mL*) vinegar
¾ cup	(*180 mL*) safflower oil

Place all ingredients into a blender.

Blend for 1 minute or until a smooth sauce is formed.

Use as required.

Green Goddess Salad Dressing

2 ½ cups (625 mL)

1 oz	(*30 g*) anchovy paste
1	garlic clove, minced
2	green onions, chopped
1 tbsp	(*15 mL*) parsley flakes
1 tbsp	(*15 mL*) chopped tarragon
1 tbsp	(*15 mL*) chopped chives
2	egg yolks
2 cups	(*500 mL*) oil
¼ cup	(*60 mL*) lemon juice

In a blender, purée the anchovy paste, garlic, green onions, parsley, tarragon and chives.

Add the egg yolks. With the machine running slowly, pour in the oil. Add the lemon juice.

Use for salads, chicken or cold seafood dishes.

Italian Salad Dressing

2¼ cups (560 mL)

2 cups	(*500 mL*) French dressing
1 tsp	(*5 mL*) salt
2 tbsp	(*30 mL*) sugar
1 tsp	(*5 mL*) dry mustard
1 tsp	(*5 mL*) paprika
½ tsp	(*3 mL*) oregano
½ tsp	(*3 mL*) basil
½ tsp	(*3 mL*) chervil
2 tsp	(*10 mL*) Worcestershire sauce

Blend the dressing with the seasonings.

Use as required.

Russian Dressing

2 cups (500 mL)

1 cup	(*250 mL*) mayonnaise
⅓ cup	(*80 mL*) chili sauce
3 tbsp	(*45 mL*) minced green onion
2 tbsp	(*30 mL*) chopped pickled beets
1 tbsp	(*15 mL*) chopped parsley
2 tbsp	(*30 mL*) chopped pitted black olives
2 tbsp	(*30 mL*) caviar

Blend all ingredients thoroughly.

Refrigerate. Use as required.

Green Goddess Salad Dressing, Italian Salad Dressing and French Dressing

Creamy Basil Dressing

1 cup (250 mL)

2	shallots, minced
2 tbsp	(30 mL) fresh basil, minced
1 tsp	(5 mL) Dijon mustard
½ cup	(125 mL) olive oil
¼ tsp	(1 mL) salt
¼ tsp	(1 mL) pepper
3 tbsp	(45 mL) lemon juice

Combine the shallots, basil, mustard, oil, salt and pepper in a blender.

With the machine running slowly, pour in the lemon juice.

Use as a salad marinade or dressing.

Piquant Dressing

2 cups (500 mL)

¼ cup	(60 mL) minced sweet red bell pepper
3 tbsp	(45 mL) minced onion
1 tsp	(15 mL) chopped capers
2 tbsp	(30 mL) minced dill pickles
¼ cup	(60 mL) sugar
1 tsp	(5 mL) salt
1 tsp	(5 mL) dry mustard
1 tsp	(5 mL) garlic powder
2 tsp	(10 mL) basil leaves
½ tsp	(3 mL) cracked black pepper
½ tsp	(3 mL) Worcestershire sauce
3 tbsp	(45 mL) lemon juice
¼ cup	(60 mL) vinegar
¾ cup	(180 mL) safflower oil

Place all the ingredients, except the oil, in a blender.

Blend on medium speed for 30 seconds. With machine running, slowly add the oil. Blend until smooth.

Use as required.

Honey Lemon Dressing

1¼ cups (310 mL)

1 cup	(250 mL) French dressing
¼ cup	(60 mL) honey
2 tbsp	(30 mL) lemon juice
1 tsp	(5 mL) ground cinnamon

Blend together the dressing, honey, lemon juice and cinnamon thoroughly.

Refrigerate. Use as required.

Ranch Dressing

2 cups (500 mL)

½ cup	(125 mL) buttermilk
1 cup	(250 mL) mayonnaise
2 tbsp	(30 mL) minced chives
1 tbsp	(15 mL) lemon juice
¼ tsp	(1 mL) salt
pinch	white pepper

Fold the buttermilk into the mayonnaise. Whip in the remaining ingredients. Refrigerate.

Use as required.

1000 Island Dressing and Blue Cheese Dressing

1000 Island Dressing

2 cups (500 mL)

1 cup	(*250 mL*) mayonnaise
1/2 cup	(*125 mL*) chili sauce
1/4 cup	(*60 mL*) pickle relish
1/2 tsp	(*3 mL*) dry mustard
1/2 tsp ·	(*3 mL*) basil
1 tbsp	(*15 mL*) pimiento
2	hard-boiled eggs, grated

Blend all the ingredients together thoroughly. Refrigerate.

Use as required.

Poppy Seed Dressing

2 cups (500 mL)

1 1/2 cups	(*375 mL*) French dressing
1/3 cup	(*80 mL*) sugar
2 tbsp	(*30 mL*) poppy seeds

Blend the ingredients together thoroughly. Refrigirate.

Use as required.

Blue Cheese Dressing

2 cups (500 mL)

1/4 cup	(*60 mL*) blue cheese
1 1/2 cups	(*375 mL*) mayonnaise
1 tbsp	(*15 mL*) lemon juice
1/2 tsp	(*3 mL*) salt
1/4 tsp	(*1 mL*) white pepper

Melt the cheese over a double boiler. Remove from heat.

Place in a mixing bowl. Fold in the mayonnaise, lemon juice and seasonings.

Refrigerate. Use as required.

If desired, crumble 1/2 cup (*125 mL*) cheese into dressing.

Eggs

I find it amazing that most people consider eggs simply as a breakfast food or as a baking ingredient. Unfortunately, many of the textbooks in our schools and colleges still place eggs only in these categories.

But in fact, eggs lend themselves to some wonderful luncheon and dinner recipes. Even when it seems there is very little in the way of ingredients in the refrigerator, you can make a wonderful meal based on eggs using one of the traditional cooking techniques — scrambled, shirred, baked, boiled, fried, poached, or in an omelette.

Eggs should always be treated to slow gentle cooking, with the notable exception of omelettes, which require relatively high heat. But in general, cooking at high heat toughens the egg. Boiling eggs at high heat causes a green ring around the yolk.

Perfect Boiled Eggs

Eggs should be at room temperature before cooking. Bring the water to a boil, add the eggs, then reduce heat to a simmer. Cook according to the following timing chart:

Soft-boiled eggs: 3 - 5 minutes
Medium-boiled eggs: 6 - 8 minutes
Hard-boiled eggs: 10 - 11 minutes

Pastry Egg Breakfast

Molded Shrimp Eggs

6 servings

6	eggs
¼ cup	(*60 mL*) heavy cream
¼ tsp	(*1 mL*) salt
pinch	pepper
1 cup	(*250 mL*) baby shrimp
6	bread rusks
1 cup	(*250 mL*) Mornay sauce, hot (see *Sauces*)

Preheat oven to 350°F (*180°C*).

Mix the eggs with the cream and seasonings. Blend in the baby shrimp.

Lightly grease six 4 oz (*125 mL*) molds. Fill with egg mixture.

Place molds in a water bath.

Bake in oven until eggs set, about 25 minutes.

Unmold onto rusks.

Cover with sauce and serve.

Pastry Egg Breakfast

8 servings

8	vol-au-vent shells
8	eggs
¼ cup	(*60 mL*) heavy cream
8	slices bacon, diced
1	green pepper, finely diced
2	green onions, minced
1 cup	(*250 mL*) grated Havarti cheese

Preheat oven to 400°F (*200°C*).

Bake the vol-au-vent shells for 15 minutes. Mix the eggs with the cream.

Fry the bacon, add the green pepper and sauté until tender. Pour off half the fat.

Add the eggs and green onions; stir until cooked.

Remove from heat.

Stir in the cheese. Fill each shell with the egg filling.

Serve at once.

Chilled Eggs Carême

8 tarts

8	eggs
1 cup	(*250 mL*) diced smoked salmon
⅓ cup	(*80 mL*) mayonnaise
8	tart shells, 3 in. (*7 cm*) each, baked
2 tbsp	(*30 mL*) red caviar

Poach the eggs gently until hard. Chill.

Bind the salmon in the mayonnaise.

Place some of the salmon in each tart shell.

Top with an egg and sprinkle with caviar.

Chilled Eggs Carême

Pickled Eggs

1 dozen

12	eggs
2 cups	(*500 mL*) white vinegar
1½ tbsp	(*22 mL*) pickling spice
1 tsp	(*5 mL*) salt
3	garlic cloves
1 tbsp	(*15 mL*) lemon zest
1 cup	(*250 mL*) water
1	onion, sliced

Hardboil the eggs. Chill and shell.

Boil together all the remaining ingredients for 10 minutes. Cool.

Place the eggs in a large jar. Pour the pickling mixture over the eggs.

Seal the jar.

Place in a refrigerator for 4 to 7 days before serving.

Eggs Hussarde

Eggs Hussarde

4 servings

8	ham slices, 2 oz (60 g) each
8	bread rusks
1 cup	(250 mL) Marchand de Vin Sauce
8	tomato slices, grilled
8	poached eggs, soft
1 cup	(250 mL) hollandaise sauce (see *Sauces*)

Broil the ham for 2 minutes. Place 1 slice on each rusk. Top ham with Marchand de Vin Sauce. Place one slice of tomato on sauce.

Top with a poached egg. Top egg with hollandaise sauce.

Marchand de Vin Sauce

¾ cup	(180 mL) butter
½ cup	(125 mL) sliced mushrooms
¼ cup	(60 mL) chopped green onions
½ cup	(125 mL) minced onions
3	garlic cloves, minced
4 oz	(115 g) ham, minced
2 tbsp	(30 mL) flour
¾ cup	(180 mL) beef stock
1 cup	(250 mL) sherry
½ tsp	(3 mL) salt
½ tsp	(3 mL) pepper
¼ tsp	(1 mL) cayenne pepper

Melt the butter; sauté the mushrooms, both onions, garlic and ham.

Add the flour and stir. Add the beef stock, sherry and seasonings.

Simmer for 40 minutes over low heat.

Poached Eggs Oscar

6 servings

12	eggs
6	English muffins
1 cup	(*250 mL*) crab meat
12	asparagus spears, blanched 5 minutes
1 cup	(*250 mL*) hollandaise sauce (see *Sauces*)

Poach the eggs in an egg poacher or hot water with a few drops of vinegar.

Halve the English muffins and toast them.

Top each muffin with an egg, a spoonful of crab meat, 1 asparagus spear and some hollandaise.

Serve hot.

Lobster Eggs

8 servings

2 tbsp	(*30 mL*) butter
2 oz	(*60 g*) mushrooms, sliced
2 tbsp	(*30 mL*) flour
1 cup	(*250 mL*) heavy cream
¼ tsp	(*1 mL*) salt
pinch	pepper
½ tsp	(*3 mL*) fresh basil, chopped
2 cups	(*500 mL*) lobster meat
8	eggs
8	bread rusks

In a skillet, heat the butter. Sauté the mushrooms. Sprinkle in flour and cook for 2 minutes.

Add the cream, seasonings and ½ cup (*125 mL*) lobster meat. Simmer until thickened.

Poach the eggs to desired doneness. Place the remaining lobster meat on the bread rusks.

Top with an egg. Smother with sauce.

Serve at once.

Eggs Parmentier

4 servings

4	medium potatoes, peeled
8	eggs
¼ cup	(*60 mL*) heavy cream
3 tbsp	(*45 mL*) butter
1	small onion, diced
½ lb	(*225 g*) ham, diced
1	tomato, diced
1 cup	(*250 mL*) grated Swiss cheese

Preheat oven to 400°F (*200°C*).

Parboil the potatoes; cool. Slice the potatoes.

Mix the eggs with the cream.

Heat the butter and sauté the potatoes. Add the onion and ham; sauté until tender.

Add the tomato and eggs.

Top with cheese and bake in oven for 15 to 20 minutes, until eggs are cooked through.

Sauté the green pepper until tender. Sprinkle with curry powder.

Add the Mornay sauce and blend well.

Slice the chicken breasts. Place on a bread rusk. Top with an egg.

Cover with sauce and serve at once.

Eggs Nantua

Eggs Nantua

4 servings

4	tomatoes
8	eggs
1 cup	(*250 mL*) chopped, cooked crayfish or shrimp
1 cup	(*250 mL*) Mornay sauce (see *Sauces*)
1 cup	(*250 mL*) grated medium Cheddar cheese
8	bread rusks

Preheat oven to 350°F (*180°C*).

Cut the tomatoes in half; scoop out the seeds and the pulp.

Heat in oven for 10 minutes. While tomatoes are heating, poach the eggs.

Remove tomatoes from oven. Place 1 egg in cavity of each tomato half.

Top with a little crayfish, 1 tbsp (*15 mL*) Mornay sauce and sprinkle cheese on top.

Place under broiler for 2 minutes or until cheese melts.

Serve with bread rusks.

Eggs Maharaja

4 servings

½ cup	(*125 mL*) water
½ cup	(*125 mL*) white wine, or chicken broth
2	chicken breasts, 7 oz (*200 g*) each
8	eggs
1 tbsp	(*15 mL*) butter
3 tbsp	(*45 mL*) green pepper, finely diced
1 tbsp	(*15 mL*) curry powder
2 cups	(*500 mL*) Mornay sauce (see *Sauces*), hot
8	bread rusks

In a saucepan, place the water and wine. Gently poach the chicken breasts, about 15 minutes. Remove. Set aside and keep hot. Strain the liquid through a fine cheesecloth.

Poach the eggs in the liquid. In a skillet, heat the butter.

Mexican Eggs

6 servings

6		eggs
¼ cup	(60 mL)	heavy cream
¼ tsp	(1 mL)	chili powder
¼ tsp	(1 mL)	salt
pinch		pepper
pinch		paprika
2 tbsp	(30 mL)	butter
½ cup	(125 mL)	tomato sauce
½ cup	(125 mL)	grated medium Cheddar

In a mixing bowl, blend together the eggs, cream and seasonings. Beat well.

Heat the butter in a skillet. Add the eggs and fry, stirring until cooked. Place on heat-proof platter.

Pour the tomato sauce on top of the eggs. Do not blend in. Sprinkle with cheese.

Place under the broiler for 1 minute or until cheese melts.

Serve at once.

Eggs à la Suisse

3 servings

1 cup	(250 mL)	grated Havarti cheese
6		eggs
½ cup	(125 mL)	light cream
¼ tsp	(1 mL)	salt
¼ tsp	(1 mL)	pepper

Preheat oven to 350°F (180°C). Butter an earthenware baking dish.

Sprinkle half the cheese in the dish. Break the eggs into a small bowl and slide on top of cheese; (don't break the yolks).

Pour in the cream. Sprinkle with salt, pepper and the remaining cheese.

Bake in oven for 15 minutes. Serve at once.

Twenty-Four Hour Omelette

8-10 servings

1		small French loaf, cut into 1 in. (2,5 cm) cubes
3 tbsp	(45 mL)	melted butter
1½ cups	(375 mL)	grated Swiss cheese
1 cup	(250 mL)	grated Colby cheese
8		slices Genoa salami, coarsely chopped
8		eggs
1½ cups	(375 mL)	milk
¼ cup	(60 mL)	dry white wine
2 tbsp	(30 mL)	chopped parsley
1½ tsp	(8 mL)	Dijon mustard
		pepper
		hot pepper sauce
¾ cup	(180 mL)	sour cream
½ cup	(125 mL)	grated Parmesan cheese

Distribute bread cubes in a greased 13 x 9 in. (33 x 23 cm) pan.

Drizzle with melted butter. Sprinkle with Swiss and Colby and salami.

Combine eggs, milk, wine, parsley and mustard.

Season with pepper and hot pepper sauce to taste; beat until well blended.

Pour over cheese mixture, cover with foil, and refrigerate 12-24 hours.

Preheat oven to 325°F (160°C). Remove pan from refrigerator 30 minutes before baking.

Bake, covered, in oven for 1 hour. Remove pan from oven; remove cover.

Spread with sour cream and sprinkle with Parmesan.

Return to 400°F (200°C) oven and bake, uncovered, for 15 minutes or until lightly browned.

Variations : Use different cheeses, chopped ham, crumbled bacon, sautéed mushrooms, chopped peppers, or cooked cubed chicken.

Quiche Lorraine

6-8 servings

Pastry

1 cup	(250 mL)	all-purpose flour
½ tsp	(3 mL)	salt
¼ cup	(60 mL)	butter
1		egg
3 tbsp	(45 mL)	cold water

(Continued on next page)

Filling

8	slices bacon, cut into 1/2- in. (1 cm) pieces
1	onion, finely chopped
1 cup	(250 mL) grated Swiss cheese
6	eggs
1½ cups	(375 mL) heavy cream

Preheat oven to 400°F (200°C).

Pastry : Combine flour and salt. Cut in butter until mixture resembles coarse meal.

In a measuring cup, beat egg and water with a fork until blended.

Gradually add just enough liquid to flour to make dough hold together. Press into a ball.

Roll out dough to ⅛-in. (0,5 cm) thickness and place in a 9-in. (23 cm) flan pan. Line with foil, fill with dried beans or rice, and bake in oven for 10 minutes.

Remove foil and beans and return to oven for about 10 minutes or until barely golden.

Filling : Fry bacon until cooked but still tender. Drain most of fat, reserving just enough to sauté the onion until tender.

Pat bacon and onion in paper towel to remove extra fat.

Sprinkle bacon, onion, and cheese over baked flan shell. Whisk together eggs and cream; pour into shell.

Bake at 375°F (190°C) for 30-40 minutes or until knife inserted in the center comes out clean.

Let stand 5 minutes before serving.

1

Place dough in flan pan, line with foil and fill with dried beans or rice. Bake in oven for 10 minutes.

2

Fry bacon, drain most of fat and sauté the onion until tender.

3

Place filling in shell; whisk together eggs and cream and pour into shell.

4

Bake in oven 30 to 40 minutes or until knife inserted in the center comes out clean.

Crustless Crab Quiche

6-8 servings

1½ cups	(*375 mL*) sliced mushrooms
2 tbsp	(*30 mL*) butter
4	eggs
1 cup	(*250 mL*) sour cream
½ cup	(*125 mL*) cottage cheese
¼ cup	(*60 mL*) grated Parmesan cheese
¼ cup	(*60 mL*) all-purpose flour
1 tsp	(*5 mL*) onion powder
¼ tsp	(*1 mL*) salt
4	drops hot pepper sauce
½ cup	(*125 mL*) crab meat, well drained
2 cups	(*500 mL*) grated medium Cheddar cheese

Preheat oven to 350°F (*180°C*).

Sauté the mushrooms in butter over high heat until tender.

Place on a paper towel.

In a blender or food processor, combine eggs, sour cream, cottage cheese, Parmesan, flour, onion powder, salt, and hot pepper sauce; process until well blended.

Combine egg mixture, mushrooms, crab meat and cheese in a large bowl; mix well.

Crustless Crab Quiche

Pour into a 10-in. (*25 cm*) quiche dish and bake in oven for 45 minutes or until mixture is set and surface is golden.

Let stand 5 minutes before cutting.

Bacon 'n Egg Crêpes

8 servings

1 lb	(*450 g*) bacon, cooked and crumbled
8	eggs
¼ cup	(*60 mL*) heavy cream
¼ cup	(*60 mL*) chopped green onions
	salt and pepper
1 cup	(*250 mL*) grated Monterey Jack cheese
8	8-in. (*20 cm*) crêpes (see *Breads*)

Cut the bacon into pieces and fry until crisp; drain well.

Whisk together eggs and cream.

Stir in bacon, onions and seasonings to taste. Pour into a hot buttered pan.

As portions cook, gently lift with a spatula so that uncooked portions can flow to bottom. Avoid constant stirring.

Sprinkle cheese over eggs when eggs are almost totally cooked.

Spoon egg mixture into crêpes and roll.

Serve with hash brown potatoes and green grapes.

Bacon 'n Egg Crêpes

Shirred Eggs Puerto Rico

4 servings

1½ cups	(*375 mL*) tomato sauce (see *Sauces*)
2 cups	(*500 mL*) ham, finely diced
2 cups	(*500 mL*) asparagus tips
8	eggs
1½ cups	(*375 mL*) Mornay sauce (see *Sauces*)

Preheat oven to 350°F (*180°C*).

In a small greased casserole dish, pour the tomato sauce. Add the ham and asparagus.

Break the eggs into a small bowl without breaking the yolks. Slide the eggs onto the asparagus.

Pour the Mornay sauce around the eggs.

Bake in oven for 20 minutes. Serve at once.

Spanish Omelette

1 serving

1 tbsp	(*15 mL*) butter
1 tbsp	(*15 mL*) green onion, finely diced
1 tbsp	(*15 mL*) green pepper, finely diced
2 tbsp	(*30 mL*) sliced mushrooms
2 tbsp	(*30 mL*) heavy cream
3	eggs

¼ cup	(*60 mL*) Creole Sauce (see *Sauces*)
¼ cup	(*60 mL*) grated medium Cheddar

Preheat oven to 450°F (*230°C*). In an omelette pan or skillet, heat the butter.

Add the onion, green pepper and mushrooms. Sauté until tender.

Carefully mix the cream with the eggs.

Cook the eggs until soft. Carefully flip the eggs over.

Pour the Creole Sauce on top and sprinkle with cheese.

Place in oven for 2-3 minutes. Remove carefully. Fold in half. Slide onto a plate and serve.

Shirred Eggs à la Reine

4 servings

2 cups	(*500 mL*) chicken, cooked and diced fine
8	eggs
2 cups	(*500 mL*) Mornay sauce (see *Sauces*)
1 cup	(*250 mL*) grated Swiss cheese

Preheat oven to 350°F (*180°C*). Lightly butter a small casserole dish. Place the chicken on the bottom.

Break the eggs into a small bowl without breaking the yolks. Slide the eggs onto the chicken.

Pour the Mornay sauce around the eggs. Sprinkle with cheese.

Bake in oven for 15 minutes.

Serve hot.

Shirred Eggs Florentine

4 servings

10 oz	(*284 g*) spinach
2 cups	(*500 mL*) Mornay sauce (see *Sauces*)
8	eggs
1½ cups	(*375 mL*) grated Havarti cheese

Preheat oven to 350°F (*180°C*).

Clean and trim the spinach. Blanch for 3 minutes.

Lightly butter a small casserole dish; line with spinach.

Cover the spinach with Mornay sauce.

Break the eggs into a small bowl, without breaking the yolks. Slide onto sauce. Sprinkle with cheese.

Bake in oven for 12 to 15 minutes.

Serve at once.

Shirred Eggs Florentine and Shirred Eggs Puerto Rico

Cheese Soufflé

4 servings

3 tbsp	(45 mL) butter
3 tbsp	(45 mL) flour
1 cup	(250 mL) scalded milk
1 tsp	(5 mL) salt
½ cup	(125 mL) grated Cheddar cheese
4	egg yolks
5	egg whites

Preheat oven to 375°F (190°C).

Melt the butter in top of a double boiler over hot water and blend in the flour.

Gradually stir in milk, blending until smooth, and then cook, stirring until the sauce is thick and smooth. Mix in the salt and cheese. Cool the sauce slightly.

Beat the egg yolks until light and lemon-colored and pour in the cream sauce. Mix together. Let this cool while you beat the egg whites until stiff but still moist.

Fold half the beaten egg whites into the sauce, then fold in the other half very lightly.

Pour the soufflé mixture into a 6-cup (1,5 L) buttered soufflé dish and bake in oven until puffed up and browned, about 35 minutes.

Serve at once.

Variations

Chicken Soufflé : Prepare the basic cream sauce adding 1 extra tbsp (15 mL) flour. (Chicken stock and sherry can be used for the liquid for the sauce instead of the scalded milk, if desired.)

Mix ⅔ cup (160 mL) finely diced chicken and 1 finely chopped pimiento.

Season with salt to taste and add ½ tsp (3 mL) pepper. Mix with egg yolks. Fold in egg whites and bake as directed.

Ham Soufflé : Follow the directions for chicken soufflé, substituting 1 cup (250 mL) finely ground ham for the chicken. Add 1 tsp (5 mL) dry mustard to seasonings.

Apricot Soufflé with Hot Brandy Sauce

4 servings

1¼ cups	(310 mL) dried apricots
1½ cups	(375 mL) water
2 tbsp	(30 mL) sugar
4	egg whites, beaten
⅛ tsp	(0,5 mL) cream of tartar
pinch	salt
⅛ tsp	(0,5 mL) almond extract
¼ cup	(60 mL) sugar
1 cup	(250 mL) chilled whipping cream
1 tbsp	(15 mL) sifted sugar
⅛ tsp	(0,5 mL) almond extract

Preheat oven to 325°F (160°C).

Simmer apricots and water together in a covered saucepan for ½ hour or until tender. Then press the mixture through a sieve.

Butter a 6-cup (1,5 L) casserole and sprinkle with 2 tbsp (30 mL) sugar.

Beat egg whites until foamy and add cream of tartar, salt and almond extract. Continue beating to form soft peaks.

Add ¼ cup (60 mL) sugar, 1 tbsp (15 mL) at a time, beating after each addition until stiff.

Gently fold apricot purée into egg whites.

Turn into casserole and set casserole in a pan of hot water.

Bake in oven for about 40 minutes or until firm.

Whip cream until stiff, then add sifted sugar and almond extract.

Serve soufflé with whipped cream and hot brandy sauce.

Hot Brandy Sauce

Cream ½ cup (125 mL) soft butter and 1 cup (250 mL) sifted icing sugar until fluffy.

Beat in 1 egg and 3 tbsp (45 mL) brandy. Pour into top of double boiler and heat, while stirring, until hot.

Chocolate Soufflé

5-6 servings

⅓ cup	(*80 mL*) light cream
1	3 oz (*90 g*) pkg. cream cheese
8 oz	(*225 g*) semi-sweet chocolate
3	egg yolks
pinch	salt
3	egg whites
3 tbsp	(*45 mL*) sugar

Preheat oven to 300°F (*150°C*).

Blend cream and cream cheese together over very low heat.

Add chocolate pieces; heat and stir until melted. Cool.

Beat egg yolks and salt until thick and lemon-colored.

Gradually blend in the chocolate mixture.

Beat egg whites until soft peaks form. Gradually add sugar, beating to stiff peaks; fold in chocolate mixture.

Pour into greased 4-cup (*1 L*) soufflé dish.

Bake in oven for 45 minutes or until knife inserted comes out clean.

Chocolate Soufflé

Beef

Most people have fond memories of their favorite meal, and it almost invariably includes beef — whether it was the Sunday roast served with potatoes and gravy, or the perfect little steak in that intimate little French restaurant.

Whichever your personal favorite, it is important to select an appropriate cut of beef from a reputable butcher, and then treat it with respect during its preparation.

Tender cuts include steaks such as T-bone, Porterhouse, club, filet, sirloin and tenderloin, as well as roasts cut from the loin, sirloin, or rib section, such as rib roast and Chateaubriand.

These cuts should be treated to a dry heat cooking method, which includes roasting, broiling, pan-broiling, barbecuing, and frying.

Less tender cuts should be treated to moist heat methods such as braising, stewing, and pot roasting. Look for cuts such as brisket, chuck, flank and neck.

Timetable for Roast Beef oven temperature 325°F (*160°C*)			
	Minutes per lb (*450g*)		
	Rare	Medium	Well done
Rib roast 6-8 lbs (*3-4 kg*)	16	21	26
Rolled roast 6-8 lbs (*3-4 kg*)	27	34	44
Broiled steak 1 in. (*2,5 cm*) thick	12	15	20
1½ in. (*3,5 cm*) thick	15	20	25
2 in. (*5 cm*) thick	25	30	35

Steak au Poivre

6 servings

6	10 oz (*280 g*) New York strip loin steaks
¼ cup	(*60 mL*) crushed black peppercorns
¼ cup	(*60 mL*) butter
2 tbsp	(*30 mL*) brandy
1 cup	(*250 mL*) demi-glace (see *Sauces*)
2 tbsp	(*30 mL*) sherry
¼ cup	(*60 mL*) heavy cream

Pat the peppercorns into the steaks.

Heat the butter and sauté the steaks to desired doneness. Remove and keep hot.

Pour in brandy and flambé; add sherry and demi-glace.

Simmer for 1 minute. Add cream and blend well.

Pour sauce over steaks and serve at once.

Steak au Poivre

Herb and Spice Steaks

6 servings

½ cup	(*125 mL*) oil
1 cup	(*250 mL*) cider vinegar
⅓ cup	(*80 mL*) brown sugar
2	garlic cloves, minced
¾ cup	(*180 mL*) minced onion
¼ tsp	(*1 mL*) cayenne pepper
¼ tsp	(*1 mL*) salt
½ tsp	(*3 mL*) marjoram
½ tsp	(*3 mL*) rosemary
6	8 oz (*225 g*) New York strip loin steaks

Heat the oil, vinegar, sugar, garlic, onions and seasonings together. Boil for 2 minutes. Remove from heat. Cool.

Place steaks in a deep pan. Pour the cool marinade over the steaks.

Refrigerate for 6 to 8 hours or overnight. Remove steaks and broil to your liking.

Steak Diane

8 servings

⅓ cup	(80 mL) butter
8	4 oz (115 g) filet steaks
4 oz	(115 g) mushrooms, sliced
2	green onions, minced
¼ cup	(60 mL) brandy
1½ cups	(375 mL) demi-glace (see *Sauces*)
¼ cup	(60 mL) sherry
¼ cup	(60 mL) heavy cream

In a large skillet, heat the butter. Fry the steaks in the butter 3½ to 4 minutes on each side. Remove and keep hot.

Add the mushrooms to the skillet; sauté until tender.

Add the green onions and sauté for 1 minute.

Carefully flame with brandy. Add the demi-glace, sherry and cream. Reduce to ¾ volume.

Pour sauce over steaks. Serve.

Filet Oscar

6 servings

3 tbsp	(45 mL) butter
6	6 oz (170 g) tenderloin steaks
8 oz	(225 g) crab meat
12	asparagus, blanched 5 minutes
6 tbsp	(90 mL) Béarnaise sauce (see *Sauces*)

Heat the butter and sauté the steaks to desired doneness.

Place on a baking sheet; top with crab meat and asparagus.

Place 1 tbsp (15 mL) of sauce on top of each steak and broil for 30 seconds or until sauce browns.

Tournedos Rossini

6 servings

¼ cup	(60 mL) butter
6	4 oz (115 g) filet steaks
12 oz	(340 g) pâté
¼ cup	(60 mL) flour
6	3-in. (7 cm) round croutons
1 cup	(250 mL) demi-glace (see *Sauces*)
¼ cup	(60 mL) sherry
¼ cup	(60 mL) heavy cream

Heat the butter in a skillet. Fry the steaks 3½ to 4 minutes on each side.

Remove to a hot platter.

Slice the pâté into rounds a little smaller than the steaks.

Dust with flour, and fry 1 minute each side in the butter.

Place the steaks on a crouton. Top with pâté.

Heat the demi-glace in a saucepan.

Add the sherry; reduce to half. Add the cream; simmer 1 minute.

Pour sauce over steaks. Serve.

NOTE : Classic Tournedos Rossini should be topped with a slice of truffle. But this is far too expensive in North America - about $60 an ounce!

Sauté lightly for 3 minutes. Chop the spinach. Add it to the skillet with the breadcrumbs, basil and broth.

Spread over steak. Sprinkle with cheese and cashews. Roll like a jelly roll. Tie with string every two inches. Bake, covered, in oven, for 2 hours.

Slice in 1-in. (2,5 cm) servings.

Swiss Steak

6 servings

¼ cup	(60 mL) oil
2	garlic cloves, minced
1	onion, sliced
1	green pepper, sliced
4 oz	(115 g) mushrooms, sliced
½ cup	(125 mL) flour
2¼ lbs	(1 kg) round steak, tenderized
2 tsp	(10 mL) salt
¼ tsp	(1 mL) pepper
½ tsp	(3 mL) basil
½ tsp	(3 mL) thyme
2 cups	(500 mL) tomato purée
1 cup	(250 mL) tomatoes, seeded and chopped

Heat oil in a large skillet.

Sauté garlic, onion, green pepper and mushrooms until tender.

Flour the meat. Brown in the oil with the vegetables. Add the seasonings, tomato purée and tomatoes.

Cover and simmer for 1½ hours over low heat.

Flank Steak Florentine

Flank Steak Florentine

6 servings

2¼ lbs	(1 kg) flank steak
3 tbsp	(45 mL) butter
1	small onion, diced
1	garlic clove, minced
2 oz	(60 g) mushrooms, sliced
10 oz	(284 g) spinach
1½ cups	(375 mL) breadcrumbs
1 tsp	(5 mL) basil
½ cup	(125 mL) chicken broth or white wine
1½ cups	(375 mL) grated Cheddar
¼ cup	(60 mL) cashews

Preheat oven to 350°F (180°C). Pound the steak on both sides with a mallet.

In a large skillet, heat the butter. Add the onion, garlic and mushrooms.

Filet de Boeuf Wellington

8 servings

Pastry

2 cups	(500 mL)	flour
¾ tsp	(4 mL)	salt
½ lb	(225 g)	butter
⅓ cup	(80 mL)	ice water

Beef

4 ½ lbs	(2 kg)	tenderloin filet
3 tbsp	(45 mL)	butter
1		onion, diced
4 oz	(115 g)	mushrooms, quartered
1 lb	(450 g)	liver pâté

Sauce

2 cups	(500 mL)	demi-glace (see *Sauces*)
¼ cup	(60 mL)	sherry
½ cup	(125 mL)	heavy cream
2 tsp	(10 mL)	green peppercorns

*Pastry : Sift the flour and salt into a bowl. Cut in ¾ of the butter. Add the water. Mix into walnut size pieces. Cover and chill for 20 minutes.

Uncover and roll out on a flour-dusted board. Dot with remaining butter. Fold into thirds.

Cover and refrigerate another 20 minutes.

1 Gather roasted beef filet, pâté and onion/mushroom mixture (duxelles). Roll out the dough for final rolling.

2 Spread pâté over pastry, then spread duxelles over pâté.

3 Lay the filet over the duxelles and carefully wrap the pastry around the filet.

4 Bake in oven for 25 minutes or until pastry is golden brown.

(Continued on next page)

Uncover. Roll out. Fold into thirds and refrigerate at least 3 more times. Refrigerate before final use. (*You may prefer to use 1 lb (450 g) of commercial puff pastry, instead.*)

Assembly : Roast the filet in a 425°F (*220°C*) oven for 20 minutes. Allow to cool.
Heat the butter in a skillet. Add the onion and mushrooms and sauté until all the liquid has evaporated. Scrape into a blender and blend on low for 20 seconds. (*This is a duxelles*).
Roll out the dough for the final rolling. Spread pâté over pastry.

Spread duxelles over pâté. Lay the filet over the duxelles.

Carefully wrap the pastry around the filet. Seal the edges. Decorate with remaining pastry.

Place filet, sealed side down, on a pastry sheet. Bake in preheated 425°F (*220°C*) oven 25 minutes or until pastry is golden brown. Let stand 5 minutes before serving.

Sauce : Pour demi-glace into a saucepan. Add sherry and reduce volume by half.

Add cream and simmer 5 minutes. Add the peppercorns. Pour into a serving bowl. Serve with beef.

Rib Roast of Beef

8 servings

¼ cup	(*60 mL*) flour
2 tbsp	(*30 mL*) dry mustard
1 tsp	(*5 mL*) oregano
1 tsp	(*5 mL*) basil
½ tsp	(*3 mL*) thyme
½ tsp	(*3 mL*) salt

Rib Roast of Beef

4½ lb	(*2 kg*) rib roast	
2 tbsp	(*30 mL*) Worcestershire sauce	
1	onion, chopped	
2	carrots, chopped	
2	celery stalks, chopped	
1	bay leaf	
1 cup	(*250 mL*) red wine	
1 cup	(*250 mL*) water	

Preheat oven to 325°F (*160°C*). Mix the flour, mustard and seasonings together.

Rub into roast. Place roast in pan. Pour over the Worcestershire sauce.

Surround the roast with the vegetables, bay leaf and pour in the wine and water. Place in oven.

Bake to desired doneness. Use juices to baste the roast.

Use juices to make a pan gravy for roast.

Serve with Yorkshire pudding (see *Breads*).

Pot-au-Feu

6 servings

2¼ lb	(*1 kg*) shoulder roast
12 cups (*3 L*) water	
1 tsp	(*5 mL*) salt
1	carrot, sliced
1	turnip, diced
1	onion, sliced
1	parsnip, diced
2	celery stalks, diced
2	small zucchini, diced
1	cabbage, quartered
1	bouquet garni*

Have the meat tied together. Place in a large pot. Add water and salt. Cover and simmer for 2 hours.

Add the vegetables, (except the cabbage) and the bouquet garni.

Simmer for an additional 1½ hours.

Add the cabbage and continue to simmer another ½ hour. Discard the bouquet garni.

Serve the meat and vegetables with a little of the broth.

*A bouquet garni is : thyme, marjoram, peppercorns, bay leaf and parsley, tied together in a cheesecloth.

Deli Corned Beef

8 servings

4 cups	(*1 L*) water
1¼ cups	(*310 mL*) salt
3 tbsp	(*45 mL*) pickling spice
1 tsp	(*5 mL*) saltpeter
1 tsp	(*5 mL*) sugar
6	bay leaves
12	garlic cloves
4½ lbs	(*2 kg*) beef brisket
1	onion
1	celery stalk
4 cups	(*1 L*) water
1 tbsp	(*15 mL*) prepared mustard
¼ cup	(*60 mL*) brown sugar

Mix 4 cups (*1 L*) water with the seasonings; bring to a boil. Allow to cool.

Place brisket in a large crock or pan. Pour mixture over brisket. Arrange so that the brisket remains completely covered with brine. Cover with tin foil and refrigerate for 7 days.

Drain and rinse the brisket. Place brisket in a large pot or Dutch oven.

Add the onion and celery. Pour in 4 cups (*1 L*) water. Bring to a boil.

Reduce heat to a simmer. Simmer for 3 hours. Cool for 30 minutes in liquid.

Remove to a pastry sheet. Brush with mustard. Sprinkle with brown sugar.

Bake in a 350°F (*180°C*) oven for 30 minutes. Slice and serve.

Boiled Beef

6 servings

2¼ lbs	(*1 kg*) beef brisket
2	leeks, washed and trimmed
1	bouquet garni
1	carrot, pared and chopped
1	onion, halved
1	celery stalk, chopped
1 tsp	(*5 mL*) salt
8 cups	(*2 L*) boiling water
12	small new potatoes
24	baby carrots

In a large pot or Dutch oven, place the brisket, leeks, bouquet garni, carrot, onion, celery and salt.

Pour in the boiling water. Bring to a boil. Reduce to low and simmer for 3 hours.

Remove any grease or scum as it floats to the top. Add the potatoes and baby carrots. Simmer for 40 more minutes.

Place brisket on a serving platter.

Surround with potatoes and carrots. Serve with horseradish, if desired.

Chef K's Fire Chili

8 servings

2¼ lbs	(*1 kg*) boneless lean beef, diced
¼ cup	(*60 mL*) oil
1	onion, sliced thin
1	green pepper, diced coarse
4 oz	(*115 g*) mushrooms, halved
2	garlic cloves, minced
4 cups	(*1 L*) tomatoes, seeded, peeled and chopped
2 tsp	(*10 mL*) salt
1 tsp	(*5 mL*) cayenne pepper
½ tsp	(*3 mL*) black pepper
2 tbsp	(*30 mL*) chili powder
2	10 oz (*284 mL*) cans kidney beans, drained

Trim the fat from the meat. Heat the oil in a large skillet. Sauté the onion, green pepper, mushrooms and garlic until tender. Add beef and brown over medium heat.

Drain excess grease. Add the tomatoes. Stir in the seasonings. Cover and simmer for 1 hour. Add beans and simmer for 10 minutes. Serve.

Chef K's Fire Chili

Old-Fashioned Beef Stew

6 servings

2¼ lbs	(*1 kg*) stewing beef
¼ cup	(*60 mL*) oil
4	potatoes, diced
1	onion, sliced thin
2	celery stalks
2	carrots, diced
8 oz	(*225 g*) button mushrooms
3 cups	(*750 mL*) beef stock
¼ cup	(*60 mL*) tomato paste
1 tsp	(*5 mL*) salt
½ tsp	(*3 mL*) black pepper
½ tsp	(*3 mL*) basil
½ tsp	(*3 mL*) paprika
1 tsp	(*5 mL*) Worcestershire sauce
1 tbsp	(*15 mL*) soya sauce

Trim the fat from the beef. Heat the oil in a pot or Dutch oven.

Add the potatoes, onion, celery, carrots, mushrooms and sauté for 3 minutes. Add the beef and brown. Add the beef stock, tomato paste, seasonings, Worcestershire and soya sauces. Bring to a boil.

Reduce and simmer for 3 hours. Serve.

English Steak and Kidney Pie

8 servings

Pastry

2 cups	*(500 mL)*	flour
¾ tsp	*(4 mL)*	salt
½ lb	*(225 g)*	butter
⅓ cup	*(80 mL)*	ice water

Filling

1 tsp	*(5 mL)*	salt
pinch		pepper
1 tsp	*(5 mL)*	thyme
½ cup	*(125 mL)*	flour
2¼ lbs	*(1 kg)*	rump steak, cut into thin 1½ in. *(4 cm)* wide strips
¼ cup	*(60 mL)*	chopped bacon
2		onions, chopped
4 oz	*(115 g)*	mushrooms, sliced
2 ½ cups	*(625 mL)*	beef broth
3		veal kidneys
2		egg yolks

*Pastry : Sift together the flour and salt into a bowl. Put ¾ of the butter into the flour.

Add the water and mix into walnut size pieces. Cover and chill 20 minutes. Uncover and roll out to ⅛ in. *(0,5 cm)* on a flour-dusted board. Dot with the remaining butter. Fold into thirds.

Cover and refrigerate for an additional 20 minutes. Uncover.

Roll out and fold into thirds. Refrigerate for 20 minutes. Repeat this process at least 3 more times.

Filling : Blend the seasonings into the flour. Dust the beef with seasoned flour.

Heat the bacon in a large skillet. Brown the beef in the bacon over high heat. Add the onions and mushrooms and sauté for 3 minutes.

Pour the beef broth into the skillet. Cover and simmer for 1½ hours.

Clean the kidneys. Using a sharp paring knife, remove the membranes. Slice the kidneys thin.

Preheat oven to 375°F *(190°C)*.

Pour the beef mixture into a large casserole dish, 9 x 12 in. *(23 x 30 cm)*.

Stir in the kidneys. Dampen the edges of the pan. Roll out the pastry.

Place on top and seal the edges. Cut a hole ½ in. *(1,2 cm)* in diameter in the center.

Roll a small piece of tin foil into a tube and place in hole.

Cut remaining pastry into designs and decorate.

Brush with egg yolk. Bake in oven for 50 minutes or until golden brown.

Beef Bordelaise

6 servings

⅓ cup	*(80 mL)*	butter
2¼ lbs	*(1 kg)*	round steak, cut in thin 1-in. *(2,5 cm)* wide strips
4 oz	*(115 g)*	button mushrooms
¼ cup	*(60 mL)*	chopped shallots
½ cup	*(125 mL)*	Bordeaux wine
2 cups	*(500 mL)*	Espagnole Sauce (see *Sauces*)
2 tbsp	*(30 mL)*	beef marrow, chopped fine
1 tbsp	*(15 mL)*	chopped parsley

In a large skillet, heat the butter. Fast fry the beef strips.

Remove and keep hot.

Add the mushrooms and shallots. Sauté for 3 minutes.

Add the wine and reduce to one third.

Add the sauce, marrow, parsley and simmer two minutes.

Pour over beef strips. Serve.

---

*Or use 1 lb (450 g) of puff pastry.

Pepper Steak

Beef and Cheese Goulash

8 servings

1½ lbs	(675 g) egg noodles
2¼ lbs	(1 kg) cooked beef, cut into ¾-in. (2 cm) cubes
¼ cup	(60 mL) butter
3	onions, chopped
3 cups	(750 mL) tomato sauce (see Sauces)
1½ tsp	(8 mL) paprika
1 tsp	(5 mL) salt
¼ tsp	(1 mL) pepper
1 tbsp	(15 mL) caraway seeds
1 cup	(250 mL) grated Colby cheese
1 cup	(250 mL) grated Caraway cheese

Preheat oven to 375°F (190°C).

Cook noodles in a large pot of boiling, salted water, about 8-10 minutes or until al dente (*tender but firm*). Drain well.

Place noodles in a greased 13 x 9 in. (33 x 23 cm) baking dish. Top with beef.

Melt the butter; sauté the onions over low heat until tender.

Add the tomato sauce and seasonings; simmer 15 minutes. Pour sauce over the beef.

Sprinkle with caraway seeds and cheeses.

Bake in oven for 30 minutes or until cheese has melted and is lightly browned.

Pepper Steak

4 servings

1½ lbs	(675 g) round steak, cut into small strips
½ cup	(125 mL) flour
3 tbsp	(45 mL) oil
1	onion, sliced
1	green pepper, sliced
1	celery stalk, sliced
2 oz	(60 g) mushrooms
2	tomatoes, quartered
½ cup	(125 mL) beef broth
¼ cup	(60 mL) sherry
2 tbsp	(30 mL) soya sauce
1 tsp	(5 mL) Worcestershire sauce

Dust the beef with flour. Heat oil in a large skillet or wok.

Fast fry the beef to brown. Add the onion, green pepper, celery and sliced mushrooms. Fry for 2 minutes. Add the remaining ingredients. Cook for 2 more minutes.

Serve with rice.

Beef and Mushrooms with Old Cheddar

8 servings

4 cups	(1 L) cooked rice
2¼ lbs	(1 kg) cooked beef, cut in thin julienne strips
1 lb	(450 g) button mushrooms, sautéed in butter
¼ cup	(60 mL) butter
¼ cup	(60 mL) all-purpose flour
2 cups	(500 mL) Espagnole Sauce (see *Sauces*)
2 cups	(500 mL) heavy cream
1 tbsp	(15 mL) green peppercorns
3 cups	(750 mL) grated old Cheddar cheese
¼ cup	(60 mL) breadcrumbs

Preheat over to 400°F (200°C).

Spread the rice in the bottom of a greased 13 x 9 in. (33 x 23 cm) baking dish.

Cover with beef strips and sautéed mushrooms.

Melt butter over medium heat; stir in flour.

Add Espagnole Sauce and cream; heat, stirring constantly, until mixture thickens and comes to a boil. Stir in green peppercorns. Pour sauce over meat mixture.

Combine cheese and breadcrumbs and sprinkle over sauce.

Bake in oven for 25 minutes or until heated through.

Beef Stroganoff

8 servings

2¼ lbs	(1 kg) round steak
¼ cup	(60 mL) oil
3 tbsp	(45 mL) butter
1	celery stalk, sliced
1	onion, sliced
1	green pepper, sliced
½ lb	(225 g) mushrooms, sliced
⅓ cup	(80 mL) flour
1¼ cups	(300 mL) beef stock
¾ cup	(180 mL) sherry
2 tbsp	(30 mL) Worcestershire sauce
2 tbsp	(30 mL) prepared mustard
¼ cup	(60 mL) tomato paste
1	bay leaf
2 tsp	(10 mL) paprika
½ tsp	(3 mL) thyme
¼ tsp	(1 mL) pepper
1 cup	(250 mL) sour cream
4 cups	(1 L) cooked egg noodles, hot

Cut the steak into slices.

Heat the oil and the butter. Brown the beef, then sauté the vegetables until tender. Add the flour and stir for 2 minutes.

Add the beef stock, sherry, Worcestershire sauce, mustard, tomato paste and seasonings.

Cover and simmer for 1¼ hours.

Add sour cream and mix thoroughly. Pour over noodles and serve.

Beef Bourguignon

8-10 servings

4½ lbs	(2 kg) chuck beef, cubed
1 tsp	(5 mL) dry mustard
1 tsp	(5 mL) basil
1 tbsp	(15 mL) salt
½ tsp	(3 mL) pepper
½ lb	(225 g) bacon
20	pearl onions
2 cups	(500 mL) red wine
1 cup	(250 mL) sherry
1	bay leaf
¼ cup	(60 mL) chopped parsley
1 tsp	(5 mL) thyme
1 lb	(450 g) mushrooms, sliced
3 tbsp	(45 mL) flour
¼ cup	(60 mL) water

Season the beef with the mustard, basil, salt and pepper.

In a Dutch oven, sauté the bacon. Remove the bacon pieces.

Brown the beef in the fat. Add onions and sauté until tender. Add wine, sherry, bay leaf, parsley and thyme. Cover and simmer for 2 hours.

Add the mushrooms and simmer another 30 minutes.

Mix the flour with water into a very smooth paste.

Add to the beef and simmer, while stirring, for 5 minutes or until mixture thickens.

Serve with new potatoes.

Beef Stroganoff

Filet Oscar Crêpes

8 servings

1	small onion, finely chopped
	margarine
3 cups	(*750 mL*) sliced mushrooms
1 lb	(*450 g*) beef tenderloin
	salt and pepper
16	asparagus spears
8	8-in. (*20 cm*) crêpes (see *Breads*)
1 cup	(*250 mL*) grated Swiss cheese
1 cup	(*250 mL*) cooked baby shrimp
1 cup	(*250 mL*) Béarnaise sauce (see *Sauces*)

Sauté onion in small amount of margarine over medium heat until tender. Set aside. Sauté mushrooms in additional margarine over high heat until tender; set aside.

Cut beef into thin slivers and sauté to desired doneness. Return onions and mushrooms to pan, reheat, and season to taste.

Meanwhile, cook asparagus in boiling, salted water just until tender, about 3 minutes; drain.

Spoon meat mixture onto each crêpe, sprinkle with cheese, and roll. Place on a baking sheet. Top with shrimp, 2 asparagus spears, and Béarnaise sauce.

Place under heated broiler until sauce is slightly browned, about 1 minute.

Filet Oscar Crêpes

Texan Short Ribs

8 servings

4 1/2 lbs	(*2 kg*) short ribs, cut into 3-in. (*7 cm*) pieces	
3 tbsp	(*45 mL*) oil	
1/3 cup	(*80 mL*) flour	
1	onion, chopped	
2 tsp	(*10 mL*) salt	
1/2 tsp	(*3 mL*) pepper	
1/2 tsp	(*3 mL*) oregano	
1/2 tsp	(*3 mL*) thyme	
1/2 tsp	(*3 mL*) paprika	
1/4 cup	(*60 mL*) boiling water	
2 cups	(*500 mL*) chili sauce	
1/3 cup	(*80 mL*) diced pickles	

Trim excess fat from ribs. Heat the oil in a large pot or Dutch oven. Dust the ribs with flour, then brown in oil. Drain excess fat, reserving about 1 tbsp (*15 mL*). Add the onion and fry to brown. Sprinkle with seasonings. Add water and reduce heat. Cover and simmer for 1 1/2 hours.

Add the chili sauce and pickles. Simmer for 1 hour more or until ribs are very tender.

Serve with rice pilaf of your choice.

Steak Tartare

4 servings

1 lb	*(450 g)* tenderloin
½ cup	*(125 g)* finely chopped green onions
1 tsp	*(5 mL)* minced garlic
2 tbsp	*(30 mL)* sherry
½ tsp	*(3 mL)* cracked pepper
1 tsp	*(5 mL)* chopped parsley
1 tsp	*(5 mL)* salt
1 tsp	*(5 mL)* Worcestershire sauce
1 tbsp	*(15 mL)* brandy
1 tsp	*(5 mL)* capers
4	egg yolks
1	pumpernickel bread

Grind the tenderloin twice.

Place the meat in a bowl, add onions and blend.

Blend in the garlic, sherry, pepper, parsley, salt, Worcestershire sauce, brandy and capers.

Divide into four servings and place on plates.

Make an indentation in the center of each portion. Place an egg yolk in the indentation.

Serve with pumpernickel.

Place ground meat in a bowl, add green onions and blend.

2

Blend in the garlic, sherry, pepper, parsley, salt, Worcestershire sauce, brandy and capers.

3

Divide meat mixture into four servings and place on plates. Make an indentation in the center of each portion.

4

Place an egg yolk in the indentation.

Meatball Soup

8 servings

Meatballs

1 lb	(*450 g*) extra lean ground beef
1 tsp	(*5 mL*) Worcestershire sauce
⅓ cup	(*80 mL*) breadcrumbs
¼ cup	(*60 mL*) milk
1	egg, beaten
¼ tsp	(*1 mL*) garlic powder
¼ tsp	(*1 mL*) oregano
¼ tsp	(*1 mL*) thyme
¼ tsp	(*1 mL*) basil
pinch	chili powder
½ tsp	(*3 mL*) paprika
1 tsp	(*5 mL*) salt
¼ tsp	(*1 mL*) pepper

Preheat oven to 350°F (*180°C*).

Combine the beef, Worcestershire sauce and breadcrumbs together.

Beat the egg with the milk and add the seasonings. Blend into meat mixture.

Bake in oven for 12 to 15 minutes. Drain excess fat and reserve.

Soup

¼ cup	(*60 mL*) oil
1	onion, sliced
1	green pepper, sliced
4 oz	(*115 g*) mushrooms, sliced
2	garlic cloves, minced
2	celery stalks, sliced
4 cups	(*1 L*) chopped tomatoes
2 cups	(*500 mL*) chicken broth
½ cup	(*125 mL*) vermicelli, broken
1 tsp	(*5 mL*) salt
1 tsp	(*5 mL*) oregano
¼ tsp	(*1 mL*) pepper
¼ cup	(*60 mL*) sherry

In a pot or Dutch oven, heat the oil. Add the onion, green pepper, mushrooms, garlic and celery; sauté until tender.

Add the tomatoes and broth; bring to a boil. Add the vermicelli and reduce to a simmer.

Simmer, covered, for 15 minutes. Add the seasonings, sherry and meatballs.

Simmer 5 more minutes. Serve.

Shepherd's Pie

4 servings

3 tbsp	(*45 mL*) oil
2	onions, minced
2	celery stalks, minced
2	carrots, finely diced
1 lb	(*450 g*) lean ground beef
½ tsp	(*3 mL*) savory
1 tsp	(*5 mL*) salt
10 oz	(*284 mL*) can creamed corn
4 cups	(*1 L*) mashed potatoes

Preheat oven to 375°F (*190°C*).

Heat the oil in a skillet. Sauté the onions, celery and carrots.

Add the beef and brown. Season with savory and salt. Drain excess fat.

Place the meat mixture in a casserole dish.

Pour the corn over the meat. Top with mashed potatoes.

Bake in oven for 20 minutes.

Cheese Burger Insane

8 servings

2¼ lbs	(*1 kg*) lean ground beef
2 tsp	(*10 mL*) seasoned salt
pinch	pepper
1	egg
¼ cup	(*60 mL*) fine dry breadcrumbs
8	slices Havarti or medium Cheddar cheese, about 1 in. (*2,5 cm*) square and ¼ in. (*0,5 cm*) thick

Combine ground beef, seasonings, egg and breadcrumbs; mix thoroughly.

Divide into 8 portions. From each portion, make 2 thin patties. Sandwich 1 cheese slice between the patties and pinch edges to seal. Place under heated broiler and cook until browned, about 6 minutes per side. Serve on fresh buns, garnished with your favorite fixin's.

Ground Sirloin Wellington

8 servings

Pastry

2½ cups	(*625 mL*) flour
1 tsp	(*5 mL*) salt
¾ cup	(*180 mL*) butter, chilled and diced
1	egg
½ cup	(*125 mL*) sour cream

Ground Sirloin Wellington

Filling

¼ cup	(*60 mL*) butter
4 oz	(*115 g*) mushrooms
¼ cup	(*60 mL*) minced onion
2¼ lbs	(*1 kg*) twice-ground sirloin
1 tbsp	(*15 mL*) parsley
1 tbsp	(*15 mL*) basil
1 tsp	(*5 mL*) salt
1 tsp	(*5 mL*) pepper
2	eggs
8 oz	(*225 g*) liver pâté

Pastry : Sift together the flour and salt. Mix in the butter until pastry is in large coarse pieces.

Mix egg with the sour cream. Blend this mixture into the flour. Mix into a smooth ball. Cover and chill 1 hour.

Preheat oven at 350°F (*180°C*).

Filling : Melt the butter and sauté the mushrooms and onion. Allow to cool. Mix the sirloin with the mushrooms, onion, seasonings and eggs. Roll out the pastry in 8 rectangles of 8 x 5 in. (*20 x 12 cm*). Spread the pâté in the center then add the filling. Wrap the meat and seal the edges. Brush with a little melted butter.

Bake for 1 hour, or until pastry is golden brown in color.

Java Beef

8 servings

2 tbsp	(*30 mL*) butter
1	onion, sliced
1	green pepper, sliced
1½ lbs	(*675 g*) lean ground beef
1 tsp	(*5 mL*) salt
1 tbsp	(*15 mL*) curry powder
½ cup	(*125 mL*) raisins
½ cup	(*125 mL*) dried, chopped apricots
1 cup	(*250 mL*) cashews
1 cup	(*250 mL*) beef stock
2 cups	(*500 mL*) peas, fresh or frozen
½ cup	(*125 mL*) chopped pimiento

Melt the butter and sauté the onion and green pepper.

Add the beef, salt and curry powder; brown. Blend in the raisins, apricots and cashews. Add the beef stock and simmer for 20 minutes.

Add the peas and pimiento. Simmer an additional 10 minutes.
Serve with rice and chutney on the side.

Java Beef

Old-Fashioned Chili 'n Cheese

8 servings

2	garlic cloves, minced
1	medium onion, chopped
2 tbsp	(*30 mL*) vegetable oil

1 lb	(*450 g*) lean ground beef	½ tsp	(*3 mL*) dried oregano leaves
28 oz	(*796 mL*) can tomatoes	½ tsp	(*3 mL*) dried basil leaves
2½ cups	(*625 mL*) water	½ tsp	(*3 mL*) cayenne pepper
2	tomatoes, peeled, seeded and chopped	1 tsp	(*5 mL*) salt
1	green pepper, chopped	14 oz	(*398 mL*) can kidney beans, rinsed
2 tbsp	(*30 mL*) chili powder	½ cup	(*125 mL*) grated old Cheddar cheese
1 tbsp	(*15 mL*) paprika	½ cup	(*125 mL*) grated Swiss cheese
1 tsp	(*5 mL*) rubbed thyme		

(Continued on next page)

Meat Loaf with Mushroom Sauce

1 tsp	(*5 mL*) basil
1½ tsp	(*0 mL*) salt
½ tsp	(*3 mL*) pepper
4	strips bacon

Preheat oven to 350°F (*180°C*). Combine the beef with the eggs, breadcrumbs and seasonings. Shape into a 9 x 5 in. (*22 x 12 cm*) loaf pan. Lay the bacon across the top.

Bake in oven for 1¼ to 1½ hours.

Sauce

3 tbsp	(*45 mL*) butter
8 oz	(*225 g*) mushrooms, sliced
3 tbsp	(*45 mL*) flour
1 cup	(*250 mL*) heavy cream
2 cups	(*500 mL*) beef stock
¼ cup	(*60 mL*) sherry
¼ cup	(*60 mL*) tomato paste

In a saucepan, heat the butter.

Sauté the mushrooms until tender.

Add the flour and cook for 2 minutes.

Add the cream, stock and sherry. Stir.

Reduce heat and simmer until thickened. Whisk in tomato paste.

Pour over meat loaf.

Sauté garlic and onion in oil until tender. Stir in ground beef and continue cooking until no pink remains; drain.

Stir in canned tomatoes, water, fresh tomatoes, green pepper, seasonings and kidney beans. Bring to a boil; reduce heat and simmer 2 ½ to 3 hours.

At serving time, spoon chili into individual bowls and sprinkle with cheese. Serve with garlic bread.

Meat Loaf with Mushroom Sauce

6 servings

Loaf

2¼ lbs	(*1 kg*) extra lean ground beef
2	eggs
⅔ cup	(*160 mL*) fine breadcrumbs
¼ cup	(*60 mL*) chopped parsley

Poultry

My customers' fondest memories are of dishes created especially for them, and more often than not, those special dishes were based on chicken. (Chicken Rombough, which is presented in this chapter, is just one of those inspirations.)

The fact is, chicken is such a wonderfully versatile item that the number of ways for preparing it is truly limitless. And even when the bones are picked clean, they can be used to create endlessly useful stocks and soup bases.

Little wonder, then, that the most famous cooking school in the world is not named after a great chef, but after a world-famous chicken dish — Cordon Bleu.

But extraordinary as this bird is, there is more to poultry than chicken alone. The category includes any domesticated bird used for human consumption, including turkey, duck, goose and Cornish hens.

You can also include game birds, such as pheasant and partridge, in the poultry category.

Poultry can be cooked using most cookery methods. Experiment with them all and you will find a never-ending menu would be possible from poultry alone.

Roasting Timetable at 325°F (160°C)		
	Weight	Time
Chicken	2-3 lbs (1 kg)	1¼-1½ hrs
	4-5 lbs (2 kg)	2¾-3½ hrs
	5-6 lbs (3 kg)	3½-4½ hrs
	6-7 lbs (4 kg)	4½-5 hrs
Turkey	6-8 lbs (3-4 kg)	3-4 hrs
	8-12 lbs (4-6 kg)	4-5 hrs
	12-16 lbs(6-8 kg)	5-6 hrs
	16-20 lbs (8-9kg)	6-7½ hrs

Test for Doneness: It is best to use a meat thermometer, inserted in the thigh, but not touching the bone. Poultry is cooked when the temperature reads 190°F (87°C).

Without a thermometer, you can tell if the bird is done when the leg moves freely in its socket, and when the juices run clear rather than pink when you stab the thickest part of the thigh.

Peach and Mango Chicken

Peach and Mango Chicken

4-6 servings

2 ½ - 3 lb	(1,1 - 1,4 kg) fryer chicken
¼ cup	(60 mL) butter
1 cup	(250 mL) diced mangos
½ cup	(125 mL) diced peaches
3	strips lemon rind
1¼ cups	(310 mL) chicken stock
1 tbsp	(15 mL) lemon juice
½ cup	(125 mL) heavy cream
	salt and pepper

Preheat oven to 350°F (180°C).

Fry the chicken in the butter until browned on all sides. Add mangos, peaches, lemon rind and chicken stock.

Cover and bake in oven for 1 hour.

Remove chicken from pan and keep warm.

Remove lemon rind. Add lemon juice and cream. Season to taste.

Bring sauce to a simmer and reduce until thickened.

Pour sauce over chicken and serve.

Rosemary Roast Chicken

4 servings

2¼ lb	(1 kg) fryer chicken
1 tbsp	(15 mL) melted butter
¼ tsp	(1 mL) salt
pinch	pepper
pinch	paprika
1 tbsp	(15 mL) rosemary

Preheat oven to 325°F (160°C).

Stuff chicken if you choose. Use your favorite stuffing.

Place chicken in a roasting pan. Brush with melted butter. Sprinkle with seasonings. Roast in oven for 60 minutes.

(*If you use a stuffing, a little longer cooking time may be required.*)

Spring Chicken Bonne Femme

4 servings

1	fryer chicken, cut into 8 pieces
3 tbsp	(*45 mL*) oil
8	slices bacon, chopped
1	small onion, diced
4 oz	(*115 g*) mushrooms, sliced
2 cups	(*500 mL*) demi-glace (see *Sauces*)

Sauté the chicken in the oil over high heat.

Reduce heat and cook, half-covered, about 15 minutes. Remove and keep warm.

Drain the oil from pan and add the bacon; sauté until tender.

Add the onion and brown.

Add the mushrooms and sauté. Swirl in the demi-glace and simmer 8 minutes.

Pour over chicken and serve at once.

Sautéed Chicken Niçoise

4 servings

⅓ cup	(*80 mL*) oil
2¼ lb	(*1 kg*) chicken, cut into 8 pieces
½ cup	(*125 mL*) white wine
¾ cup	(*180 mL*) tomato sauce (see *Sauces*)
2	artichokes
8	very small potatoes
1 cup	(*250 mL*) julienned zucchini
12	black olives, pitted
2 tsp	(*10 mL*) tarragon

In a large skillet, heat the oil. Brown the chicken in the oil.

Add the wine and tomato sauce and reduce heat. Cover and simmer for 50 minutes.

Clean and trim the artichokes. Remove the core. Sauté the potatoes.

One half hour before the chicken is ready, add the potatoes and artichokes.

Ten minutes before the chicken is ready, add the zucchini and olives.

Sprinkle with tarragon just before serving.

Sautéed Chicken Petit-Duc

4 servings

⅓ cup	(*80 mL*) butter
2¼ lb	(*1 kg*) chicken, cut into 8 pieces
4 oz	(*115 g*) button mushrooms
¼ cup	(*60 mL*) Madeira wine
2½ cups	(*625 mL*) demi-glace (see *Sauces*)

Heat the butter in a large skillet.

Sauté the chicken until browned. Remove and set aside.

Add the mushrooms and sauté. Swirl the pan with the wine.

Return chicken to skillet. Pour over the demi-glace.

Cover and simmer on low heat for 50 to 55 minutes or until chicken is tender.

Sautéed Chicken Petit-Duc, Sautéed Chicken Niçoise and Spring Chicken Bonne Femme

Chicken with Espagnole Sauce

4 servings

3 lbs	*(1,4 kg)* chicken pieces
¼ cup	*(60 mL)* vegetable oil
	salt and pepper
	paprika
	dried oregano leaves
	rubbed thyme
¼ cup	*(60 mL)* brandy
½ cup	*(125 mL)* heavy cream
¼ cup	*(60 mL)* sherry
5 tbsp	*(75 mL)* all-purpose flour
½ cup	*(125 mL)* Espagnole Sauce (see *Sauces*)
1⅓ cups	*(330 mL)* grated mild Cheddar cheese

Preheat oven to 350°F *(180°C)*.

Brown the chicken in oil, about 5 minutes, then transfer to a baking dish.

Sprinkle lightly with seasonings and bake in oven for 45 minutes or until cooked through. Drain fat, pour brandy over and flame.

Remove chicken from pan and keep warm.

Combine cream and sherry; stir in flour until smooth.

Pour cream mixture and Espagnole Sauce into pan juices; cook and stir until thickened. Add the cheese; stir just until melted.

Transfer chicken pieces to a serving dish and pour sauce over.

Southern Fried Chicken Marylands

8 servings

2¼ lbs	*(1 kg)* chicken marylands*
1 tbsp	*(15 mL)* salt
1 tbsp	*(15 mL)* paprika
1 tsp	*(5 mL)* each : oregano, thyme, sage, basil, garlic powder, black pepper, onion powder, marjoram
4 cups	*(1 L)* fine breadcrumbs
4	eggs
½ cup	*(125 mL)* milk
2 cups	*(500 mL)* flour
3 cups	*(750 mL)* oil

Preheat oven to 350°F *(180°C)*.

Wash the chicken and pat dry. Mix the seasonings in the breadcrumbs. Mix the eggs in the milk.

Dust chicken with flour. Dip in egg mixture. Roll in seasoned breadcrumbs.

Heat oil to 325°F *(160°C)*. Fry chicken in oil until golden brown. Remove from oil and place in paper towels to soak excess oil.

Place on baking sheet and bake in oven 12 to 15 minutes.

* A maryland is the leg and thigh of a chicken left whole.

Chicken Sauté Chasseur

4 servings

1	fryer chicken, cut into 8 pieces
1½ tbsp	*(22 mL)* butter
1½ tbsp	*(22 mL)* oil
¼ cup	*(60 mL)* sweet white wine
⅔ cup	*(160 mL)* Chasseur Sauce (see *Sauces*)
1 tbsp	*(15 mL)* chopped parsley

Sauté the chicken in the butter and oil.

Once cooked, remove from heat and keep warm.

Add the wine and reduce by half. Add the sauce and simmer 5 minutes.

Pour over chicken and sprinkle with parsley.

Serve.

Chicken Sauternes Veronique

Chicken Sauternes Veronique

8 servings

2	fryer chickens, cut into quarters
2 tbsp	(*30 mL*) melted butter
1 tbsp	(*15 mL*) sugar
	salt and white pepper

Sauce

3 tbsp	(*45 mL*)	butter
3 tbsp	(*45 mL*)	flour
½ cup	(*125 mL*)	sauternes wine
½ cup	(*125 mL*)	chicken stock
½ cup	(*125 mL*)	light cream
2 cups	(*500 mL*)	green grapes, halved

Preheat oven to 350°F (*180 °C*).

Brush chicken with melted butter. Sprinkle with sugar, salt and pepper.

Bake in over for 45 minutes.

Sauce : In a saucepan, melt butter and add flour. Cook for 2 minutes without browning.

Add wine and chicken stock. Reduce to half.

Add cream and simmer until sauce thickens. Add grapes.

Place cooked chicken on a platter, pour sauce over chicken and serve.

Chicken Paprika

8 servings

½ cup	(125 mL)	flour
1 tbsp	(15 mL)	salt
1 tbsp	(15 mL)	paprika
1 tsp	(5 mL)	pepper
2		fryer chickens, cut into 8 pieces
⅓ cup	(80 mL)	oil
2½ cups	(625 mL)	chicken stock
1 cup	(250 mL)	sour cream

Mix the flour with the seasonings. Wash the chicken and coat with seasoned flour.

In a large skillet, heat the oil and brown the chicken. Add the chicken stock and simmer for 40 minutes.

Remove chicken and keep warm.

Swirl in the sour cream and simmer for 5 minutes.

Pour sauce over chicken and serve with buttered noodles.

Chicken Paprika

Polynesian Chicken

4 servings

1 tsp	(5 mL)	salt
1 tsp	(5 mL)	paprika
½ cup	(125 mL)	flour
2¼ lb	(1 kg)	fryer chicken, cut into 8 pieces
½ cup	(125 mL)	shortening
1 cup	(250 mL)	orange juice
2 tbsp	(30 mL)	brown sugar
2 tbsp	(30 mL)	vinegar
1 tsp	(5 mL)	basil
1 tsp	(5 mL)	ground nutmeg
1¼ cups	(310 mL)	sliced peaches

Combine salt, paprika and flour. Lightly coat chicken.

Heat shortening in a large skillet. Sauté chicken until golden brown on all sides.

Mix the orange juice, brown sugar, vinegar, basil and nutmeg in a bowl.

Add to chicken. Cover and simmer 35 to 40 minutes until chicken is tender.

Add peaches and simmer 5 more minutes. Serve.

Coq au Vin

8 servings

4 lb	(1,8 kg) chicken, cut into pieces
3 tbsp	(45 mL) flour
¼ cup	(60 mL) butter
½ cup	(125 mL) brandy
1 tsp	(5 mL) thyme
1 tsp	(5 mL) paprika
2 tsp	(10 mL) salt
1½ cups	(375 mL) dry red wine
1½ cups	(375 mL) strong chicken stock
4	slices bacon, diced
1 cup	(250 mL) pearl onions
1 cup	(250 mL) button mushrooms

Dust the chicken in the flour. Brown in butter over low heat. Flame with brandy.

Add seasonings, red wine and chicken stock. Cover and simmer until chicken is tender, about 40 minutes.

In a sauté pan, brown diced bacon and sauté the onions and mushrooms. Drain any oil.

Add to chicken 5 minutes before chicken is done.

1

Flame browned chicken with brandy.

2

Add seasonings, red wine and chicken stock. Cover and simmer until chicken is tender, about 40 minutes.

3

In a sauté pan, brown the diced bacon and sauté the onions and mushrooms.

4

Add to chicken 5 minutes before chicken is done.

Swiss Chicken

8 servings

8	boneless chicken breasts
	salt and pepper
	paprika
	vegetable oil
8 oz	(*225 g*) Black Forest ham, thinly sliced
16	cooked asparagus spears
8	slices Swiss cheese

Sprinkle the chicken breasts lightly with salt, pepper and paprika.

Sauté in vegetable oil over medium heat or grill until cooked through.

Top each breast with ham, 2 spears of asparagus, and a slice of cheese.

Place under a heated broiler just until cheese melts.

Serve immediately.

Chicken à la Nantua

8-10 servings

8-10	boneless chicken breasts
6 cups	(*1,5 L*) chicken stock or water
¾ lb	(*340 g*) cooked baby shrimp
1½ cups	(*375 mL*) crab meat
1 cup	(*250 mL*) Velouté Sauce (see *Sauces*)
2 cups	(*500 mL*) Supreme Sauce (see *Sauces*)
⅓ cup	(*80 mL*) grated Parmesan cheese

Preheat oven to 350°F (*180°C*).

Drop chicken breasts into simmering stock; simmer just until cooked through, about 10 minutes. Remove from stock and cover tightly.

Combine shrimp, crab meat, and Velouté Sauce; spoon into a greased shallow baking dish.

Place the poached breasts over the seafood mixture. Spoon Supreme Sauce over.

Sprinkle with Parmesan cheese and bake in oven until heated through and browned, about 15 minutes.

Three Pepper Chicken Breasts

6 servings

6	boneless chicken breasts, 6 oz (*170 g*) each
1 tbsp	(*15 mL*) fresh cracked black peppercorns
1 tbsp	(*15 mL*) green Madagascar peppercorns
1 tbsp	(*15 mL*) fresh cracked white peppercorns
3 tbsp	(*45 mL*) oil
2 cups	(*500 mL*) demi-glace (see *Sauces*)
¼ cup	(*60 mL*) heavy cream
¼ cup	(*60 mL*) sherry

Wash the chicken breasts.

Mix together the peppercorns and press into chicken, making sure to cover the entire chicken breast.

Heat the oil in a skillet. Sauté each breast in the oil, about 2½ minutes each side. Remove from oil and keep hot.

Add the demi-glace, cream and sherry. Simmer for 5 minutes.

Pour sauce over chicken and serve.

Mix the cornstarch with 1 tbsp (*15 mL*) water, add to sauce and bring back to a boil. Pour sauce over chicken

Chicken Supremes en Papillote

6 servings

6	boneless chicken breasts, 6 oz (*170 g*) each
3 tbsp	(*45 mL*) butter
6	wax paper hearts, buttered
12	slices Black Forest ham, 1 oz (*30 g*) each
¾ cup	(*180 mL*) Italienne Sauce (see *Sauces*)

Preheat oven to 425°F (*220°C*).

Brown the breasts in the butter. Remove and cool.

On one half of the paper heart, place a slice of ham and 1 tbsp (*15 mL*) of sauce on top of the ham.

Then top the ham with a breast. Add 1 tbsp (*15 mL*) of sauce then another slice of ham.

Fold the paper over to encase the chicken. Pleat the edge so that no air escapes during cooking.

Bake in oven until the papillotes puff up with air. Serve at once.

Lemon Chicken

Lemon Chicken

4 servings

3 tbsp	(*45 mL*) oil
4	boneless chicken breasts, 6 oz (*170 g*) each
1 tbsp	(*15 mL*) sesame seeds
2 tbsp	(*30 mL*) butter
¼ cup	(*60 mL*) sugar
¼ cup	(*60 mL*) water
¼ cup	(*60 mL*) lemon juice
2 tsp	(*10 mL*) cornstarch
1 tbsp	(*15 mL*) water

Heat the oil in a sauté pan.

Flatten the chicken breasts and sauté 2½ minutes each side. Top with sesame seeds. Remove and keep warm.

Melt the butter in a saucepan. Add the sugar. Stir constantly and cook until the sugar turns a caramel color.

Add ¼ cup (*60 mL*) water and lemon juice and bring to a boil.

Chicken Washington

6 servings

2 tbsp	(30 mL) butter
1/4 cup	(60 mL) finely chopped mushrooms
2 tbsp	(30 mL) flour
1/2 cup	(125 mL) light cream
1/4 tsp	(1 mL) salt
pinch	cayenne pepper
1 1/4 cups	(310 mL) grated old Cheddar cheese
6	boneless chicken breasts, 6 oz (170 g) each
1/4 cup	(60 mL) flour
2	eggs, slightly beaten
3/4 cup	(180 mL) fine breadcrumbs
1/2 cup	(125 mL) shortening

In a saucepan, melt the butter. Sauté the mushrooms until tender.

Blend in the flour and stir until smooth. Add the cream, salt and pepper and simmer until thick. Stir in cheese and continue to stir until it melts. Remove from heat and chill 2 hours. Cut into six even pieces.

Preheat oven to 350°F (180°C).

While the filling chills, pound chicken breasts, then add filling to each and fold in two. Dust with flour, dip in eggs and roll in breadcrumbs.

Heat shortening and fry chicken enough to brown on each side.

Place on pastry sheet and bake 10 minutes in oven. Serve at once.

Chicken Sauté Cumberland

6 servings

6	boneless chicken breasts
2 tbsp	(30 mL) butter
2 tbsp	(30 mL) oil

Sauce

1 cup	(250 mL) red currant jelly
1 tbsp	(15 mL) grated orange rind
1 tbsp	(15 mL) grated lemon rind
1 cup	(250 mL) orange juice
1/4 cup	(60 mL) lemon juice
1 1/2 tsp	(8 mL) ginger
1/4 cup	(60 mL) sherry
1 tbsp	(15 mL) Dijon mustard
1 tbsp	(15 mL) cornstarch
2 tbsp	(30 mL) water

Sauté the chicken in the butter and oil over medium-low heat until the meat is tender, about 8 minutes per side. Remove and keep warm.

In a saucepan, combine the jelly, orange and lemon rinds, juices, ginger, sherry and mustard. Bring to a gentle boil (coddle).

Mix the cornstarch with the water. Mix in sauce and simmer for 5 minutes or until sauce has thickened.

Place chicken on plate and cover with sauce.

Chicken Rombough

4 servings

4	boneless chicken breasts
6 oz	(170 g) Brie cheese
16	medium-size shrimp
1/4 cup	(60 mL) crushed pineapple, drained
3 tbsp	(45 mL) cashews
3 tbsp	(45 mL) sultana raisins
2 tbsp	(30 mL) melted butter
1 cup	(250 mL) heavy cream
1 tbsp	(15 mL) peach flavoring
2 tsp	(10 mL) cornstarch
3 tbsp	(45 mL) peach schnapps

Preheat oven to 350°F (180°C).

Pound the chicken flat. Place 1 1/2 oz (45 g) of cheese, 4 shrimp, 1 tbsp (15 mL) of pineapple and a sprinkle of cashews and raisins on each breast.

Wrap the chicken around the filling. Brush with melted butter. Bake in oven 15 to 20 minutes.

Mix the cream with peach flavoring and heat to a boil.

Combine cornstarch with peach schnapps and add to cream. Simmer until thick.

Remove chicken from oven. Place on plates and cover with sauce.

Chicken Melba

6 servings

6	boneless chicken breasts
1 cup	(*250 mL*) peach slices (if using canned, drain well)
6 oz	(*170 g*) Brie cheese
2 tbsp	(*30 mL*) melted butter
1 cup	(*250 mL*) raspberry coulis (see *Sauces*)
½ cup	(*125 mL*) heavy cream

Preheat oven 350°F (*180°C*).

Pound each breast flat. Top with peach slices and cheese. Roll to fill the breast.

Place on a greased sheet and brush with butter. Place in oven and bake 15 minutes.

Pour raspberry coulis in saucepan, add cream and simmer 5 minutes.

Pour sauce over chicken and serve.

Chicken Melba

Chicken Cordon Bleu

6 servings

6	boneless chicken breasts, 6 oz (*170 g*) each
6 oz	(*170 g*) Black Forest ham
6 oz	(*170 g*) Swiss cheese
2	eggs
¼ cup	(*60 mL*) milk
¼ cup	(*60 mL*) flour
2 cups	(*500 mL*) fine breadcrumbs
½ cup	(*125 mL*) oil
1 cup	(*250 mL*) Mornay Sauce (see *Sauces*)

Preheat oven to 350°F (*180°C*).

Pound the chicken breasts flat. Cut the ham and cheese in six equal portions.

Place 1 piece each of ham and cheese on a chicken breast.

Fold the breast to encase the ham and cheese.

Mix eggs with milk.

Dust each breast with flour. Dip in egg mixture. Roll in breadcrumbs.

Heat oil and shallow fry.

Bake in oven for 8 to 10 minutes.

Serve with Mornay sauce on the side.

Ginger Garlic Chicken Wings

Ginger Garlic Chicken Wings

4 servings

¼ cup	(*60 mL*) soya sauce
2 tsp	(*10 mL*) ground ginger
3 tbsp	(*45 mL*) brown sugar
1 tsp	(*5 mL*) garlic powder
2¼ lbs	(*1 kg*) chicken wings

Preheat oven to 350°F (*180°C*).

Mix the soya sauce, ginger, sugar and garlic powder together.

Pour over chicken wings and marinate for 2 hours.

Bake in oven for 1 hour.

Moo Goo Gai Pan

4 servings

2 tbsp	(*30 mL*) soya sauce
2 tbsp	(*30 mL*) white wine
½ tsp	(*3 mL*) salt
½ tsp	(*3 mL*) sugar
2 tsp	(*10 mL*) oil
1 tsp	(*5 mL*) vinegar
1 lb	(*450 g*) diced chicken
¼ cup	(*60 mL*) oil
1 cup	(*250 mL*) Chinese cabbage
4 oz	(*115 g*) mushrooms, sliced
1	green pepper, diced
1	carrot, sliced
8 oz	(*225 g*) bamboo shoots
¼ cup	(*60 mL*) sliced water chestnuts

Mix the soya sauce, wine, salt, sugar, 2 tsp (*10 mL*) oil and vinegar together.

Pour over chicken and marinate for 1 hour.

Heat ¼ cup (*60 mL*) oil in a wok or large frying pan.

Discard the marinade and brown the chicken.

Add vegetables and cook for 3 minutes.

Serve with a rice pilaf.

Chicken à la King

6 servings

½ lb	(*225 g*) button mushrooms
¼ cup	(*60 mL*) diced green peppers
1	small onion, diced
2	celery stalks, sliced
¼ cup	(*60 mL*) butter
¼ cup	(*60 mL*) flour
2 cups	(*500 mL*) heavy cream
1½ lbs	(*675 g*) chicken, cooked and diced
3	egg yolks
½ tsp	(*3 mL*) paprika
¼ cup	(*60 mL*) sherry
¼ cup	(*60 mL*) diced pimiento
	salt and pepper to taste

Sauté the mushrooms, peppers, onion and celery in the butter until tender.

Add flour and blend well. Add cream, chicken and simmer until slightly thickened.

Whip together the egg yolks, paprika, sherry and pimiento. Fold into sauce. Simmer for 5 minutes.

Season to taste and serve in vol-au-vent shells or over toast.

Chicken Newburg

4 servings

¼ cup	(*60 mL*) butter
2 oz	(*60 g*) mushrooms, sliced
2 tbsp	(*30 mL*) minced onion
1 lb	(*450 g*) chicken, cooked and diced
¼ cup	(*60 mL*) sherry
1 cup	(*250 mL*) light cream
½ tsp	(*3 mL*) salt
½ tsp	(*3 mL*) paprika
pinch	white pepper
3	egg yolks
8 cups	(*2 L*) water
2 cups	(*500 mL*) raw rice

In a saucepan, heat the butter and sauté the mushrooms and onion until tender.

Add the chicken and the sherry. Simmer for 5 minutes.

Add the cream and the seasonings and simmer 5 more minutes.

Remove a little of the hot sauce and mix with the egg yolk.

Return this mixture to the chicken and simmer until sauce has thickened.

In another pan, heat the water. Add the rice and stir 2 minutes. Once rice has cooked, drain.

Place rice in a serving dish. Pour Chicken Newburg over rice and serve.

Pamela's Favorite Chicken and Rice

8-10 servings

1 lb	(*450 g*) boneless chicken, diced
1 lb	(*450 g*) sliced tender veal, pounded very thin, in julienne strips
¼ cup	(*60 mL*) butter
2	medium carrots, coarsely grated
2	celery stalks, finely chopped
4	green onions, thinly sliced
¼ cup	(*60 mL*) flour
2 cups	(*500 mL*) chicken stock
2 cups	(*500 mL*) heavy cream
3 cups	(*750 mL*) cooked rice
1½ cups	(*375 mL*) coarsely grated Swiss cheese
1½ cups	(*375 mL*) coarsely grated medium Cheddar cheese

Preheat oven to 450°F (*230°C*).

In a heavy skillet, sauté the chicken and veal in butter over medium heat until cooked through. Stir in the vegetables, and sauté just until tender, about 2 to 3 minutes. Add the flour, chicken stock and cream. Simmer until thickened. Spread the rice in a greased 13 x 9 in. (*33 x 23 cm*) baking dish; pour the chicken mixture over it, and sprinkle with the grated cheeses.

Bake in oven 6 to 8 minutes or just until the cheese melts.

1

In a skillet, sauté the chicken and veal in butter over medium heat until cooked through.

2

Add the flour, chicken stock and cream; simmer until thickened.

3

Spread the rice in a greased baking dish and pour chicken mixture over it.

4

Sprinkle with grated cheeses and bake in oven 6 to 8 minutes, or until cheese melts.

Chicken Chili

Chicken Chili

8 servings

3 cups	(750 mL) kidney beans
¼ cup	(60 mL) butter
1 cup	(250 mL) diced onions
1	green pepper, diced
3	celery stalks, diced
4 oz	(115 g) mushrooms, sliced
4 cups	(1 L) cooked, diced chicken
4 cups	(1 L) tomatoes, seeded and chopped
½ cup	(125 mL) tomato paste
2 tsp	(10 mL) salt
1 tsp	(5 mL) basil
1 tsp	(5 mL) oregano
2 tsp	(10 mL) paprika
2 tsp	(10 mL) pepper
1¼ tbsp	(20 mL) chili powder

Soak beans overnight.

In a large pot or Dutch oven, melt the butter.

Add the onions, green pepper, celery and mushrooms. Sauté until tender.

Stir in the chicken. Add the tomatoes, tomato paste, beans, salt and seasonings.

Simmer for 40 minutes. Serve.

Chicken Divan

4 servings

4 cups	(*1 L*) broccoli florets
2 cups	(*500 mL*) Golden Mashed Potatoes (see *Vegetables*)
1 lb	(*450 g*) cooked boneless chicken breasts, diced
1⅓ cups	(*330 mL*) Mornay Sauce (see *Sauces*)
3	slices toast, cut into quarters diagonally

Preheat oven to 300°F (*150°C*).

Blanch broccoli florets just until tender crisp.

In a greased shallow baking dish, spread potatoes evenly.

Sprinkle with broccoli and diced chicken.

Drizzle with Mornay sauce and bake, uncovered, in oven 25 to 30 minutes or until heated through.

Place toast around rim of baking dish with points up.

Creamed Mace Chicken

6 servings

¼ cup	(*60 mL*) butter
¼ cup	(*60 mL*) flour
1 cup	(*250 mL*) chicken broth
2 cups	(*500 mL*) light cream
1 tsp	(*5 mL*) salt
¼ tsp	(*1 mL*) mace
¼ tsp	(*1 mL*) pepper
4 cups	(*1 L*) cooked boneless chicken, diced
8 cups	(*2 L*) cooked rice, hot

In a saucepan, heat the butter.

Add the flour and cook 2 minutes, while stirring.

Add the broth, cream and seasonings. Simmer until thickened, 10 to 12 minutes.

Stir in the chicken and simmer an additional 5 minutes.

Pour over rice and serve.

Rock Cornish Game Hens with Prune Stuffing

4 servings

Stuffing

2 cups	(*500 mL*) chicken stock
¼ cup	(*60 mL*) butter
1 cup	(*250 mL*) raw long-grain rice
1 tsp	(*5 mL*) salt
1 cup	(*250 mL*) finely chopped prunes
½ cup	(*125 mL*) walnuts

Rock Cornish Hens

4	rock Cornish game hens, 1 lb (*450 g*) each
¼ cup	(*60 mL*) melted butter
1 tbsp	(*15 mL*) salt

Preheat oven to 400°F (*200°C*).

In a saucepan, heat the chicken stock and melt the butter. Add the rice and salt and stir for 2 minutes. Cover and simmer 18 to 20 minutes.

Once cooked, rinse rice in a strainer under cold water. Mix the rice with the prunes and walnuts.

Carefully stuff the cavities of the birds with the stuffing. Brush each bird with the melted butter then season with salt.

Roast 35 to 50 minutes, basting with drippings every 10 to 15 minutes. Serve at once.

Roast Stuffed Cornish Hens

Roast Stuffed Cornish Hens

6 servings

8 cups	(2 L)	chicken stock
2 cups	(500 mL)	wild rice
1 tsp	(5 mL)	salt
½ tsp	(3 mL)	pepper
½ cup	(125 mL)	butter
¼ tsp	(1 mL)	chervil
¼ tsp	(1 mL)	basil
1 tsp	(5 mL)	chives
1 tbsp	(15 mL)	chopped parsley
¼ cup	(60 mL)	minced celery
2 tbsp	(30 mL)	minced onion
6		Cornish game hens, 12 oz (340 g) each
2 tsp	(10 mL)	paprika

Pour chicken stock into large pot or Dutch oven. Add wild rice, salt and pepper.

Bring to a boil, reduce heat, cover and simmer for 45 to 50 minutes.

Preheat oven to 350°F (180°C).

Drain and stir the rice.

Blend in ¼ cup (60 mL) butter, chervil, basil, chives, chopped parsley, celery and onion. Stuff into cavity of hens and tie hens with string. Place hens in a roasting pan.

Melt the remaining butter. Brush the hens with butter. Sprinkle with paprika.

Bake in oven for 45 to 60 minutes or until hens are tender. Serve.

NOTE : A hunter's sauce (Chasseur Sauce, see Sauces) is exceptionally good with this dish.

Chicken Curry

4 servings

2 tbsp	(30 mL)	butter
2		garlic cloves, minced
1½ cups	(375 mL)	chopped apples
½ cup	(125 mL)	chopped onions
1 tsp	(5 mL)	salt
1 tbsp	(15 mL)	curry powder
2 tbsp	(30 mL)	flour
2 cups	(500 mL)	light cream
2 cups	(500 mL)	cooked, diced chicken

In a saucepan, melt butter and add garlic, apples and onions. Sauté until tender.

Add salt, curry powder and flour. Blend well.

Gradually add cream, chicken and simmer 5 minutes. Serve over rice.

Thanksgiving Turkey

8-10 servings

Stuffing

½ cup	(125 mL)	diced celery
1		large onion, diced
2		small carrots, diced
1 cup	(250 mL)	butter
1 tsp	(5 mL)	sage
1 tsp	(5 mL)	basil
1 tsp	(5 mL)	oregano
1 tsp	(5 mL)	thyme
1 tsp	(5 mL)	black pepper
2 tsp	(10 mL)	salt
2¼ lbs	(1 kg)	breadcrumbs
1 cup	(250 mL)	raisins
2		eggs
½ cup	(125)	cashews (optional)

Preheat oven to 375°F (190°C).
Sauté the celery, onion and carrots in the butter until tender. Add seasonings and sauté 1 minute. Pour mixture into a bowl; add breadcrumbs, raisins, eggs and cashews. Mix thoroughly. Stuff into a 12-14 lb (5,4-6,3 kg) turkey.

Turkey

12-14 lb (5,4-6,3 kg) turkey		
½		lemon
1		garlic clove
2 tsp	(10 mL)	salt

Rub turkey with garlic and lemon. Sprinkle with salt. Roast 4-5 hours, basting often.

Roast Duckling Grand Marnier

4 servings

1		duck, cut into 8 pieces
		salt and pepper
¼ cup	(60 mL)	oil
2 cups	(500 mL)	orange juice
¼ cup	(60 mL)	Grand Marnier liqueur
1 cup	(250 mL)	apricots, pitted and chopped
1 cup	(250 mL)	plums, pitted and chopped
2 tbsp	(30 mL)	flour
2 tbsp	(30 mL)	water
4 cups	(1 L)	cooked rice, hot

Remove the fat and trim the meat of the duck. Season with salt and pepper.

Brown in the oil. Add the orange juice and Grand Marnier and simmer until meat is tender.

Add the apricots and plums and simmer an additional 45 minutes.

Mix the flour with the water into a paste.

Add to the sauce and simmer until thickened.

Pour over rice and serve.

Roast Duck Bigarade

4 servings

4½ lb	(2 kg)	duck
1 tbsp	(15 mL)	butter
		salt and pepper
¾ cup	(180 mL)	white wine
1		lemon
1		orange
1 tbsp	(15 mL)	sugar
1 tbsp	(15 mL)	sherry
1 cup	(250 mL)	orange juice
2 tbsp	(30 mL)	brandy
1 tbsp	(15 mL)	cornstarch

Preheat oven to 375°F (190°C).

Rub the duck with the butter and season with salt and pepper. Place in a roasting pan and add the wine. Place in oven and roast for 2 to 2½ hours. Baste every 15 to 20 minutes with the wine.

Grate the lemon and orange rinds into a sauté pan. Melt the sugar in the pan with the sherry and cook until caramel in color, being careful not to let it burn.

Add the orange juice, the juice of the lemon and brandy. Simmer for 5 minutes. Cut the orange into segments and add to the sauce.

Remove duck from oven when done. Carve and place on platter. Drain fat from roasting pan and add the sauce to the duck drippings.

Mix a little water with the cornstarch and add to sauce. Bring to a boil for 2 minutes.

Pour over duck and serve.

Roast Duck Bigarade

Preheat oven to 350°F (*180°C*).

Prick skin of duck all over with a fork. Place duck in a roasting pan, surround with vegetables, and add 3 cups (*750 mL*) water.

Roast, uncovered, in oven 25 minutes per pound (*450 g*), or until cooked through.

Meanwhile, bring Espagnole Sauce to a boil and reduce to 1¼ cups (*310 mL*).

Drain cherries, reserving ½ cup (*125 mL*) juice.

Combine reduced Espagnole Sauce, reserved cherry juice, sherry, orange rind, and orange juice.

Remove duck from roasting pan; keep warm.

Discard vegetables from pan juices and drain off all fat.

Stir 1 cup (*250 mL*) pan juices into Espagnole Sauce mixture.

Bring to a boil and reduce, stirring constantly, to about 1¼ cups (*310 mL*).

Add icing sugar, cinnamon and cream cheese; stir until smooth.

Stir in cherries. Carve duck and serve accompanied with sauce.

Roast Duckling Montmorency

4 servings

1	4-5 lb (*2-2,5 kg*) duck
1	medium onion, quartered
2	carrots, coarsely chopped
2	celery stalks, coarsely chopped
2½ cups	(*625 mL*) Espagnole Sauce (see *Sauces*)
14 oz	(*398 mL*) can sweet cherries
½ cup	(*125 mL*) Brights Cream Sherry
2 tsp	(*10 mL*) grated orange rind
¼ cup	(*60 mL*) orange juice
3 tbsp	(*45 mL*) icing sugar
pinch	cinnamon
1	(*250 g*) pkg. cream cheese, cut into cubes

Sautéed Quails Provençale

3 servings

6	quails
¼ cup	(60 mL) butter
3	garlic cloves, minced
½ cup	(125 mL) diced green peppers
¼ cup	(60 mL) diced onions
3 cups	(750 mL) tomatoes, peeled, seeded and chopped
¼ cup	(60 mL) sherry
1 tsp	(5 mL) paprika
	salt and pepper

Using poultry shears, split the quails down the back.

Melt the butter and sauté the quails 3 minutes each side or until golden brown. Remove from pan and keep warm.

Add garlic, peppers and onions; sauté until tender.

Add tomatoes and bring to a simmer. Add sherry and quails and continue to simmer until most of liquid evaporates.

Season with paprika, salt and pepper.

Pour sauce on a platter and arrange quails on sauce.

Roast Quails Cumberland

5 servings

¼ cup	(60 mL) butter
	salt and pepper
10	quails
3 tbsp	(45 mL) lemon juice
1 cup	(250 mL) sherry

Sauce

¾ cup	(180 mL) red currant jelly
¾ cup	(180 mL) orange juice
¼ cup	(60 mL) lemon juice
¼ tsp	(1 mL) ground ginger
pinch	cayenne pepper
2 tbsp	(30 mL) cornstarch
2 tbsp	(30 mL) water

Preheat oven to 350°F (180°C).

Butter and season the quails. Place the quails in a roasting pan.

Pour the lemon juice and sherry over them. Bake for 1 hour, basting every 15 to 20 minutes.

In a small saucepan, heat jelly and simmer until melted. Slowly add the juices. Mix in the seasonings.

Mix the cornstarch with the water and add to the sauce. Bring to a boil and remove from heat at once.

Place quails on a platter. Pour sauce over quails and serve.

Apple Duckling

6 servings

2¼ lb	(1 kg) duck
2 tsp	(10 mL) salt
1 cup	(250 mL) apple juice
1 cup	(250 mL) diced apples
¾ cup	(180 mL) cashews
¼ tsp	(1 mL) cinnamon
2 cups	(500 mL) wild rice, cooked
1 cup	(250 mL) Calvados
1 tsp	(5 mL) sugar

Preheat oven to 500°F (260°C).

Rub the outside of the duck with the salt. Roast in oven for 10 minutes.

Reduce heat to 375°F (190°C). Baste with apple juice. Remove duck after 20 minutes.

Mix together the apples, cashews, cinnamon, wild rice and half the Calvados. Stuff the duck with this mixture.

Return duck to oven. Bake for an additional 40 minutes.

Place duck on platter. Sprinkle with sugar.

Pour the remaining Calvados over the duck. Ignite carefully.

Serve while flaming.

Sautéed Quails Provençale and Roast Quails Cumberland

Guinea Fowl with Ceps

6 servings

3 tbsp	(45 mL) oil
6	guinea fowl breasts, 6 oz (170 g) each
¼ cup	(60 mL) minced shallots
½ cup	(125 mL) white wine
3 tbsp	(45 mL) butter
1 cup	(250 mL) oil
8 oz	(225 g) cep mushrooms
pinch	salt
pinch	pepper
1 cup	(250 mL) seasoned breadcrumbs

Heat oil in a sauté pan. Sauté the breasts 2½ minutes on each side. Remove and keep warm.

Drain oil from pan and sauté the shallots. Swirl in the wine and reduce by half. Finish by adding the butter; remove from heat.

Ceps

Heat oil to very hot. Season the ceps with salt and pepper, then fry in oil until they are very wrinkled.

Toss the ceps in the breadcrumbs.

Place the guinea fowl breasts on a platter and pour pan sauce over.

Top with the ceps and serve.

Guinea Fowl Champagne

Guinea Fowl Champagne

6 servings

6	guinea fowl breasts
3 tbsp	(45 mL) oil
3 tbsp	(45 mL) butter
4	carrots, cut in julienne
2	zucchini, cut in julienne
4	celery stalks, cut in julienne
½ lb	(225 g) yellow beans
½ lb	(225 g) green beans
¼ cup	(60 mL) butter
2 tsp	(10 mL) caraway seeds
2 cups	(500 mL) Champagne Sauce (see *Sauces*)

Sauté breasts in oil and 3 tbsp (45 mL) butter, 10 minutes each side. Blanch the vegetables for 5 minutes in salted water.

Sauté the vegetables in butter and sprinkle with caraway. Heat sauce.

Arrange vegetables on plate, top with breasts and pour sauce over breasts.

Sautéed Pheasant with Clementine Sauce

6 servings

3 tbsp	*(45 mL)* oil
6	pheasant breasts, 6 oz *(170 g)* each
	salt and pepper to taste
1/3 cup	*(80 mL)* tangerine concentrate
1/2 cup	*(125 mL)* chicken stock
1/4 cup	*(60 mL)* heavy cream
2 tbsp	*(30 mL)* butter
1 tsp	*(5 mL)* lime juice
	fresh cracked black pepper

Heat the oil in a large skillet.

Sauté the pheasant 4 to 6 minutes each side. Season with salt and pepper. Keep warm.

In a saucepan, add the tangerine concentrate and chicken stock. Bring to a boil and reduce heat.

Add cream and simmer 6 minutes or until sauce coats a spoon.

Whisk in the butter and lime juice. Add just a touch of pepper. Pour sauce over pheasant breasts and serve.

Pheasant Casserole

4 servings

1/2 cup	*(125 mL)* butter
2	onions, thinly sliced
4	carrots, pared and julienned

Sautéed Pheasant with Clementine Sauce

2	pheasants, 2¼ lbs *(1 kg)* each, cut into 4 pieces each
2 tbsp	*(30 mL)* flour
1 cup	*(250 mL)* red wine
1/2 cup	*(125 mL)* sherry
1/4 cup	*(60 mL)* brandy
1/2 cup	*(125 mL)* chicken stock
	salt and pepper
1/4 lb	*(115 g)* bacon, diced
12	pearl onions
20	button mushrooms

Preheat oven to 325°F *(160°C)*.

In a large pot, heat half the butter and sauté the sliced onions and carrots until tender.

Add the pheasant and brown. Sprinkle in the flour and stir until the flour has absorbed the butter. Pour in the wine, sherry, brandy, stock and sprinkle with salt and pepper. Bring to a boil. Reduce heat and simmer 20 minutes.

In a saucepan, sauté the bacon, pearl onions and mushrooms until brown.

Place pheasant in a casserole dish. Spoon on the onions, bacon and mushrooms. Pour over the sauce. Cover.

Bake in oven for 60 minutes.

Pork

The great French chef Escoffier apparently thought pork was unworthy of classic cuisine, although he held ham in high regard.

Fortunately, today's chefs realize that pork, both fresh and cured, can play an important role in menu planning. In fact, pork is the second most popular red meat, next to beef.

Fresh pork is usually from young animals, and therefore tender. And although some people consider pork to be a fatty meat, certain cuts, including lean roasts and tenderloin, are lean enough to be adopted even in the most calorie-conscious diets.

Pork, unlike beef, should always be fresh, never aged. And it should always be cooked until well done, in order to eliminate the possibility of trichinosis.

Pork roasts should be cooked for 30 minutes per lb (*450 g*) at 325°F (*160°C*). It's a safe practice to use a meat thermometer, which should read 170°F (*76°C*) when the meat is properly cooked.

Hams are available fresh, cured or partly cured. Some of the most famous hams are Parma (prosciutto), Virginia (cured up to 2 years), Danish and York.

In this chapter you will find a number of pork recipes for ham and sausage as well as for fresh pork, including steaks, cutlets and stir fries.

Pork Dijonnaise

Pork Dijonnaise

6 servings

6	pork shoulder chops
2 tbsp	(*30 mL*) butter
1 tsp	(*5 mL*) oil
2	green onions, diced
2	garlic cloves, minced
12	gherkins, julienned
½ cup	(*125 mL*) sherry
½ cup	(*125 mL*) heavy cream
2 tbsp	(*30 mL*) Dijon mustard

Sauté the pork chops in half the butter and oil, about 8-10 minutes each side.

In a saucepan, heat the rest of the butter. Sauté the onions and garlic until tender.

Add the gherkins and sherry. Simmer until most of liquid has evaporated.

Mix the mustard with the cream. Add to sauce; simmer 2 minutes.

Pour over pork chops and serve.

Pork Chops Baked in Mushroom Cream

8 servings

8	pork chops, 1-in. (2,5 cm) thick
2 tbsp	(30 mL) oil
4 oz	(115 g) mushrooms, sliced
2 tbsp	(30 mL) flour
1 cup	(250 mL) heavy cream
¼ cup	(60 mL) sherry
2 tsp	(10 mL) paprika
1 tsp	(5 mL) salt
½ tsp	(3 mL) black pepper

Preheat oven to 375°F (190°C).

Trim the chops of excess fat. Sauté the chops in a skillet in the oil, browning each side.

Transfer chops to a large casserole.

Place the mushrooms in the skillet and sauté until tender.

Sprinkle with flour and cook 2 minutes. Add the cream, sherry and seasonings.

Stir and gently simmer for 5 minutes. Pour sauce over chops.

Bake in oven for 30 minutes.

Serve with rice pilaf.

Breaded Pork Chops with Raisin Sauce

4 servings

1	egg
¼ cup	(60 mL) milk
8	pork chops
⅓ cup	(80 mL) flour
2 cups	(500 mL) breadcrumbs
¼ cup	(60 mL) oil

Sauce

1½ tbsp	(22 mL) cornstarch
½ cup	(125 mL) water
3 tbsp	(45 mL) brown sugar
1¼ cups	(310 mL) orange juice
2 tbsp	(30 mL) lemon juice
½ tsp	(3 mL) cinnamon
pinch	allspice
½ cup	(125 mL) raisins

Mix the egg in the milk. Dip the chops into the flour, then into the egg. Dredge in the breadcrumbs.

Heat the oil in a skillet. Fry the chops in the oil.

Sauce : Blend the cornstarch in the water. Dissolve the sugar in the orange juice.

Heat the orange juice in a saucepan.

Add the lemon juice and seasonings. Add the raisins and simmer for 5 minutes. Blend in the water and simmer until thick. Pour sauce over the chops and serve.

Orange Thyme Pork Chops

6 servings

6	pork shoulder chops
1 tsp	(5 mL) thyme
½ tsp	(3 mL) grated orange rind
1 cup	(250 mL) orange juice
2 tbsp	(30 mL) oil
pinch	salt and pepper

Trim the excess fat from the pork chops.

Mix the thyme, orange rind and orange juice together and pour over pork chops.

Marinate for 1 hour at room temperature.

Preheat oven to 375°F (190°C).

Remove pork chops and reserve marinade.

In a skillet, heat the oil and brown the chops. Place in a baking pan.

Pour marinade over chops, season and bake, covered, for 20 minutes.

Uncover and bake for another 5 minutes.

Stuffed Pork Chops

4 servings

¼ cup	(*60 mL*) minced onions
2 tbsp	(*30 mL*) minced celery
1 cup	(*250 mL*) breadcrumbs
½ cup	(*125 mL*) raisins
¼ cup	(*60 mL*) walnut pieces
½ tsp	(*3 mL*) thyme
½ tsp	(*3 mL*) basil
1 tbsp	(*15 mL*) chopped parsley
1 tsp	(*5 mL*) salt
⅓ cup	(*80 mL*) heavy cream
4	double rib pork chops
2 tbsp	(*30 mL*) oil
2 cups	(*500 mL*) Mornay Sauce (see *Sauces*)

Preheat oven to 350°F (*180°C*).

In a mixing bowl, blend together onions, celery, breadcrumbs, raisins, walnuts and seasonings. Blend in the cream and mix thoroughly.

Trim the chops of any excess fat. Slice between the bones, creating a pocket. Stuff the filling into the pockets.

Heat the oil in a skillet. Brown the chops in the oil. Transfer to a casserole dish.

Cover the chops with the Mornay Sauce.

Cover and bake in oven for 45 minutes. Remove cover and degrease.

Place chops on platter. Smother with sauce.

1

In a mixing bowl, blend together onions, celery, breadcrumbs, raisins, walnuts and seasonings. Blend in the cream and mix thoroughly.

2

Trim the pork chops of fat and slice between the bones to create a pocket.

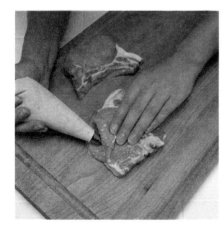

3

Stuff the filling into the pockets.

4

Pour Mornay Sauce over browned chops, cover and bake in oven for 45 minutes. Remove cover and degrease.

Crown Roast of Pork

8 servings

1	16-chopped crown pork roast
1 tbsp	(*15 mL*) salt
¼ cup	(*60 mL*) diced celery
¼ cup	(*60 mL*) butter
2 tbsp	(*30 mL*) sugar
1 cup	(*250 mL*) chopped cranberries
2 tsp	(*10 mL*) grated orange rind
½ tsp	(*3 mL*) ground cinnamon
¼ tsp	(*1 mL*) ground allspice
¼ cup	(*60 mL*) orange juice
½ cup	(*125 mL*) chopped pecans
4 cups	(*1 L*) cubed white bread
¼ cup	(*60 mL*) flour

Preheat oven to 350°F (*180°C*).

Sprinkle pork with salt. Place roast, rib ends up, on a piece of foil in a shallow roasting pan. (Foil with hold stuffing in roast when it is removed from pan).

Wrap ends of bones with foil to prevent darkening.

Roast in oven 1 hour.

While roast cooks, sauté celery in butter in large frying pan until soft.

Stir in sugar until dissolved, then add cranberries, orange rind, cinnamon and allspice; remove from heat.

Stir in orange juice, pecans and bread cubes until evenly moistened.

Spoon into the hollow of the roast and cover with foil to prevent browning.

Continue roasting 1 hour or until pork is tender. Lift out roast; remove foil. Keep warm.

Pour drippings from pan into a 2-cup (*500 mL*) measure. Let stand a few minutes until fat rises to the top, then skim off.

Measure ¼ cup (*60 mL*) of drippings and return to pan. Add water to make 2 cups.

Blend in the flour and let thicken. Use as gravy.

Pork Tenderloin with Apricots

6 servings

2 lbs	(*900 g*) pork tenderloin
3 tbsp	(*45 mL*) butter
3 tbsp	(*45 mL*) oil
½ cup	(*125 mL*) coarsely chopped dried apricots
2 cups	(*500 mL*) demi-glace (see *Sauces*)
¼ cup	(*60 mL*) sherry

Clean the tenderloin of any fat or membranes.

Sauté the tenderloin in butter and oil until well done.

Remove from heat and keep hot in oven.

Place apricots in pan and gently sauté for 2 minutes.

Add demi-glace and sherry; simmer for 6 to 8 minutes.

Pour sauce over tenderloin and serve.

Pork Tenderloin Stuffed with Prunes and Apples

4 servings

2	pork tenderloins
1 tsp	(5 mL) salt
1 tsp	(5 mL) pepper
12	pitted prunes
1	apple, peeled, cubed
1 tsp	(5 mL) lemon juice
3 tbsp	(45 mL) oil
3 tbsp	(45 mL) butter
¾ cup	(180 mL) white wine
¾ cup	(180 mL) heavy cream

Cut a pocket in the center along the length of each tenderloin. Season.

Cover prunes with water and bring to boil. Remove from heat and soak 30 minutes. Drain.

Preheat oven to 350°F (180°C).

Sprinkle apple with lemon juice. Stuff pork with prunes and apples. Tie meat in several places.

Heat the oil and butter in a Dutch oven. Brown the meat on all sides. Pour off the fat, pour in wine and cream. Simmer, then cover and cook in oven for 15 minutes.

Place meat on platter. Skim fat from liquid, bring to boil and simmer to reduce. Serve with meat.

1

Cut a pocket in the center along the length of each tenderloin.

2

Stuff pork with prunes and apples.

3

Tie the meat in several places.

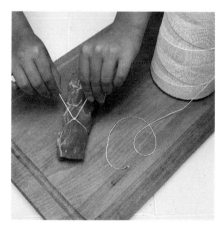

4

Brown the meat on all sides. Pour off the fat; pour in wine and cream.

Roast Loin of Pork Provençale

8 servings

¼ cup	(60 mL) oil
7 lb	(3 kg) boneless pork loin, tied
¼ cup	(60 mL) minced onions
¼ cup	(60 mL) celery stalks, minced
¼ cup	(60 mL) green peppers, minced
3	garlic cloves, minced
1 cup	(250 mL) water
1 cup	(250 mL) red wine
2 cups	(500 mL) chopped tomatoes
2 tbsp	(30 mL) chopped parsley
½ tsp	(3 mL) thyme
1 tsp	(5 mL) salt
½ tsp	(3 mL) black pepper

Preheat oven to 350°F (180°C).

Heat the oil in a roasting pan. Brown the roast in the oil.

Add the onion, celery, green peppers and garlic. Pour the water and wine over the roast.

Add the tomatoes and seasonings. Cover and roast in oven 2½ hours. Remove roast, and keep warm.

Reduce sauce by simmering gently. Degrease.

Slice roast and serve with sauce.

Pork Steak with Mushroom Sauce

Pork Steak with Mushroom Sauce

8 servings

8	slices bacon
8	very lean pork steaks, 6 oz (170 g) each
¼ cup	(60 mL) butter
2 tbsp	(30 mL) minced onion
3 tbsp	(45 mL) diced green pepper
4 oz	(115 g) mushrooms
3 tbsp	(45 mL) flour
2 cups	(500 mL) demi-glace (see *Sauces*)
¼ cup	(60 mL) sherry
½ cup	(125 mL) heavy cream
¼ cup	(60 mL) diced green onions

Wrap the bacon around the steaks. Broil steaks over a charbroiler or in the oven until well done. Heat the butter in a skillet. Add the vegetables and sauté until tender. Sprinkle in flour. Cook for 2 minutes. Add the demi-glace and sherry and simmer for 5 minutes. Add the cream. Simmer 1 minute, add the green onions and simmer for 3 minutes.

Pour sauce over steaks. Serve at once.

Fry the cutlets in the oil, 2½ minutes each side. Remove and place on a pastry sheet.

Spoon 2 tbsp (*30 mL*) of sauce onto each cutlet. Sprinkle with cheese. Top with green peppers and mushrooms.

Broil in the oven 3 to 5 minutes until golden brown. Serve hot.

Pork Steak with Pepper Apple Sauce

4 servings

4	small pork steaks
2 tbsp	(*30 mL*) crushed black peppercorns
2 tbsp	(*30 mL*) flour
1 tbsp	(*15 mL*) brown sugar
2 tbsp	(*30 mL*) butter
2 tsp	(*10 mL*) green peppercorns
½ tsp	(*3 mL*) crushed white peppercorns
pinch	salt
2 tbsp	(*30 mL*) sherry
3 tbsp	(*45 mL*) applesauce

Pat the steaks in the crushed black peppercorns. Mix 1 tbsp (*15 mL*) flour with the sugar. Roll steaks in the sugared flour. Heat the butter and sauté the steaks. Remove and keep warm.

Add 1 tbsp (*15 mL*) flour to pan. Stir until browned.

Add the green peppercorns, white peppercorns, salt, sherry and applesauce. Simmer until thickened.

Pour over pork steaks and serve.

Pork Schnitzel Milanese

Pork Schnitzel Milanese

6 servings

6	pork cutlets, 4 oz (*115 g*) each
1	egg
¼ cup	(*60 mL*) milk
½ cup	(*125 mL*) flour
2 cups	(*500 mL*) seasoned breadcrumbs
¼ cup	(*60 mL*) olive oil
1½ cups	(*375 mL*) tomato sauce (see *Sauces*)
2 cups	(*500 mL*) grated mozzarella cheese
½ cup	(*125 mL*) sliced green peppers
½ cup	(*125 mL*) sliced mushrooms

Pound the cutlets very thin. Blend egg with the milk. Dust the cutlets in the flour, dip into the egg and dredge in breadcrumbs.

Heat the oil in a large skillet.

Stuffed Pork Cutlets

6 servings

6	pork cutlets, 6 oz (*170 g*) each
6	slices Cheddar, 1½ oz (*40 g*) each
12 oz	(*340 g*) hot sausage
½ cup	(*125 mL*) flour
1	egg
¼ cup	(*60 mL*) milk
2 cups	(*500 mL*) seasoned fine breadcrumbs
1 cup	(*250 mL*) oil
2 tbsp	(*30 mL*) butter
¼ cup	(*60 mL*) minced onions
¼ cup	(*60 mL*) minced green pepper
¼ cup	(*60 mL*) minced celery
1	garlic clove, minced
2 tbsp	(*30 mL*) flour
½ cup	(*125 mL*) heavy cream
¼ cup	(*60 mL*) sherry
2 cups	(*500 mL*) tomato sauce (see *Sauces*)

Preheat oven to 425°F (*220°C*).

Pound the pork cutlets flat. Place 1 cheese slice in the center of each.

Dice the hot sausage and divide among the cutlets. Wrap the cutlets around cheese and sausage. Dust with flour.

Blend the egg into the milk. Dip the cutlets into the milk. Dredge with breadcrumbs.

Heat the oil in a large skillet. Brown the cutlets in the oil. Transfer to a baking sheet. Bake in oven for 15 minutes.

While cutlets are baking, heat the butter in a saucepan.

Sauté the onions, green pepper, celery and garlic until tender. Sprinkle with flour and cook 2 minutes.

Add the cream and the sherry; simmer until very thick. Add the tomato sauce. Simmer for 7 minutes.

Cover the cutlets with sauce. Serve at once.

Pork Cutlets Robert

6 servings

6	pork cutlets, 4 oz (*115 g*) each
½ cup	(*125 mL*) flour
1	egg
¼ cup	(*60 mL*) milk
2 cups	(*500 mL*) seasoned fine breadcrumbs
⅓ cup	(*80 mL*) oil

Sauce

¼ cup	(*60 mL*) butter
¼ cup	(*60 mL*) minced onions
¼ cup	(*60 mL*) red wine vinegar
1½ cups	(*375 mL*) Espagnole Sauce (see *Sauces*)
⅓ cup	(*80 mL*) chopped gherkins
2 tsp	(*10 mL*) prepared mustard
3 tbsp	(*45 mL*) chopped parsley

Pound the cutlets thin. Dust with flour.

Mix the egg into the milk. Dip the cutlets into the milk. Dredge in breadcrumbs.

Heat the oil in a large skillet.

Fry the cutlets in the oil 2½ minutes each side, or until golden brown.

Sauce : Heat the butter in a saucepan. Sauté the onions for 5 minutes. Stir in the vinegar and reduce by half.

Add the Espagnole Sauce; simmer over low heat for 15 minutes.

Add the gherkins, mustard and parsley; stir.

Pour over cutlets before serving.

Italian Pork Tenderloin

Italian Pork Tenderloin

8 servings

¼ cup	(60 mL)	olive oil
2¼ lbs	(1 kg)	pork tenderloin, cubed
1		garlic clove, minced
1		onion, finely diced
1		green pepper, finely diced
2		celery stalks, finely diced
½ lb	(225 g)	button mushrooms
3 cups	(750 mL)	tomatoes, seeded and chopped
1 tsp	(5 mL)	thyme
1 tsp	(5 mL)	salt
½ tsp	(3 mL)	cracked pepper
½ tsp	(3 mL)	oregano
½ tsp	(3 mL)	basil
1 lb	(450 g)	fettuccine

Heat the oil in a large skillet. Sauté the pork until browned. Remove and keep warm.

Add the garlic, onion, green pepper, celery and mushrooms; sauté until tender.

Stir in the tomatoes and seasonings. Simmer gently for 20 minutes.

Return the pork to skillet and simmer 5 to 7 minutes.

While the sauce is reducing, boil water in a large pot. Add salt and fettuccine. Cook al dente.

Place drained fettucine on a platter.

Serve pork mixture over noodles.

Pork Tenderloin in Sour Cream Sauce

8 servings

¼ cup	(60 mL) oil
3 lbs	(1,4 kg) pork tenderloin, cubed
2 tbsp	(30 mL) butter
¼ cup	(60 mL) minced onions
4 oz	(115 g) mushrooms, sliced
1	garlic clove, minced
3 tbsp	(45 mL) flour
1 cup	(250 mL) chicken broth
1 cup	(250 mL) sour cream
1 tsp	(5 mL) paprika
½ tsp	(3 mL) cracked pepper
1 tsp	(5 mL) salt

Heat the oil in a large skillet. Sauté the tenderloin to brown. Remove and keep warm.

Add the butter to the skillet.

Sauté the onions, mushrooms and garlic until tender. Sprinkle with the flour. Cook for 2 minutes.

Add the broth, sour cream and seasonings. Simmer for 5 minutes.

Return the pork to skillet. Gently simmer for 10 minutes.

Serve with hot buttered noodles.

Pork Tenderloin Stroganoff

8 servings

¼ cup	(60 mL) butter
1	onion, thinly sliced
4 oz	(115 g) mushrooms, sliced
2¼ lbs	(1 kg) pork tenderloin, diced
2 tbsp	(30 mL) flour
1 cup	(250 mL) beef broth
½ cup	(125 mL) white wine
1 cup	(250 mL) sour cream
2 tsp	(10 mL) salt
½ tsp	(3 mL) cracked pepper
2 tsp	(10 mL) paprika
1 tbsp	(15 mL) prepared mustard

Heat the butter in a large skillet.

Add the onion and mushrooms. Sauté until tender.

Add the pork and brown. Sprinkle with flour. Cook 2 minutes.

Add the broth, wine and sour cream. Stir and simmer for 5 minutes.

Add seasonings and mustard. Simmer 30 more minutes.

Serve over noodles or rice.

Pork Tenderloin Diane

6 servings

¼ cup	(60 mL) butter
2¼ lbs	(1 kg) pork tenderloin, cubed
4 oz	(115 g) mushrooms, sliced
6	green onions, diced
¼ cup	(60 mL) brandy
¼ cup	(60 mL) sherry
2 cups	(500 mL) demi-glace (see *Sauces*)
½ cup	(125 mL) heavy cream

In a skillet, heat the butter. Sauté the tenderloin in the butter. Remove and keep warm.

Add the mushrooms and onions to the butter and cook until tender.

Add the brandy and flame carefully. Add the sherry and demi-glace. Simmer gently for 5 minutes. Finish by swirling in the cream.

Return the pork to skillet and simmer for an additional 3 minutes.

Serve at once.

Pork Tenderloin Diane

Pork Tenderloin and Mushrooms Lucullus

6 servings

⅓ cup	(*80 mL*) butter
2¼ lbs	(*1 kg*) pork tenderloin, cubed
1 lb	(*450 g*) mushrooms, sliced
2 tbsp	(*30 mL*) flour
1 cup	(*250 mL*) sherry
2 cups	(*500 mL*) heavy cream
1 tsp	(*5 mL*) salt
1 tsp	(*5 mL*) paprika
¼ tsp	(*1 mL*) pepper

Preheat oven to 350°F (*180°C*).

Heat the butter in a large skillet. Brown the pork in the butter. Remove and keep hot in a casserole dish.

Add the mushrooms to the butter. Sauté until tender.

Sprinkle in flour. Cook 2 minutes.

Add the sherry, cream and seasonings. Simmer for 5 minutes.

Pour sauce over pork. Cover.

Bake in oven for 20 minutes. Serve.

Pork aux Pommes

8 servings

2 lbs	(*900 g*) pork leg, diced
½ tsp	(*3 mL*) salt
1 tsp	(*5 mL*) paprika
2 tbsp	(*30 mL*) oil
1 cup	(*250 mL*) apple juice
1 cup	(*250 mL*) sherry
4	Granny Smith apples, peeled, cored and sliced
2 tbsp	(*30 mL*) flour
3 tbsp	(*45 mL*) water
4 cups	(*1 L*) cooked rice, hot

Remove the fat and trim the meat; season with salt and paprika. Brown in the oil.

Add the apple juice and sherry and simmer until meat is tender.

Add the apples and simmer an additional 5 minutes.

Mix the flour with the water into a paste. Add to the sauce and simmer until thickened.

Pour over rice and serve.

Chinese Sweet-and-Sour Pork

4 servings

1	egg, beaten
½ cup	(*125 mL*) flour
½ tsp	(*3 mL*) salt
¼ tsp	(*1 mL*) baking powder
1¼ cups	(*310 mL*) water
1 lb	(*450 g*) pork shoulder, cubed small
4 cups	(*1 L*) oil
½ cup	(*125 mL*) vinegar
¼ cup	(*60 mL*) brown sugar
1 tbsp	(*15 mL*) molasses
1 cup	(*250 mL*) pineapple chunks, drained
1	green pepper, sliced
2 tbsp	(*30 mL*) cornstarch

Mix the egg with flour, salt, baking powder and ¼ cup (*60 mL*) water.

Season the pork with a little salt and pepper.

Coat the pork with the batter and deep fry in the oil until golden brown. Remove and keep warm.

In a saucepan, heat to boiling the following : ¾ cup (*180 mL*) water, vinegar, brown sugar and molasses.

Add the pineapple and green pepper. Simmer 2 minutes.

Mix the cornstarch with ¼ cup (*60 mL*) water. Pour into sauce. Bring to a boil; remove from heat.

Pour over pork cubes and serve.

Almonds, Peas and Pork

Almonds, Peas and Pork

4 servings

¼ cup	(60 mL) oil
1 lb	(450 g) lean pork, sliced thin
2 cups	(500 mL) snow peas
1 cup	(250 mL) toasted almonds
¼ cup	(60 mL) sherry
1 tbsp	(15 mL) curry powder*
2 cups	(500 mL) plain yogurt
4 cups	(1 L) cooked rice, hot

Heat the oil in a large skillet until very hot. Add the pork and fast fry.

Add the snow peas and almonds. Toss and cook for 1 minute.

Stir in the sherry, curry powder and yogurt. Simmer for 3 minutes.

Serve over rice.

* Curry Powder

1 tbsp	(15 mL) ground coriander
1 tbsp	(15 mL) ground cumin
1 tsp	(5 mL) ground ginger
2 tsp	(10 mL) turmeric
¼ tsp	(1 mL) cayenne pepper
pinch	pepper
1½ tsp	(8 mL) cardamom

Mix all spices together thoroughly.

Breakfast Sausage Patties

32 2-oz (60 g) patties

4 lbs	(1,8 kg) ground pork
1 tbsp	(15 mL) salt
1 tbsp	(15 mL) ground sage
1 tbsp	(15 mL) black pepper
2 tsp	(10 mL) ground oregano
½ tsp	(3 mL) nutmeg
½ tsp	(3 mL) allspice
½ tsp	(3 mL) ginger
¼ tsp	(1 mL) mace
1 tbsp	(15 mL) sugar
½ cup	(125 mL) water

Preheat oven to 450°F (230°C).

Place the pork in a mixing bowl. Add the seasonings and blend thoroughly.

Add the water gradually, blending in a little at a time. Shape into patties.

Place patties on a baking sheet. Bake in oven for 8 minutes or until done.

Barbecued Back Ribs

8 servings

5 lbs	(2,2 kg) pork back ribs
2 cups	(500 mL) beer
10 cups	(2,5 L) water
1	onion, diced
2	carrots, diced
2	celery stalks, diced
1	garlic clove, minced
¼ cup	(60 mL) pickling spice
2 tsp	(10 mL) salt
2 cups	(500 mL) Barbecue Sauce (see *Sauces*)

Place the ribs in a large pot. Pour the beer and water over the ribs.

Add the vegetables and seasonings. Bring to a boil. Reduce to a gentle simmer. Simmer for 2 hours.

Preheat oven to 400°F (200°C).

Remove the ribs and run under cool water. When cooled enough to be handled, remove the back membranes. Place ribs on a baking sheet.

Brush with Barbecue Sauce and bake in oven for 15 minutes, or, broil on a charbroiler, brushing with sauce. Serve hot.

Honey Ginger Ribs

6 servings

2¼ lbs	(1 kg) spareribs
1 tsp	(5 mL) salt
1 tsp	(5 mL) ground ginger
¼ tsp	(1 mL) garlic powder
¼ cup	(60 mL) soya sauce
1 cup	(250 mL) liquid honey

Have the butcher cut the ribs into serving portions.

Preheat oven to 350°F (180°C).

Sprinkle ribs with salt, ginger and garlic powder.

Mix the soya sauce with the honey. Brush onto ribs.

Bake in oven for 1½ hours or until very tender, basting frequently with sauce.

Cabbage Rolls

18 rolls — 6 servings

1	cabbage
2 tbsp	(*30 mL*) bacon drippings
1 cup	(*250 mL*) diced onion
2	garlic cloves, minced
1 lb	(*450 g*) lean ground pork
¾ cup	(*180 mL*) cooked rice
2	eggs, beaten
2 tbsp	(*30 mL*) paprika
¼ tsp	(*1 mL*) oregano
1 tsp	(*5 mL*) salt
1 tsp	(*5 mL*) pepper
1 lb	(*450 g*) sauerkraut
½ cup	(*125 mL*) chicken stock
½ cup	(*125 mL*) tomato purée
2 cups	(*500 mL*) sour cream

Preheat oven to 350°F (*180°C*).

Boil cabbage until leaves are tender enough to roll.

Heat the bacon drippings and brown the onion and garlic.

Mix the pork, browned onion and garlic, rice, eggs and seasonings together. Stuff into leaves and roll.

Place sauerkraut on the bottom of a casserole dish. Place rolls on top of sauerkraut.

Mix chicken stock with tomato purée.

Pour over rolls. Cover and bake in oven for 1¾ hours. Serve with sour cream.

1

Mix the ground pork, browned onion and garlic, rice, eggs and seasonings together.

2

Stuff mixture into cabbage leaves and roll.

3

Spread sauerkraut on the bottom of casserole dish and place cabbage rolls on top.

4

Mix chicken stock with tomato purée and pour over rolls.

Clove-Studded Black Forest Ham

8 servings

5 lb	(2,2 kg) smoked Black Forest ham
20	cloves
½ cup	(125 mL) apricot preserves
½ cup	(125 mL) white grape jelly, or apple jelly
1 tbsp	(15 mL) Dijon mustard
1½ cups	(375 mL) demerara sugar*
¼ tsp	(1 mL) ground cinnamon
¼ tsp	(1 mL) allspice

Preheat oven to 325°F (160°C).

Cut ⅛-in. (0,5 cm) deep criss-cross lines in the ham. Stud each diamond with 1 clove.

In a saucepan, heat the preserves, jelly, mustard, sugar, cinnamon and allspice. Boil down into a glaze.

Bake the ham in oven for 2¼ hours.

Brush with glaze every 5 minutes during the final ½ hour.

Serve.

* brown crystallized cane sugar

Clove-Studded Black Forest Ham

Jambon au Gratin

Apricot-Glazed Ham

8 servings

5 lb	*(2,2 kg)* smoked boneless ham
1 lb	*(450 g)* dried apricots
2 cups	*(500 mL)* water
½ cup	*(125 mL)* brown sugar
1 tsp	*(5 mL)* allspice

Soak the ham overnight in enough water to cover it. Refrigerate (this removes excess salt).

In a saucepan, mix the apricots with the water, sugar and allspice.

Cook, mashing into a purée. Simmer until most of the liquid has evaporated. Reserve.

Preheat oven to 325°F *(160°C)*.

Cut the ham in criss-cross lines ⅛-in. *(0,5 cm)* deep on top.

Place in a roasting pan and roast for 2¼ to 2½ hours.

During the last half hour, spoon purée on top.

Jambon au Gratin

8 servings

8	1-in. *(2,5 cm)* thick slices of uncooked ham
	vegetable oil
¼ cup	*(60 mL)* soft butter
1 cup	*(250 mL)* grated old Cheddar cheese
pinch	cayenne pepper
¼ cup	*(60 mL)* chopped chives

Brush both sides of ham with oil. Place under heated broiler 6 minutes on each side, or until cooked through.

Combine butter, cheese, cayenne and chives.

Spread over ham and place under broiler until lightly browned.

Veal, Lamb and other Meats

North Americans have not been as adventurous as people in other parts of the world when it comes to meats.

Lamb, especially, is far more common on menus in other countries than it is here. However, more and more, our finest restaurants are featuring lamb dishes, and receiving an enthusiastic response. And these are not simply the old standbys of lamb chops or rack of lamb, but variations based on a whole gamut of cuts : steaks, crown roast, leg, loin roast, saddle roast and shoulder roast.

Cook lamb as you would beef. If you prefer your beef cooked rare or medium, chances are you'll like lamb done the same way.

Veal is a delicate meat that requires little cooking. "True" veal comes from calves no more that 14 weeks old, but in fact an acceptable product is obtained from animals up to a year old.

Because veal comes from young animals, it has not had the chance to develop much fat. The best veal is very pale pink, but is darker from older animals.

Veal is a relatively expensive meat, so beware of cheap "veal cutlets" in second-class restaurants. It's quite likely that pork has been substituted for the veal.

Game meats are becoming increasingly popular and available in North America. They can make a wonderful change from more common meats, and are not really complicated to prepare. Consider one of the game recipes in this chapter on those occasions when you want to surprise your guests with something really different.

Veal Medallions with Oyster Mushrooms and Brandy Sauce

Veal Medallions with Oyster Mushrooms and Brandy Sauce

6 servings

2 lbs	(900 g) veal tenderloin
¼ cup	(60 mL) butter
1 lb	(450 g) oyster mushrooms
3 tbsp	(45 mL) brandy
3 tbsp	(45 mL) sherry
2 cups	(500 mL) demi-glace (see *Sauces*)
½ cup	(125 mL) heavy cream

Cut the tenderloin into medallions.

Sauté the medallions in the butter, 2 minutes each side.

Remove the medallions and keep warm in oven.

Add the mushrooms to the butter and sauté until tender. Flame with the brandy.

Stir in the sherry and demi-glace. Simmer for 3 minutes and add cream. Simmer 3 more minutes.

Pour sauce over medallions and serve.

Veal Medallions in Shrimp Sauce

4 servings

2 tbsp	(*30 mL*) oil
2 tbsp	(*30 mL*) butter
8	veal medallions, 3 oz (*90 g*) each
3 tbsp	(*45 mL*) flour
¾ cup	(*180 mL*) veal or chicken stock (see *Soups*)
½ cup	(*125 mL*) heavy cream
¼ cup	(*60 mL*) sherry
½ tsp	(*3 mL*) salt
¼ tsp	(*1 mL*) pepper
¾ cup	(*180 mL*) baby shrimp

Heat the oil and butter in a skillet.

Sauté the veal in the butter 3½ minutes each side. Transfer to a heat-proof plate. Keep warm in oven.

Sprinkle the flour into the skillet; cook for 2 minutes.

Add the stock, cream, sherry and seasonings. Simmer for 2 minutes over low heat.

Add the shrimp and simmer 2 more minutes.

Pour sauce over veal. Serve at once.

Veal Piccata

4 servings

4	veal escalopes, 6 oz (*170 g*) each
2 tbsp	(*30 mL*) flour
¼ cup	(*60 mL*) butter
1	garlic clove, minced
¼ cup	(*60 mL*) dry sherry
1 tbsp	(*15 mL*) lemon juice
½	lemon, sliced

Place the veal between 2 pieces of wax paper. Pound very thin.

Dust the veal with flour.

Melt the butter and sauté the garlic. Remove the garlic bits and sauté the veal 2 ½ minutes each side.

Remove and keep warm.

Pour the sherry and lemon juice in the pan; simmer 3 minutes.

Pour sauce over veal.

Garnish with lemon slices and serve.

Escalope of Veal Cordon Bleu

8 servings

8	veal escalopes, pounded to a thickness of ⅛ in. (*0,5 cm*), about 3 oz (*90 g*) each
8 oz	(*250 g*) thinly sliced Black Forest ham
8	slices Swiss cheese
½ cup	(*125 mL*) all-purpose flour
3	eggs, well-beaten
2 tbsp	(*30 mL*) milk
2 cups	(*500 mL*) fine dry breadcrumbs
½ tsp	(*3 mL*) salt
½ tsp	(*3 mL*) pepper
	oil for frying
	Mushroom and Parmesan Cream Sauce (see *Sauces*)

Preheat oven to 400°F (*200°C*).

On one side of each veal escalope, place 1 oz (*30 g*) ham and 1 slice of cheese. Fold the other side over and pinch edges to seal.

Dip each escalope in flour, then into a mixture of eggs and milk, and then into breadcrumbs seasoned with salt and pepper.

Fry in ½ in. (*1 cm*) hot oil until browned, about 3 minutes each side.

Bake 12 minutes in oven to make outside crisp.

Serve with Mushroom and Parmesan Cream Sauce.

Veal Scaloppine Velez

8 servings

8	veal escalopes
½ cup	(*125 mL*) all-purpose flour
2	eggs, beaten
¾ cup	(*180 mL*) fine dry breadcrumbs
1 tsp	(*5 mL*) salt
pinch	pepper
pinch	rubbed thyme
pinch	dried basil leaves
⅓ cup	(*80 mL*) butter
¼ cup	(*60 mL*) vegetable oil
1 lb	(*450 g*) thinly sliced ham
16	cooked asparagus spears
2 cups	(*500 mL*) coarsely grated Havarti cheese

Dip each veal escalope first into flour, then into the beaten eggs, and then into a mixture of breadcrumbs, salt, pepper, thyme and basil.

Heat butter and oil in a large skillet. Sauté the escalopes over high heat, about 2 ½ minutes each side.

Top each escalope with 2 oz (*60 g*) ham and 2 asparagus spears. Sprinkle with grated cheese and place under a heated broiler just until cheese melts.

Veal Scaloppine Velez

Veal John B. Hoyle

8 servings

8	veal escalopes about 5 oz (*150 g*) each pounded to a thickness of about ⅛ in. (*0,5 cm*)
½ lb	(*225 g*) cooked baby shrimp
2	Granny Smith apples, peeled and chooped
2 cups	(*500 mL*) grated Colby cheese
	salt and pepper
¼ cup	(*60 mL*) melted butter
1⅓ cups	(*330 mL*) Mornay Sauce (see *Sauces*)

Preheat oven to 350°F (*180°C*)

Top each veal escalope with shrimp, chopped apples and cheese. Roll tightly and place, seam side down, in a greased, shallow baking dish. Season and brush with butter.

Bake, covered, in oven 15 to 20 minutes or until veal is cooked through.

Transfer rolls to a serving plate and drizzle with Mornay Sauce.

Veal à la Carte

6 servings

6	veal cutlets, 6 oz (*170 g*) each
2	eggs
½ cup	(*125 mL*) milk
½ cup	(*125 mL*) flour
2 cups	(*500 mL*) seasoned breadcrumbs
⅓ cup	(*80 mL*) butter
8 oz	(*225 g*) baby shrimp
1 cup	(*250 mL*) asparagus, blanched 5 minutes
1	recipe Béarnaise Sauce (see *Sauces*)

Pound the veal flat between 2 pieces of wax paper.

Mix the eggs with milk.

Dust the veal with the flour. Dip in the egg mixture. Roll in the breadcrumbs.

Heat the butter and sauté the cutlets 2 ½ minutes each side.

Place on a baking sheet. Top each cutlet with shrimp, asparagus and Béarnaise Sauce.

Place under broiler and brown lightly about 30 seconds.

Veal Helena

6 servings

6	veal cutlets
10 oz	(*284 g*) spinach
6 oz	(*170 g*) Havarti cheese
6 oz	(*170 g*) smoked salmon
3 tbsp	(*45 mL*) butter
2 cups	(*500 mL*) Chicken Velouté (see *Sauces*)

Preheat oven to 350°F (*180°C*).

Pound the veal flat. Chop the spinach fine.

Place 1 ½ oz (*45 g*) spinach, 1 oz (*30 g*) cheese and 1 oz (*30 g*) salmon on top of each cutlet.

Roll veal and secure with toothpick. Brush with butter and bake 18 minutes in oven.

Slice veal, pour velouté over and serve.

Veal Chops in Papillote

4 servings

3 tbsp	(*45 mL*) butter
1 cup	(*250 mL*) minced onions
6 oz	(*170 g*) mushrooms, sliced
3 tbsp	(*45 mL*) flour
½ cup	(*125 mL*) light cream
¼ tsp	(*1 mL*) pepper
½ tsp	(*3 mL*) salt
¼ cup	(*60 mL*) oil
4	veal chops, 6 oz (*170 g*) each
8	slices ham, 1 oz (*30 g*) each
8	heart-shaped wax paper cut-outs (slightly larger than chop size)

Preheat oven to 450°F (*230°C*).

Heat the butter in a saucepan. Add the onions and mushrooms. Sauté until all moisture has evaporated.

Add the flour and cook 2 minutes. Add the cream and seasonings. Simmer until very thick.

Heat 3 tbsp (*45 mL*) oil in a skillet. Brown the chops in the oil.

Brush the wax paper cut-outs with remaining oil.

Place one slice of ham on each of 4 hearts. Top with sauce and place a chop on the sauce.

Spread more sauce on the chop and place another slice of ham on the sauce.

Cover with the other 4 hearts and seal the edges by rolling up the paper.

Bake in oven for 10 minutes or until hearts are puffed up and slightly brown.

Serve while puffed up.

Veal Helena and Veal Chops in Papillote

Veau Sauvage

8 servings

3 lb	(*1,3 kg*) veal shoulder roast, boned and tied
	salt and pepper
½ lb	(*225 g*) oyster mushrooms
½ lb	(*225 g*) morels
½ lb	(*225 g*) chanterelles
¼ cup	(*60 mL*) butter
¼ cup	(*60 mL*) sherry
2 cups	(*500 mL*) demi-glace (see *Sauces*)
1 cup	(*250 mL*) heavy cream

Preheat oven to 350°F (*180°C*).

Rub roast with seasonings and roast for about 1 ¼ hours.

Sauté mushrooms in butter and set aside.

Remove roast from pan and degrease.

Pour sherry, demi-glace and cream in pan and simmer for 10 minutes.

Add mushrooms and simmer another 3 minutes.

Serve roast with sauce on the side.

Serve with new potatoes, fresh peas, broccoli or julienned vegetables.

Veau Sauvage

Veal Pizzaïola

8 servings

¼ cup	(*60 mL*) oil
2¼ lbs	(*1 kg*) veal, cut in 2-in. (*5 cm*) strips
1	onion, finely diced
2	celery stalks, finely diced
1	small green pepper, finely diced
3 cups	(*750 mL*) tomatoes, peeled, seeded and chopped
3	garlic cloves, crushed
2 tbsp	(*30 mL*) chopped oregano
¼ tsp	(*1 mL*) salt
pinch	pepper

Heat the oil in a large skillet. Brown the veal.

Add the onion, celery and green pepper. Sauté 2 minutes.

Add the tomatoes, garlic and seasonings. Reduce heat and simmer for 20 to 30 minutes.

Serve with hot buttered linguine.

Blanquette de Veau

Blanquette de Veau

6 servings

1½ lbs	(*675 g*) veal shoulder, coarsely diced
4 cups	(*1 L*) chicken stock (see *Soups*)
1 tbsp	(*15 mL*) salt
¼ tsp	(*1 mL*) thyme
1	bay leaf
20	pearl onions
4	carrots, julienned
2 tbsp	(*30 mL*) butter
2 tbsp	(*30 mL*) flour
2 tbsp	(*30 mL*) lemon juice
2	egg yolks
pinch	cayenne pepper
1 tbsp	(*15 mL*) chopped parsley

In a Dutch oven, put in the veal, stock, salt, thyme and bay leaf.

Cover and simmer for 1 ¼ hours.

Add the onions and carrots; cook for 15 minutes. Remove 2 cups (*500 mL*) of liquid.

Melt the butter in a small saucepan, add the flour and cook 3 minutes without browning.

Slowly add the 2 cups (*500 mL*) of liquid, stirring until thickened.

Whisk the lemon juice in the egg yolks. Blend into the sauce. DO NOT BOIL.

Add the sauce to the veal; do not boil. Add the cayenne. Pour into a serving dish. Garnish with parsley.

Serve with cooked egg noodles.

Veal Meatballs

4 servings

2	slices bacon, finely chopped
1	onion, finely chopped
1 lb	(*450 g*) ground veal
¼ tsp	(*1 mL*) rubbed thyme
¼ tsp	(*1 mL*) dried oregano leaves
¼ tsp	(*1 mL*) dried basil leaves
¼ tsp	(*1 mL*) garlic powder
1 tsp	(*5 mL*) salt
1	egg
½ cup	(*125 mL*) fine dry breadcrumbs
1 cup	(*250 mL*) grated Parmesan cheese
2 tbsp	(*30 mL*) vegetable oil
½ cup	(*125 mL*) beef stock (see *Soups*)
½ cup	(*125 mL*) white wine
2 tbsp	(*30 mL*) minced parsley
	cooked pasta or rice, hot

In a large skillet, sauté bacon until cooked but still tender; set aside. In the bacon fat, sauté onion until tender.

Combine bacon, onion, veal, seasonings, egg, breadcrumbs, and cheese; blend well with your fingers. Shape into 1-in. (*2,5 cm*) meatballs.

Brown the meatballs in bacon fat, adding vegetable oil if necessary, until the sides of the meatballs are crisp; drain.

Add beef stock and wine; simmer meatballs, uncovered, 15 to 20 minutes until cooked through.

Spoon the meatballs over hot, cooked pasta or rice, drizzle with about half the stock, and sprinkle with parsley.

Veal Meatballs

Veal Croquettes

6 servings

1 ½ lbs	(*675 g*) ground veal
2 tbsp	(*30 mL*) vegetable oil
3 tbsp	(*45 mL*) butter
3	mushrooms, finely chopped
3 tbsp	(*45 mL*) all-purpose flour
1 cup	(*250 mL*) heavy cream
½ cup	(*125 mL*) beef stock (see *Soups*)
1 tbsp	(*15 mL*) chopped fresh parsley
¼ tsp	(*1 mL*) nutmeg
¼ tsp	(*1 mL*) salt
¼ tsp	(*1 mL*) pepper

(Continued on next page)

6 oz	(175 g) Swiss cheese, in a block
¼ tsp	(1 mL) salt
¼ tsp	(1 mL) pepper
2 cups	(500 mL) fine dry breadcrumbs
¼ cup	(60 mL) all-purpose flour
2	eggs, well beaten
	oil for frying

Sauté the veal in oil and half the butter until no pink remains; drain and set aside.

Sauté the mushrooms in the remaining butter, stir in 3 tbsp (45 mL) flour. Add the cream, stock, parsley, nutmeg, salt and pepper; simmer stirring, until thickened.

Stir in the meat; cool completely.

Cut cheese into six sticks. Pat meat around each stick.

Add salt and pepper to breadcrumbs.

Roll each croquette in flour, then in eggs, and finally in seasoned breadcrumbs. Heat the oil to 375°F (190°C) and deep fry until golden.

Carré d'Agneau

Carré d'Agneau

1 serving

1	rack of lamb
2 tbsp	(30 mL) Dijon mustard
¼ cup	(60 mL) ground hazelnuts
2 tbsp	(30 mL) fine breadcrumbs
1 tbsp	(15 mL) Romano cheese
1 tbsp	(15 mL) melted butter

Have the butcher remove the backbone of the rack of lamb.

Preheat oven to 400°F (200°C).

Trim all the fat. Trim the meat from top and in between each rib bone. Crack the bones at the joints.

Spread the mustard over the meat.

Mix the hazelnuts, breadcrumbs and cheese together. Sprinkle over the mustard, covering completely.

Sprinkle with melted butter. Roast in oven for 30 minutes.

Serve with your choice of Béarnaise Sauce or mint jelly preserves.

Roast Lamb Rack

1 serving

1		rack of lamb
2 tbsp	(30 mL)	olive oil
1 tsp	(5 mL)	coarse salt
½ tsp	(3 mL)	rosemary
½ tsp	(3 mL)	cracked pepper
¼ tsp	(1 mL)	oregano
¼ tsp	(1 mL)	basil
¼ tsp	(1 mL)	paprika

Have the butcher remove the backbone of the rack of lamb.

Preheat oven to 400°F (200°C).

Trim all the fat. Trim meat from top and in between each rib bone. Crack bones at the joint.

Rub meat with olive oil. Sprinkle with seasonings and salt.

Roast in oven for 30 minutes. Serve with Apple Mint Sauce.

Apple Mint Sauce (*per serving*)

1 tbsp	(15 mL)	butter
2 tbsp	(30 mL)	brown sugar
½ cup	(125 mL)	apples, pared, cored and diced
1½ tsp	(8 mL)	chopped fresh mint
¼ cup	(60 mL)	apple juice

Heat the butter in a saucepan. Add the sugar and caramelize. Add the apples, mint and juice. Simmer 5 to 6 minutes. Serve on the side with rack of lamb.

Lamb Loaf with Chasseur Sauce

8 servings

2¼ lbs	(1 kg)	lean ground lamb
½ cup	(125 mL)	breadcrumbs
2		eggs
1 tsp	(5 mL)	salt
½ tsp	(3 mL)	pepper
1 tbsp	(15 mL)	chopped chives
1 tbsp	(15 mL)	chopped parsley
½ tsp	(3 mL)	basil
1 tsp	(5 mL)	grated lemon rind

Preheat oven to 350°F (180°C).

In a large mixing bowl, blend the lamb, breadcrumbs and eggs.

Add the seasonings and lemon rind. Combine thoroughly. Shape into a loaf. Bake in oven for 60 minutes. Remove and serve with Chasseur Sauce (see *Sauces*).

New Zealand Roast Lamb

8 servings

5 lb	(2,2 kg)	lamb shoulder, boned, rolled and tied
¼ cup	(60 mL)	oil
2 tsp	(10 mL)	salt
½ tsp	(3 mL)	black pepper
2 cups	(500 mL)	Honey-Mustard Sauce (see *Sauces*)

Preheat oven to 350°F (180°C).

Rub the lamb with the oil. Sprinkle with salt and pepper. Roast in oven for 1 ½ hours. During the final 15 minutes, brush with sauce every 5 minutes, then once more just before serving.

Serve remaining sauce with the roast.

Shish Kebab Flambé

6 servings

2 tsp	(10 mL)	garlic powder
½ tsp	(3 mL)	basil
½ tsp	(3 mL)	oregano
2 tsp	(10 mL)	salt
½ tsp	(3 mL)	coriander
½ tsp	(3 mL)	cumin
¼ tsp	(1 mL)	turmeric
pinch		ginger
1 cup	(250 mL)	sherry
⅓ cup	(80 mL)	olive oil
1 tbsp	(15 mL)	lemon juice
2¼ lbs	(1 kg)	lamb, cut in 1½ in. (4 cm) cubes
⅓ cup	(80 mL)	brandy

Blend all the seasonings together with the sherry, oil and lemon juice in a mixing bowl. Add the cubed lamb.

Marinate overnight or for 8 hours. Place meat on skewers. Leave small gaps between each piece. Broil 3 minutes each side, preferably on a charcoal broiler.

Place skewers on a platter when cooked. Pour brandy over. Ignite carefully. Serve while flaming.

Herb and Cheese Lamb Cutlets

6 servings

6	lamb cutlets, 4 oz (*115 g*) each
½ tsp	(*3 mL*) basil
½ tsp	(*3 mL*) marjoram
1 tsp	(*5 mL*) chopped chives
½ tsp	(*3 mL*) cracked pepper
12 oz	(*340 g*) cream cheese
1	egg
¼ cup	(*60 mL*) milk
⅓ cup	(*80 mL*) flour
2 cups	(*500 mL*) breadcrumbs
½ cup	(*125 mL*) oil
2 cups	(*500 mL*) Mornay Sauce (see *Sauces*)

Preheat oven to 350°F (*180°C*).

Pound the cutlets thin.

Blend the herbs and the pepper into the cheese.

Place 2 oz (*60 g*) of blended cheese on each cutlet. Wrap meat around the cheese.

Mix the egg in the milk. Dust cutlets with flour. Dip into milk. Dredge in breadcrumbs.

Heat oil in a skillet. Brown the cutlets in the oil.

Transfer to a baking sheet.

Bake 12 minutes in oven.

Heat Mornay Sauce. Serve sauce with cutlets.

Pound the lamb cutlets thin. Blend the herbs and the pepper into the cream cheese.

2 Place 2 oz (*60 g*) of blended cheese on each cutlet.

3 Wrap meat around the cheese.

4 Bake breaded cutlets 12 minutes in oven.

Lamb Chops in Almond Mushroom Cream

4 servings

8	lamb chops, 3 oz (*85 g*) each
pinch	salt and pepper
¼ cup	(*60 mL*) butter
4 oz	(*115 g*) mushrooms, sliced
3 tbsp	(*45 mL*) flour
1 cup	(*250 mL*) chicken stock (see *Soups*)
1 cup	(*250 mL*) heavy cream
¼ cup	(*60 mL*) blanched ground almonds
½ tsp	(*3 mL*) almond extract
½ cup	(*125 mL*) toasted slivered almonds

Broil the chops 3 minutes each side. Season with salt and pepper. Set aside and keep warm.

Heat the butter in a saucepan.

Add the mushrooms and sauté until tender. Sprinkle in the flour. Cook for 2 minutes.

Add the chicken stock and cream. Simmer for 5 minutes.

Add ground almonds and almond extract. Simmer 10 more minutes.

Sprinkle with toasted almonds.

Arrange chops on a platter. Serve with sauce.

Lamb Chops Provençale

Lamb Chops Provençale

3 servings

½ tsp	(*3 mL*) salt
¼ tsp	(*1 mL*) thyme
¼ tsp	(*1 mL*) marjoram
¼ tsp	(*1 mL*) black pepper
6	loin lamb chops
¼ cup	(*60 mL*) milk
1	egg
¼ cup	(*60 mL*) flour
1 cup	(*250 mL*) breadcrumbs
2 tbsp	(*30 mL*) olive oil
2 tbsp	(*30 mL*) butter

Mix the seasonings together. Rub into the chops.

Blend the milk together with the egg. Dust the chops with flour. Dip into the egg. Dredge in the breadcrumbs.

Heat the oil and butter. Fry the chops 5 minutes each side.

Serve very hot.

Venison Baden Baden

6 servings

6	venison filet steaks
3 tbsp	(*45 mL*) butter
3 tbsp	(*45 mL*) oil
2	pears
½ cup	(*125 mL*) cranberries
2 cups	(*500 mL*) Chasseur Sauce (see *Sauces*)

Sauté the venison in the butter and oil; cook to desired doneness.

Remove from heat, save drippings and keep venison hot.

Peel, core and dice the pears.

In the drippings, sauté the pears and cranberries until tender.

Add sauce and simmer 5 minutes. Pour sauce over venison and serve.

Venison Steaks

4 servings

4	venison steaks, 6 oz (*170 g*) each
3 tbsp	(*45 mL*) oil
2 tsp	(*10 mL*) salt
½ tsp	(*3 mL*) pepper
½ tsp	(*3 mL*) paprika

Brush steaks with oil. Season. Broil to desired doneness. Serve with sauce.

Sauce

2 tbsp	(*30 mL*) butter
⅓ cup	(*80 mL*) minced onions
⅓ cup	(*80 mL*) grated carrots
2 cups	(*500 mL*) Espagnole Sauce (see *Sauces*)
½ cup	(*125 mL*) red wine
pinch	ground cloves
1 tbsp	(*15 mL*) lemon juice
¼ cup	(*60 mL*) red currant preserves
⅓ cup	(*80 mL*) light cream
3 tbsp	(*45 mL*) chopped parsley

Heat the butter in a saucepan. Sauté the onions and carrots until tender.

Add the Espagnole Sauce, wine, cloves and lemon juice. Reduce by half.

Stir in the preserves and finish by adding the cream and parsley.

Venison Baden Baden

Buffalo Burgers

8 servings

2¼ lbs	(*1 kg*) ground buffalo meat
1 cup	(*250 mL*) breadcrumbs
2	eggs
1 tsp	(*5 mL*) salt
½ tsp	(*3 mL*) pepper
1 tbsp	(*15 mL*) Worcestershire sauce
1 tsp	(*5 mL*) basil
1 tsp	(*5 mL*) paprika

In a large mixing bowl, blend together the buffalo meat, breadcrumbs, eggs and seasonings. Shape into patties.

Broil over a charcoal broiler to desired doneness.

Buffalo Filets in Peppercorn Sauce

6 servings

6	buffalo filets, 6 oz (*170 g*) each
1 cup	(*250 mL*) demi-glace (see *Sauces*)
¼ cup	(*60 mL*) sherry
⅓ cup	(*80 mL*) heavy cream
¼ cup	(*60 mL*) red currant preserves
1 tbsp	(*15 mL*) green peppercorns

Broil the filets over a charcoal broiler to desired doneness.

Heat the demi-glace in a saucepan.

Add the sherry and reduce by half. Add the cream and the preserves and simmer for 3 minutes.

Add the peppercorns. Serve the sauce over the steaks.

Braised Buffalo Steak with Mushrooms

6 servings

2¼ lbs	(*1 kg*) buffalo round steak
1	egg, lightly beaten
3 tbsp	(*45 mL*) milk
2 cups	(*500 mL*) seasoned breadcrumbs
¼ cup	(*60 mL*) light oil
10 oz	(*284 g*) can mushrooms, with liquid
1 tbsp	(*15 mL*) flour

Cut steak to 1-in. (*2,5 cm*) thickness and serving size.

Dip into egg and milk mixture and then into the breadcrumbs.

Heat the oil in a large skillet. Brown the steaks 2 ½ minutes each side.

Pour mushrooms over the steaks with the liquid. Cover and simmer for 45 minutes.

Mix the flour with a little water; add to sauce a little at a time.

Simmer until thick. Serve at once.

Moose Roast

6-8 servings

1 lb	(*450 g*) salt pork (optional)
4 lb	(*1,8 kg*) rump moose roast
1 tbsp	(*15 mL*) dry mustard
2 tsp	(*10 mL*) salt
1 tsp	(*5 mL*) pepper
2	onions, sliced
2	carrots, chopped
2	celery stalks, chopped
2 cups	(*500 mL*) tomatoes, seeded, chopped and strained

Roll the salt pork out thin. Wrap the roast with the pork. Refrigerate overnight or 10 to 12 hours.*

Preheat oven to 300°F (*150°C*).

Remove and discard the pork. Rub thoroughly with dry mustard. Season with salt and pepper.

Place in a roasting pan. Surround with vegetables.

Pour tomatoes over vegetables.

Cover and bake in oven for 2 hours for medium doneness.

For well done, bake an additional 35 to 45 minutes.

* This adjusts the meat if it has a wild gamey odor which will affect the taste. This is dictated by the animals feeding ground and not age.

Moose Roast

Rabbit with Plums

3 servings

⅓ cup	(*80 mL*) butter
3 tbsp	(*45 mL*) oil
3½ lbs	(*1,5 kg*) rabbit, cut into pieces
3	large carrots, coarsely diced
1	medium onion, coarsely diced
1½ lbs	(*750 g*) plums, pitted
1½ cups	(*375 mL*) sherry
1 tsp	(*5 mL*) basil
1 tsp	(*5 mL*) parsley
¼ tsp	(*1 mL*) black pepper
3 tbsp	(*45 mL*) flour

In a large pot or Dutch oven, heat half the butter and the oil.

Brown the rabbit. Remove and keep warm.

Add the carrots and onion; sauté until tender.

Add the plums and sherry. Return the rabbit to pot.

Sprinkle with seasonings.

Cover and simmer for 45 minutes.

Remove rabbit and keep warm. Blend the remaining butter with the flour.

Whisk into the liquid a little at a time. Simmer until thickened.

Pour over rabbit and serve.

Rabbit and Oyster Casserole

3 servings

3½ lbs	(*1,5 kg*) rabbit, cut into pieces
¼ cup	(*60 mL*) flour
½ tsp	(*3 mL*) salt
1 cup	(*250 mL*) chicken stock, hot (see *Soups*)
1 cup	(*250 mL*) heavy cream
2 cups	(*500 mL*) oysters
2 tbsp	(*30 mL*) butter

Preheat oven to 350°F (*180°C*).

Dredge the rabbit with flour.

Place in a large casserole dish. Season with salt. Pour stock over the rabbit.

Cover and bake 1 hour in oven.

Add the cream, oysters and dot with butter.

Cover and bake 15 more minutes.

Rabbit Provençale

6 servings

3½ lb	(*1,5 kg*) rabbit
1½ tbsp	(*22 mL*) oil
1½ tbsp	(*22 mL*) butter
¼ lb	(*115 g*) bacon, diced
1	garlic clove, minced
1	large onion, diced
2	green peppers, diced
¼ lb	(*115 g*) mushrooms
1 lb	(*450 g*) tomatoes, peeled, seeded and chopped
1 tsp	(*5 mL*) basil
1 tsp	(*5 mL*) thyme
1 tsp	(*5 mL*) marjoram
1 tbsp	(*15 mL*) parsley
1 tbsp	(*15 mL*) Dijon mustard

Preheat oven to 325°F (*160°C*).

Cut the rabbit into serving-size pieces.

Heat the oil and butter in a large skillet.

Add the bacon and brown. Place bacon into a casserole dish.

Brown the rabbit in the fat.

Place into the casserole dish. Sauté the vegetables in the oil. Drain.

Place into the casserole dish.

Pour tomatoes over rabbit. Sprinkle with herbs and mustard.

Bake in oven 1¼ to 1½ hours.

Paprika Rabbit with Caraway Noodles

Paprika Rabbit with Caraway Noodles

6 servings

2 tsp	*(10 mL)* salt	
2 tsp	*(10 mL)* pepper	
1 cup	*(250 mL)* flour	
2	rabbits, each cut into 6 pieces	
½ cup	*(125 mL)* butter	
1 tbsp	*(15 mL)* paprika	
1½ cups	*(375 mL)* heavy cream	
¼ cup	*(60 mL)* sherry	
3 cups	*(750 mL)* egg noodles	
2 tsp	*(10 mL)* caraway seeds	

Mix the salt and pepper in the flour.

Roll rabbit in flour.

Heat half the butter in a large skillet and brown the rabbit.

Mix the paprika with the cream.

Add the sherry to the rabbit, then the cream. Reduce heat to low; simmer for 1 hour.
A little water may be required half-way through cooking.

Boil egg noodles al dente. Drain.

Melt in the remaining butter and sprinkle in caraway seeds.

Serve with rabbit.

Fish and Seafood

These days, people are eating more fish and shellfish than ever, and with good reason. Modern transportation makes good fresh fish available no matter where you live, and almost everyone likes at least some kind of fish — even many vegetarians!

And fish is a healthy choice, too. It's high in protein, low in calories and saturated fats.

But as far as I'm concerned, the best thing about fish is its succulent flavor, which serves as the inspiration for so many creative recipes.

In this chapter, you will find a variety of recipes for fish and shellfish, some of them almost sinfully rich and elegant, some of them incredibly simple, and all of them delicious.

Whatever recipes you try, remember that the most important thing is to start with perfectly fresh fish.

Plan to use fish the same day you buy it. If you must store it, keep it in the coldest part of the refrigerator. Shellfish keep best on ice.

How To Choose Fresh Fish

Fishermen will tell you the best fish they ever ate was the fish freshly-caught and put straight in the pan.

If you live near the seacoast, your best bet is to head to the markets where fishermen sell their catch fresh off the boat. But in the rest of the country, here are the signs of freshness you should look for:

1. Fresh fish has almost no smell. Never buy fish that has an objectionable odor or a particularly "fishy" smell.

2. The skin should be bright and shiny with the scales clinging closely. Eyes should be round and bright, not milky or sunken. The flesh inside the gills should be red or bright pink.

3. The flesh should feel firm to the touch, not soft.

Basic Cooking Tips

Whatever the species or cooking method, plan on cooking for 10 minutes per inch (2,5 cm) of thickness (measured at the thickest part of the fish or filet). If possible, choose to pan-fry, steam, bake, or deep fry fish. Fish cooked in water tends to dry out. If you want to poach your fish, be sure to use a fish fumet or court bouillon. (See the section on *Soups*).

Salmon Filets with Raspberry, Kiwi and Green Peppercorn Sauce

Salmon Filets with Raspberry, Kiwi and Green Peppercorn Sauce

4 servings

4	salmon filets
1 tbsp	(*15 mL*) melted butter
½ cup	(*125 mL*) heavy cream
1 cup	(*250 mL*) raspberries
¼ cup	(*60 mL*) sugar
1 tbsp	(*15 mL*) green peppercorns
2	kiwis

Preheat oven to 350°F (*180°C*).

Brush salmon with melted butter.

Bake in oven for 12 to 15 minutes.

In a saucepan, heat cream, raspberries, sugar and peppercorns. Simmer for 5 minutes.

Peel the kiwis and chop; add to sauce.

Remove salmon from oven.

Place filets on plates and pour sauce over salmon and serve.

Apples Stuffed with Smoked Salmon

6 servings

6	very large apples
1 lb	(*450 g*) fresh spinach
½ cup	(*125 mL*) butter
3 tbsp	(*45 mL*) all-purpose flour
1 tbsp	(*15 mL*) dried basil leaves
2½ cups	(*625 mL*) heavy cream
2	egg yolks
½ cup	(*125 mL*) grated Havarti cheese
1 lb	(*450 g*) smoked salmon

Preheat oven to 350°F (*180°C*).

Cut a ½-in. (*1,5 cm*) slice from the top of each apple. Hollow out the apple, leaving a ¼-in. (*0,5 cm*) shell all around. Take care not to pierce the apple skin.

Arrange the apple shells in a baking dish.

Quickly sauté the spinach in ¼ cup (*60 mL*) butter over high heat until wilted and tender. Chop and set aside.

Melt the remaining ¼ cup (*60 mL*) butter and stir in the flour. Add the basil and 2 cups (*500 mL*) cream; simmer until sauce has thickened.

Whisk the yolks into the remaining cream and stir into the sauce. Stir in the cheese and set aside.

Place half the salmon in the bottom of the apples. Spoon spinach over.

Place the remaining salmon on top. Fill with sauce.

Replace apple tops and bake in oven until apple skins are tender, 15 to 20 minutes.

Serve with rice pilaf and kernel corn mixed with pieces of sweet red pimiento.

Cheese scones are very nice with this as well.

Salmon with Crab and Béarnaise Sauce

4 servings

4 cups	(*1 L*) court bouillon (see *Soups*)
4	salmon filets, 6 oz (*170 g*) each
1 cup	(*250 mL*) crab meat, cooked
1 cup	(*250 mL*) Béarnaise Sauce (see *Sauces*)

Heat the court bouillon. Gently simmer the salmon in court bouillon 10 to 12 minutes.

Remove and place in a shallow pan. Top each filet with ¼ cup (*60 mL*) crab meat and 2 tbsp (*30 mL*) of Béarnaise Sauce.

Place under broiler for 1 minute or until brown.

Serve the remaining sauce on the side.

Baked Stuffed Salmon

8 servings

5 lb	(*2,2 kg*) fresh salmon
½ lb	(*225 g*) bacon, diced
1	onion, minced
1	celery stalk, minced
2	carrots, minced
2 cups	(*500 mL*) crackers, crushed fine
1 cup	(*250 mL*) lobster, shrimp or crab meat, cooked and chopped
1 tsp	(*5 mL*) paprika
¼ tsp	(*1 mL*) pepper
½ cup	(*125 mL*) water

Preheat oven to 375°F (*190°C*).

Thoroughly clean the salmon. Prepare stuffing by frying the bacon until tender.

Add the onion, celery and carrots. Sauté until tender. Drain excess fat. Cool.

Mix the crackers with the seafood and seasonings. Add the fried mixture.

Stuff into the cavity of the fish. Tie with string.

Bake in a greased covered baking pan 40 to 45 minutes with ½ cup (*125 ml*) water.

Poached Salmon with Blue Cheese Sauce

until fish flakes with a fork, about 8 to 12 minutes, depending on size of filets.

Serve hot or cold, accompanied with Blue Cheese Sauce.

Sauce : Combine all ingredients; mix well. Chill.

Salmon with Orange and Pecans

6 servings

3 tbsp	(*45 mL*) butter
6	salmon filets, 6 oz (*170 g*)
2 tbsp	(*30 mL*) flour
1 cup	(*250 mL*) heavy cream
¼ cup	(*60 mL*) sherry
1	orange
½ cup	(*125 mL*) chopped pecans

Preheat oven to 350°F (*180°C*).

Melt the butter in a saucepan. Use 1 tbsp (*15 mL*) of melted butter to brush on salmon. Bake salmon 12 to 15 minutes in oven.

Add the flour to the remaining butter. Stir and cook for 2 minutes.

Add the cream and sherry. Simmer until thickened.

Grate the orange peel and add to sauce. Stir in the pecans.

Remove fish from oven. Place on a serving platter. Smother with sauce.

Slice the orange and use as a garnish. Serve.

Poached Salmon with Blue Cheese Sauce

6 servings

6	salmon filets
	court bouillon (see *Soups*)

Blue Cheese Sauce

1 tbsp	(*15 mL*) pickle relish
2 tbsp	(*30 mL*) chopped parsley
2 tbsp	(*30 mL*) chopped chives
2 tbsp	(*30 mL*) heavy cream
2 tsp	(*10 mL*) lemon juice
1 tsp	(*5 mL*) Worcestershire sauce
¼ cup	(*60 mL*) crumbled blue cheese
1 cup	(*250 mL*) mayonnaise

Place the salmon filets in a large heavy skillet.

Cover with court bouillon. Bring to a boil over high heat; reduce heat and simmer just

Filet of Sole Olga

4 servings

4	large potatoes
4	sole filets 6 oz (*170 g*) each
4 cups	(*1 L*) court bouillon (see *Soups*)
1 cup	(*250 mL*) baby shrimp
1 cup	(*250 mL*) White Wine Sauce (see *Sauces*)
1 cup	(*250 mL*) grated Cheddar cheese

Preheat oven to 400°F (*200°C*).

Wash and scrub the potatoes.

Bake potatoes until tender in oven. Remove from oven.

Cut away the tops. Scoop out the pulp, leaving the shell.

Fold filets in half. Heat court bouillon. Gently poach the filets in the court bouillon.

Spoon 2 tbsp (*30 mL*) of shrimp into potatoes. Add the poached filets. Spoon in 2 tbsp (*30 mL*) of White Wine Sauce.

Sprinkle with cheese.

Return to over and bake 8 to 10 minutes or until cheese is golden brown. Serve.

Sole Meunière

4 servings

4	sole filets
⅓ cup	(*80 mL*) milk
½ cup	(*125 mL*) flour
⅓ cup	(*125*) butter
2 tbsp	(*30 mL*) freshly chopped parsley
1	lemon

Dip the filets in the milk. Dust the filets with the flour.

Heat the butter in a skillet. Sauté the filets in the butter 2½ to 3 minutes each side.

Remove filets to a heated platter.

Add the parsley and lemon juice to butter; cook for 1 minute.

Pour over filets and serve.

Sole Walewaska

4 servings

4 cups	(*1 L*) court bouillon (see *Soups*)
4	sole filets, 6 oz (*170 g*) each
1 cup	(*250 mL*) Mornay Sauce (see *Sauces*)
8 oz	(*225 g*) lobster meat
1 cup	(*250 mL*) grated Swiss cheese

Heat the court bouillon.

Gently poach the filets in the court bouillon 8 to 10 minutes.

Heat the Mornay Sauce in a saucepan.

Remove filets and place on an ovenproof platter.

Top each filet with 2 oz (*30 g*) of lobster meat. Cover with sauce. Sprinkle with cheese.

Broil in oven for 1 minute or until golden brown.

Filet of Sole Florentine

4 servings

4	sole filets, 8 oz (*225 g*) each
8 oz	(*225 g*) spinach leaves, chopped fine
6 cups	(*1,5 L*) court bouillon (see *Soups*)
½ cup	(*125 mL*) sherry
1½ cups	(*375 mL*) Mornay Sauce (see *Sauces*)

Top each filet with spinach, then roll each up like a jelly roll.

Hold together with toothpicks.

Bring court bouillon to a gentle boil and add the sherry.

Cook the fish in the court bouillon until opaque in color.

Place on serving platter. Keep hot.

Heat Mornay Sauce.

Pour sauce over fish and serve at once.

1

Top each sole filet with chopped spinach.

2

Roll each filet up like a jelly roll; hold together with toothpicks.

3

Boil the fish in the court bouillon and sherry until opaque in color.

4

Pour heated Mornay Sauce over fish and serve at once.

Filet of Sole with Mushrooms

4 servings

8 oz	(*225 g*) mushrooms, sliced
2 cups	(*500 mL*) water
1 cup	(*250 mL*) white wine
4	sole filets, 6 oz (*170 g*) each
3 tbsp	(*45 mL*) butter
3 tbsp	(*45 mL*) flour
1 cup	(*250 mL*) light cream
1 cup	(*250 mL*) Mornay Sauce (see *Sauces*)
¼ cup	(*60 mL*) fine breadcrumbs

Preheat oven to 500°F (*260°C*).

Boil the mushrooms in the water and wine for 7 minutes. Strain the mushrooms and reserve the liquid.

Poach fish in the mushroom liquid and keep hot in a casserole dish.

In a saucepan, melt the butter, add the flour and make a paste (roux).

Add the cream and mushrooms. Simmer until very thick. Mix in Mornay Sauce.

Pour this mixture over the fish.

Sprinkle with breadcrumbs.

Bake in oven until golden brown. Serve.

Filet of Sole Nantua

1 serving

1	sole filet, 8 oz (*225 g*)
6 cups	(*1,5 L*) court bouillon (see *Soups*)
2 tsp	(*10 mL*) butter
2 tsp	(*10 mL*) flour
3 tbsp	(*45 mL*) heavy cream
3 tbsp	(*45 mL*) fish stock (see *Soups*)
1 tbsp	(*15 mL*) chopped crayfish, or lobster meat
1 tbsp	(*15 mL*) shrimp, cooked and chopped
pinch	paprika
2 tsp	(*10 mL*) sherry

Gently poach the fish in the court bouillon.

Remove 1 cup (*250 mL*) of the court bouillon and simmer; reduce to 3 tbsp (*45 mL*).

In a saucepan, melt the butter and add the flour to make a paste (roux).

Add the cream and stock. Simmer 1 minute, add crayfish, shrimp, paprika and sherry.

Simmer 1 more minute.

Pour sauce over fish and serve.

Sole Normandy

4 servings

4	apples
1 cup	(*250 mL*) Béchamel Sauce (see *Sauces*)
1 cup	(*250 mL*) baby shrimp
½	sheet puff pastry
⅓ cup	(*80 mL*) butter
4 tsp	(*20 mL*) oil
4	sole filets, 7 oz (*200 g*) each
1 tsp	(*5 mL*) parsley
2 tsp	(*10 mL*) lemon juice

Preheat oven to 350°F (*180°C*).

Cut the tops from the apples. Scoop away the core and pulp, leaving a shell.

Mix the Béchamel Sauce with the shrimp. Stuff into the cavity of the apple. Bake in oven 20 to 25 minutes until the apples are tender.

Cut the puff pastry into 1 x 3-in. (*2,5 x 7,5 cm*) rectangles.

Bake in oven with the apples on a separate shelf.

In a skillet, melt 4 tsp (*20 mL*) butter together with the oil. Reduce heat.

Gently sauté the filets 2½ to 3 minutes each side. Remove fish to a heated serving platter.

Add the remaining butter, parsley and lemon juice.

Cook to very hot. Pour over fish.

Place the apples around the platter and garnish with pastries. Serve.

Sole Normandy

Baked Orange Roughy

4 servings

4	orange roughy filets
1½ cups	(*375 mL*) sliced mushrooms
½ cup	(*125 mL*) grated medium Cheddar cheese
	salt and pepper

Preheat oven to 450°F (*230°C*).

Place filets on individual pieces of heavy-duty foil.

Top with raw mushroom slices and cheese. Sprinkle with salt and pepper.

Wrap each filet tightly and place on a baking sheet.

Bake in oven 10 to 12 minutes.

Broiled Orange Roughy Parmesan

4 servings

4	orange roughy filets
¼ cup	(*60 mL*) melted butter
	salt and pepper
½ cup	(*125 mL*) grated Parmesan cheese

Place filets in a shallow baking pan, drizzle with half the melted butter, and season with salt and pepper.

Place under a heated broiler 3 to 4 minutes.

Turn filets over and drizzle with remaining butter.

Sprinkle with cheese and return to oven for 3-4 minutes or until cooked through and fish flakes with a fork.

Fennel Orange Roughy

4 servings

1 tbsp	(*15 mL*) crushed fennel seeds
½ cup	(*125 mL*) flour
¼ cup	(*60 mL*) light cream
3 tbsp	(*45 mL*) butter
4	orange roughy filets, 6 oz (*170 g*) each

Mix the fennel with the flour.

Dip the filets in the cream and dust with flour.

Heat the butter in a skillet.

Sauté the filets 2½ minutes each side.

Peppered Orange Roughy and Lime Butter

6 servings

6	orange roughy filets
2 tbsp	*(30 mL)* oil
2 tbsp	*(30 mL)* crushed dried green peppercorns
2 tbsp	*(30 mL)* cracked black peppercorns
2 tbsp	*(30 mL)* cracked white peppercorns
¼ cup	*(60 mL)* butter

Lime Butter

½ cup	*(125 mL)* softened butter
1 tbsp	*(15 mL)* grated lime rind
2 tbsp	*(30 mL)* lime juice
1	garlic clove, minced

Brush the fish with oil. Mix the peppercorns and coat each side of fish with pepper mixture.

Heat butter and gently sauté fish.

To prepare Lime Butter, combine butter with other ingredients.

Place on wax paper and roll. Refrigerate until firm.

Once fish is cooked, slice butter and place a slice on each filet.

1

Brush the fish filets with oil and coat each side with mixed peppercorns.

2

To make Lime Butter, combine butter with lime rind, lime juice and garlic.

3

Place on wax paper, roll and refrigerate until firm.

4

Once fish is cooked, slice butter and place a slice on each filet.

Dill Swordfish

6 servings

6	swordfish steaks
1 tbsp	(*15 mL*) oil
2 tbsp	(*30 mL*) dill weed
¼ cup	(*60 mL*) butter
1 tsp	(*5 mL*) lemon juice

Brush steaks with oil.

Broil the steaks 5 minutes each side, for each inch (*2,5 cm*) of thickness, (over coals is best).

Blend together the dill, butter and lemon juice.

Brush onto steaks as they grill and just before serving.

Grilled Swordfish with Walnut Sauce

Grilled Swordfish with Walnut Sauce

4 servings

4	swordfish steaks, 6 oz (*170 g*) each
1 tbsp	(*15 mL*) melted butter

Sauce

1 tsp	(*5 mL*) Dijon mustard
2 tsp	(*10 mL*) lemon juice
pinch	salt
¼ tsp	(*1 mL*) fresh cracked pepper
2 tbsp	(*30 mL*) walnut oil
¼ cup	(*60 mL*) olive oil

Brush fish with butter.

Grill in an oven broiler or over coals 4 minutes each side.

To prepare sauce, blend together the mustard, lemon juice, salt, pepper and oils thoroughly.

Brush fish with sauce and serve.

Whitefish Rolls

Whitefish Rolls

6 servings

3	slices bacon
1	carrot, finely diced
1	celery stalk, finely diced
1	small onion, finely diced
1 cup	(*250 mL*) grated Havarti cheese
6	whitefish filets
2 tbsp	(*30 mL*) butter
2 cups	(*500 mL*) Mornay Sauce (see *Sauces*)

Preheat oven to 350°F (*180°C*).

Finely dice the bacon and sauté.

Add the vegetables and sauté until tender. Allow to cool.

Combine sautéed mixture with cheese.

Press cheese mixture onto each filet and roll.

Bake in a buttered pan for 15 to 20 minutes.

Remove from oven, place on plates and cover with heated Mornay Sauce.

Trout Jodee

2 servings

2	small trout
3 tbsp	(*45 mL*) butter
3 tbsp	(*45 mL*) oil
2	carrots, cut in julienne
1	zucchini, cut in julienne
2	celery stalks, cut in julienne
1 cup	(*250 mL*) commercial oyster sauce
½ lb	(*225 g*) oyster mushrooms
¼ cup	(*60 mL*) butter

Sauté the trout in the butter and oil, 4 to 5 minutes each side.

Remove from heat and keep hot.

Blanch the carrots, zucchini and celery for 5 minutes. Heat the sauce.

Sauté the vegetables and mushrooms in butter.

Place on a plate, top with trout and pour sauce over fish.

Bass Amandine

4 servings

¼ cup	(60 mL) butter
4	bass filets, 6 oz (170 g) each
¼ cup	(60 mL) milk
¼ cup	(60 mL) flour
⅓ cup	(80 mL) slivered blanched almonds
1	lemon

Heat the butter in a skillet.

Dip the bass in the milk then dust with flour.

Fry 2½ to 3 minutes each side. Remove fish to a heated platter.

Add almonds to butter and sauté until browned.

Squeeze the juice from the lemon into the butter. Swirl.

Pour over fish and serve.

Baked Red Snapper with Crab Stuffing

8 servings

¼ cup	(60 mL) butter
1	small onion, minced
½ tsp	(3 mL) basil
1 tbsp	(15 mL) chopped parsley
½ cup	(125 mL) heavy cream
½ lb	(225 g) crab meat
2 cups	(500 mL) diced bread
3 tbsp	(45 mL) lemon juice
5 lb	(2,2 kg) red snapper

Preheat oven to 400°F (200°C).

In a saucepan, heat the butter.

Add the onion and sauté until tender.

In a mixing bowl, combine the remaining stuffing ingredients. Add to the butter and onion. Mix well.

Stuff into the fish. Tie together. Place in a baking pan.

Cover tail with tin foil so it won't burn.

Bake in oven 45 to 50 minutes.

Monkfish en Brochette

4 servings

1½ lbs	(675 g) monkfish filets
3 tbsp	(45 mL) oil
½ tsp	(3 mL) basil
½ tsp	(3 mL) thyme
½ tsp	(3 mL) oregano
½ tsp	(3 mL) salt
1 tbsp	(15 mL) minced garlic
1 tsp	(5 mL) parsley flakes
1½ tsp	(8 mL) lemon juice
⅓ cup	(80 mL) softened butter

Dice filets into 1-in. (2,5 cm) cubes.

Mix oil with basil, thyme, oregano and salt in a mixing bowl. Add fish.

Stir to cover fish with seasoned oil.

Blend the garlic, parsley and lemon juice into butter.

Skewer fish cubes with wooden (bamboo) skewers.

Broil in oven 5 minutes each side, brushing with butter.

Serve on rice.

Halibut with Rémoulade Sauce

Halibut with Rémoulade Sauce

4 servings

4	halibut steaks, 6 oz (170 g) each
1 tbsp	(15 mL) melted butter
3	egg yolks
¾ cup	(180 mL) oil
2 tbsp	(30 mL) fresh chopped parsley
1	garlic clove, minced
2	green onions, diced
1 tsp	(5 mL) paprika
3	drops Tabasco sauce

Heat the broiler (oven or gas).

Brush the halibut with butter.

Broil 4 minutes each side.

In a food processor with steel blades, blend the eggs. Slowly pour in the oil. Blend in the parsley, garlic, onions and seasonings; combine well.

Remove steaks and place on a platter.

Drop 1 tbsp (15 mL) of sauce in the center of each steak.

Serve with the remaining sauce.

Cod Soufflé

4 servings

1 tbsp	(*15 mL*) flour
¼ cup	(*60 mL*) heavy cream
1 tbsp	(*15 mL*) butter
1	egg
1	egg white
pinch	salt
⅛ tsp	(*0,5 mL*) cream of tartar
⅓ cup	(*80 mL*) cooked, flaked cod
½ cup	(*125 mL*) grated Parmesan cheese

Preheat oven to 350°F (*180°C*).

Blend the flour with a little of the cream into a paste.

Heat remaining cream and butter together until butter melts. Pour flour paste into cream. Stir until boiling. Remove from heat.

Whip the egg. Blend a little hot cream into the egg. Stir into sauce.

Beat the egg white with the salt and cream of tartar until stiff. Stir one quarter of the egg white into the sauce. Fold in the fish.

Add the remaining egg white in a folding motion. Try not to lose too much of the lightness of the egg white.

Fold into a greased casserole dish, which has been dusted with the grated cheese.

Bake in a water bath in oven for 35 minutes or until golden brown.

English-Style Fish

8 servings

1 cup	(*250 mL*) flour
½ tsp	(*3 mL*) baking powder
⅛ tsp	(*0,5 mL*) baking soda
¾ tsp	(*4 mL*) salt
pinch	white pepper
1 cup	(*250 mL*) beer
4 cups	(*1 L*) vegetable oil
1	egg white
2 lbs	(*900 g*) cod filet, cut into ¾-in. (*2 cm*) strips

In a mixing bowl, sift together all the dry ingredients.

Slowly add the beer. Whisk briskly. Let stand for 1½ hours.

Heat the oil to 375°F (*190°C*).

Whip the egg white. Fold into batter.

Dip fish into batter, allowing any excess batter to run off.

Using a slotted spoon, place fish in hot oil. Fry 2½ to 3 minutes or until golden brown.

Remove and keep hot on a paper towel-lined platter.

Pike Baked in Cream

4 servings

1 lb	(*450 g*) pike filets
3 tbsp	(*45 mL*) butter
1	small onion, diced
½	green pepper, diced
1	celery stalk, diced
½ cup	(*125 mL*) tomatoes, peeled, seeded and chopped
1½ cups	(*375 mL*) heavy cream
1 cup	(*250 mL*) grated Swiss cheese
½ cup	(*125 mL*) breadcrumbs
½ tsp	(*3 mL*) salt

Preheat oven to 350°F (*180°C*).

Wash and dry the fish. Place fish in a greased casserole dish.

Heat the butter in a saucepan.

Add the onion, pepper and celery; sauté until tender.

Add the tomatoes and simmer until liquid has evaporated. Spoon over fish.

Add the cream and sprinkle with cheese and breadcrumbs.

Bake in oven for 30 minutes.

Perch Filets with Shrimp Sauce

4 servings

1 lb	(*450 g*) perch filets
1 cup	(*250 mL*) flour
1	egg
½ cup	(*125 mL*) milk
1½ cups	(*375 mL*) fine breadcrumbs
3 tbsp	(*45 mL*) butter
3 tbsp	(*45 mL*) flour
1 cup	(*250 mL*) heavy cream
½ cup	(*125 mL*) fish stock (see *Soups*)
¼ cup	(*60 mL*) sherry
½ tsp	(*3 mL*) salt
½ lb	(*225 g*) baby shrimp
1 cup	(*250 mL*) oil

Wash and dry the filets. Dust with flour.

Mix the egg with the milk. Dip filets in egg mixture. Dredge with breadcrumbs. Reserve.

Heat the butter in a saucepan. Add 3 tbsp (*45 mL*) flour and stir into a paste (roux). Cook for 2 minutes.

Add the cream, stock and sherry. Simmer until thick.

Add the salt and shrimp. Simmer for 5 minutes.

Heat oil in a large skillet.

Fry the fish in the oil 1½ to 2 minutes each side.

Place on a platter. Pour half the sauce over the fish. Serve the remainder separately.

Perch Filets with Eggs and Brown Butter

Perch Filets with Eggs and Brown Butter

3 servings

4 cups	(*1 L*) court bouillon (see *Soups*)
1 lb	(*450 g*) perch filets
⅓ cup	(*80 mL*) butter
1 tsp	(*5 mL*) parsley flakes
1½ tsp	(*8 mL*) lemon juice
2	hard-boiled eggs, chopped

Heat court bouillon. Gently simmer the fish in the court bouillon for 6 minutes.

In a saucepan, heat the butter until it turns hazelnut-brown in color.

Add the parsley and lemon juice.

Place fish on a serving platter. Pour butter over fish.

Sprinkle with chopped eggs.

Three-Pepper Prawns

Three-Pepper Prawns

8 servings

2 tbsp	(*30 mL*) oil
¼ cup	(*60 mL*) butter
2	garlic cloves, crushed
2 tbsp	(*30 mL*) green peppercorns
2 tbsp	(*30 mL*) cracked black pepper
1 tsp	(*5 mL*) cayenne pepper
3 lbs	(*1,3 kg*) prawns, shelled and deveined
½ cup	(*125 mL*) red pimiento
1 tsp	(*5 mL*) sugar
2 tbsp	(*30 mL*) brandy

Heat the oil and butter in a large frying pan.

Add the garlic and peppers and sauté 2 minutes.

Add the prawns and sauté until tender. Stir in pimiento.

Sprinkle with sugar and flame with brandy. Serve at once.

Shrimp Aïoli

4 servings

4 cups	(*1 L*) court bouillon, (see *Soups*)
1 lb	(*450 g*) prawns, peeled and deveined
4	garlic cloves, pressed
1½ tsp	(*8 mL*) vinegar
2 tbsp	(*30 mL*) breadcrumbs
pinch	salt
1	egg yolk
¾ cup	(*180 mL*) olive oil

Bring court bouillon to a boil. Cook the shrimp in the court bouillon for 3 to 4 minutes. Remove and chill.

Place garlic in blender. Add vinegar and breadcrumbs. Blend for 30 seconds.

Add the salt and egg yolk and blend until smooth. With blender running, slowly pour in the oil. Blend into a thick sauce.

Place shrimp on a platter.

Serve with sauce in the center.

Shrimp à l'Étouffée

Shrimp à l'Étouffée

6 servings

½ cup	(*125 mL*) butter
1	onion, diced
1	green pepper, diced
2¼ lbs	(*1 kg*) shrimp, peeled and deveined
2 cups	(*500 mL*) tomato sauce
1 tsp	(*5 mL*) salt
1 tsp	(*5 mL*) pepper
1 tsp	(*5 mL*) paprika
½ tsp	(*3 mL*) oregano
½ tsp	(*3 mL*) thyme
½ tsp	(*3 mL*) cayenne pepper
½ tsp	(*3 mL*) garlic powder
½ tsp	(*3 mL*) white pepper
3 tbsp	(*45 mL*) diced green onions
1 tbsp	(*15 mL*) parsley flakes

Melt the butter and sauté the onion and green pepper.

Add the shrimp and cook gently.

Add the tomato sauce and seasonings. Simmer, half-covered, for 20 minutes.

Stir in the green onions and parsley flakes.

Serve over noodles or rice.

Tempura Shrimp

6 servings

½ cup	(125 mL)	milk
2¾ cups	(680 mL)	flour
2 tbsp	(30 mL)	cornstarch
1 tsp	(5 mL)	baking powder
1 tsp	(5 mL)	salt
2		eggs, beaten
4 cups	(1 L)	oil
2¼ lbs	(1 kg)	prawns, peeled and deveined

Blend the milk, ¾ cup (180 mL) flour, cornstarch, baking powder, salt, eggs and 2 tbsp (30 mL) oil into a smooth batter.

Heat the remaining oil to 375°F (190°C).

Dip the shrimp into the remaining flour, then into the batter.

Cook in the oil 2½ to 3 minutes. Serve hot.

Jumbo Fantail Shrimp

8 servings

2¼ lbs	(1 kg)	large shrimp, peeled and deveined
2 cups	(500 mL)	flour
½ cup	(125 mL)	cornmeal
1 tsp	(5 mL)	baking powder
1 tsp	(5 mL)	salt
½ tsp	(3 mL)	oregano
½ tsp	(3 mL)	thyme
½ tsp	(3 mL)	basil
1 tsp	(5 mL)	paprika
½ tsp	(3 mL)	pepper
2		eggs
1 cup	(250 mL)	heavy cream
4 cups	(1 L)	oil

Butterfly the shrimp.

Sift 1 cup (250 mL) of flour into cornmeal.

Add the baking powder and seasonings.

Beat the eggs into the cream. Stir into the seasoned flour.

Dust the shrimp with the remaining flour. Dip into batter.

Fry in the oil, which has been heated to 375°F (190°C). Serve at once.

B.B.Q. Shrimp

8 servings

3 lbs	(1,4 kg)	large shrimp
¼ cup	(60 mL)	butter
½ cup	(125 mL)	olive oil
1 tbsp	(15 mL)	Worcestershire sauce
4		garlic cloves, minced
4 tsp	(20 mL)	lemon juice
2 tsp	(10 mL)	chopped parsley
½ tsp	(3 mL)	paprika
½ tsp	(3 mL)	basil
½ tsp	(3 mL)	thyme
½ tsp	(3 mL)	oregano
½ tsp	(3 mL)	cayenne pepper
½ tsp	(3 mL)	hot pepper sauce
½ tsp	(3 mL)	salt

Place the shrimp in a large mixing bowl.

Add the remaining ingredients to a saucepan.

Combine well and heat without boiling, then chill. Pour over shrimp.

Marinate 30 minutes, stirring from time to time.

Preheat oven to 325°F (160°C).

Pour shrimp and sauce on a baking sheet; bake 8 to 10 minutes in oven.

Serve at once.

Jumbo Stuffed Shrimp

4 servings

2 tbsp	(*30 mL*) butter
1 tbsp	(*15 mL*) minced green onion
1 tbsp	(*15 mL*) Dijon mustard
1 tsp	(*5 mL*) chopped sage
1 cup	(*250 mL*) breadcrumbs
1 cup	(*250 mL*) crab meat
1	egg
¼ cup	(*60 mL*) heavy cream
24	large prawns, butterflied

Preheat oven to 425°F (*220°C*).

In 2 tsp (*10 mL*) butter, sauté the onion. Blend in the mustard and sage. Remove from heat.

In a mixing bowl, blend together the breadcrumbs, crab meat, egg, cream, sage mixture and remaining butter.

Place 2 tbsp (*30 mL*) of mixture on each butterflied shrimp. Place on a lightly greased baking sheet.

Bake in oven 8 to 10 minutes, or until golden brown. Serve hot.

1

Sauté the green onion in 2 tsp (*10 mL*) butter; blend in the mustard and sage and remove from heat.

2

Blend together the breadcrumbs, crab meat, egg, cream, sage mixture and remaining butter.

3

Place 2 tbsp (*30 mL*) of mixture on each butterflied shrimp.

4

Bake in oven 8 to 10 minutes, or until golden brown.

Shrimp Creole au Gratin

4-6 servings

3 cups	*(750 mL)* court bouillon (see *Soups*)
1½ lbs	*(675 g)* large fresh shrimp
2 cups	*(500 mL)* cooked and drained fettuccine noodles
1½ cups	*(375 mL)* Creole Sauce (see *Sauces*)
½ cup	*(125 mL)* coarsely grated medium Cheddar cheese
½ cup	*(125 mL)* coarsely grated old Cheddar cheese
½ cup	*(125 mL)* coarsely grated Swiss or Havarti cheese

Preheat oven to 400°F (*200°C*).

Bring court bouillon to a boil. Add shrimp and simmer just until cooked through, about 3 to 5 minutes.

Cool, peel, and devein shrimp.

Place noodles in a greased shallow baking dish. Spread shrimp over noodles; pour sauce evenly over shrimp.

Combine cheeses and sprinkle over sauce.

Bake in oven 25 to 30 minutes or until the cheese is melted and golden.

Coquilles St. Jacques à l'Indienne

4 servings

1 cup	*(250 mL)* white wine
1 lb	*(450 g)* scallops
¼ cup	*(60 mL)* butter
1	small onion, diced
1	green pepper, diced
1	celery stalk, diced
3 tbsp	*(45 mL)* flour
1 cup	*(250 mL)* heavy cream
⅓ cup	*(80 mL)* sherry
½ tsp	*(3 mL)* salt
2 tsp	*(10 mL)* curry powder
1 cup	*(250 mL)* tomatoes, peeled, seeded and chopped
1	recipe Risi e Bisi (see *Rice*)

Heat the wine. Add the scallops and cook for 6 minutes. Set aside.

In a saucepan, heat the butter. Sauté the vegetables until tender.

Add the flour and stir. Cook for 2 minutes.

Add the cream, sherry and seasonings. Simmer until thickened.

Add the tomatoes and scallops. Simmer for 5 minutes.

Serve with Risi e Bisi.

Coquilles St. Jacques Florentine

2 servings

10 oz	*(284 g)* spinach
1 tbsp	*(15 mL)* butter
1 cup	*(250 mL)* white wine
½ lb	*(225 g)* scallops
1 cup	*(250 mL)* Mornay Sauce (see *Sauces*)
¼ cup	*(60 mL)* grated Parmesan cheese

Preheat oven to 450°F (*230°C*).

Clean and stem the spinach. Cook in boiling, salted water for 5 minutes. Drain. Cool.

Coarsely chop the spinach.

Heat butter in a skillet. Add spinach and sauté 3 minutes.

Place spinach in a greased casserole dish.

Heat wine. Add scallops and cook for 6 minutes. Remove and place on spinach.

Cover with Mornay Sauce. Sprinkle with Parmesan.

Place in oven 3 to 5 minutes or until golden brown.

Coquilles St. Jacques à l'Indienne and Coquilles St. Jacques Florentine

Paprika Scallops

4 servings

3 tbsp	*(45 mL)*	butter
1 lb	*(450 g)*	scallops
3 tbsp	*(45 mL)*	flour
1 cup	*(250 mL)*	heavy cream
¼ cup	*(60 mL)*	sherry
1 tbsp	*(15 mL)*	Hungarian paprika
3		green onions, minced

Heat the butter in a large skillet. Add the scallops and sauté for 5 minutes.

Sprinkle in the flour. Cook 2 minutes. Add the cream, sherry and paprika.

Reduce heat and simmer 8 to 10 minutes or until thickened.

Sprinkle with green onions. Serve over rice or fettuccine.

Paprika Scallops

Coquilles St. Jacques Meunière

8 servings

2 lbs	*(900 g)*	scallops
1 tsp	*(5 mL)*	salt
½ tsp	*(3 mL)*	pepper
½ tsp	*(3 mL)*	paprika
2 cups	*(500 mL)*	flour
1½ cups	*(375 mL)*	milk
4 cups	*(1 L)*	oil
½ cup	*(125 mL)*	butter
1 tbsp	*(15 mL)*	parsley
2 tsp	*(10 mL)*	lemon juice

Wash and dry the scallops. Mix the seasonings into the flour.

Heat oil to 375°F (*190°C*). Dip scallops in milk, then into seasoned flour.

Fry in the oil to golden brown. Place in a serving dish.

Slowly cook the butter until it turns to a hazelnut-brown color.

Sprinkle with parsley and lemon juice. Pour over scallops and serve.

Scallops au Gratin

Meanwhile, sauté mushrooms in butter over high heat.

Stir mushrooms and shrimp into Mornay Sauce.

Place scallops in 4 individual shells or baking dishes.

Spoon sauce mixture over and sprinkle with grated cheeses.

Place under heated broiler until cheese melts.

Kentucky Scallops

8 servings

2 lbs	(900 g)	scallops
½ tsp	(3 mL)	oregano
½ tsp	(3 mL)	thyme
½ tsp	(3 mL)	basil
½ tsp	(3 mL)	garlic powder
½ tsp	(3 mL)	onion powder
½ tsp	(3 mL)	paprika
½ tsp	(3 mL)	pepper
1 tsp	(5 mL)	salt
2 cups	(500 mL)	flour
4 cups	(1 L)	oil
1½ cups	(375 mL)	milk

Wash the scallops, then dry them. Blend all the seasonings into the flour.

Heat the oil to 375°F (190°C).

Dip scallops in milk then into the seasoned flour.

Deep fry in the oil 2 to 3 minutes or until golden brown.

Scallops au Gratin

4 servings

1 lb	(450 g)	scallops
	court bouillon (see *Soups*) or salted water	
1½ cups	(375 mL)	sliced mushrooms
2 tbsp	(30 mL)	butter
½ cup	(125 mL)	cooked baby shrimp
2 cups	(500 mL)	Mornay Sauce (see *Sauces*)
½ cup	(125 mL)	grated mild Cheddar cheese
½ cup	(125 mL)	grated mozzarella cheese
¾ cup	(180 mL)	grated Parmesan cheese

Place scallops in a medium saucepan and cover with court bouillon or water.

Bring to a simmer and cook 3 to 5 minutes or until scallops are cooked through; drain.

Sylvia's Jumbo Crab Claws

8 servings

2 tbsp	(*30 mL*)	butter
2¼ cups	(*560 mL*)	flour
1 cup	(*250 mL*)	milk
4 cups	(*1 L*)	crab meat, cooked
½ tsp	(*3 mL*)	thyme
½ tsp	(*3 mL*)	basil
½ tsp	(*3 mL*)	oregano
½ tsp	(*3 mL*)	pepper
1 tsp	(*5 mL*)	paprika
1 tsp	(*5 mL*)	salt
2		eggs
1 cup	(*250 mL*)	milk
3 cups	(*750 mL*)	fine breadcrumbs
4 cups	(*1 L*)	oil

Heat the butter in a saucepan. Add ¼ cup (*60 mL*) of flour and stir. Cook two minutes.

Add 1 cup (*250 mL*) milk and cook very slowly over low heat until very thick. Cool.

Add the crab meat and blend.

Shape into 8 crab claws. Place on a wax paper-lined pastry sheet.

Chill in refrigerator for 2 hours.

Blend the seasonings with the remaining flour. Beat the eggs and add the milk. Dust crab claws with seasoned flour and dip into eggs. Dredge with breadcrumbs.

Heat oil to 375°F (*180°C*). Fry one or two claws at a time until golden brown.

Serve at once.

1

Add crab meat to thickened, cooled milk.

2

Shape into 8 crab claws.

3

Dust claws with seasoned flour, dip into eggs and dredge with breadcrumbs.

4

Fry one or two claws at a time in heated oil until golden brown.

Crab Louis

Add cream and simmer, stirring, until thickened. Stir in crab meat and season to taste.

Spoon hot mixture into a greased shallow baking dish. Sprinkle with almonds and cheese. Bake in oven just until cheese is golden.

Crab Louis

4 servings

1 lb	(*450 g*) crab meat
2	heads butter lettuce
3	tomatoes, sliced
4	hard-boiled eggs, quartered
16	green olives

Sauce

¾ cup	(*180 mL*) chili sauce
½ cup	(*125 mL*) mayonnaise
1 tsp	(*5 mL*) minced onion
½ tsp	(*3 mL*) sugar
¼ tsp	(*1 mL*) Worcestershire sauce
¼ tsp	(*1 mL*) salt
pinch	pepper

Check crab meat and remove any cartilage. On four plates, arrange the lettuce leaves. Place 4 oz (*115 g*) of crab meat in the center of lettuce. Place 4 slices of tomato and egg around the crab meat. Pour over 2 tbsp (*30 mL*) of sauce. Garnish with the olives. Serve remaining sauce separately.

Sauce : Blend together all the ingredients thoroughly. Chill 30 minutes before serving.

Baked Crab au Gratin

6-8 servings

1	medium onion, chopped
1	green pepper, chopped
1	red pepper, chopped
8	large mushrooms, sliced
2	large tomatoes, peeled, seeded and diced
¼ cup	(*60 mL*) butter
¼ cup	(*60 mL*) all-purpose flour
1¼ cups	(*310 mL*) heavy cream
2¼ lbs	(*1 kg*) cooked crab meat
	salt and pepper
¼ cup	(*60 mL*) sliced almonds
2 cups	(*500 mL*) grated medium Cheddar cheese

Preheat oven to 450°F (*230°C*). Sauté the vegetables in butter until tender. Sprinkle with flour; stir until well blended.

Lobster Mornay

4 servings

4	live lobsters, about 1½ lbs (*675 g*) each
	court bouillon (see *Soups*)
3 tbsp	(*45 mL*) finely chopped onion
3 tbsp	(*45 mL*) finely chopped celery
3 tbsp	(*45 mL*) finely chopped carrot
8	large mushrooms, sliced
2 tbsp	(*30 mL*) butter
1 cup	(*250 mL*) cooked diced chicken
1¾ cups	(*430 mL*) Mornay Sauce (see *Sauces*)
1 cup	(*250 mL*) grated Swiss cheese

Holding lobsters by the back, plunge them, head first, into a large pot of boiling court bouillon.

Simmer 12 to 15 minutes, or until lobsters rise to the surface. Drain.

Sauté the vegetables in butter. Stir in the chicken and hot Mornay Sauce. Simmer over low heat until mixture is thickened.

Slice lobsters in half horizontally, crack claws, and remove all lobster meat and tamale or coral roe.

Discard the claws. Slice lobster meat and stir into the Mornay mixture with tamale or roe; spoon mixture into the half shells and tail.

Sprinkle with cheese and place under heated broiler until golden.

Lobster Thermidor

6 servings

3	lobsters, 1½ lbs (*675 g*) each
¼ cup	(*60 mL*) butter
2 tbsp	(*30 mL*) oil
3	shallots, chopped
¼ cup	(*60 mL*) white wine
¼ cup	(*60 mL*) sherry
2 cups	(*500 mL*) Mornay Sauce (see *Sauces*)
1 tbsp	(*15 mL*) parsley
1 tsp	(*5 mL*) dry mustard
1 tbsp	(*15 mL*) heavy cream
½ cup	(*125 mL*) grated Parmesan cheese

Preheat oven to 400°F (*200°C*).

Split the lobsters in half. Remove and crack the claws.

Melt 2 tbsp (*30 mL*) butter and drizzle over the lobster.

Pour oil on large pastry sheet. Place lobster and claws on pastry sheet. Place in oven for 10 minutes.

While lobster is cooking, heat remaining butter in a saucepan.

Add shallots and simmer until tender. Add wine and sherry and reduce to ¼ cup (*60 mL*).

Add the Mornay Sauce, parsley and dry mustard. Cook 3 minutes on high heat, stirring constantly with a whisk.

Remove lobster from oven. Take meat out of shells. Reserve shells.

Dice the meat and place in a mixing bowl. Add ⅔ of the sauce. Combine. Spoon a little of the sauce into the shells. Fill shells with lobster mixture.

Pour remaining sauce and cream over mixture. Sprinkle with cheese.

Return to oven and brown. Serve.

Lobster Medallions in Pernod Cream

6 servings

6	lobster tails
1	small onion, minced
1	garlic clove, minced
1 tbsp	(*15 mL*) butter
2 cups	(*500 mL*) crushed tomatoes
1 tsp	(*5 mL*) fennel seeds
¼ cup	(*60 mL*) Pernod
½ cup	(*125 mL*) heavy cream

Cut the lobster tails into medallions.

Sauté the onion and garlic in the butter until tender.

Add the tomatoes, fennel seeds and Pernod; simmer for 12 minutes.

Add the cream and lobster and simmer 10 more minutes. Serve at once.

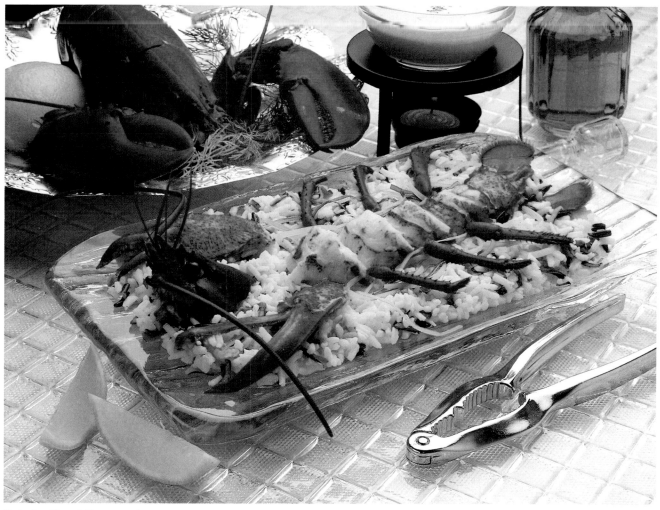

Lobster Henri Duvernois

Lobster Henri Duvernois

6 servings

2¼ lbs	(1 kg) lobster meat
¼ cup	(60 mL) butter
½ cup	(125 mL) leeks, julienned
⅔ cup	(160 mL) sherry
2 tbsp	(30 mL) brandy
2 cups	(500 mL) heavy cream
4 cups	(1 L) cooked rice, hot

Sauté the lobster meat in the butter. Add the leeks and cook until tender.

Add the sherry and brandy and simmer for 5 minutes.

Remove lobster and keep hot.

Add cream and reduce to half the volume.

Place lobster over rice, pour sauce over the lobster and serve.

Pamela's Seafood Sloppy Joes

6 servings

¼ cup	(*60 mL*) oil
2	garlic cloves, minced
1	small onion, finely diced
1	green pepper, finely diced
4 oz	(*115 g*) mushrooms, sliced
2	celery stalks, minced
1 lb	(*450 g*) small shrimp, peeled and deveined
2 cups	(*500 mL*) tomato purée
¼ tsp	(*1 mL*) oregano
¼ tsp	(*1 mL*) thyme leaves
¼ tsp	(*1 mL*) basil
¼ tsp	(*1 mL*) chili powder
¼ tsp	(*1 mL*) paprika
¼ tsp	(*1 mL*) pepper
1 tsp	(*5 mL*) salt
1 lb	(*450 g*) crab meat, cooked
1	french loaf, cut into 6 thick slices
2 cups	(*500 mL*) grated Cheddar cheese

Heat the oil in a large skillet. Add the garlic, onion, pepper, mushrooms and celery; sauté until tender.

Add the shrimp; cook until pink. Add the tomato purée and seasonings; stir. Cook for 10 minutes over low heat.

Add the crab meat and simmer for 5 more minutes.

Hollow the sliced bread to form a cavity. Place bread under oven broiler and toast.

Remove and fill the bread cavity with seafood mixture.

Sprinkle with cheese and return under the broiler for 1 minute or until browned.

Seafood Crêpes Mornay

8 servings

Crêpes

3	eggs
¼ tsp	(*1 mL*) salt
1 cup	(*250 mL*) milk
¾ cup	(*180 mL*) flour
3 tbsp	(*45 mL*) butter

Filling

¼ cup	(*60 mL*) butter
1 cup	(*250 mL*) tiny scallops
1 cup	(*250 mL*) baby shrimp
1 cup	(*250 mL*) crab meat, cooked
2 cups	(*500 mL*) Mornay Sauce (see *Sauces*)
2 cups	(*500 mL*) grated Cheddar cheese

Crêpes : Whip the eggs until very light. Add the salt and milk. Fold in the flour a little at a time.

Lightly grease a heated skillet with a little butter. Pour in enough batter to cover the bottom of the pan.

Rotate the pan to spread the batter into a thin layer.

Grill the crêpe until browned. Turn over, grill 30 seconds and remove to a plate.

Filling : Preheat oven to 350°F (*180°C*).

Heat the butter in a saucepan. Add the scallops and sauté.

Add the shrimp and crab meat. Simmer for 3 minutes.

Stir in the sauce. Simmer for 5 minutes.

Spoon 3 tbsp (*45 mL*) of seafood mixture onto each crêpe. Roll crêpes.

Place crêpes in a greased casserole dish. Sprinkle with cheese.

Bake in oven for 15 minutes.

Seafood Crêpes Mornay

Lobster Crab Casserole

4 servings

1 cup	(*250 mL*) crab meat, cooked	
1 cup	(*250 mL*) lobster meat, cooked	
½ cup	(*125 mL*) finely diced celery	
1	green pepper, finely diced	
1	onion, finely diced	
¾ cup	(*180 mL*) mayonnaise	
½ tsp	(*3 mL*) salt	
¼ tsp	(*1 mL*) pepper	
½ tsp	(*3 mL*) paprika	
1 tsp	(*5 mL*) Worcestershire sauce	
½ cup	(*125 mL*) breadcrumbs	
½ cup	(*125 mL*) grated Cheddar cheese	

Preheat oven to 350°F (*180°C*).

Combine the seafood with the vegetables. Stir in the mayonnaise and seasonings.

Scrape mixture into a greased casserole.

Sprinkle with breadcrumbs and cheese. Bake in oven for 30 minutes.

Escargots à la Bourguignonne

8 servings

48	snails, canned	
3 cups	(*750 mL*) court bouillon (see *Soups*)	
1¾ cups	(*430 mL*) softened butter	
3	garlic cloves, crushed	
1 cup	(*250 mL*) chopped fresh parsley	
2 tsp	(*10 mL*) black pepper	
1 tbsp	(*15 mL*) brandy	
48	snail shells	

Preheat oven to 400°F (*200°C*).

Gently simmer the snails in the court bouillon for 30 minutes.

While snails are cooking, blend the butter, garlic, parsley, pepper and brandy together.

Drain the snails and stuff into shells. Fill each shell with butter mixture.

Bake in oven for 5 minutes. Serve with garlic bread.

John Hoyle's Fresh Oysters

3-6 servings

36	fresh New Orleans oysters	
2	green onions, minced	
⅓ cup	(*80 mL*) red wine vinegar	
1 tsp	(*5 mL*) lemon juice	
3	lemons, quartered	

Scrub and shuck the oysters. Detach the bivalve from the shell. Leave in the larger shell. Discard the top shell.

Blend the green onions, vinegar and lemon juice together.

Place oysters on a serving platter. Spoon ½ tsp (*3 mL*) of sauce on each oyster.

Serve with lemons.

Oysters Bienville

Oysters Bienville

4 servings

2 tbsp	(*30 mL*) butter
3 oz	(*90 g*) mushrooms, sliced
3	green onions, diced
2 tbsp	(*30 mL*) flour
⅔ cup	(*160 mL*) fish stock (see *Soups*)
⅓ cup	(*80 mL*) sherry
½ tsp	(*3 mL*) salt
pinch	cayenne pepper
1	egg yolk

24	oysters on the half shell
½ cup	(*125 mL*) fine breadcrumbs
2 tbsp	(*30 mL*) grated Parmesan cheese

Preheat oven to 400°F (*200°C*).

In a saucepan, heat the butter. Sauté the mushrooms and green onions.

Add the flour, stir and cook 2 minutes. Add the fish stock, sherry and seasonings. Simmer for 5 minutes.

Whip the egg yolk. Stir into sauce. Cook for 5 minutes over low heat.

Place oysters on a baking sheet. Bake in oven 5 minutes.

Remove from oven and top with sauce. Sprinkle with breadcrumbs and cheese.

Return to oven and bake until golden brown. Serve at once.

International Cooking

Foreign and regional cuisines are becoming more and more popular, and no wonder. Sampling another country's cuisine is almost as good as going there, and not nearly so expensive!

Of course, many North Americans have been broadening their culinary horizons for years. In fact, most of us no longer even stop to think that everyday meals such as spaghetti and stir-fries were once regarded as very exotic.

You may find the recipes in this chapter a little more exotic, but once you have tried some of the great dishes from countries as far afield as Mexico and Russia, Poland and Japan, I feel sure they will become favorites as well.

Some of my personal favorite dishes come from the regional cuisine of Louisiana — Cajun and Creole. No other food strikes me as being as lively and as filled with the spirit of its people. Its roots are in French country cooking, which the Acadians who were banished from the Canadian east coast took with them to Louisiana. But Spanish settlers, African slaves, native Indians and the local conditions of heat, humidity and plenty of alligators all played a role in the development of this wonderful cooking style.

Don't be misled by the idea that Cajun cooking is always hot and spicy. Spice is just part of its mystique, but should never overwhelm the other flavors.

I like to match up ethnic and regional food with the appropriate music. For me, that means a Cajun feast with the sounds of Bourbon Street and Pete Fountain's clarinet in the background. Now this is living.

Chicken and Shrimp Gumbo

Chicken and Shrimp Gumbo

8 servings

¼ cup	(60 mL) oil
1¼ lbs	(565 g) shrimp, peeled and deveined
1¼ lbs	(565 g) boneless chicken meat, diced
1	onion, coarsely diced
2	green peppers, coarsely diced
3	celery stalks, coarsely diced
½ lb	(225 g) hot sausage, sliced
2 cups	(500 mL) tomatoes, peeled, seeded and chopped
1½ cups	(375 mL) water
1 cup	(250 mL) raw rice
2 tsp	(10 mL) salt
1 tsp	(5 mL) oregano
1 tsp	(5 mL) cayenne pepper
1 tsp	(5 mL) thyme
1 tsp	(5 mL) paprika
1 tsp	(5 mL) pepper
2 tsp	(10 mL) garlic powder
1 lb	(450 g) okra
3 tbsp	(45 mL) gumbo filé* (optional)

In a large pot, heat the oil. Sauté the shrimp and chicken.

Add the vegetables and hot sausage; sauté until tender.

Add tomatoes, water, rice and the seasonings. Simmer for 30 minutes.

While gumbo is simmering, slice the okra and simmer for 15 minutes in water.

Drain and add to gumbo. Just before serving, add gumbo filé and serve at once.

*ground sassafras leaves

Bayou Short Ribs

8 servings

3 tbsp	(45 mL)	oil
2¼ lbs	(1 kg)	short ribs, cut up
1 cup	(250 mL)	flour
1		onion, diced
4		garlic cloves, minced
2		celery stalks, diced
1		green pepper, diced
1 cup	(250 mL)	crushed tomatoes
2 tbsp	(30 mL)	tomato paste
1 cup	(250 mL)	water
2 tsp	(10 mL)	salt
1 tsp	(5 mL)	pepper
¼ tsp	(1 mL)	oregano
½ tsp	(3 mL)	thyme
½ tsp	(3 mL)	cayenne pepper
½ tsp	(3 mL)	basil
3		bay leaves
2 tbsp	(30 mL)	brown sugar

Heat oil in large skillet. Coat ribs with flour and place in skillet.

Add onion, garlic, celery and pepper; sauté until tender.

Add tomatoes, tomato paste and water; stir.

Add seasonings, bay leaves and sugar.

Reduce heat and simmer for 3 hours, adding more water as needed.

Black Bean Soup

8 servings

1½ cups	(375 mL)	black beans
6⅔ cups	(1,6 L)	beef stock (see *Soups*)
1⅓ tbsp	(20 mL)	butter
1		Spanish onion, minced
1		celery stalk, minced
1 tbsp	(15 mL)	flour
1 tbsp	(15 mL)	freshly chopped parsley
2 tsp	(10 mL)	freshly chopped coriander
1		small ham bone
6 oz	(170 g)	large pieces ham rind
1		leek, thinly sliced
1		bay leaf
½ tsp	(3 mL)	pepper
¼ tsp	(1 mL)	cayenne pepper
⅓ cup	(80 mL)	Madeira wine
⅔ cup	(160 mL)	sour cream

Wash the beans. Soak for 6 hours or overnight.

Drain the beans and simmer in the beef stock for 1½ hours.

In a large pot, melt the butter and sauté the onion and celery until tender.

Blend in the flour, parsley and coriander. Cook for 2 minutes.

Add the beans and stock. Stir thoroughly.

Add the ham bone and rind, leek, bay leaf and peppers.

Simmer over low heat 1 to 1½ hours. Remove ham bone, rind and bay leaf.

Force through a coarse sieve or process in a food processor into a smooth liquid.

Add the Madeira, bring soup to a boil and serve with sour cream on the side.

Red Beans and Rice

8 servings

1½ cups	(375 mL) kidney beans
6 cups	(1,5 L) water
3 tbsp	(45 mL) oil
1	onion, diced
6	green onions, diced
3	garlic cloves, crushed
1	green pepper, diced
3	celery stalks, diced
1 lb	(450 g) hot sausage
1 lb	(450 g) ham, diced
3 cups	(750 mL) chopped tomatoes
1 tsp	(5 mL) paprika
1 tsp	(5 mL) chili powder
½ tsp	(3 mL) cayenne pepper
1 tsp	(5 mL) thyme
¼ tsp	(1 mL) pepper
1 tsp	(5 mL) oregano
8 cups	(2 L) cooked rice, hot

Soak the beans in the water overnight. Simmer for 1 hour. Drain.

Heat the oil. Sauté the onion, garlic, green pepper, celery, sausage and ham for 2 minutes.

Add the tomatoes and seasonings. Mix with the beans.

Continue to simmer until thick, about 2 hours.

Place hot rice on a platter. Pour kidney beans on rice.

Serve at once.

Red Beans and Rice

New Orleans Bouillabaisse

8 servings

3 tbsp	(*45 mL*) butter
3 tbsp	(*45 mL*) minced onion
3 tbsp	(*45 mL*) minced green pepper
1	celery stalk, minced
1	garlic clove, minced
1 tsp	(*5 mL*) chopped parsley
2/3 cup	(*160 mL*) chopped tomatoes
1 2/3 cups	(*410 mL*) fish stock (see *Soups*)
6 oz	(*170 g*) shrimp, peeled and deveined
6 oz	(*170 g*) oyster meat
6 oz	(*170 g*) crab meat
6 oz	(*170 g*) crayfish tails
1/2 tsp	(*3 mL*) thyme
1/2 tsp	(*3 mL*) basil
1/2 tsp	(*3 mL*) marjoram
1/2 tsp	(*3 mL*) paprika
1/3 cup	(*80 mL*) sherry
10 oz	(*300 g*) red snapper, cut in 2-in. (*5 cm*) strips

In a large pot or Dutch oven, heat the butter.

Sauté the onion, green pepper, celery, garlic and parsley.

Add the tomatoes and fish stock. Simmer for 15 minutes.

Add the shellfish, seasonings and sherry.

Simmer for an additional 10 minutes.

Add the red snapper and simmer for 5 more minutes. Serve.

Shrimp Jambalaya

6 servings

1/2 lb	(*225 g*) hot Italian sausage, diced
2 tbsp	(*30 mL*) oil
1/2 cup	(*125 mL*) diced green onions
2	garlic cloves, minced
2	green peppers, diced
2 tbsp	(*30 mL*) parsley flakes
2 cups	(*500 mL*) tomatoes, peeled, seeded and crushed
2 tsp	(*10 mL*) salt
1 tsp	(*5 mL*) pepper
1/2 tsp	(*3 mL*) oregano
1/2 tsp	(*3 mL*) thyme
1/2 tsp	(*3 mL*) basil
1 1/2 cups	(*375 mL*) water
1 cup	(*250 mL*) raw rice
2 1/4 lbs	(*1 kg*) large shrimp, peeled and deveined

Sauté the sausage in the oil. Add the onions, garlic and green peppers. Sauté until tender.

Add the parsley, tomatoes, seasonings, water and rice. Mix thoroughly.

Add the shrimp. Bring to a boil, then reduce heat to low.

Cover and simmer for 30 minutes.

Taste, adjust seasonings and serve.

Frog Legs Creole

6 servings

¼ cup	(*60 mL*) butter
1	onion, finely diced
1	green pepper, finely diced
2	celery stalks, finely diced
3 cups	(*750 mL*) chopped tomatoes
½ tsp	(*3 mL*) oregano
½ tsp	(*3 mL*) thyme
½ tsp	(*3 mL*) basil
1 tsp	(*5 mL*) paprika
1 tsp	(*5 mL*) salt
½ tsp	(*3 mL*) cayenne pepper
½ tsp	(*3 mL*) black pepper
4	green onions, sliced
2 tbsp	(*30 mL*) chopped parsley
24	pairs frog legs
¼ cup	(*60 mL*) garlic butter

Heat the butter in a saucepan. Sauté the vegetables.

Add the tomatoes and seasonings. Simmer for 20 minutes.

Add the green onions and parsley.

Split the frog legs.

Heat the garlic butter in a large skillet. Sauté the frog legs for 5 minutes.

Pour the sauce over the frog legs.

Simmer for 8 minutes. Serve.

1

Sauté the vegetables in a saucepan. Add the tomatoes and seasonings and simmer 20 minutes.

2

Add the green onions and parsley.

3

In a large skillet, sauté the frog legs in garlic butter for 5 minutes.

4

Pour the sauce over the frog legs, simmer 8 minutes and serve.

Shrimp Creole

6 servings

2¼ lbs	(*1 kg*) shrimp, peeled and deveined
¼ cup	(*60 mL*) oil
¼ cup	(*60 mL*) flour
1	Spanish onion, finely diced
2	green peppers, finely diced
3	celery stalks, finely diced
2 cups	(*500 mL*) tomatoes, peeled, seeded and chopped
2 tsp	(*10 mL*) salt
1 tsp	(*5 mL*) garlic powder
1 tsp	(*5 mL*) pepper
1 tsp	(*5 mL*) white pepper
½ tsp	(*3 mL*) cayenne pepper
1 tsp	(*5 mL*) oregano
1 tsp	(*5 mL*) thyme
1 tsp	(*5 mL*) basil
1½ cups	(*375 mL*) water
1 tbsp	(*15 mL*) brown sugar
¼ cup	(*60 mL*) minced green onions
3 tbsp	(*45 mL*) chopped parsley

Sauté the shrimp in the oil. Remove shrimp and set aside.

Add the flour and make a light brown roux (paste).

Add the onion, peppers and celery; sauté until tender, stirring constantly.

Add the tomatoes, seasonings, water and sugar.

Simmer, covered, for 20 minutes.

Return the shrimp to sauce, add the green onions and parsley.

Simmer for 7 minutes and serve on cooked rice.

Bananas Foster

6 servings

⅓ cup	(*80 mL*) butter
¾ cup	(*180 mL*) brown sugar
1 tsp	(*5 mL*) cinnamon
3 oz	(*90 mL*) banana liqueur
6 oz	(*180 mL*) dark rum
6	bananas
6 cups	(*1,5 L*) vanilla ice cream

In a skillet, melt the butter. Caramelize the sugar in the butter.

Add the cinnamon. Flame carefully with the banana liqueur and rum. Add the bananas. Heat for 2 minutes.

Pour mixture over ice cream.

Serve one banana per serving.

Cornish Hens Rochambeau

6 servings

3	Cornish hens, halved and boned
3 tbsp	(*45 mL*) oil
1 tsp	(*5 mL*) salt
1 tsp	(*5 mL*) paprika
1 tsp	(*5 mL*) pepper
1 tsp	(*5 mL*) oregano
6	slices ham, 2 oz (*60 g*) each
½ cup	(*125 mL*) butter
3 tbsp	(*45 mL*) flour
1 cup	(*250 mL*) pineapple juice
1 tbsp	(*15 mL*) brown sugar
½ cup	(*125 mL*) sherry
6	bread rusks
½ cup	(*125 mL*) Béarnaise Sauce (see *Sauces*)

Preheat oven to 350°F (*180°C*).

Brush the Cornish hens with oil. Sprinkle with seasonings. Roast for 40 minutes in oven.

Broil ham slices for 2 minutes.

Melt the butter, add the flour and make a roux (paste).

Add the pineapple juice, sugar and sherry. Simmer until thickened.

Place half a Cornish hen on a bread rusk. Top with ham slice. Pour pineapple sauce over ham.

Top with heated Béarnaise Sauce and serve.

Chicken Normandy

Daube de Bœuf Provençale

8 servings

2¼ lbs	(*1 kg*) round steak, cut into thin strips
1 tsp	(*5 mL*) salt
½ tsp	(*3 mL*) pepper
½ tsp	(*3 mL*) basil
2	bay leaves, crushed
2 cups	(*500 mL*) red or white wine
1½ tbsp	(*22 mL*) olive oil
6	slices bacon, diced
4	carrots, sliced
4 oz	(*115 g*) mushrooms, sliced
2 cups	(*500 mL*) tomatoes, seeded and chopped
2	garlic cloves, minced
8	pitted black olives, sliced
1	bouquet garni
6 cups	(*1,5 L*) cooked rice, hot

Season the beef with the salt, pepper, basil and bay leaves.

Pour wine and olive oil over the beef. Marinate for 2 hours.

Mix together the bacon, carrots, mushrooms, tomatoes, garlic and olives. Drain the beef. Reserve liquid.

In a greased casserole dish, alternate layers of beef and vegetable mix. Place the bouquet garni in the center. Pour reserved liquid over. Refrigerate for 2 hours.

Bake in a 325°F (*160°C*) oven for 4 hours. Serve with rice.

Chicken Normandy

4 servings

1	fryer chicken, cut into 8 pieces
3 tbsp	(*45 mL*) butter
1 lb	(*450 g*) apples, peeled and sliced
¼ cup	(*60 mL*) Calvados (apple brandy)

Preheat oven to 350°F (*180°C*).
Sauté the chicken in the butter until half done.

Place the apples in a casserole dish. Top with the chicken pieces.

Swirl the Calvados in the pan and pour over the chicken.

Cover and bake in oven 25 to 30 minutes.

Rouladen

8 servings

2¼ lbs	(*1 kg*) round steak	
1 lb	(*450 g*) lean ground veal	
1 cup	(*250 mL*) minced onions	
½ cup	(*125 mL*) breadcrumbs	
1	egg, beaten	
1 cup	(*250 mL*) chili sauce	
pinch	cayenne pepper	
5	dill pickles, cut into spears	
½ cup	(*125 mL*) seasoned flour	
⅓ cup	(*80 mL*) oil	
1 cup	(*250 mL*) beef stock (see *Soups*)	

Preheat oven to 375°F (*190°C*).

Trim the steak of excess fat. Pound thin.

Mix together the veal, onions, breadcrumbs, egg, chili sauce and cayenne. Spread across the beef.

Arrange the pickles over the meat. Roll and tie the meat. Dust with seasoned flour.

Heat oil in a large skillet. Brown meat. Place in a roasting pan. Pour in the stock.

Roast in oven for 1½ hours.

Thicken the broth to make a gravy. Pour over the Rouladen.

Sauerbraten

6 servings

3 tbsp	(*45 mL*) vinegar	
½ cup	(*125 mL*) red or white wine	
12 oz	(*341 mL*) beer	
1½ cups	(*375 mL*) water	
1	carrot, sliced	
1	onion, sliced	
1	celery stalk, sliced	
1 tsp	(*5 mL*) salt	
3 tbsp	(*45 mL*) pickling spice	
2¼ lbs	(*1 kg*) round roast	

In saucepan, heat the vinegar, wine, beer, water, carrot, onion, celery and seasonings. Bring to a boil and simmer 15 minutes. Allow to cool completely.

Place roast in a large bowl. Pour cool mixture over roast. Cover and place in refrigerator for 24 hours.

Preheat oven to 350°F (*180°C*).

Drain roast and discard liquid and vegetables. Place in roasting pan. Roast for 2½ hours or until desired doneness.

Once done, place on a platter, carve and serve.

Sachertorte

8-10 servings

1 tbsp	(*15 mL*) cocoa powder	
⅔ cup	(*160 mL*) pastry flour, sifted	
12 oz	(*340 g*) semi-sweet chocolate	
⅓ cup	(*80 mL*) butter	
⅓ cup	(*80 mL*) sugar	
4	egg yolks	
5	egg whites	
¼ cup	(*60 mL*) apricot jam	
¾ lb	(*340 g*) almond paste*	
1½ tsp	(*8 mL*) oil	

Preheat oven to 325°F (*160°C*).

Sift together the cocoa powder and flour. Melt the chocolate in a double boiler.

Cream the butter with the sugar until light. Slowly add ½ cup (*125 mL*) of melted chocolate to creamed mixture.

Add the egg yolks one at a time. Slowly add the flour mixture. Incorporate but do not overmix.

Beat the egg whites until stiff. Fold carefully into cake mixture. Pour batter into a deep 8-in. (*20 cm*) springform pan, which has been lightly greased.

Bake in oven for 1¼ hours. Remove. Cool 10 minutes.

Heat the jam and brush on cake. On a board lightly dusted with icing sugar, roll out the almond paste thin.

Cover the entire cake. Trim to fit the cake.

Add the oil to the remaining chocolate. Pour over cake. Refrigerate 1 hour. Serve.

At Vienna's Sacher Hotel where this recipe originated, they serve plenty of unsweetened whipped cream alongside.

*Almond paste may be purchased from any cake decorating store or bakery.

Roast Pork Loin and Red Cabbage

Roast Pork Loin and Red Cabbage

8 servings

5 lb	(*2,2 kg*) pork loin roast, tied
¼ cup	(*60 mL*) oil
1 tsp	(*5 mL*) salt
½ tsp	(*3 mL*) pepper
½ tsp	(*3 mL*) paprika
¼ tsp	(*1 mL*) cinnamon
4 oz	(*115 g*) bacon, diced
2¼ lbs	(*1 kg*) red cabbage, shredded
1 tsp	(*5 mL*) caraway seeds
2 tbsp	(*30 mL*) sugar
½ cup	(*125 mL*) sherry

Preheat oven to 350°F (*180°C*).

Rub the pork loin with oil. Season by sprinkling salt, pepper, paprika and cinnamon over the roast.

Place in a roasting pan. Bake 2 hours in oven.

While loin is roasting, fry the bacon in a large skillet. Remove and set aside. Drain all the bacon fat. Reserve ¼ cup (*60 mL*).

Place cabbage in skillet. Sauté 3 minutes in reserved bacon fat. Add the caraway seeds, sugar, bacon and sherry.

Cover and simmer for 15 minutes, or until tender. Place on platter.

Remove roast, slice and serve on cabbage.

Moussaka

8 servings

2 tbsp	(30 mL)	butter
1		onion, minced
1		garlic clove, minced
1½ lbs	(675 g)	ground lamb
2 cups	(500 mL)	crushed tomatoes
1 tbsp	(15 mL)	salt
½ tsp	(3 mL)	oregano
½ tsp	(3 mL)	thyme
1 tsp	(5 mL)	paprika
1 tsp	(5 mL)	basil
½ tsp	(3 mL)	pepper
½ tsp	(3 mL)	cinnamon
1 tbsp	(15 mL)	cornstarch
3 tbsp	(45 mL)	red wine
2		eggplants, 1¼ lbs (565 g) each
½ cup	(125 mL)	melted butter
1 cup	(250 mL)	grated Cheddar cheese
3 cups	(750 mL)	Mornay Sauce (see *Sauces*)

Melt the butter in a Dutch oven. Add onion and garlic; sauté until tender.

Add the lamb and brown. Add tomatoes, 1½ tsp (8 mL) salt and seasonings.

Reduce heat and simmer for 30 minutes.

Mix the cornstarch with the wine. Add to sauce and simmer until thickened.

Halve the eggplants lengthwise. Slice crosswise, ½ in. (1 cm) thick.

Brush with butter and sprinkle with the remaining salt. Broil for 4 minutes. Remove from oven.

To assemble, layer in a greased 12x7x2-in. (30x18x5 cm) pan: 1 layer eggplant, 1 layer meat sauce, sprinkle with cheese. Repeat. Top with Mornay Sauce.

Bake at 350°F (180°C) for 35 minutes. Serve.

Greek-Style Leg of Lamb

8 servings

2		garlic cloves, minced
¼ cup	(60 mL)	lemon juice
½ tsp	(3 mL)	black pepper
¼ tsp	(1 mL)	crushed fennel seeds
1 cup	(250 mL)	plain yogurt
6 lb	(2,7 kg)	leg of lamb (boned, trimmed and butterflied)

Combine the garlic, lemon juice, pepper, fennel and yogurt.

Brush on lamb and refrigerate 12 hours.

Preheat oven to 400°F (200°C).

Place the lamb in a shallow roasting pan.

Roast 40 minutes, turn and baste. Roast another 20 minutes. Serve.

Lamb Brochettes

6 servings

¼ cup	(60 mL)	olive oil
1 tsp	(5 mL)	oregano
½ tsp	(3 mL)	salt
¼ tsp	(1 mL)	pepper
1 tbsp	(15 mL)	lemon juice
2¼ lbs	(1 kg)	lean, boneless lamb, cut into 48 small cubes
48		mushroom caps
48		green pepper pieces

Blend together the oil, seasonings and lemon juice.

Marinate the lamb in the dressing for 8 hours, covered.

Skewer pieces of lamb, mushrooms and pepper, alternating meat and vegetables.

Broil in a very hot oven or over a broiler. Brush with marinade while cooking, 5 to 6 minutes.

Serve with rice pilaf.

Greek Salad

8 servings

Dressing

½ cup	(125 mL) oil
2 tbsp	(30 mL) white vinegar
1 tbsp	(15 mL) lemon juice
½ tbsp	(7 mL) Worcestershire sauce
½ tbsp	(7 mL) dried basil
1 tbsp	(15 mL) dried oregano
1 tbsp	(15 mL) seasoned salt

Salad

2	large tomatoes, seeded
1	Spanish onion
1	green pepper
1	seedless cucumber
½ lb	(225 g) button mushrooms
½ cup	(125 mL) black olives
1 cup	(250 mL) crumbled feta cheese

In food processor or jar with tight-fitting lid, combine all of dressing ingredients.

Process or shake until well blended.

Cut tomatoes, onion, pepper, and cucumber into bite-size pieces.

Mix in mushrooms, olives and cheese.

Pour dressing over and toss gently.

Greek Pilaf of Chicken

4 servings

1 lb	(450 g) chicken meat, cubed
3 tbsp	(45 mL) butter
1	small onion, minced
1	small green pepper, diced
2 tbsp	(30 mL) flour
2 cups	(500 mL) chicken stock
¼ cup	(60 mL) sultana raisins
3 cups	(750 mL) cooked rice, hot

Sauté the chicken in the butter. Add the onion and green pepper; sauté until tender. Add the flour and stir. Pour in the stock and simmer for 10 minutes.

Add the raisins and simmer for another 3 minutes.

Pour over rice and serve at once.

Greek Pilaf of Chicken

Hungarian Goulash

Hungarian Goulash

8 servings

2 tbsp	(30 mL) butter
½ cup	(125 mL) finely diced onions
3	garlic cloves, minced
3 tbsp	(45 mL) paprika
2¼ lbs	(1 kg) stewing beef, cubed
1 tsp	(5 mL) caraway seeds
4 cups	(1 L) beef stock
1 tsp	(5 mL) salt
½ tsp	(3 mL) black pepper
2 cups	(500 mL) tomatoes, peeled, seeded and chopped
8 oz	(225 g) button mushrooms
½ tsp	(3 mL) oregano
1 tbsp	(15 mL) cornstarch

In a 16-cup (4 L) saucepan, heat the butter and sauté the onions and garlic until lightly browned.

Add the paprika and stir until well blended. Add the beef, caraway seeds, stock, salt and pepper. Simmer for 1 hour.

Add the tomatoes, mushrooms and oregano and simmer another 40 minutes, uncovered.

Mix the cornstarch with a little water, add to goulash and bring to a boil.

Simmer until sauce thickens slightly.

Hungarian Paprika Potatoes

6 servings

2 tbsp	*(30 mL)* oil
⅓ cup	*(80 mL)* butter
2¼ lbs	*(1 kg)* large potatoes, diced
1½ cups	*(375 mL)* sour cream
1½ cups	*(375 mL)* heavy cream
1 tbsp	*(15 mL)* paprika
1½ tsp	*(8 mL)* salt
¼ tsp	*(1 mL)* pepper
3	green onions, chopped

Preheat oven to 350°F (*180°C*).

Heat the oil and butter in a large skillet.

Sauté the potatoes in the oil and butter for 5 minutes.

Blend together the sour cream, cream and seasonings.

Place the potatoes in a casserole dish. Pour the cream over the potatoes.

Sprinkle with green onions. Cover and bake in oven for 1 hour.

Uncover and continue to bake for 10 more minutes. Serve.

1

Sauté the diced potatoes in the oil and butter for 5 minutes.

2

Blend together the sour cream, cream and seasonings.

3

Place the potatoes in a casserole dish, pour the cream over and sprinkle with green onions.

4

Bake, covered, in oven for 1 hour; uncover and bake 10 more minutes.

Hungarian Paprikache

6 servings

2 tbsp	(*30 mL*) oil
2	onions, chopped
2 tbsp	(*30 mL*) paprika
½ cup	(*125 mL*) red wine
1 cup	(*250 mL*) beef stock (see *Soups*)
½ tsp	(*3 mL*) salt
2¼ lbs	(*1 kg*) round steak, diced
5	potatoes, peeled and thinly sliced

Heat the oil and sauté the onions until golden brown.

Add paprika and blend. Add wine, beef stock and salt.

Add the beef and simmer for 40 minutes.

Lay potatoes on top of beef and simmer, covered, for 20 minutes. Serve at once.

Gulyassuppe

6 servings

¼ cup	(*60 mL*) oil
1 lb	(*450 g*) lean beef, diced
2	potatoes, peeled and diced
1	onion, chopped
3	celery stalks, chopped
1	green pepper, chopped
6 cups	(*1,5 L*) beef stock (see *Soups*)
1	garlic clove, minced
2 tsp	(*10 mL*) paprika
½ tsp	(*3 mL*) caraway seeds
1 tsp	(*5 mL*) salt
3 cups	(*750 mL*) tomatoes, seeded and chopped
3	sausages, diced
¾ cup	(*180 mL*) water
⅓ cup	(*80 mL*) flour

Heat the oil in a pot. Add beef and brown. Add the vegetables and sauté until tender.

Add the beef stock, garlic and seasonings. Simmer for 30 minutes.

Add the tomatoes and sausages. Simmer for 10 more minutes.

Mix the water and flour together. Add to soup.

Simmer until thickened, about 10 minutes.

Gnocchi with Sour Cream and Beef

8 servings

¼ cup	(*60 mL*) oil
2¼ lbs	(*1 kg*) lean beef, diced
8 cups	(*2 L*) beef stock (see *Soups*)
2 cups	(*500 mL*) crushed tomatoes
1 tsp	(*5 mL*) Worcestershire sauce
1 tsp	(*5 mL*) salt
1 cup	(*250 mL*) sour cream
1	recipe gnocchi (see *Pasta*)

Heat the oil in a large pot. Add the beef and brown.

Pour in the stock and bring to boil. Reduce and simmer beef for 45 minutes.

Remove meat and reduce stock to 2 cups (*500 mL*).

Add the tomatoes and simmer, reducing total volume to 3 cups (*750 mL*).

Add the seasonings and sour cream; simmer, further reducing the sauce to 2½ cups (*625 mL*). Stir in the beef.

Cook gnocchi as instructed. Pour beef mixture over gnocchi. Serve.

Curried Lamb

Curried Lamb

8 servings

⅓ cup	(80 mL)	butter
2¼ lbs	(1 kg)	boneless lamb, cut into 2-in. (5 cm) strips
1		large onion, diced
2 cups	(500 mL)	diced celery
3 tbsp	(45 mL)	flour
1 cup	(250 mL)	tomato sauce
1 cup	(250 mL)	chicken broth
1 cup	(250 mL)	plain yogurt
1 tsp	(5 mL)	salt
2 tbsp	(30 mL)	curry powder

In a large skillet, heat the butter.

Add the lamb, onion and celery. Sauté for 5 minutes.

Sprinkle with flour and continue cooking for 3 minutes.

Add the tomato sauce, broth, yogurt and seasonings.

Reduce heat and simmer gently for 30 to 40 minutes, or until lamb is tender.

Serve with noodles or rice.

Kedgeree

6 servings

2 cups	(*500 mL*) cooked rice
4	hard-boiled eggs, chopped
1 lb	(*450 g*) salmon, cooked and flaked
2 tbsp	(*30 mL*) butter
½ cup	(*125 mL*) minced onions
¼ cup	(*60 mL*) minced celery
1 tbsp	(*15 mL*) flour
½ cup	(*125 mL*) heavy cream
¼ cup	(*60 mL*) chopped parsley
¼ tsp	(*1 mL*) salt
¼ tsp	(*1 mL*) pepper
½ tsp	(*3 mL*) curry powder
2 cups	(*500 mL*) grated Cheddar cheese

Preheat oven to 350°F (*180°C*).

In a mixing bowl, combine the rice, eggs and salmon.

Heat the butter in a saucepan. Add the onions and celery; sauté until tender. Add the flour and stir. Cook for 2 minutes without browning.

Add cream and seasonings. Cook until thickened. Stir into fish. Combine thoroughly.

Pour mixture into a greased casserole dish. Top with cheese.

Bake in oven 25 to 30 minutes. Serve.

Indian Omelette

1 serving

3	eggs
2 tbsp	(*30 mL*) heavy cream
2 tbsp	(*30 mL*) butter
3 tbsp	(*45 mL*) finely diced ham
3 tbsp	(*45 mL*) finely diced chicken
1 tbsp	(*15 mL*) finely diced green onions
¼ cup	(*60 mL*) curry sauce, hot (see *Sauces*)
2 tbsp	(*30 mL*) chopped tomatoes

Beat the eggs with the cream.

In a skillet, heat the butter. Add the ham, chicken and green onions. Sauté until the onions are tender.

Add the eggs. Cook until firm enough to turn over.

Flip over and cook for 1½ to 2 minutes. Fold in half. Place on serving plate.

Pour sauce over the omelette and sprinkle with tomatoes. Serve at once.

Indian Omelette

Chicken Cacciatore

6 servings

2¼ lb	(1 kg) fryer chicken, cut into 8 pieces
¼ cup	(60 mL) flour
½ cup	(125 mL) oil
1	small onion, finely diced
1	small green pepper, diced
2	garlic cloves, minced
½ tsp	(3 mL) oregano
½ tsp	(3 mL) thyme
1 tsp	(5 mL) salt
1 tsp	(5 mL) pepper
1 tsp	(5 mL) paprika
3½ cups	(875 mL) tomatoes, seeded and chopped
½ cup	(125 mL) red wine or sherry

Chicken Cacciatore

Dust the chicken with the flour. Brown in the oil on all sides.

Add the onion, green pepper and garlic. Sauté until tender.

Drain off the oil. Add the seasonings, tomatoes and wine.

Cover and simmer slowly for 45 to 50 minutes.

Serve with fresh Italian garlic bread.

Chicken Parmigiana

6 servings

6	boneless chicken breasts
2	eggs
¼ cup	(60 mL) milk
½ cup	(125 mL) flour
1 cup	(250 mL) fine breadcrumbs
3 tbsp	(45 mL) oil
3 tbsp	(45 mL) butter
1 cup	(250 mL) tomato sauce (see *Sauces*)
1 cup	(250 mL) grated mozzarella cheese

Pound the chicken into flat cutlets. Mix the eggs with the milk. Dust the cutlets in the flour, then dip in the egg mixture. Pat the cutlets in the breadcrumbs.

Sauté in the oil and butter 3 minutes each side.

Place on a greased pan, top with sauce and cheese and broil in oven until cheese melts.

Chicken Tetrazzini

6 servings

1 lb	(450 g) spaghetti
1	onion, finely diced
1 cup	(250 mL) diced celery
⅓ cup	(80 mL) diced green pepper
⅓ cup	(80 mL) diced red pepper
⅓ cup	(80 mL) diced yellow pepper
10 oz	(300 g) mushrooms, sliced
¼ cup	(60 mL) butter
¼ cup	(60 mL) flour
2 cups	(500 mL) light cream
2 cups	(500 mL) grated Havarti cheese
1 tsp	(5 mL) salt
½ tsp	(3 mL) pepper
1 tsp	(5 mL) basil
½ tsp	(3 mL) oregano
½ tsp	(3 mL) marjoram
3 cups	(750 mL) diced cooked chicken
¼ cup	(60 mL) sweet white wine
¾ cup	(180 mL) grated Parmesan cheese

Boil the spaghetti in a large pot until al dente. Drain and keep hot.

Sauté the onion, celery, peppers and mushrooms in butter until tender.

Stir in the flour and blend to smooth. Add cream and stir until thickened.

Add Havarti cheese, seasonings, chicken and wine; simmer for 8 minutes.

Pour spaghetti into a large casserole dish; top with sauce.

Sprinkle with Parmesan and brown quickly in the oven on broil.

Veal Parmigiana

6 servings

6	veal cutlets
2	eggs
¼ cup	(60 mL) milk
½ cup	(125 mL) flour
1 cup	(250 mL) fine breadcrumbs
3 tbsp	(45 mL) oil
3 tbsp	(45 mL) butter
1 cup	(250 mL) tomato sauce (see *Sauces*)
1 cup	(250 mL) grated mozzarella cheese

Pound the cutlets flat. Mix the eggs with the milk.

Dust cutlets with flour and dip in egg mixture. Pat the cutlets in the breadcrumbs.

Sauté cutlets in oil and butter 3 minutes each side.

Top with tomato sauce and cheese.

Broil in oven until cheese melts.

Italian Meatballs for Spaghetti

4 servings

¾ lb	(340 g) lean ground beef
¼ lb	(115 g) Italian sausage meat, minced
½ cup	(125 mL) breadcrumbs
½ cup	(125 mL) grated Parmesan cheese
1 tbsp	(15 mL) chopped parsley
2 tbsp	(30 mL) oil
2	garlic cloves, minced
½ cup	(125 mL) milk
1	egg, beaten
1 tsp	(5 mL) salt
¼ tsp	(1 mL) oregano
¼ tsp	(1 mL) thyme
¼ tsp	(1 mL) basil
½ tsp	(3 mL) pepper
½ tsp	(3 mL) paprika

Preheat oven to 375°F (190°C).

Mix together the beef with the sausage meat.

Blend in the breadcrumbs, Parmesan, parsley and oil.

Add all the remaining ingredients and combine well.

Roll into meatballs. Bake in oven for 12 minutes.

Serve with spaghetti and tomato sauce.

Veal Parmigiana

Guadalajara Special

6 servings

2 tbsp	(*30 mL*) butter
1	onion, finely diced
1	green pepper, finely diced
1 cup	(*250 mL*) chopped tomatoes
2 cups	(*500 mL*) tomato sauce (see *Sauces*)
1 tsp	(*5 mL*) salt
1 tsp	(*5 mL*) chili powder
¼ tsp	(*1 mL*) pepper
¼ tsp	(*1 mL*) paprika
2 cups	(*500 mL*) diced, cooked chicken
1 cup	(*250 mL*) shrimp meat
1 cup	(*250 mL*) crab meat
6	tortilla shells
2 cups	(*500 mL*) grated Cheddar cheese

Preheat oven to 350°F (*180°C*).

Heat the butter in skillet. Sauté the onion and green pepper.

Add the tomatoes, tomato sauce and seasonings.

Reduce heat to low and simmer for 15 minutes.

Wrap the chicken, shrimp and crab meat in the tortilla shells.

Place in a casserole dish. Pour the sauce over the tortillas.

Sprinkle with cheese. Bake for 12 minutes in oven.

Enchiladas

6 servings

1 lb	(*450 g*) lean ground beef
2 tbsp	(*30 mL*) oil
1	garlic clove, minced
1	medium onion, finely diced
1 tsp	(*5 mL*) salt
1 tsp	(*5 mL*) paprika
1 tsp	(*5 mL*) pepper
2 tsp	(*10 mL*) chili powder
6	tortillas
1 cup	(*250 mL*) sour cream
2 cups	(*500 mL*) sharp Cheddar, crumbled

Preheat oven to 350°F (*180°C*).

Sauté the ground beef in the oil. When half done, add garlic and onion. Sauté until tender.

Drain excess fat and add seasonings; stir. Divide filling evenly over tortillas.

Place about 2 tbsp (*30 mL*) of sour cream on meat.

Roll tortillas. Place folded edges down in a casserole dish.

Pour sauce over, sprinkle with cheese and bake for 20 minutes in oven.

Sauce

1	medium onion, finely diced
2	garlic cloves, minced
1	green pepper, finely diced
¼ cup	(*60 mL*) oil
1 cup	(*250 mL*) tomatoes, peeled and diced
1 cup	(*250 mL*) water
½ cup	(*125 mL*) tomato paste
1 tbsp	(*15 mL*) chili powder
1 tsp	(*5 mL*) salt
1 tsp	(*5 mL*) pepper
½ tsp	(*3 mL*) cayenne pepper
1 tsp	(*5 mL*) paprika
1 tsp	(*5 mL*) vinegar
½ tsp	(*3 mL*) oregano
½ tsp	(*3 mL*) thyme
2 tsp	(*10 mL*) brown sugar

Sauté the onion, garlic and green pepper in the oil until tender.

Add the tomatoes, water and tomato paste. Simmer for 3 minutes.

Reduce heat and add all remaining ingredients.

Simmer for 15 more minutes. Use as required.

Guacamole

1¼ cups (310 mL)

1	avocado, mashed
¼ cup	(60 mL) mayonnaise
1 tbsp	(15 mL) lemon juice
1 tsp	(5 mL) minced onion
½ tsp	(3 mL) salt
¼ tsp	(1 mL) garlic powder
¼ tsp	(1 mL) chili powder
¼ tsp	(1 mL) paprika

Blend together the avocado, mayonnaise, lemon juice and onion.

Mix in the seasonings.

Serve with chips, nachos, enchiladas, tacos or tortillas (see *Sandwiches*).

Guacamole

Irish Stew

6-8 servings

2¼ lbs	(1 kg) potatoes
2¼ lbs	(1 kg) boneless lamb, cut in 1½-in. (4 cm) cubes
2	large onions, sliced
2 tsp	(10 mL) salt
½ tsp	(3 mL) pepper
½ tsp	(3 mL) thyme
2	celery stalks, diced
2 tbsp	(30 mL) chopped parsley
4 cups	(1 L) chicken or beef stock (see *Soups*)

Preheat oven to 350°F (180°C).

Peel and quarter potatoes.

In a large Dutch oven, arrange the lamb, potatoes and onions in layers.

Sprinkle in the seasonings, celery and parsley. Pour in the stock.

Cover and bake in oven for 2½ hours. Serve at once.

Sushi Rice

about 2 cups (500 mL)

1 cup	(*250 mL*) water	
¾ cup	(*180 mL*) short grain rice	
1½ tbsp	(*22 mL*) vinegar	
1½ tbsp	(*22 mL*) lemon juice	
2 tbsp	(*30 mL*) sugar	
½ tsp	(*3 mL*) salt	

Bring water to a boil and add rice. Reduce heat. Cover and cook until rice absorbs all the liquid.

In a second saucepan, heat together the vinegar, lemon juice, sugar and salt.

Bring to a boil. Stir until sugar is completely dissolved.

Remove from heat. Stir liquid mixture into rice. Let stand until absorbed.

Sushi 1

8 slices

1	piece nori*, 7x8 in. (*18x20 cm*)	
1½ cups	(*375 mL*) sushi rice	
2 oz	(*60 g*) crab sticks	
2 oz	(*60 g*) baby shrimp	

Place nori on a slightly damp tea towel. Top with rice. Pack down firmly.

On one of the short ends, lay a strip of crab, then beside the crab, a shrimp.

Roll up jelly roll fashion. Using a very sharp knife, slice in 1-in. (*2,5 cm*) slices.

Serve with savory sauces of your choice.

Sushi 2

8 slices

1	piece nori	
1 cup	(*250 mL*) sushi rice	
3 oz	(*90 g*) smoked salmon, thinly sliced	
½ cup	(*125 mL*) apple butter, (see *Vegetables*)	
2 tsp	(*10 mL*) fresh mint	

Place nori on a damp tea towel. Pack rice onto nori.

About 1 in. (*2,5 cm*) from the short end, place a line of salmon.

Roll up jelly roll fashion. Slice with a very sharp knife.

Mix the apple butter with the mint. Serve separately as a sauce.

Sushi 3

8 slices

1	piece nori	
1½ cups	(*375 mL*) sushi rice	
4 oz	(*115 g*) ham, very thinly sliced	
4 oz	(*115 g*) lobster meat, minced	

Place nori on a damp towel. Pack a thin layer of rice on top. Lay across the rice a thin layer of ham.

Pack onto the ham another layer of rice. Top with lobster meat. Roll up jelly roll fashion.

Slice with a very sharp knife. Serve with your choice of savory sauces.

Nori is a toasted dried seaweed product available in most Asian food stores and the gourmet section of some supermarkets.

Sushi 1, Sushi 2 and Sushi 3

Shrimp Egg Foo Yong

2 servings

2 tbsp	(*30 mL*) oil
½ cup	(*125 mL*) shrimp meat
2 tbsp	(*30 mL*) minced onion
4	eggs, beaten

Sauce

¼ tsp	(*1 mL*) salt
¼ tsp	(*1 mL*) black pepper
3 tbsp	(*45 mL*) soya sauce
1 tsp	(*5 mL*) minced green onion
¼ tsp	(*1 mL*) garlic powder
pinch	ground ginger
2 tsp	(*10 mL*) brown sugar
1 tbsp	(*15 mL*) water

Heat oil in wok. Sauté the shrimp until pink. Remove.

Sauté onion until tender. Return shrimp to wok and stir in eggs. Fry.

Remove and serve with sauce.

To prepare sauce, combine all the ingredients and whisk together.

Shrimp Egg Foo Yong

Sandacz Na Winie

4 servings

1 cup	*(250 mL)* dry white wine
1	medium onion, chopped
1	carrot, chopped
1	celery stalk, chopped
4	perch filets, 8 oz *(225 g)* each
2 tbsp	*(30 mL)* butter
2 tbsp	*(30 mL)* flour
½ cup	*(125 mL)* fish stock (see *Soups*)
2 tsp	*(10 mL)* chopped parsley

Heat the wine in a saucepan with the vegetables.

Gently poach the filets in the wine for 5 to 6 minutes, depending on thickness of filets. Remove and keep hot.

Strain wine. Heat the butter in a saucepan.

Add the flour and cook for 1½ to 2 minutes.

Add the wine and fish stock. Simmer for 5 minutes or until thick. Pour over fish.

Sprinkle with parsley and serve.

Polish Sausage in Pastry

Polish Sausage in Pastry

8 slices

1	sheet frozen puff pastry, 7x8 in. *(18x20 cm)*
1 lb	*(450 g)* Polish sausage
1	egg, lightly beaten

Preheat oven to 425°F *(220°C)*.

Thaw the pastry. Remove casing from sausage. Wrap the sausage with the pastry. Brush with egg.

Bake in oven for 20 to 25 minutes, or until golden brown.

Remove, slice and serve with savory sauce of your choice.

Paella

8 servings

½ lb	(225 g)	clams
½ lb	(225 g)	mussels
½ cup	(125 mL)	oil
2¼ lb	(1 kg)	chicken, cut into 12 pieces
1		onion, minced
1		green pepper, minced
3		celery stalks, minced
2		garlic cloves, minced
½ tsp	(3 mL)	ground saffron
1 tsp	(5 mL)	thyme
1 tsp	(5 mL)	oregano
8 cups	(2 L)	chicken stock (see *Soups*)
2 cups	(500 mL)	crushed tomatoes
4 cups	(1 L)	long grain, converted rice
1 lb	(450 g)	crab, legs and claws cut
1 lb	(450 g)	shrimp, peeled and deveined
½ lb	(225 g)	diced ham
½ lb	(225 g)	peas

Preheat oven to 375°F (190°C).

Clean clams and mussels.

In a large pot, heat the oil. Sauté the chicken to brown.

Add the onion, green pepper, celery and garlic. Sauté until tender. Remove chicken. Drain excess oil.

Add the saffron, thyme and oregano. Cook 1 minute.

Add the chicken stock and tomatoes. Bring to a boil.

Place rice in a large casserole dish.

Top with chicken, clams, mussels, crab, shrimp, ham and peas.

Pour the stock over the mixture.

Bake in oven for 30 minutes or until rice is tender. Do not stir.

Remove from oven. Cover for 5 minutes. Serve.

Arroz con Pollo

6 servings

¼ cup	(60 mL)	flour
½ tsp	(3 mL)	oregano
½ tsp	(3 mL)	thyme
½ tsp	(3 mL)	basil
1 tsp	(5 mL)	salt
1 tsp	(5 mL)	pepper
2¼ lb	(1 kg)	fryer chicken, cut in 8 pieces
½ cup	(125 mL)	olive oil
1		green pepper, diced
1 cup	(250 mL)	diced onions
2 cups	(500 mL)	tomatoes, seeded and chopped
4 oz	(115 g)	mushrooms, sliced
1½ cups	(375 mL)	raw rice
4 cups	(1 L)	chicken stock (see *Soups*)
1 tbsp	(15 mL)	diced pimiento
1		garlic clove, minced
1		bay leaf
¼ tsp	(1 mL)	cayenne pepper
¼ tsp	(1 mL)	cracked black pepper
¼ tsp	(1 mL)	saffron
½ cup	(125 mL)	sherry
1 cup	(250 mL)	frozen green peas

Preheat oven to 350°F (180°C).

Season the flour with oregano, thyme, basil, salt and pepper.

Wash and dry the chicken. Dredge in the seasoned flour.

Heat the oil and brown the chicken on all sides. Place the chicken in a large casserole dish.

Sauté the green pepper and onions in the oil until tender.

Add the tomatoes, mushrooms, rice, stock, pimiento, seasonings and sherry.

Simmer for 3 minutes and pour over chicken.

Cover and bake for 55 to 60 minutes.

Add the peas and continue to bake for 15 more minutes.

Gravlax

Gravlax

8 servings

1½ lb	(675 g) fresh salmon
8 oz	(225 g) bunch fresh dill
½ cup	(125 mL) sugar
¼ cup	(60 mL) rock salt
1 tbsp	(15 mL) cracked black peppercorns
1 tbsp	(15 mL) cracked white peppercorns
1	lemon, sliced

Cut two fish filets very carefully from bones. Coarsely chop the dill.

Crush together the sugar, salt and peppercorns, using a mortar and pestle.

Lay one filet on a platter, skin side down. Coat with half the salt mixture.

Place the dill on top. Coat with the remaining salt mixture.

Lay top filet over salt-dill mixture. Wrap platter with plastic wrap.

Weigh with a brick and refrigerate for 3 days. (Every 12 hours unwrap and discard any liquid, rewrap and refrigerate).

Remove fish after refrigeration time. Scrape away marinade (salt-dill mixture). Lay filets skin side down.

Using a sharp knife, slice flesh across the grain very thinly. Slice away from skin.

Arrange on a serving platter and garnish with lemon slices.

Swedish Meatballs

6 servings

½ cup	(125 mL) fine breadcrumbs
¼ cup	(60 mL) heavy cream
1 lb	(450 g) ground veal
1	egg
1 tbsp	(15 mL) minced onion
¼ tsp	(1 mL) paprika
¼ tsp	(1 mL) onion powder
pinch	allspice
½ tsp	(3 mL) black pepper
¼ tsp	(1 mL) garlic powder
¼ cup	(60 mL) oil
¼ cup	(60 mL) beef stock (see *Soups*)
1 cup	(250 mL) sour cream (optional)

Soak the breadcrumbs in the cream; mix together with veal, egg and seasonings. Shape into small balls.

Heat the oil and brown meatballs. Drain oil. Add beef stock, cover and simmer 15 to 20 minutes.

Serve hot over noodles, with sour cream.

Russian Salmon Kulebyaka

10-12 servings

2 lbs	*(900 g)* salmon filets, skinless
2 tsp	*(10 mL)* salt
3 tbsp	*(45 mL)* chopped parsley
1/2 cup	*(125 mL)* butter
1	large onion, minced
3/4 cup	*(180 mL)* raw rice
2 cups	*(500 mL)* chicken stock (see *Soups*)
1/4 lb	*(115 g)* mushrooms, cooked and chopped
3	hard-boiled eggs, chopped
1/2 tsp	*(3 mL)* chervil
1/2 tsp	*(3 mL)* basil
3/4 cup	*(190 mL)* chicken velouté (see *Sauces*)
1	recipe brioche dough (see *Breads*)
1	egg yolk
2 tbsp	*(30 mL)* light cream

Cut salmon into 3/4-in. *(2 cm)* strips. Sprinkle with salt and 1 tbsp *(15 mL)* parsley. Chill.

Heat half the butter in a saucepan. Sauté 1/4 of the onions until tender.

Add the rice and swirl in the butter to glaze it.

Add the chicken stock and cook rice until tender. Cool.

In a second saucepan, heat the remaining butter and sauté the remaining onions; allow to cool.

Combine together the cooked rice, fried onions, remaining parsley, mushrooms, chopped eggs, seasonings and velouté.

Roll out half the brioche dough into a rectangle. Place 1/4 of the rice mixture on the pastry, leaving a 3/4-in. *(2 cm)* rim from each edge.

Top the rice with strips of salmon. Continue to make layers of rice, then salmon.

You should finish with 4 layers of rice and 3 layers of salmon.

Roll out the remaining brioche dough a little larger than the first.

Mix the egg yolk with the cream. Brush onto the edges of the dough stacked with rice/salmon. Place the second piece of dough on top. Press the edges firmly to seal.

Cut away any excess pastry.

Brush with egg mixture. Cut a hole in the center of the dough to allow steam to escape.

Decorate with excess dough. Brush with egg one final time.

Bake in a 400°F *(200°C)* oven for 45 minutes.

Remove and serve hot, warm or cold.

Borscht

10 servings

6	large beets
1/4 cup	*(60 mL)* butter
1 lb	*(450 g)* beef, diced
1	onion, minced
1/4	head cabbage, shredded
8 cups	*(2 L)* chicken stock (see *Soups*)
1 tsp	*(5 mL)* sugar
2 tsp	*(10 mL)* salt
1 tsp	*(5 mL)* pepper
1 1/2 cups	*(375 mL)* sour cream

Blanch the beets in boiling water for 5 minutes. Drain and remove the skins. Dice the beets.

Heat the butter in a large pot. Brown the beef. Add the onion and beets. Sauté for 5 minutes.

Add the cabbage and stock; simmer for 2 hours, or until beef is tender.

Add sugar, salt and pepper.

Serve with a tablespoon of sour cream per bowl.

Chicken Kiev

6 servings

½ cup	(*125 mL*) softened butter
2	garlic cloves, minced
2 tbsp	(*30 mL*) minced chives
2 tbsp	(*30 mL*) parsley flakes
6	boneless chicken breasts, 6 oz (*170 g*) each
¼ cup	(*60 mL*) flour
2	eggs, beaten
1 cup	(*250 mL*) fine breadcrumbs
3 cups	(*750 mL*) oil

Mix butter with garlic, chives and parsley flakes.

Wrap butter in wax paper and freeze for 2½ to 3 hours.

Preheat oven to 350°F (*180°C*).

Place chicken in plastic wrap and pound flat. Divide frozen butter into 6 even pieces.

Place one piece of butter on each breast. Fold to completely encase butter.

Dust with flour. Dip in egg. Roll in breadcrumbs.

Fry in hot oil until browned on all sides.

Bake in oven for 8 to 10 minutes.

1

Mix softened butter with garlic, chives and parsley flakes. Wrap in wax paper and freeze.

2

Place chicken in plastic wrap and pound flat.

3

Place one piece of butter on each chicken breast and fold to completely encase butter.

4

Fry breaded chicken in hot oil until browned and bake in oven 8 to 10 minutes.

Holubsti (Cabbage Rolls)

8-10 servings

1	large head cabbage
3 tbsp	(*45 mL*) oil
1	onion, minced
1	celery stalk, minced
1	carrot, minced
½ lb	(*225 g*) ground pork
½ lb	(*225 g*) lean ground beef
3 cups	(*750 mL*) cooked rice
½ tsp	(*3 mL*) basil
½ tsp	(*3 mL*) thyme
½ tsp	(*3 mL*) marjoram
1	egg
1½ cups	(*375 mL*) tomato juice
½ cup	(*125 mL*) sour cream

Preheat oven to 350°F (*180°C*).

Remove core from center of cabbage. Immerse in boiling water. Cook until leaves are soft.

Remove leaves without tearing. Remove ribs from center of leaves. Cut leaves into 2 to 3 sections.

Line the bottom of a large pan with a few leaves.

Heat the oil in a large skillet. Sauté the vegetables and the meats until cooked thoroughly. Cool.

Blend in the rice, herbs and egg.

Place 2 tbsp (*30 mL*) or more of mixture into leaves; fold over the ends and roll together.

Arrange rolls in layers over the leaves in the pan.

Whip the tomato juice together with sour cream and pour over the rolls. Cover with additional leaves.

Cover tightly with a lid or foil. Bake in oven for 1½ to 2 hours.

Fruit Varenyky

24 pieces

2 cups	(*500 mL*) flour
1 tsp	(*5 mL*) salt
1	egg
½ cup	(*125 mL*) cold water

In a mixing bowl, mix the flour with the salt. Add the egg and enough water to make a medium firm dough. Knead until smooth. Cover and rest the dough.

Cut into two. Roll very thin. Cut into 2½ to 3 in. (*6 cm*) squares. Brush with water.

Place 1 tsp (*5 mL*) of filling on each, or 1 pitted plum. Fold over. Seal the edges.

Cook by dropping into a pot of boiling water, a few at a time.

Cook 3 to 4 minutes. Serve with a fruit sauce.

Filling

24	plums
⅓ cup	(*80 mL*) sugar
1 tbsp	(*15 mL*) cinnamon

Stone the plums. Mix the sugar with cinnamon.

Stuff the pit holes with the sugar.

Baked Chicken Kasha

6-8 servings

1 cup	(*250 mL*) buckwheat groats
1	egg
2 tbsp	(*30 mL*) oil
2 cups	(*500 mL*) boiling water
¼ lb	(*115 g*) ham, diced
¼ lb	(*115 g*) mushrooms, sliced
1	medium onion, diced
1 tbsp	(*15 mL*) chopped parsley
1 tsp	(*5 mL*) marjoram
1 tsp	(*5 mL*) thyme
1 tsp	(*5 mL*) salt
½ tsp	(*3 mL*) pepper
4 lb	(*1,8 kg*) chicken

Preheat oven to 350°F (*180°C*).

Place groats in a shallow pan.

Blend in the egg. Bake in oven until lightly browned.

Place in a saucepan with the oil and water. Boil until most of liquid is absorbed.

Stir in the ham, mushrooms, onion and seasonings. Stuff into the chicken cavity.

Place chicken in a roasting pan and cook in oven about 1½ hours, basting often.

Baked Chicken Kasha

Vegetables

"Eat up your vegetables" is a constant refrain in many households. The sad truth is that the vegetables served in many homes and restaurants are not worth eating. Why is it that so many people treat vegetables as an after-thought, or boil the life out of them until they are nothing but mush?

Vegetables properly cooked are a pleasure to look at and a real delight to the taste buds. And really good cooks know that vegetables add more than vitamins and minerals to a meal. They are an important source of color and texture, adding infinitely to the overall aesthetic pleasure of the dining experience.

When you plan a meal, think of the vegetables as part of the "total package". Consider the following points :

Color : No matter how good the ingredients, no meal is interesting unless it has visual appeal. Since vegetables come in such a wide choice of colors, they are an easy way to liven up a boring plate.

Flavor : Always choose vegetables at their peak of freshness. New, small or "baby" vegetables have the finest flavor.

Shape : Select vegetables that will provide variation in shape. A plate of meatballs would look quite silly served with cherry tomatoes and small whole potatoes. Add variation by using different shapes — dice, sticks, ovals and rings.

Texture : Again, variety is the catchword. A meal in which everything is mashed or puréed is tedious. Texture adds excitement.

Tips For Cooking Vegetables

When boiling vegetables, use only enough salted water to cover them. Do not try to cook large quantities at a time.

If you use frozen vegetables, thaw them first, and cut down on the recommended cooking time.

Broccoli in Puff Pastry

Broccoli in Puff Pastry

8 servings

1½ cups	(*375 mL*) sliced mushrooms
2 tbsp	(*30 mL*) butter
2 cups	(*500 mL*) chopped broccoli
14 oz	(*398 g*) pkg. frozen puff pastry, thawed
1 cup	(*250 mL*) grated Swiss cheese
1	egg, beaten
2 tbsp	(*30 mL*) milk

Preheat oven to 425°F (*220°C*).

Sauté mushrooms in butter over high heat until tender, about 3 minutes; set aside.

Cook broccoli in boiling, salted water until almost tender; drain and set aside.

Roll puff pastry into a 16 x 8-in. (*40 x 20 cm*) rectangle.

Cut into eight 4-in. (*10 cm*) squares.

Place some of the mushrooms, broccoli, and cheese on each square.

Moisten the edges with water, and fold diagonally; pinch pastry edges to seal.

Combine egg and milk; brush over turnovers.

Bake in oven 12 to 15 minutes or until golden brown.

Asparagus Shrimp Béarnaise

4 servings

1	bunch asparagus
4 cups	(*1 L*) water
2 tsp	(*10 mL*) salt
1 cup	(*250 mL*) baby shrimp, minced
1 cup	(*250 mL*) Béarnaise Sauce (see *Sauces*)

Cook the asparagus in the water and salt until tender. Drain well.

Place on a heat-proof serving platter. Sprinkle with shrimp.

Pour sauce over asparagus.

Place under a broiler for 30 seconds. Serve.

Asparagus Casserole

8 servings

2¼ lbs	(*1 kg*) fresh asparagus, cut into 1-in. (*2,5 cm*) pieces
10 oz	(*284 mL*) can condensed cream of mushroom soup
2 cups	(*500 mL*) crushed plain crackers
½ cup	(*125 mL*) melted butter
2 cups	(*500 mL*) grated old Cheddar cheese
1 cup	(*250 mL*) cashews

Preheat oven to 350°F (*180°C*).

Cook asparagus in boiling, salted water, covered, until almost tender, about 3 to 5 minutes.

Drain, reserving 1¼ cups (*310 mL*) cooking liquid.

Combine mushroom soup with reserved cooking liquid; blend until smooth.

Combine crushed crackers, butter, and cheese; mix well.

Sprinkle half the crumb mixture into a 13 x 9 in. (*33 x 23 cm*) greased baking dish.

Top with half the asparagus, half the nuts, and half the mushroom soup mixture.

Repeat layers.

Bake in oven 30 to 40 minutes.

Artichokes au Gratin

6 servings

6	artichokes
2 cups	(*500 mL*) Mornay Sauce (see *Sauces*)
1 tsp	(*5 mL*) salt
¼ tsp	(*1 mL*) pepper
½ cup	(*125 mL*) grated Parmesan cheese
2 tbsp	(*30 mL*) butter

Preheat oven to 375°F (*190°C*).

Remove the outer leaves and bottoms of the artichokes.

Parboil in salted water until tender. Arrange in a casserole dish.

Pour sauce over artichokes. Season with salt and pepper. Sprinkle with cheese.

Dot with butter.

Bake in oven until cheese melts.

Asparagus Shrimp Béarnaise and Artichokes au Gratin

Green Beans Provençale

6 servings

1 lb	(450 g) green beans
3 tbsp	(45 mL) butter or oil
1	onion, finely diced
3	garlic cloves, minced
2 cups	(500 mL) tomatoes, seeded and chopped
1 tsp	(5 mL) salt
¼ tsp	(1 mL) pepper
1 tsp	(5 mL) thyme

Trim the beans. Cook in boiling, salted water for 10 minutes. Keep hot.

Heat the butter in a skillet. Add the onion and garlic. Sauté until tender.

Add the tomatoes and seasonings. Simmer for 5 minutes. Stir into beans.

Serve hot.

Barbecued Baked Beans

10 servings

1½ lbs	(675 g) navy beans
1½ cups	(375 mL) dark brown sugar
1 cup	(250 mL) molasses
4 cups	(1 L) tomato juice
¼ tsp	(1 mL) allspice
1½ tsp	(8 mL) dry mustard
1 tsp	(5 mL) salt
¼ tsp	(1 mL) pepper
1 tbsp	(15 mL) chili powder
1 tsp	(5 mL) paprika
2 tbsp	(30 mL) butter
1	onion, minced
4 oz	(115 g) bacon, diced

Soak the beans overnight in water, covering beans.

Drain and cover with fresh water. Bring to a boil and simmer until tender.

Preheat oven to 300°F (150°C).

Drain beans and rinse under cold water. Place in a mixing bowl.

Combine sugar, molasses, tomato juice and seasonings. Pour over beans and blend.

Heat the butter in a skillet and sauté the onion until tender. Stir into the beans with the bacon.

Pour into a large casserole dish. Cover and bake in oven for 3 hours. Uncover and bake an additional 30 minutes.

If beans become too dry while cooking, add a little water.

Serve hot or cold.

Green Beans Amandine

4 servings

1 lb	(450 g) green beans
¼ cup	(60 mL) butter
1½ cups	(375 mL) sliced almonds
2 tbsp	(30 mL) lemon juice

Trim the beans. Cook in boiling, salted water 8 to 10 minutes. Keep hot.

In a large skillet, heat the butter. Reduce heat. Add almonds and sauté until browned.

Add the lemon juice and beans. Sauté for 3 minutes.

Serve hot.

Broccoli Cake

0 servings

2 cups	(*500 mL*) broccoli, mostly stalks
4	eggs, beaten
½ cup	(*125 mL*) flour
½ tsp	(*3 mL*) baking powder
½ cup	(*125 mL*) milk
½ tsp	(*3 mL*) nutmeg
1 tsp	(*5 mL*) salt
½ tsp	(*3 mL*) pepper

Preheat oven to 350°F (*180°C*).

In a food processor, mince the broccoli. Add the eggs and blend.

Sift together the flour and baking powder. Blend in.

Slowly add the milk. Add the seasonings.

Pour into a well-greased loaf pan.

Bake in oven for 30 to 35 minutes.

Test for doneness.

French Beans Lyonnaise and Green Beans Amandine

French Beans Lyonnaise

4 servings

1 lb	(*450 g*) green beans
4 oz	(*115 g*) bacon, diced
2 tbsp	(*30 mL*) butter
1	onion, finely diced
¼ cup	(*60 mL*) finely diced pimiento
1 tsp	(*5 mL*) salt
¼ tsp	(*1 mL*) pepper

Trim the beans. Blanch the beans for 6 minutes in boiling water.

Fry the bacon in a skillet. Drain the grease.

Add the butter, onion and pimiento. Sauté until tender.

Add the beans. Fast fry for 3 minutes.

Season with salt and pepper. Serve.

Broccoli Surprise

Broccoli and Cauliflower in Orange Almond Sauce

8 servings

¾ lb	(*340 g*) broccoli florets
¾ lb	(*340 g*) cauliflower florets
2 tbsp	(*30 mL*) butter
2 tbsp	(*30 mL*) flour
1¼ cups	(*310 mL*) orange juice
¼ cup	(*60 mL*) brown sugar
⅓ cup	(*80 mL*) toasted slivered almonds

Cook the broccoli and cauliflower in boiling, salted water until tender.

Heat the butter in a saucepan. Stir in the flour and cook for 2 minutes.

Stir in the orange juice and sugar. Simmer until thick. Stir in the almonds.

Place vegetables in a serving bowl.

Pour sauce over vegetables and serve.

Broccoli Surprise

6 servings

2 cups	(*500 mL*) cooked broccoli
1½ cups	(*375 mL*) heavy cream
1 cup	(*250 mL*) grated Havarti cheese
4	eggs, beaten

Preheat oven to 350°F (*180°C*).

In a food processor, purée the broccoli. Add the cream and cheese. Process 30 seconds. Add the eggs; process another 30 seconds.

Generously grease a muffin tin. Pour mixture into muffin cups.

Place in a hot water bath and bake in over for 40 to 45 minutes.

Remove, turn out and serve.

Brussels Sprouts Paprika

6 servings

1½ lbs	(675 g) Brussels sprouts
4 cups	(1 L) chicken broth
¼ cup	(60 mL) butter
¼ cup	(60 mL) flour
1 cup	(250 mL) milk
1 tsp	(5 mL) salt
¼ tsp	(1 mL) white pepper
2 tsp	(10 mL) paprika

Wash and trim the Brussels sprouts.

Heat the chicken broth. Cook the sprouts in 3 cups (750 mL) chicken broth. Drain and keep hot.

Heat the butter in a saucepan. Stir in the flour. Cook for 2 minutes.

Stir in the remaining broth and the milk.

Add seasonings. Simmer until thick.

Pour over sprouts and serve.

Brussels Sprouts Bonne Femme

Brussels Sprouts Bonne Femme

4 servings

1 lb	(450 g) Brussels sprouts
4 oz	(115 g) bacon
1 tbsp	(15 mL) flour
1 cup	(250 mL) chicken broth
½ cup	(125 mL) finely diced onions

Trim the sprouts. Blanch 10 to 12 minutes in boiling, salted water.

Dice the bacon. Fry until tender. Drain all but 1 tbsp (15 mL) of grease.

Sprinkle with flour and cook 2 minutes. Add the broth, onions and the sprouts.

Reduce heat and simmer gently until thickened.

Serve hot.

Appled Brussels Sprouts

6 servings

1½ lbs	(*675 g*) Brussels sprouts
1 lb	(*450 g*) apples, cored, peeled and sliced
2 tbsp	(*30 mL*) lemon juice
8	slices bacon, diced
1	small onion, minced
2 cups	(*500 mL*) sour cream

Cook Brussels sprouts until tender. Soak apples in lemon juice to prevent discoloring.

Sauté the bacon, add the onion and cook until tender.

Drain the grease. Drain apples, add to pan and cook until tender.

Add the Brussels sprouts and sour cream.

Simmer five minutes. Serve.

Cauliflower with Shrimp Sauce

6 servings

1	head cauliflower
1 cup	(*250 mL*) Mornay Sauce (see *Sauces*)
½ lb	(*225 g*) baby shrimp
½ cup	(*125 mL*) sour cream
½ tsp	(*3 mL*) salt
¼ tsp	(*1 mL*) pepper
¼ cup	(*60 mL*) toasted slivered almonds
½ cup	(*125 mL*) fine breadcrumbs
4 oz	(*115 g*) Cheddar cheese, grated

Preheat oven to 350°F (*180°C*).

Separate the cauliflower. Blanch for 4 minutes. Drain and run under cold water until cool.

Grease a casserole dish. Mix the Mornay Sauce, shrimp, sour cream and seasonings together. Pour over cauliflower.

Sprinkle almonds on top, then breadcrumbs and cheese.

Bake 20 minutes in oven.

Corn Puffs

8 servings

3 cups	(*750 mL*) fresh corn kernels
3	egg yolks, beaten
¼ cup	(*60 mL*) flour
¾ tsp	(*4 mL*) salt
¼ tsp	(*1 mL*) pepper
½ tsp	(*3 mL*) baking powder
3	egg whites, stiffly beaten
4 cups	(*1 L*) oil

Mix the corn with the egg yolks and blend.

Sift together the flour, salt, pepper and baking powder, then sift into the corn.

Fold in the egg whites.

Heat oil over medium heat to about 350°F (*180°C*).

Drop in 1 tbsp (*15 mL*) size batter into hot oil.

Cook on one side. Turn over.

Remove when golden brown.

Cauliflower with Shrimp Sauce

Just Peachy Carrots

4 servings

1 lb	(*450 g*) frozen baby carrots
1½ cups	(*375 mL*) apple juice
3 tbsp	(*45 mL*) butter
2 tbsp	(*30 mL*) brown sugar
3	peaches, peeled and sliced

In a saucepan, cook the carrots in the apple juice until tender. Drain.

Heat the butter in a skillet. Add the brown sugar, stir until sugar melts.

Sauté the peach slices until tender. Add the carrots.

Toss only to glaze. Serve.

Baked Carrots and Apples

4 servings

6	carrots, thinly sliced
1	apple, peeled, cored and sliced
1 tsp	(*5 mL*) grated lemon rind
½ tbsp	(*8 mL*) softened butter
3 tbsp	(*45 mL*) water
	salt and pepper
½ cup	(*125 mL*) grated old Cheddar cheese

Preheat oven to 400°F (*200°C*).

Combine sliced carrots and apples with the lemon rind in a 3-cup (*750 mL*) greased baking dish.

Top with butter, drizzle with water, sprinkle with salt and pepper.

Cover and bake in oven for 20 to 25 minutes or until carrots are tender.

Remove cover, drain, and sprinkle with cheese.

Serve as soon as cheese melts.

Julienned Carrots with Cheddar Sauce

6 servings

1 lb	(*450 g*) carrots, cut in julienne
3 tbsp	(*45 mL*) butter
3 tbsp	(*45 mL*) flour
¾ cup	(*180 mL*) chicken broth
½ cup	(*125 mL*) heavy cream
1 cup	(*250 mL*) grated medium Cheddar
1 tsp	(*5 mL*) salt
¼ tsp	(*1 mL*) white pepper

Boil the carrots in salted water until tender.

Place in a serving bowl and keep hot.

Heat the butter in a saucepan. Stir in the flour. Cook for 2 minutes.

Add the broth and cream. Simmer 8 minutes.

Stir in the cheese and seasonings; simmer 4 more minutes.

Pour sauce over carrots. Serve hot.

Cashew Carrots

8 servings

8	medium carrots, cut in julienne
¾ cup	(*180 mL*) orange juice
¼ cup	(*60 mL*) melted butter
2 tsp	(*10 mL*) honey
½ tsp	(*3 mL*) salt
¼ tsp	(*1 mL*) white pepper
1 tbsp	(*15 mL*) lemon juice
¼ tsp	(*1 mL*) lemon zest
½ cup	(*125 mL*) cashews, coarsely chopped

Cook the carrots in the orange juice until tender. Drain.

Melt the butter in a skillet.

Add the honey, salt, pepper, lemon juice and lemon zest.

Add the carrots and toss to coat.

Add the cashews and serve.

Cashew Carrots

Ratatouille

8 servings

¼ cup	(*60 mL*) olive oil
2	onions, diced
2	garlic cloves, minced
2	medium eggplants, diced
3	zucchini, sliced
2	green peppers, sliced
3 cups	(*750 mL*) tomatoes, seeded and chopped
1 tsp	(*5 mL*) basil
1 tsp	(*5 mL*) chervil
1 tsp	(*5 mL*) salt
2 tsp	(*10 mL*) chopped parsley

Preheat oven to 350°F (*180°C*).

Heat the oil in a saucepan.

Add the vegetables, tomatoes and seasonings. Stir well.

Place in a casserole dish. Cover and bake in oven 40 to 45 minutes.

Serve either hot or cold.

1

In a saucepan, sauté the vegetables in the oil.

2

Add tomatoes and seasonings. Stir well.

3

Place mixture in a casserole dish and bake in oven 40 to 45 minutes.

4

Serve either hot or cold.

Eggplant and Shrimp au Gratin

4 servings

1	large eggplant, peeled
¼ cup	(*60 mL*) butter
2 cups	(*500 mL*) baby shrimp
2 cups	(*500 mL*) Mornay Sauce (see *Sauces*)
⅓ cup	(*80 mL*) grated Parmesan cheese
1 tsp	(*5 mL*) salt
¼ tsp	(*1 mL*) pepper
⅓ cup	(*80 mL*) fine breadcrumbs

Preheat oven to 350°F (*180°C*).

Slice the eggplant lengthwise.

Heat the butter in a skillet.

Sauté the eggplant in the butter. Arrange in a casserole dish. Top with shrimp. Cover with sauce.

Sprinkle with cheese, seasonings and breadcrumbs. Drizzle with melted butter from skillet.

Bake in oven for 30 minutes.

Baked Endives in Tomato Cream

Baked Endives in Tomato Cream

8 servings

8	endives
3 tbsp	(*45 mL*) butter
3 tbsp	(*45 mL*) flour
1 cup	(*250 mL*) light cream
1 cup	(*250 mL*) tomatoes, seeded and chopped
½ tsp	(*3 mL*) thyme
½ tsp	(*3 mL*) basil
½ tsp	(*3 mL*) chervil
¼ tsp	(*1 mL*) pepper
1 tsp	(*5 mL*) salt

Preheat oven to 350°F (*180°C*).

Blanch the endives in boiling salted water 4 to 5 minutes.

Place in a casserole dish.

Heat the butter in a saucepan.

Add the flour and cook for 2 minutes. Stir in the cream. Simmer until thick.

Add the tomatoes and seasonings. Simmer 3 minutes. Pour over endives.

Bake uncovered in oven for 35 minutes. Serve hot.

Kohlrabi in Sour Cream

6 servings

1½ lbs	(675 g) kohlrabi
¼ tsp	(1 mL) salt
½ tsp	(3 mL) basil
1 cup	(250 mL) sour cream

Peel and dice the kohlrabi.

Cook in boiling, salted water until tender.

Mash into a purée.

Stir in the seasonings and sour cream.

Serve hot.

Onion Rings

6 servings

2	large onions
2 cups	(500 mL) flour
2 tsp	(10 mL) baking powder
½ tsp	(3 mL) salt
¼ tsp	(1 mL) white pepper
1	egg
½ cup	(125 mL) milk
4 cups	(1 L) oil

Slice the onions into rings, ¼-in. (1 cm) thick.

Sift together 1 cup (250 mL) flour, baking powder and seasonings.

Beat the egg into the milk. Blend into the flour.

Dip the rings into the remaining flour, then into the batter.

Heat the oil to 360°F (183°C). Drop the rings into the oil.

Cook, browning all sides.

Remove and drain on paper towels. Serve hot.

Gourmet Peas

4 servings

8	slices bacon, diced
3 tbsp	(45 mL) minced onion
10 oz	(284 g) frozen peas
¼ cup	(60 mL) chicken broth
¼ cup	(60 mL) sour cream
¼ cup	(60 mL) grated Parmesan cheese

Sauté the bacon in a skillet, add the onion and sauté until tender.

Drain off excess fat. Add the peas and chicken broth.

Simmer until peas are tender but not mushy. Drain off liquid.

Add sour cream and Parmesan.

Stir until blended. Serve.

Stir-Fried Mushrooms and Peas

6 servings

3 tbsp	(*45 mL*) oil
8 oz	(*225 g*) snow peas
8 oz	(*225 g*) mushrooms, sliced
4 oz	(*115 g*) bamboo shoots
½ tsp	(*3 mL*) salt
2 tsp	(*10 mL*) curry powder
½ cup	(*125 mL*) chicken broth
1 tsp	(*5 mL*) cornstarch
1 tbsp	(*15 mL*) water

Heat the oil in a wok or skillet. Add the peas, mushrooms and bamboo shoots. Sauté for 3 minutes.

Add the salt and curry powder and cook for 1 more minute. Add the chicken broth.

Blend the cornstarch with the water.

Add to the vegetables. Cook for 1 minute.

Serve hot.

1

In a wok or skillet, sauté peas, mushrooms and bamboo shoots in oil for 3 minutes. Add salt and curry powder and cook 1 more minute.

2

Add the chicken broth.

3

Blend the cornstarch with the water and add to vegetables.

4

Cook 1 minute and serve hot.

Crab and Spinach Soufflé

8 servings

10 oz	(284 g) spinach
4	eggs, separated
2 tbsp	(30 mL) butter
2 tbsp	(30 mL) flour
⅓ cup	(80 mL) heavy cream
1 tsp	(5 mL) salt
¼ tsp	(1 mL) pepper
10 oz	(280 g) crab meat, cooked
⅓ cup	(80 mL) grated Parmesan cheese

Preheat oven to 375°F (190°C).

Steam and finely chop the spinach.

Whip the egg whites until stiff.

Heat the butter in a saucepan. Stir in the flour. Cook for 2 minutes.

Add the cream, seasonings, spinach and crab meat.

Remove from heat. Beat in the egg yolks and cheese.

Fold in the egg whites. Pour into a lightly greased soufflé dish.

Bake in oven 30 to 35 minutes.

Minted Peas

8 servings

4 cups	(1 L) peas, fresh or frozen
3 tbsp	(45 mL) butter
2 tsp	(10 mL) crushed mint
½ tsp	(3 mL) salt
¼ tsp	(1 mL) pepper

Cook the peas in boiling, salted water 3 to 5 minutes (shorten time for frozen). Drain.

Stir in the butter, mint, salt and pepper.

Serve.

Caraway Red Cabbage

6 servings

½	medium-size head red cabbage
½ cup	(125 mL) boiling water
1 tbsp	(15 mL) lemon juice
1 tbsp	(15 mL) butter
2 tbsp	(30 mL) brown sugar
½ cup	(125 mL) pineapple juice
1 tbsp	(15 mL) vinegar
1 tbsp	(15 mL) cornstarch
1 tsp	(5 mL) crushed caraway seeds

Shred the cabbage. Boil in the water and lemon juice for 12 minutes. Drain. Stir in the butter.

Dissolve the brown sugar in the pineapple juice and add the vinegar. Blend in the cornstarch.

Pour over the cabbage and cook until sauce thickens.

Stir in the caraway and serve.

Caraway Red Cabbage and Minted Peas

Zucchini Provençale

6 servings

3 tbsp	(*45 mL*) butter
3	zucchini, cut in julienne
2	garlic cloves, minced
1	onion, sliced
3 cups	(*750 mL*) tomatoes, seeded and chopped
1 tsp	(*5 mL*) salt
¼ tsp	(*1 mL*) pepper
1 tsp	(*5 mL*) chervil
½ tsp	(*3 mL*) basil
½ cup	(*125 mL*) sweet white wine

Heat the butter in a large skillet.

Sauté the zucchini, garlic and onion until tender.

Add the tomatoes, seasonings and wine. Reduce heat.

Simmer slowly until liquid is completely reduced.

Serve as a side dish, or over rice.

Zucchini Provençale

Cinnamon Spaghetti Squash

8 servings

1	spaghetti squash
¾ cup	(*180 mL*) brown sugar
1 tsp	(*5 mL*) ground cinnamon
¼ cup	(*60 mL*) butter

Bake the squash whole in a 350°F (*180°C*) oven for 1¼ hours.

With a fork, grate out pulp of squash. Place the squash in a lightly buttered casserole dish.

Sprinkle with sugar and cinnamon. Dot with butter.

Return to oven for 15 more minutes. Serve very hot.

Tomatoes Provençale

Tomatoes Provençale

4 servings

4	tomatoes
1 tbsp	(15 mL) olive oil
2 tbsp	(30 mL) butter
1	garlic clove, minced
2 tbsp	(30 mL) minced onion
¼ tsp	(1 mL) salt
¼ tsp	(1 mL) pepper
½ tsp	(3 mL) chervil
1 tbsp	(15 mL) chopped parsley
⅓ cup	(80 mL) grated Parmesan cheese

Slice the tomatoes in half. Seed and scoop out the pulp; reserve.

Heat the oil in a skillet. Place tomatoes, cut side into the oil.

Cook until the sides are caramelized. Remove and place on a pastry sheet.

Add the butter to the skillet. Add the garlic and onion. Sauté until tender.

Stir in the seasonings and tomato pulp.

Sauté for 1 minute. Fill the tomato cavities with mixture.

Sprinkle with cheese. Place under broiler until browned, about 2 minutes.

Serve hot or cold.

Almond Potato Fritters

6 servings

4	eggs
¼ cup	(*60 mL*) heavy cream
2 cups	(*500 mL*) mashed potatoes
½	recipe choux pastry (see *Desserts*)
1½ cups	(*375 mL*) ground almonds
4 cups	(*1 L*) oil

Blend 1 egg and the cream into the potatoes.

Thoroughly blend together the potatoes with the choux pastry.

Shape into small balls or croquettes.

Beat the remaining eggs. Dip fritters into egg. Roll in the almonds.

Heat the oil to 350°F (*180°C*).

Deep fry fritters until golden brown. Serve hot.

Parisienne Potatoes

Parisienne Potatoes

6 servings

6	medium potatoes
3 tbsp	(*45 mL*) butter
½ cup	(*125 mL*) demi-glace (see *Sauces*)
¼ tsp	(*1 mL*) thyme
¼ tsp	(*1 mL*) chervil
1 tbsp	(*15 mL*) chopped parsley
pinch	pepper

Pare the potatoes. Scoop out small balls with a melon scoop.

Parboil in boiling salted water for 5 minutes. Drain.

Heat the butter in a skillet.

Add the potatoes and brown.

Cover with the demi-glace and add the seasonings.

Simmer 5 minutes before serving.

Potato Broccoli Casserole

6 servings

1½ lbs	(675 g) potatoes
¼ cup	(60 mL) butter
3 tbsp	(45 mL) flour
2½ cups	(625 mL) milk
½ tsp	(3 mL) salt
¼ tsp	(1 mL) pepper
1 lb	(450 g) broccoli
½ cup	(125 mL) grated Parmesan cheese

Preheat oven to 350°F (180°C).

Wash and pare the potatoes. Cut into very thin slices.

Heat the butter in a saucepan. Sprinkle with flour, cook for 2 minutes.

Add the milk and seasonings. Simmer until boiling. Remove from heat.

In a large greased casserole dish, layer the potatoes, alternating with sauce and broccoli pieces.

Finish with a top layer of sauce. Sprinkle with Parmesan.

Bake, covered, for 15 minutes and continue to bake for an additional 5 minutes, uncovered.

Remove from oven. Cool for 5 minutes. Serve.

Potato Broccoli Casserole

Creamed Potatoes with Peas

4 servings

4	large potatoes
1½ cups	(*375 mL*) heavy cream
1 cup	(*250 mL*) peas, fresh or frozen
1 tsp	(*5 mL*) salt
¼ tsp	(*1 mL*) pepper

Pare and slice the potatoes. Parboil 10 minutes.

Bring the cream to a boil.

Place the potatoes in a saucepan. Add the peas and seasonings.

Pour in the cream and simmer until the cream is reduced by half.

Potatoes should thicken the cream.

Chantilly Potatoes

6 servings

1 cup	(*250 mL*) heavy cream
1 cup	(*250 mL*) grated Havarti cheese
2 tsp	(*10 mL*) salt
4 cups	(*1 L*) mashed potatoes, hot

Preheat oven to 400°F (*200°C*).

Whip the cream until stiff. Fold in the cheese and salt.

Place the mashed potatoes in a casserole dish.

Spread the cream over the potatoes.

Bake, uncovered, in oven 15 to 20 minutes, or until golden brown.

Maitre d'Hôtel Potatoes

4 servings

6	medium potatoes
2 cups	(*500 mL*) milk
½ tsp	(*3 mL*) salt
¼ tsp	(*1 mL*) white pepper
2 tbsp	(*30 mL*) chopped parsley
1 tsp	(*5 mL*) basil

Parboil the potatoes for 10 minutes in boiling, salted water. Drain.

Peel and slice the potatoes into ¼-in. (*1 cm*) thick slices. Place in a large saucepan.

Heat the milk to a boil. Pour over the potatoes.

Simmer, reducing the milk until the sauce thickens.

Sprinkle with seasonings.

Place in a serving bowl. Serve at once.

Chantilly Potatoes and Maître d'Hôtel Potatoes

Potatoes in Wine and Cream

4 servings

1 lb	(*450 g*) potatoes, pared and thinly sliced
2 tbsp	(*30 mL*) butter
1	onion, minced
½ cup	(*125 mL*) chicken broth
½ cup	(*125 mL*) heavy cream
½ cup	(*125 mL*) white wine
1 tsp	(*5 mL*) salt
½ tsp	(*3 mL*) pepper

Preheat oven to 375°F (*190°C*).

Arrange potatoes in a greased casserole dish.

Melt butter and sauté onion until tender. Spoon onto potatoes.

Mix the chicken broth, cream, wine, salt and pepper together. Pour onto potatoes.

Bake in oven 35 to 40 minutes. Serve.

Mojo Potatoes

6 servings

6	large potatoes
½ tsp	(*3 mL*) thyme
½ tsp	(*3 mL*) basil
½ tsp	(*3 mL*) oregano
1 tsp	(*5 mL*) salt
½ tsp	(*3 mL*) pepper
1½ tsp	(*8 mL*) paprika
¼ tsp	(*1 mL*) cayenne pepper
½ tsp	(*3 mL*) chili powder
1½ cups	(*375 mL*) flour
1	egg
⅓ cup	(*80 mL*) milk
¼ cup	(*60 mL*) oil

Preheat oven to 450°F (*230°C*).

Wash and brush the potatoes. Slice into wedges.

Mix the seasonings into the flour. Mix the egg with the milk.

Dip potato wedges into milk. Dust with seasoned flour. Place on a pastry sheet. Drizzle with oil.

Bake in oven 20 to 25 minutes, until browned and tender. Serve hot.

Soufflé Potatoes

8 servings

8	potatoes
8 cups	(*2 L*) oil

Place 4 cups (*1 L*) of oil in one pot. Heat to 325°F (*160°C*).

Place the remaining oil in a second pot and heat to 375°F (*190°C*).

Pare the potatoes. Slice ⅛-in. (*0,3 cm*) thick. Wash and dry the slices.

Fry a few potatoes in the lower temperature until they float to the top.

Plunge the potatoes at once into the hotter oil. This will induce the potatoes to puff up.

Fry to golden brown. Drain, season as you wish. Serve hot.

Mojo Potatoes

Potato Croquettes

6 servings

1 lb	(*450 g*) potatoes
2 tbsp	(*30 mL*) butter
4	eggs
¼ cup	(*60 mL*) heavy cream, heated
1 cup	(*250 mL*) flour
½ tsp	(*3 mL*) salt
½ tsp	(*3 mL*) pepper
½ tsp	(*3 mL*) paprika
½ tsp	(*3 mL*) thyme
½ tsp	(*3 mL*) chili powder
2 cups	(*500 mL*) fine breadcrumbs
4 cups	(*1 L*) oil

Pare and boil the potatoes. Mash and press through a sieve or process in a food processor until no longer lumpy.

Add the butter, 1 egg yolk and cream; blend until very smooth.

Divide into rounds. Cool. Shape into cigar shapes.

Mix the flour with the seasonings. Beat the remaining eggs.

Roll the potatoes in the flour, then dip in the eggs and roll in the breadcrumbs.

Heat the oil. Deep fry the croquettes until golden brown.

1

Add butter, 1 egg yolk and cream to the processed potatoes and blend until very smooth.

2

Divide into rounds and cool.

3

Shape into cigar shapes.

4

Deep fry breaded croquettes in heated oil until golden brown.

Chive Potato Pancakes

8 servings

Pancakes

2	eggs
3	medium potatoes, pared and shredded
2 tbsp	*(30 mL)* flour
⅓ cup	*(80 mL)* minced chives
¼ tsp	*(1 mL)* pepper
½ tsp	*(3 mL)* salt
	oil for frying

Sauce

2 cups	*(500 mL)* sour cream
1 cup	*(250 mL)* bacon, cooked and crumbled
½ cup	*(125 mL)* minced chives

In a mixing bowl, blend the eggs, potatoes and flour together.

Add the chives and seasonings. Combine well.

Heat a little oil in a large skillet. Drop the batter into the hot oil by tablespoons.

Fry each side crisp and brown. Serve with sauce.

To make sauce, blend the ingredients together well.

Chive Potato Pancakes

Potato Nests

6 servings

8	medium potatoes
4 cups	*(1 L)* oil

Pare and shred the potatoes. Place some of the potatoes in a small sieve or basket.

Press a second sieve or basket into the first, forcing the potatoes to hollow in the center.

Heat the oil to 375°F *(190°C)*.

Fry the potatoes in the baskets until golden brown.

Remove the smaller sieve. Turn out the remaining baskets or nests when cooked.

Fill with your choice of accompaniment to the main course.

Scalloped Potatoes au Gratin

6 servings

1½ lbs	(675 g) raw potatoes
2 tbsp	(30 mL) flour
3 tbsp	(45 mL) butter
½ tsp	(3 mL) salt
¼ tsp	(1 mL) pepper
1 cup	(250 mL) milk
1 cup	(250 mL) heavy cream
½ cup	(125 mL) grated Parmesan cheese

Preheat oven to 375°F (190°C).

Pare and slice the potatoes very thin.

Arrange in a casserole dish. Sprinkle the flour over the potatoes. Dot with butter.

Sprinkle on the seasonings. Pour milk and cream over potatoes. Sprinkle with cheese.

Bake in oven for 40 minutes or until potatoes are tender.

Marjoram Potatoes

6 servings

6	large potatoes, pared and diced
1½ cups	(375 mL) demi-glace (see *Sauces*)
1 tbsp	(15 mL) chopped marjoram

Parboil the potatoes.

In a skillet, heat the demi-glace. Add the potatoes and marjoram.

Simmer gently until most of the liquid has evaporated. Serve at once.

Lyonnaise Potatoes

4 servings

4	large potatoes
3 tbsp	(45 mL) butter
1	large onion, sliced
1 tsp	(5 mL) salt
½ tsp	(3 mL) pepper

Pare and dice the potatoes. Parboil the potatoes for 10 minutes.

Heat the butter in a large skillet. Brown both the onion and potatoes in the butter.

Season with the salt and pepper. Serve hot.

Pamela's Sweet Potato Marshmallow Croquettes

8 servings

8	medium yams
3	eggs
½ cup	(125 mL) light cream
2 tbsp	(30 mL) butter
3 tbsp	(45 mL) brown sugar
¼ tsp	(1 mL) cinnamon
16-20	large marshmallows
2 cups	(500 mL) fine breadcrumbs
4 cups	(1 L) oil

Pare, dice and boil the yams to a soft mash.

Stir in 1 egg, ¼ cup (60 mL) cream, the butter, sugar and cinnamon. Cool.

Shape the potatoes around the marshmallows.

Mix the eggs in the remaining cream. Dip the croquettes into cream, then dredge in breadcrumbs.

Heat the oil to 375°F (190°C).

Fry the croquettes until golden brown. Serve hot.

Timothy's Tummy Tickler

Timothy's Tummy Tickler

6 servings

½ cup (*125 mL*) sour cream

6	baked potatoes, chilled	Cut the potatoes in wedges and fry without crowding in ¾ in. (*2 cm*) hot oil, until golden.
	vegetable oil	
	seasoned salt	Place the potatoes on a baking sheet, sprinkle lightly with seasoned salt, the grated cheeses, and the crumbled bacon.
¾ cup	(*180 mL*) grated medium Cheddar cheese	
¾ cup	(*180 mL*) grated Havarti cheese	Place under the broiler until the cheese melts.
4	slices bacon, cooked and crumbled	Serve hot with sour cream on the side.

Potato Tomato Bake

8 servings

¼ lb	(*115 g*) bacon
2	garlic cloves, minced
1	onion, diced
2	celery stalks, diced
1	green pepper, diced
3 oz	(*90 g*) mushrooms, sliced
1½ lbs	(*675 g*) tomatoes, seeded and chopped
1 tsp	(*5 mL*) oregano
1 tsp	(*5 mL*) thyme
1 tsp	(*5 mL*) basil
1 tsp	(*5 mL*) salt
½ tsp	(*3 mL*) pepper
1½ lbs	(*675 g*) potatoes, pared and sliced
½ lb	(*225 g*) zucchini, sliced
2 cups	(*500 mL*) grated Havarti cheese

Preheat oven to 350°F (*180°C*).

Dice the bacon and sauté in a large skillet, with the garlic, onion, celery, green pepper and mushrooms. Drain excess grease.

Add the tomatoes and seasonings. Simmer for 10 minutes. In a large greased casserole dish, alternate layers of potatoes, sauce and zucchini, finishing with a layer of sauce.

Cover and bake in oven for 1 hour.

Uncover, sprinkle with cheese and bake an additional 10 minutes.

Potatoes Anna

6 servings

8	potatoes, pared
¼ tsp	(*1 mL*) salt
¼ tsp	(*1 mL*) pepper
⅔ cup	(*160 mL*) melted butter

Preheat oven to 400°F (*200°C*).

Slice the potatoes ¼-in. (*0,5 cm*) thick. Rinse in cold water.

Arrange the potatoes in layers in a round casserole dish. Season.

Pour the melted butter over the potatoes.

Bake in oven for 30 minutes.

Turn out onto a round serving platter. Serve hot.

Golden Mashed Potatoes

8 servings

8	medium potatoes
1 tbsp	(*15 mL*) minced onion
2 tbsp	(*30 mL*) butter
⅓ cup	(*80 mL*) heavy cream
⅓ cup	(*80 mL*) white wine
1½ cups	(*375 mL*) grated old Cheddar cheese
	salt and pepper

Peel and quarter potatoes. Cook in boiling, salted water until tender; drain and mash.

Sauté minced onion in butter over medium heat until tender.

Add to the mashed potatoes with cream and wine; beat until fluffy.

Stir in the cheese, season to taste and serve immediately.

Twice Baked Herb Potatoes

8 servings

8	baked potatoes, hot
3 tbsp	(*45 mL*) butter
3 tbsp	(*45 mL*) sour cream
½ tsp	(*3 mL*) dried thyme leaves
¼ tsp	(*1 mL*) dried chervil
1 tsp	(*5 mL*) chopped chives
	salt and pepper
1 cup	(*250 mL*) grated Swiss cheese
½ tsp	(*3 mL*) paprika

Preheat oven to 450°F (*230°C*).

Cut tops off potatoes and scoop out the centers; mash.

Stir butter, sour cream, herbs, and seasonings into mashed potatoes.

Re-stuff the potatoes, sprinkle with cheese and paprika and bake in oven until heated through and cheese is melted.

Twice Baked Blue Cheese Potatoes

6 servings

6	baked potatoes, hot
¾ cup	(*180 mL*) crumbled blue cheese
¼ cup	(*60 mL*) milk
2 tbsp	(*30 mL*) butter

Preheat oven to 450°F (*230°C*).

Cut tops off potatoes and scoop out the centers; mash.

Stir blue cheese, milk, and butter into mashed potatoes.

Re-stuff the potatoes and bake in oven until heated through and golden brown.

Twice Baked Blue Cheese Potatoes

Bread and Butter Pickles

12 cups (3 L)

2¼ lbs	(1 kg) cucumbers
3 tbsp	(45 mL) salt
4 cups	(1 L) vinegar
3 cups	(750 mL) sugar
2 tsp	(10 mL) celery seeds
2 tsp	(10 mL) mustard seeds
1 tsp	(5 mL) mace
1 tsp	(5 mL) ginger
1 tsp	(5 mL) turmeric

Slice the cucumbers. Sprinkle with salt. Marinate 1 hour.

Drain well through cheesecloth.

Boil together the vinegar, sugar and seasonings for 10 minutes.

Pack sliced cucumbers in sterilized jars. Pour brine over. Seal.

Place in a 170°F (77°C) water bath for 15 minutes.

Dill Pickles

16 cups (4 L)

40	pickling cucumbers
7 cups	(1,7 L) water
2 cups	(500 mL) vinegar
½ cup	(125 mL) non-iodized salt
6	dill sprigs
12	garlic cloves
6 tbsp	(90 mL) pickling spice
6	onions, sliced thick

Wash and scrub the cucumbers carefully. Remove the blossom end of pickle.

Mix water, vinegar and salt in a large pot. Boil.

Place 1 dill sprig, 2 garlic cloves, 1 tbsp (15 mL) pickling spice, 1 onion slice in jars.

Pack with cucumbers. Cover with hot brine, filling jars to within ½ in. (1,2 cm) from top. Seal.

Immerse jars in boiling water for 10 minutes.

Pickled Beets

12 cups (3 L)

5 lbs	(2,2 kg) beets
2 tbsp	(30 mL) pickling spice
2 tsp	(10 mL) dry mustard
2½ cups	(625 mL) vinegar
½ cup	(125 mL) lemon juice
2 tbsp	(30 mL) salt
1 cup	(250 mL) sugar
8	thick slices onion

Cook the beets in boiling water until tender. Remove the skins.

Mix the pickling spice, mustard, vinegar, lemon juice, salt and sugar. Bring to a boil. Boil 5 minutes.

Remove from heat and allow to cool. Slice beets.

Place 1 onion slice in each sterilized jar. Pack with beets.

Pour brine over beets, filling jars to within ½ in. (1,2 cm) from top. Seal.

Leave set for 30 days before using.

Pickled Mushrooms

12 cups (3 L)

2¼ lbs	(*1 kg*) very small button mushrooms
2	onions, diced
3 cups	(*750 mL*) vinegar
3	garlic cloves, minced
1 tbsp	(*15 mL*) salt
2 tbsp	(*30 mL*) oregano

Sterilize jars.

Wash, peel and destem the mushrooms. Pack in jars.

Place a little onion in each jar.

Boil the vinegar, garlic, salt and oregano together for 5 minutes.

Pour onto mushrooms, filling jars to within ½ in. (*1,2 cm*) from top. Seal.

Leave set for 30 days before using.

Pickled Beets, Pickled Mushrooms (and marinated mixed vegetables)

Tomato Ketchup

4 cups (1 L)

3 lbs	(1,4 kg) tomatoes
½ tsp	(3 mL) ginger
½ tsp	(3 mL) allspice
½ tsp	(3 mL) mace
½ tsp	(3 mL) cinnamon
½ tsp	(3 mL) cloves
1 tsp	(5 mL) pepper
¼ tsp	(1 mL) cayenne pepper
1 tbsp	(15 mL) salt
1 cup	(250 mL) vinegar
⅔ cup	(160 mL) brown sugar

Wash, chop and cook the tomatoes for 10 minutes. Press through a sieve.

Dissolve the seasonings in the vinegar.

Add to the tomatoes. Blend in the sugar. Bring to a boil; reduce to a simmer.

Simmer for 1 to 1½ hours, until very thick.

Pour into hot, sterilized jars. Seal.

Place jars in a 170°F (77°C) water bath for 30 minutes.

Chili Sauce

12 cups (3 L)

8 cups	(2 L) tomatoes, peeled and chopped
1 cup	(250 mL) minced onions
1½ cups	(375 mL) minced green peppers
2	garlic cloves, minced
1 tsp	(5 mL) dry mustard
¼ cup	(60 mL) salt
¼ tsp	(1 mL) ground cloves
½ tsp	(3 mL) allspice
1 tsp	(5 mL) basil
1 tsp	(5 mL) cinnamon
1 cup	(250 mL) vinegar
1 cup	(250 mL) brown sugar

In a large saucepan, combine the tomatoes, onions, green peppers and garlic together.

Dissolve the seasonings in the vinegar. Add to tomatoes. Blend in the sugar.

Bring to a boil; reduce to a simmer. Simmer until thick.

Pour in sterilized jars. Seal.

Place in a 170°F (77°C) water bath for 30 minutes.

Sweet Relish

6 cups (1,5 L)

2	large cucumbers, finely diced
2	onions, minced
2 tbsp	(30 mL) salt
2	apples, pared, cored and diced
1 tsp	(5 mL) mustard seeds
1 tsp	(5 mL) celery seeds
1 cup	(250 mL) sugar
2 cups	(500 mL) vinegar

Mix the cucumbers and onions in a bowl. Sprinkle with salt.

Marinate for 2 hours. Drain well.

Blend in the apples.

In a saucepan, dissolve the seasonings and sugar in the vinegar. Boil.

Reduce to a simmer for 3 minutes.

Pack cucumber mix into sterilized jars. Pour in vinegar. Seal.

Place in a 180°F (82°C) water bath for 15 minutes.

Leave set for 4 weeks before using.

Spiced Crab Apples

16 cups (4 L)

5 lbs	(2,2 kg) crab apples
5 cups	(1,2 L) sugar
3 cups	(750 mL) vinegar
2 cups	(500 mL) water
1 tsp	(5 mL) salt
¾ tsp	(4 mL) allspice
¾ tsp	(4 mL) whole cloves
¼ tsp	(1 mL) ginger
¼ tsp	(1 mL) mace
1 tbsp	(15 mL) cinnamon
5	drops red food coloring

Wash the apples. Remove the blossom ends. Pierce center of apples with a wooden skewer.

Mix the sugar, vinegar, water and seasonings in a saucepan.

Cook the apples in small batches, 7 minutes each batch. Place in sterilized jars.

Add the food coloring to the syrup. Pour over the apples. Seal.

Place in a 170°F (77°C) water bath for 20 minutes.

Apple Butter

Apple Butter

4 cups (1 L)

4 cups	(1 L) apple juice
4 cups	(1 L) apples, pared, cored and diced
¾ cup	(180 mL) sugar
½ tsp	(3 mL) ground cinnamon
¼ tsp	(1 mL) ground cloves
¼ tsp	(1 mL) ground ginger

Heat the apple juice in a pot. Reduce to 2 cups (500 mL).

Add apples. Heat to boiling, reduce heat, simmer for 30 minutes or until apples are very tender.

Press through a sieve or process in a food processor until smooth.

Place with remaining ingredients in a saucepan. Heat to boiling. Reduce heat; simmer for about 1 hour, or until thick.

Pour into sterilized jars. Seal.

Pasta

There's much more to pasta than spaghetti with tomato sauce. In fact, pasta has been around a lot longer than the tomato, which Europeans only discovered during one of their 16th century forays to South America. Legend has it that Marco Polo brought pasta back from the Orient, but chances are, it was around even before that.

You'll find a wide choice of pasta recipes in this chapter, but few of them involve tomatoes. Pasta seems to pair up wonderfully with almost everything — meat, seafood, vegetables, any number of cheeses. I hope you'll experiment and find some new favorites.

Once you get used to preparing different types of pasta dishes, you'll find that you will be able to improvise with ingredients you have on hand and create new recipes of your very own.

You might even want to try making your own pasta. I've included a basic recipe for pasta dough. Once you master it, you can vary it by adding fresh herbs, spinach or tomato purée to make colored pastas.

Once you have rolled out your homemade pasta dough, you can cut it to the desired shape. It's easy to make your own lasagne or fettucine noodles and you can even make your own ravioli.

But you can also buy many good brands of commercially-made pasta in wonderful and exotic shapes, with names to match. Don't be afraid to experiment.

Fettuccine Primavera

Fettuccine Primavera

8 servings

¼ lb	(*115 g*) broccoli florets
¼ lb	(*115 g*) cauliflower florets
¼ cup	(*60 mL*) butter
1	small onion, finely diced
1	small carrot, finely diced
3 oz	(*90 g*) mushrooms, sliced
¼ cup	(*60 mL*) flour
3 cups	(*750 mL*) light cream
2 tbsp	(*30 mL*) pimiento, finely diced
½ cup	(*125 mL*) grated Parmesan cheese
1 tsp	(*5 mL*) cracked black pepper
1 lb	(*450 g*) fettuccine

Blanch the broccoli and cauliflower in boiling water. Drain and set aside.

Heat the butter in a saucepan; sauté the onion, carrot and mushrooms until tender.

Add the flour and stir. Cook for 2 minutes. Add the cream, broccoli and cauliflower.

Reduce to a simmer. Simmer 15 minutes.

Add the pimiento, Parmesan and pepper.

Cook the noodles al dente in a pot of boiling, salted water. Drain.

Place noodles in a large serving bowl. Pour sauce over and serve.

Basic Pasta Dough

8 servings

4 cups	(1 L)	flour
½ tsp	(3 mL)	salt
4		eggs
⅓ cup	(80 mL)	cold water

Sift the flour and salt together. Place in a mixing bowl. Mix on slow speed.

Add one egg at a time. Blend slightly after each addition.

Slowly add the water until a stiff dough is formed. Knead the dough for 10 minutes. Divide into 3 parts.

Wrap the dough in a damp cloth and allow it to rest for at least 30 minutes.*

To roll, use a lightly flour-dusted surface and rolling pin.

Roll the ball away from you, turning it one quarter of the way at a time and repeat rolling.

Roll out the dough to ⅛-in. (0,3 cm) thickness.

The dough is now ready for cutting or stuffing according to the recipe you are following.

The dough can be frozen at this point. Defrost dough in refrigerator overnight, then remove it to room temperature for 1 hour before using.

Pasta Topped with Cheese-Stuffed Tomatoes

6 servings

½ lb	(225 g)	penne noodles
6		tomatoes
1 tsp	(5 mL)	basil
½ tsp	(3 mL)	chervil
½ tsp	(3 mL)	oregano
¼ tsp	(1 mL)	pepper
½ tsp	(3 mL)	salt
¼ lb	(115 g)	grated mozzarella cheese
¼ lb	(115 g)	grated Cheddar cheese
½ cup	(125 mL)	grated Parmesan cheese
3 oz	(90 g)	butter

Preheat oven to 350°F (180°C).

Cook the noodles al dente in a large pot of boiling, salted water. Drain.

Plunge the tomatoes in boiling water for 1 minute. Remove and skin the tomatoes. Cut the tops from the tomatoes.

Carefully scoop out the centers and discard. Sprinkle centers with seasonings and pack with mozzarella and Cheddar.

Bake in oven until tomatoes are soft and cheese melts.

Place noodles on a large greased platter.

Top with the tomatoes. Sprinkle with Parmesan and dot with butter.

Return to oven for 5 minutes. Serve.

Pasta Ragu

8 cups (2 L)

½ lb	(225 g)	ground beef
½ lb	(225 g)	ground veal
¼ lb	(115 g)	ground bacon
1		onion, minced
1		carrot, minced
4 oz	(115 g)	mushrooms, sliced
1		garlic clove, minced
1		bouquet garni
1 tsp	(5 mL)	salt
4 cups	(1 L)	tomato purée
1½ cups	(375 mL)	water

Brown the beef, veal and bacon together.

Add the vegetables and sauté until tender.

Add the garlic, bouquet garni, salt, tomato purée and water.

Reduce heat to low and simmer for 2 hours, skimming off any fat that rises to the top.

Serve over your choice of cooked pasta.

Pasta Topped with Cheese-Stuffed Tomatoes

Fettuccine My Way

8 servings

1 lb	(450 g) fettuccine
1 lb	(450 g) large shrimp, sliced in halves
2	small onions, diced
½ cup	(125 mL) sliced mushrooms
1	green pepper, diced
¼ cup	(60 mL) olive oil
¼ cup	(60 mL) chopped, seeded tomatoes
2 tbsp	(30 mL) sliced black olives
1 cup	(250 mL) heavy cream
½ cup	(125 mL) grated Parmesan cheese
2 tsp	(10 mL) black pepper

In a large pot, cook the fettuccine in salted, boiling water until al dente.

Sauté the shrimp, onions, mushrooms and green pepper in the oil until tender. Add the tomatoes and olives and toss to heat.

Stir in the cream, cheese and pepper. Simmer until thick.

Toss the noodles with the sauce and serve at once.

Fettuccine Niagara

Fettuccine Niagara

8 servings

1 lb	(450 g) fettuccine
3 tbsp	(45 mL) butter
1 cup	(250 mL) diced apples
3 tbsp	(45 mL) flour
2 cups	(500 mL) heavy cream
¼ cup	(60 mL) white wine (very sweet)
1 cup	(250 mL) baby shrimp
1 cup	(250 mL) diced peaches or apricots

In a large pot, cook the fettuccine in boiling, salted water until al dente.

In a saucepan, heat the butter. Sauté the apples until tender.

Add the flour and stir into a paste (roux). Add the cream and wine. Simmer for 5 minutes. Add the shrimp and peaches.

Pour sauce over pasta. Serve at once.

Fettuccine with Scallops and Sherry

8 servings

1 lb	(*450 g*) fettuccine
1 lb	(*450 g*) baby scallops
1	onion, minced
1 cup	(*250 mL*) sliced mushrooms
½ cup	(*125 mL*) butter
2 cups	(*500 mL*) Béchamel Sauce (see *Sauces*)
½ cup	(*125 mL*) sherry
1	egg yolk, beaten
½ cup	(*125 mL*) fresh chopped parsley

Cook fettuccine al dente in a large pot of boiling, salted water.

Sauté the scallops, onion and mushrooms in the butter.

Add the Béchamel and sherry. Whisk in the egg yolk and simmer for 5 minutes.

Place noodles on plates and top with sauce. Garnish with parsley.

Fettuccine with Scallops and Sherry

Fettuccine with Smoked Chicken

8 servings

1	small onion, minced
½ lb	(*225 g*) boneless smoked chicken, diced
3 tbsp	(*45 mL*) olive oil
1½ cups	(*375 mL*) tomatoes, seeded and puréed
8 oz	(*250 g*) mascarpone (cream cheese)
pinch	sweet basil
1 lb	(*450 g*) cooked fettuccine noodles

Sauté the onion and chicken in the oil, add tomatoes and simmer until most of moisture has evaporated.

Sprinkle in mascarpone and basil.

Pour sauce over noodles and serve.

Cannelloni

8 servings

½	recipe basic pasta dough
¾ cup	(*180 mL*) grated Parmesan cheese
1 cup	(*250 mL*) ricotta cheese
½ cup	(*125 mL*) grated mozzarella cheese
½ cup	(*125 mL*) grated white Cheddar
8 oz	(*225 g*) butter
1 tbsp	(*15 mL*) chopped parsley
1 tsp	(*5 mL*) basil
1 tsp	(*5 mL*) thyme
1 tsp	(*5 mL*) oregano
1 tsp	(*5 mL*) salt
2	eggs
½ cup	(*125 mL*) breadcrumbs
⅓ cup	(*80 mL*) flour
2 cups	(*500 mL*) heavy cream
2 cups	(*500 mL*) chicken stock (see *Soups*)

Preheat oven to 350°F (*180°C*).

Roll out dough as instructed in basic pasta dough recipe. Cut into 4 x 6-in. (*10 x 15 cm*) rectangles.

Cook in boiling water for 1 minute. Remove and place on a cloth.

Blend together the cheeses, half the butter, seasonings, eggs and breadcrumbs thoroughly.

Place the filling evenly over pasta sheets. Roll and seal ends and bottom edge.

Place in a large greased casserole dish.

Melt the remaining butter in a saucepan. Stir in the flour and blend. Cook 2 minutes. Do not brown.

Add the cream and stock. Simmer until sauce thickens.

Pour sauce over pasta and bake for 30 minutes or until browned.

Fusilli with Cheese and Tomatoes

8 servings

¼ cup	(*60 mL*) olive oil
¾ lb	(*340 g*) tomatoes, seeded and chopped
2 tsp	(*10 mL*) oregano
1 tsp	(*5 mL*) chervil
1 tsp	(*5 mL*) thyme
1 tsp	(*5 mL*) salt
¼ tsp	(*1 mL*) pepper
1 lb	(*450 g*) fusilli
¼ cup	(*60 mL*) grated Romano cheese
½ lb	(*225 g*) grated mozzarella cheese

Heat the oil, add the tomatoes and cook, mashing into a purée with the seasonings.

Cook the noodles al dente in a pot of boiling, salted water. Drain.

Blend the hot noodles into the hot sauce. Stir in the cheeses and serve.

Gnocchi

6 servings

3	medium potatoes, mashed
1 cup	(*250 mL*) flour
1	egg
1 tsp	(*5 mL*) salt
¼ tsp	(*1 mL*) pepper

Place the hot mashed potatoes in a mixing bowl. Blend in the flour a little at a time.

Add the egg, salt and pepper. Beat until smooth.

Knead into a smooth, soft ball.

If dough is sticky, a little more flour can be added. Roll out the dough into long oblong shapes. Cut into ¾-in. (*2 cm*) pieces. With a floured fork, press each piece firmly.

Cook immediately or freeze, if desired.

To cook, boil water and a little salt. Drop gnocchi in a few at a time.

Cook five minutes, remove and serve with sauce of your choice such as Alfredo, Mornay, tomato or Bolognese.

Fusilli, Prosciutto and Mustard Sauce

Fusilli, Prosciutto and Mustard Sauce

8 servings

1 lb	*(450 g)* fusilli
¼ cup	*(60 mL)* olive oil
2 cups	*(500 mL)* tomato purée
1½ tsp	*(8 mL)* dry mustard
1 cup	*(250 mL)* light cream
1 lb	*(450 g)* prosciutto
½ cup	*(125 mL)* grated Parmesan cheese

Cook the noodles al dente in a pot of boiling, salted water.

Heat the oil in a saucepan. Add the tomatoes and mustard; simmer until very thick.

Add the cream and chopped prosciutto. Simmer for 8 minutes.

Pour over noodles. Sprinkle with Parmesan and serve.

Lasagne Seafood Rolls

8 servings

1 lb	(*450 g*) lasagne noodles
1 cup	(*250 mL*) baby shrimp
1 cup	(*250 mL*) cooked, flaked salmon
¾ cup	(*180 mL*) grated Parmesan cheese
2	eggs
1 cup	(*250 mL*) ricotta cheese
½ cup	(*125 mL*) breadcrumbs
⅓ cup	(*80 mL*) butter
⅓ cup	(*80 mL*) flour
1 cup	(*250 mL*) light cream
1 cup	(*250 mL*) chicken stock (see *Soups*)
1 cup	(*250 mL*) grated Romano cheese

Preheat oven to 350°F (*180°C*).

Cook the noodles in a large pot until al dente. Rinse under cold water and drain.

Mix the shrimp, salmon, Parmesan, eggs, ricotta and breadcrumbs together.

Lay the noodles flat. Top with filling. Roll up end to end like a jelly roll. Place in a greased casserole dish.

Heat the butter in a saucepan. Add the flour and stir into a roux (paste). Do not brown. Cook 2 minutes.

Add the cream and chicken stock. Simmer until thickened. Pour over noodles. Sprinkle with Romano.

Bake in oven for 30 minutes or until browned.

Cheese Lasagne Verdi

6 servings

1 lb	(*450 g*) green lasagne noodles
¼ cup	(*60 mL*) butter
¾ lb	(*340 g*) ricotta cheese
4	eggs
½ cup	(*125 mL*) breadcrumbs
½ lb	(*225 g*) grated mozzarella cheese
½ lb	(*225 g*) grated medium Cheddar
1 tsp	(*5 mL*) chervil
1 tsp	(*5 mL*) basil
1 tsp	(*5 mL*) salt
2 cups	(*500 mL*) tomato sauce (see *Sauces*)
1 cup	(*250 mL*) tomato sauce, heated

Preheat oven to 400°F (*200°C*).

Cook the noodles al dente in a large pot of boiling water. Rinse under cold water. Drain.

In a food processor, blend together the butter, ricotta, eggs and breadcrumbs.

Remove and mix in the mozzarella, Cheddar and seasonings.

Grease a large casserole dish. Lay a layer of noodles on the bottom.

Cover with a thin layer of tomato sauce. Top with cheese mixture.

Repeat until all fillings are used, finishing with a layer of cheese mixture.

Bake in oven for 30 minutes or until browned.

Remove and serve with 3 tbsp (*45 mL*) of heated tomato sauce poured over each portion.

Macaroni with Gruyère and Parmesan

8 servings

1 lb	(*450 g*) elbow macaroni
2 tbsp	(*30 mL*) butter
1 cup	(*250 mL*) grated Gruyère cheese
1 cup	(*250 mL*) grated Parmesan cheese
¼ cup	(*60 mL*) heavy cream
1 tsp	(*5 mL*) salt
½ tsp	(*3 mL*) white pepper

Cook the macaroni al dente in a pot of boiling, salted water. Drain.

While macaroni is still hot, stir in the butter, cheeses, cream and seasonings.

Combine well. Serve.

My Lasagne

10 servings

Sauce

2¼ lbs	(*1 kg*) ground beef
1 lb	(*450 g*) Italian sausage, diced
3	onions, finely diced
1	green pepper, finely diced
4 oz	(*115 g*) mushrooms, sliced
2	celery stalks, finely diced
2 tbsp	(*30 mL*) olive oil
2 cups	(*500 mL*) tomatoes, seeded and chopped
½ cup	(*125 mL*) tomato paste
2 tsp	(*10 mL*) salt
1 tsp	(*5 mL*) pepper
1 tsp	(*5 mL*) garlic powder
1 tsp	(*5 mL*) rosemary
1 tsp	(*5 mL*) oregano
1 tsp	(*5 mL*) basil
1 tsp	(*5 mL*) thyme

1 lb	(*450 g*) lasagne noodles
1 lb	(*450 g*) cottage cheese
1½ lbs	(*675 g*) mozzarella cheese, grated
1 lb	(*450 g*) Cheddar cheese, grated
1 cup	(*250 mL*) grated Parmesan cheese

My Lasagne

Sauce : Brown meats together with vegetables in the oil.

Add tomatoes and tomato paste; simmer 15 minutes.

Add seasonings, reduce heat and simmer for 2 hours.

Cook noodles al dente.

Preheat oven to 350°F (*180°C*).

Grease a 15 x 10 x 2-in. (*37 x 25 x 5 cm*) casserole or baking dish. Layer noodles, cottage cheese, sauce, grated mozzarella and Cheddar.

Finish so that grated cheese is on top. Sprinkle with Parmesan cheese.

Bake in oven for 45 to 50 minutes.

Remove, slice and serve.

Pasta Stuffed Peppers

6 servings

¾ lb	(*340 g*) macaroni
6	sweet peppers
2 tbsp	(*30 mL*) butter
2 cups	(*500 mL*) tomato sauce (see *Sauces*)
1 tsp	(*5 mL*) basil
2 cups	(*500 mL*) grated mozzarella cheese
½ cup	(*125 mL*) grated Parmesan cheese

Cook the macaroni al dente in a large pot of boiling, salted water. Drain and cool.

Preheat oven to 350°F (*180°C*).

Cut the tops from the peppers. Mince them and sauté them in the butter until tender.

Add the tomato sauce and basil and simmer for 5 minutes.

Mix the sauce with the noodles. Stuff the noodles tightly into the peppers.

Sprinkle with mozzarella and Parmesan. Cover loosely with foil.

Bake in oven for 25 minutes or until the peppers are tender.

Serve at once.

1

Cut the tops from the peppers.

2

Mince tops and sauté in butter. Add the tomato sauce and basil and simmer 5 minutes.

3

Mix sauce with cooked noodles and stuff tightly into peppers. Sprinkle with cheeses.

4

Bake in oven 25 minutes, or until peppers are tender.

Linguine with Prosciutto and Smoked Salmon

8 servings

1 lb	(450 g) linguine
2 tbsp	(30 mL) butter
1	small onion, finely diced
¼ lb	(115 g) prosciutto
⅓ cup	(80 mL) sherry
2 cups	(500 mL) tomatoes, peeled, seeded and chopped
1 tsp	(5 mL) salt
1 tsp	(5 mL) paprika
1 tsp	(5 mL) basil
½ tsp	(3 mL) pepper
¼ lb	(115 g) smoked salmon
½ cup	(125 mL) heavy cream

Linguine with Prosciutto and Smoked Salmon

Cook the linguine al dente in a large pot of boiling, salted water.

Heat the butter and sauté the onion. Cut the prosciutto into slices. Cook only to heat.

Add the sherry and tomatoes; simmer for 15 minutes. Mash the tomatoes and add the seasonings.

Dice the salmon and add to sauce. Stir in the cream.

Combine the noodles into the sauce and serve at once.

Linguine and Crayfish Diable

6 servings

1 lb	(450 g) linguine
3	garlic cloves, minced
1	onion, minced
½ cup	(125 mL) olive oil
4	tomatoes, chopped
pinch	sweet basil
½ tsp	(3 mL) salt
1 tsp	(5 mL) black pepper
2 tsp	(10 mL) cayenne pepper
1 tsp	(5 mL) chopped parsley
½ cup	(125 mL) white wine
1 lb	(450 g) crayfish tails, cooked
¼ cup	(60 mL) grated Parmesan cheese

Cook linguine al dente.

Sauté garlic and onion in the oil. Add the tomatoes, basil, salt, peppers, parsley and wine.

Simmer 5 minutes, add crayfish and simmer 5 more minutes.

Serve linguine on plates topped with sauce and sprinkle with Parmesan.

Linguine Fisherman-Style

8 servings

¼ cup	(*60 mL*) olive oil
1	medium onion, finely diced
1	green onion, diced
1	celery stalk, diced
2	garlic cloves, crushed
8 oz	(*225 g*) shrimp, peeled and deveined
8 oz	(*225 g*) small scallops
2 cups	(*500 mL*) tomatoes, seeded and chopped
1 tbsp	(*15 mL*) basil
1 tbsp	(*15 mL*) oregano
1 tbsp	(*15 mL*) parsley
1 tsp	(*5 mL*) salt
1 tsp	(*5 mL*) pepper
2¼ lbs	(*1 kg*) linguine, cooked

Heat the oil in a saucepan. Sauté the vegetables and garlic until tender.

Add the shrimp and scallops and cook 5 minutes.

Add the tomatoes and seasonings and simmer 15 minutes.

Pour sauce over hot linguine. Serve.

Old-Fashioned Macaroni and Cheese

8 servings

1 lb	(*450 g*) elbow macaroni
3 tbsp	(*45 mL*) butter
3 tbsp	(*45 mL*) flour
4 cups	(*1 L*) heavy cream
pinch	nutmeg
1 tsp	(*5 mL*) salt
½ tsp	(*3 mL*) pepper
1 cup	(*250 mL*) grated sharp Cheddar cheese
2 cups	(*500 mL*) grated medium Cheddar cheese
1 cup	(*250 mL*) fine breadcrumbs

Cook the macaroni in boiling water until al dente. Drain and set aside.

Preheat oven to 350°F (*180°C*).

Heat the butter in a saucepan. Add the flour and stir into a smooth paste (roux); cook for 2 minutes. Do not brown.

Add the cream and stir. Add the seasonings. Reduce heat and simmer to a thick sauce.

Mix the cheeses and add 1½ cups (*375 mL*) to the sauce.

Butter a casserole dish; sprinkle with half the breadcrumbs.

Add the macaroni. Pour sauce over noodles. Sprinkle with the remaining cheese and breadcrumbs.

Bake in oven until browned. Serve.

Panzerotti

4 servings

3 tbsp	(*45 mL*) butter
1	small onion, minced
½ cup	(*125 mL*) minced green peppers
1	celery stalk, minced
2	garlic cloves, crushed
1 cup	(*250 mL*) chopped cooked chicken
1 cup	(*250 mL*) tomatoes, seeded and chopped
1 tsp	(*5 mL*) salt
2 tsp	(*10 mL*) basil
1 cup	(*250 mL*) ricotta cheese
1	recipe basic pasta dough
3 cups	(*750 mL*) oil

Heat the butter in a saucepan.

Add the vegetables and garlic and sauté until tender.

Add the chicken and the tomatoes. Simmer until very thick.

Add the seasonings. Remove from heat and cool. Once cool, blend in the ricotta cheese.

Roll out dough as instructed in basic pasta dough recipe. Cut into 4-in. (*10 cm*) squares.

Divide the filling among the squares. Fold in half. Seal the edges.

Heat the oil to 350°F (*180°C*).

Fry the pasta in the oil until golden brown on all sides.

Feta Penne with Veal Tomato Sauce

Feta Penne with Veal Tomato Sauce

8 servings

¼ cup	(60 mL) oil
1½ lbs	(675 g) veal, thinly sliced
2	garlic cloves, minced
1	small onion, minced
1	green pepper, finely diced
2	celery stalks, minced
4 oz	(115 g) mushrooms, sliced
1 tsp	(5 mL) salt
½ tsp	(3 mL) pepper
¼ tsp	(1 mL) oregano
¼ tsp	(1 mL) basil
¼ tsp	(1 mL) thyme
2 cups	(500 mL) crushed tomatoes
½ lb	(225 g) penne noodles
½ cup	(125 mL) crumbled feta cheese

Heat the oil in a large skillet. Brown the veal in the oil. Remove and set aside.

Add the garlic, onion, green pepper, celery and mushrooms; sauté until tender.

Add the seasonings and the tomatoes; reduce heat and simmer for 15 minutes.

Add the veal and simmer for another 10 minutes.

While sauce is simmering, heat 8 cups (2 L) of salted water in a pot to boiling. Add the penne and cook al dente. Drain.

Place the noodles on a serving platter. Top with veal sauce.

Sprinkle with crumbled feta cheese.

Pheasant and Penne

8 servings

3 tbsp	(*45 mL*) butter
3 tbsp	(*45 mL*) flour
¼ cup	(*60 mL*) sherry
1½ cups	(*375 mL*) heavy cream
1 tsp	(*5 mL*) salt
¼ tsp	(*1 mL*) pepper
1 lb	(*450 g*) pheasant meat, cooked and diced
¼ lb	(*115 g*) prosciutto, diced
1 lb	(*450 g*) penne noodles
3 oz	(*90 mL*) grated Parmesan cheese

Heat the butter in a saucepan. Add the flour and stir into a roux (paste). Do not brown.

Cook roux 2 minutes. Add the sherry and cream. Simmer until sauce thickens.

Add the seasonings, pheasant meat and prosciutto. Simmer another 5 minutes.

Cook noodles al dente in a pot of boiling, salted water. Drain.

Place on a platter. Pour sauce over noodles.

Sprinkle with Parmesan. Serve.

Penne with Four Cheeses

8 servings

½ cup	(*125 mL*) crumbled ricotta cheese
½ cup	(*125 mL*) grated Gruyère cheese
½ cup	(*125 mL*) grated Gouda cheese
½ cup	(*125 mL*) grated Romano cheese
¼ cup	(*60 mL*) heavy cream
1 tsp	(*5 mL*) salt
½ tsp	(*3 mL*) fresh cracked pepper
2 tsp	(*10 mL*) parsley flakes
1 lb	(*450 g*) penne noodles
3 tbsp	(*45 mL*) butter

Blend the cheeses together. Add the cream, salt and pepper.

Sprinkle in the parsley and combine.

Cook the penne in boiling, salted water until al dente. Drain well.

Blend in the butter and toss in the cheese mixture. Serve at once.

Penne with Smoked Salmon and Snow Peas

4 servings

4 oz	(*115 g*) snow peas, strings discarded
8 oz	(*225 g*) penne noodles
¼ cup	(*60 mL*) butter
¼ cup	(*60 mL*) flour
1 cup	(*250 mL*) chicken stock (see *Soups*)
1 cup	(*250 mL*) heavy cream
3 oz	(*90 g*) smoked salmon, diced
1 tbsp	(*15 mL*) parsley flakes
½ cup	(*125 mL*) grated Romano cheese

Blanch the snow peas for 30 seconds.

In a large pot, boil salted water and cook the penne al dente. Drain and set aside.

In a small saucepan, melt the butter, add the flour and stir into a paste (roux).

Add the chicken stock and cream. Simmer for 10 minutes, stirring occasionally.

Add the salmon and snow peas. Pour sauce over penne.

Sprinkle with parsley. Serve with cheese.

Penne with Smoked Salmon and Snow Peas

Rigatoni alla Vodka

8 servings

1 lb	(450 g) rigatoni
2 tbsp	(30 mL) butter
1	small onion, minced
1	garlic clove, minced
2 tbsp	(30 mL) flour
2 cups	(500 mL) light cream
¼ cup	(60 mL) vodka
¼ cup	(60 mL) tomato paste
1 tsp	(5 mL) salt
1 tsp	(5 mL) white pepper
1 tsp	(5 mL) sweet basil
½ cup	(125 mL) grated Romano cheese

In a large pot, boil the rigatoni in salted water.

In a saucepan, melt the butter and add the onion and garlic; sauté until tender.

Add the flour and stir into a smooth paste (roux).

Add the cream, vodka, tomato paste and seasonings. Simmer for 8 minutes.

Toss the noodles in the sauce and serve with Romano.

Rigatoni with Beef, Tomatoes and Mushrooms

8 servings

1 lb	(450 g) rigatoni
2 tbsp	(30 mL) butter
2 tbsp	(30 mL) oil
4 oz	(115 g) mushrooms, sliced
½ lb	(225 g) beef, thinly sliced
2 cups	(500 mL) tomatoes, seeded and chopped
1 tsp	(5 mL) salt
1 tsp	(5 mL) oregano
1 tsp	(5 mL) basil
½ tsp	(3 mL) black pepper

In a large pot, cook the rigatoni al dente in boiling, salted water.

Heat the butter with the oil; sauté the mushrooms and the beef until tender.

Add the tomatoes and seasonings. Simmer sauce until thick.

Pour over rigatoni and serve.

Rotini Bolognese

8 servings

¼ lb	(115 g) streaky bacon, diced
1	onion, diced
1	celery stalk, diced
1	carrot, diced
1 lb	(450 g) lean ground beef
1 lb	(450 g) tomatoes, seeded and chopped
6 oz	(180 mL) sherry
2 cups	(500 mL) beef stock (see *Soups*)
1	bay leaf
2 tsp	(10 mL) thyme
2 tsp	(10 mL) oregano
2 tsp	(10 mL) salt
1 lb	(450 g) rotini
¼ cup	(60 mL) grated Parmesan cheese

In a large pot, fry the bacon. Add the onion, celery and carrots; sauté until tender.

Add the beef and brown. Add the tomatoes, sherry, stock, and seasonings.

Bring to a boil then reduce heat. Simmer for 1 hour or until sauce is reduced to a nice thickness.

Cook the rotini al dente in a pot of salted water. Drain. Pour into a large bowl.

Smother with sauce. Sprinkle with cheese. Serve.

Ricotta Ravioli

8 servings

3 cups	(*750 mL*) ricotta cheese
2	eggs
½ tsp	(*3 mL*) salt
¼ tsp	(*1 mL*) pepper
½ tsp	(*3 mL*) basil
¾ cup	(*180 mL*) grated Parmesan cheese
1	recipe basic pasta dough

Mix the ricotta with the eggs. Add the seasonings and the Parmesan. Blend thoroughly.

Mix the pasta dough. Roll and cut the dough into strips 6 in. (*15 cm*) wide.

Place 2 tsp (*10 mL*) of ricotta mixture 3 ½ in. (*9 cm*) apart along strips. Fold the dough over the filling and seal the edges by pressing with a fork .

Cut between each mound of filling, sealing these edges.

Boil a large pot of salted water. Add the ravioli a few at a time. Cook for about 20 minutes.

Serve with your favorite tomato or cheese sauce.

Ricotta Ravioli

Spaghetti Marsala

4 servings

½	recipe basic pasta dough
3 tbsp	(*45 mL*) butter
3 tbsp	(*45 mL*) flour
1 cup	(*250 mL*) heavy cream
½ cup	(*125 mL*) Marsala wine
½ cup	(*125 mL*) grated Parmesan cheese

Roll and cut the dough as instructed in basic pasta dough recipe.

Cut the dough into spaghetti noodles and cook al dente.

Heat the butter in a saucepan.

Add the flour and stir into a roux (paste). Cook 2 minutes.

Add the cream and the wine. Simmer until slightly thickened.

Add the cheese and simmer until thickened.

Pour sauce over noodles. Serve.

Spaghetti Carbonara

8 servings

1 tbsp	(15 mL)	salt
1 lb	(450 g)	spaghetti
3/4 lb	(340 g)	bacon, diced
3/4 lb	(340 g)	fresh mushrooms
6		garlic cloves, minced
2		onions, finely diced
1/4 cup	(60 mL)	olive oil
3		eggs
1/4 cup	(60 mL)	heavy cream
1 tbsp	(15 mL)	cracked black pepper
1/2 lb	(225 g)	grated Parmesan cheese

Boil water in a large pot; add salt and cook spaghetti.

Sauté the bacon, mushrooms, garlic and onions in the oil until tender. Drain oil.

Mix the eggs, cream, black pepper and Parmesan in a bowl. Stir in the bacon and mushroom mixture.

Drain the spaghetti and toss with the sauce, mixing well. Serve.

Spaghetti, Prosciutto and Gorgonzola

8 servings

1 lb	(450 g)	spaghetti
2 tbsp	(30 mL)	olive oil
1/2 lb	(225 g)	prosciutto, diced
1 1/2 cups	(375 mL)	heavy cream
1/2 lb	(225 g)	Gorgonzola cheese
3 oz	(90 g)	Romano, grated

Cook the spaghetti al dente in a large pot of boiling, salted water. Drain.

Heat the oil and add the prosciutto. Cook only to heat.

Add the cream and bring to a simmer. Crumble in the Gorgonzola and stir until sauce thickens.

Pour sauce over noodles. Sprinkle with Romano.

Spaghetti with Pickerel and Herbs

8 servings

1 lb	(450 g)	spaghetti
3 tbsp	(45 mL)	olive oil
1 lb	(450 g)	pickerel filets
3 tbsp	(45 mL)	butter
1/4 cup	(60 mL)	flour
3 cups	(750 mL)	heavy cream
1/2 tsp	(3 mL)	basil
1/2 tsp	(3 mL)	chervil
2 tsp	(10 mL)	chopped parsley
1 tsp	(5 mL)	rosemary
1 tsp	(5 mL)	salt
1/4 tsp	(1 mL)	pepper
1 cup	(250 mL)	ricotta cheese
1/4 cup	(60 mL)	grated Parmesan Cheese

Cook the spaghetti in a large pot of boiling, salted water until al dente. Drain.

Preheat oven to 350°F (180°C).

Place noodles in a large greased casserole dish.

Heat the oil in a skillet and sauté the pickerel filets 1 1/2 minutes each side. Lay the filets over the noodles.

Heat the butter in a saucepan, add the flour and stir into a roux (paste). Cook for 2 minutes.

Reduce heat, add the cream and the seasonings. Simmer until sauce thickens slightly.

Add the ricotta and simmer until melted.

Pour sauce over fish and noodles. Sprinkle with Parmesan.

Bake in oven until browned.

Tortellini

8 servings

10 oz	(*280 g*) ricotta cheese
3 oz	(*90 g*) grated Parmesan cheese
2	eggs
1 tbsp	(*15 mL*) chopped parsley
1 tsp	(*5 mL*) oregano
1 tsp	(*5 mL*) thyme
1 tsp	(*5 mL*) basil
1 tsp	(*5 mL*) salt
½ tsp	(*3 mL*) cracked black pepper
1	recipe basic pasta dough

Cream the ricotta in a food processor.

Add the Parmesan and eggs and blend. Add the seasonings and blend.

Roll out the dough as instructed in basic pasta dough recipe.

Cut into circles 1-in. (*2,5 cm*) in diameter. Place 1½ tsp (*8 mL*) of cheese mixture in each circle. Fold circles in half. Seal the edges and shape into tortellini.

Cook by dropping a few at a time in boiling water. Remove as soon as they rise to the surface.

Serve with your choice of tomato, cheese or cream sauce.

1

Roll out dough.

2

Cut into 1-inch (*2,5 cm*) circles and place 1½ tsp (*8 mL*) of cheese mixture in each circle.

3

Fold circles in half, seal the edges and shape into tortellini.

4

Cook by dropping a few at a time in boiling water. Remove as soon as they rise to the surface.

Tortellini Marinara

Tortellini Marinara

10 servings

2¼ lbs	(*1 kg*) tortellini
1½ lbs	(*675 g*) mussels or kiwi clams
1 lb	(*450 g*) medium-size shrimp
1 tbsp	(*30 mL*) oil
1	garlic clove, crushed
3 cups	(*750 mL*) tomatoes, seeded and finely chopped
2 tbsp	(*30 mL*) tomato paste
¼ cup	(*60 mL*) sherry
1½ lbs	(*675 g*) baby scallops
½ cup	(*125 mL*) grated Parmesan cheese

Cook tortellini in rapidly boiling water for 10 minutes or according to directions.

Cook mussels in boiling, salted water until they open. Drain, remove and discard any that do not open.

Remove the flesh and discard the shells. Shell and devein the shrimp.

Heat the oil and sauté the garlic. Add the tomatoes, tomato paste and sherry.

Bring to a boil and reduce heat; simmer for 20 minutes.

Add seafood and continue to simmer an additional 15 minutes.

Serve sauce over tortellini. Sprinkle with Parmesan.

Tortellini Salad

8 servings

½	recipe tortellini
1	onion, diced
1	green pepper, chopped
2	celery stalks, diced
4 oz	(*115 g*) mushrooms, sliced
2 cups	(*500 mL*) chopped tomatoes
1 cup	(*250 mL*) olive oil
⅓ cup	(*80 mL*) vinegar
1 tsp	(*5 mL*) oregano
1 tsp	(*5 mL*) basil
1 tsp	(*5 mL*) thyme
1 tsp	(*5 mL*) salt
½ tsp	(*3 mL*) pepper

Prepare and cook the tortellini according to recipe directions. Drain and cool.

Toss the vegetables and tomatoes together.

Mix the oil with the vinegar and seasonings.

Mix the vegetables with the tortellini. Pour the dressing over the salad.

Tortellini Salad

Tortellini au Gratin

8 servings

¼ lb	(*115 g*) bacon, sliced and diced
3 cups	(*750 mL*) tomato purée
1 tsp	(*5 mL*) chervil
1 tsp	(*5 mL*) thyme
1 tsp	(*5 mL*) oregano
1 tsp	(*5 mL*) salt
1 cup	(*250 mL*) heavy cream
1	recipe tortellini
2 cups	(*500 mL*) grated mozzarella cheese
1 cup	(*250 mL*) grated medium Cheddar

Fry the bacon in a saucepan. Drain excess fat.

Add the tomato purée and seasonings. Simmer and reduce to 2 cups (*500 mL*). Stir in the cream.

Cook the tortellini according to recipe directions. Drain well.

Preheat oven to 350°F (*180°C*).

Place tortellini in a large greased casserole dish.

Pour sauce over tortellini.

Sprinkle with cheeses.

Bake 15 minutes in oven. Serve.

Curried Tortellini and Prawns

6 servings

½ cup	(*125 mL*) butter
1 lb	(*450 g*) prawns, shelled and deveined
4 oz	(*115 g*) mushrooms, sliced
1 tbsp	(*15 mL*) curry powder
¼ cup	(*60 mL*) flour
1 cup	(*250 mL*) chicken stock (see *Soups*)
2 cups	(*500 mL*) heavy cream
2 tsp	(*10 mL*) salt
½	recipe tortellini
2 cups	(*500 mL*) grated mozzarella cheese

Heat the butter in a saucepan. Sauté the prawns and the mushrooms. Remove and set aside.

Add the curry and flour; stir in a roux (paste). Cook 2 minutes.

Stir in the chicken stock, cream and salt; reduce to a simmer and cook until thickened.

Return the prawns and mushrooms to saucepan.

Cook tortellini according to recipe directions.

Preheat oven to 400°F (*200°C*).

Place tortellini in a large greased casserole dish. Pour sauce over tortellini.

Sprinkle with cheese and brown in oven. Serve.

Tortellini Seafood Soup

8 servings

¼ cup	(*60 mL*) oil
1	onion, minced
1	green pepper, minced
2	celery stalks, minced
1	garlic clove, minced
3 cups	(*750 mL*) tomatoes, chopped
8 cups	(*2 L*) fish stock (see *Soups*)
1 tsp	(*5 mL*) salt
1 tbsp	(*15 mL*) chopped parsley
1 tsp	(*5 mL*) basil
1 tsp	(*5 mL*) oregano
1 tsp	(*5 mL*) thyme
1 tsp	(*5 mL*) paprika
½ cup	(*125 mL*) Marsala wine
1 lb	(*450 g*) red snapper, sliced
1 lb	(*450 g*) shrimp, shelled and deveined
24	clams
24	mussels
½	recipe tortellini, cooked

In a large pot, heat the oil.

Add onion, green pepper, celery and garlic; sauté until tender.

Add the tomatoes, fish stock, seasonings and wine; bring to boil. Reduce heat and simmer 40 minutes.

Add the red snapper and shrimp; simmer 10 more minutes.

Add the clams and mussels and continue to simmer 5 minutes. Add the tortellini.

Remove from heat; wait 3 minutes and serve.

Seashell Seafood Salad

8 servings

1 lb	(*450 g*) seashell pasta
1	onion, finely diced
1	green pepper, finely diced
1	celery stalk, finely diced
½ lb	(*225 g*) cooked baby shrimp
½ lb	(*225 g*) cooked crab meat
½ lb	(*225 g*) cooked salmon
1 cup	(*250 mL*) mayonnaise
2 tsp	(*10 mL*) basil
1 cup	(*250 mL*) tomatoes, seeded and chopped

Cook the pasta al dente in a pot of boiling, salted water. Rinse under cold water and drain.

Combine the pasta with vegetables and seafood. Mix the mayonnaise, basil and tomatoes together and blend into the pasta. Serve.

Seashell Seafood Salad

Seashell Artichoke Salad

8 servings

1 lb	(*450 g*) seashell pasta
6	artichokes
½ cup	(*125 mL*) olive oil
3 tbsp	(*45 mL*) lemon juice
1 tsp	(*5 mL*) sweet basil
1 tsp	(*5 mL*) salt
½ tsp	(*3 mL*) pepper
1 cup	(*250 mL*) fresh tomatoes, peeled, seeded and chopped

Boil the pasta in salted water until al dente. Drain and rinse under cold water.

Clean, trim and quarter the artichokes.

Remove the core (choke) then boil the quarters in salted water until tender. Drain and cool.

Blend the oil, lemon juice and seasonings together with the tomatoes.

Toss the pasta with the artichokes and pour over the tomato dressing.

Vermicelli Pesto

8 servings

1 lb	(450 g) vermicelli
¼ cup	(60 mL) basil leaves
3 oz	(90 g) Romano cheese, grated
¼ cup	(60 mL) chopped parsley
2	garlic cloves
1 tbsp	(15 mL) pine nuts
2 tbsp	(30 mL) olive oil
2 tbsp	(30 mL) beef stock (see *Soups*)

Cook the vermicelli al dente in a large pot. Drain.

Pound the basil, Romano, parsley, garlic and nuts into a smooth paste.

Mix in the oil and beef stock. Pour over noodles.

Vermicelli Edmonton-Style

8 servings

1 lb	(450 g) vermicelli
¼ cup	(60 mL) olive oil
1	medium onion, finely diced
1	green pepper, finely diced
1	celery stalk, finely diced
2	garlic cloves, crushed
4 cups	(1 L) tomatoes, seeded and chopped
1 tbsp	(15 mL) basil
1 tbsp	(15 mL) oregano
1 tsp	(5 mL) black pepper
2 tsp	(10 mL) salt
1 lb	(450 g) cooked diced chicken
8 oz	(225 g) kolbassa (Polish sausage), diced
½ cup	(125 mL) grated Parmesan cheese

In a large pot of boiling, salted water, cook the vermicelli al dente.

In a saucepan, heat the oil. Sauté the vegetables and garlic until tender.

Add the tomatoes, seasonings, chicken and kolbassa. Simmer for 20 minutes.

Pour sauce over pasta and serve with cheese.

Vermicelli with Apples

8 servings

2¼ lbs	(1 kg) apples, pared, cored and diced
¼ cup	(60 mL) oil
1	celery stalk, minced
4 cups	(1 L) crushed tomatoes
1 tsp	(5 mL) salt
1 tsp	(5 mL) basil
¼ tsp	(1 mL) cayenne pepper
1 tsp	(5 mL) thyme
1 tsp	(5 mL) oregano
1 lb	(450 g) vermicelli

Purée the apples in a food processor.

Heat the oil in a saucepan. Add the celery and sauté until tender.

Add the tomatoes and seasonings. Simmer for 10 minutes.

Add the puréed apples, reduce heat and simmer for 40 minutes until very thick.

Boil the vermicelli in a pot of salted water until al dente. Drain.

Smother noodles with the sauce and serve.

Breaded Ravioli

8 servings

3 tbsp	(*45 mL*) butter
1½ cups	(*375 mL*) shredded chicken
1 cup	(*250 mL*) ricotta or cream cheese
2	eggs
1 tsp	(*5 mL*) salt
1 tsp	(*5 mL*) basil
½ tsp	(*3 mL*) pepper
1	recipe basic pasta dough
4 cups	(*1 L*) breadcrumbs
2 tsp	(*10 mL*) salt
½ tsp	(*3 mL*) pepper
1 tsp	(*5 mL*) thyme
¼ tsp	(*1 mL*) oregano
3 cups	(*750 mL*) oil

Heat the butter in a skillet. Sauté the chicken thoroughly. Remove and cool. Once cooled, blend the cheese and chicken together.

Add the eggs and seasonings.

Prepare the dough as instructed in basic pasta dough recipe. Cut and roll out.

Cut the dough into strips 5 in. (*12 cm*) wide. Place 2 tsp (*10 mL*) of filling 3 ½ in. (*9 cm*) apart along strips.

Fold the dough over the filling and seal the edges by pressing with a fork.

Cut between the mounds and seal the edges.

Breaded Ravioli

Blend the breadcrumbs with the seasonings.

Roll each ravioli in the seasoned breadcrumbs.

Heat the oil to 350°F (*180°C*); deep fry a few ravioli at a time.

Cook for about 2½ minutes. Serve with tomato sauce.

Rice

Rice is the main starchy food of two-thirds of the world's population, so it should come as no surprise that it lends itself to a variety of creative uses. In this chapter, you will find some of my favorite rice dishes, including several which will serve quite handily as the main dish for a light lunch or supper.

One of the easiest ways to add a little excitement to plain boiled rice is to substitute a different liquid for the water called for in the instructions. Try fruit juice, chicken or beef broth, or vegetable juice.

White Rice

White rice has had the outer bran layer removed in the milling process. It is sometimes sold as buffed or polished rice. Whether you buy short-, medium-, or long-grain rice, the basic cooking technique is the same : Add 1 cup (*250 mL*) rice to 3 cups (*750 mL*) boiling salted water. This yields 3 cups (*750 mL*) cooked rice.

Precooked or **quick-cooking rice** has been dehydrated after cooking.

Basmati Rice

This fragrant, flavorful rice comes from India or Pakistan, and is available in Asian or specialty stores. You can prepare it like white rice, but it is so tasty that it seldom benefits from the addition of other flavorings or ingredients.

Wild Rice

Wild rice is not actually a rice, but the seeds of a grass that grows in North America. It is harvested by hand, usually by native Indians, and as a result is quite expensive. But its wonderful nutty flavor makes it worth every penny. To prepare : Cook 1 cup (*250 mL*) wild rice in 6 cups (*1,5 L*) boiling, salted water for 50-60 minutes.

Cheese Rice with Fruit and Nuts

Cheese Rice with Fruit and Nuts

6 servings

4 cups	(*1 L*) beef stock (see *Soups*)
2 cups	(*500 mL*) brown rice
3 tbsp	(*45 mL*) butter
4 oz	(*115 g*) mushrooms, thinly sliced
½ cup	(*125 mL*) apples, peeled and diced
½ cup	(*125 mL*) dried apricots, sliced
1 tsp	(*5 mL*) salt
1 tsp	(*5 mL*) thyme
½ cup	(*125 mL*) cashews
2 cups	(*500 mL*) grated Cheddar cheese

Bring beef stock to a boil. Add rice and cook, covered, over low heat for 45 minutes.

Remove from heat. Drain. Keep hot.

Melt the butter and sauté the mushrooms. Add the apples and apricots and sauté until tender.

Season with salt and thyme. Mix into the rice with the cashews.

Blend in the cheese and stir until cheese has melted. Serve.

Rice-Stuffed Tomatoes

8 servings

8	large tomatoes
2 cups	(*500 mL*) cooked rice, cooled
1 tsp	(*5 mL*) basil
1 tsp	(*5 mL*) salt
¼ tsp	(*1 mL*) pepper
2 tbsp	(*30 mL*) chopped chives
3 tbsp	(*45 mL*) lemon juice
¼ cup	(*60 mL*) oil
1 cup	(*250 mL*) grated Cheddar cheese

Preheat oven to 400°F (*200°C*).

Slice the tops from the tomatoes. Scoop out the pulp. Do not break the skin.

Mix the rice together with seasonings, tomato pulp, lemon juice and oil.

Fill the tomato shells. Sprinkle with cheese.

Bake in oven for 20 minutes.

1

Slice tops from tomatoes and scoop out the pulp.

2

Mix the rice with seasonings, tomato pulp, lemon juice and oil.

3

Fill the tomato shells with mixture.

4

Sprinkle with cheese and bake in oven 20 minutes.

Chicken Tomato Rice with Old Cheddar

6 servings

¼ cup	(60 mL) butter
¼ cup	(60 mL) finely diced onions
¼ cup	(60 mL) finely diced celery
¼ cup	(60 mL) finely diced green peppers
4 oz	(115 g) mushrooms, sliced
1 cup	(250 mL) chopped tomatoes
1½ cups	(375 mL) tomato sauce (see *Sauces*)
1 lb	(450 g) chicken, cooked and diced
4 cups	(1 L) cooked rice
2 cups	(500 mL) sharp (old) Cheddar, crumbled

Preheat oven to 400°F (200°C).

Heat the butter in a skillet. Add the onions, celery, green peppers and mushrooms. Sauté until tender.

Add the tomatoes and tomato sauce. Simmer for 7 minutes.

Place chicken and rice in a mixing bowl. Blend in the sauce.

Pour into a lightly greased casserole dish. Sprinkle with Cheddar.

Bake in oven for 20 to 30 minutes.

Orange Rice

Orange Rice

6 servings

3 tbsp	(45 mL) butter
½ cup	(125 mL) diced celery
½ cup	(125 mL) chopped green onions
1½ cups	(375 mL) raw rice
4 cups	(1 L) chicken broth
2 cups	(500 mL) orange juice
2 tsp	(10 mL) grated orange rind
½ tsp	(3 mL) salt
1 cup	(250 mL) seedless raisins
1 cup	(250 mL) toasted almonds

Preheat oven to 350°F (180°C).

Melt the butter in a flame-proof casserole dish. Sauté the celery, onions and rice until rice is golden brown.

Add the broth, orange juice, orange rind, salt and raisins. Cover and bake in oven for 35 minutes.

Remove from oven and stir in almonds. Serve hot.

Chicken Florentine Rice

8 servings

10 oz	(284 g) spinach
4	eggs
1 cup	(250 mL) heavy cream
½ tsp	(3 mL) black pepper
1 tsp	(5 mL) paprika
1 tsp	(5 mL) salt
1 tsp	(5 mL) minced garlic
1	small onion, minced
4 cups	(1 L) cooked long grain rice
1 lb	(450 g) chicken, cooked and diced
½ cup	(125 mL) grated Parmesan cheese
12	tomato slices

Preheat oven to 350°F (180°C).

Remove the stems and chop the spinach. Steam for 5 minutes.

Beat the eggs into the cream and add the seasonings, garlic and onion.

Place the spinach on the bottom and sides of a large, lightly greased casserole dish.

Layer the rice over the spinach. Top with chicken.

Pour the egg mixture over the chicken. Sprinkle with cheese. Top with tomato slices.

Bake in oven 45 to 55 minutes, or until golden brown. Serve hot.

Cajun Dirty Rice

8-10 servings

¼ lb	(115 g) chicken gizzards
¼ lb	(115 g) chicken hearts
¼ lb	(115 g) chicken livers
½ cup	(125 mL) butter
2¼ lbs	(1 kg) hot sausage
1	Spanish onion, diced
1	green pepper, diced
3	celery stalks, diced
6	green onions, diced
4 oz	(115 g) ham
2¼ lbs	(1 kg) cooked rice
1 tsp	(5 mL) cayenne pepper
2 tsp	(10 mL) salt
1 tsp	(5 mL) pepper
1 tsp	(5 mL) paprika

Boil the chicken parts in salted water until cooked. Drain and reserve both chicken parts and broth.

In a large skillet, heat the butter and fry the sausage.

Add the Spanish onion, green pepper and celery. Sauté until tender. Add the green onions and simmer for 10 minutes.

Chop the ham, chicken parts and sausage and add to the fried vegetables.

Add 1 cup (250 mL) of reserved broth. Simmer for 15 minutes.

Fold in rice and seasonings. Serve.

Indian Curry Rice

8 servings

2 tbsp	(30 mL) butter
2	onions, diced
3	celery stalks, diced
2 tsp	(10 mL) salt
2 tbsp	(30 mL) curry powder
8 cups	(2 L) chicken broth
4 cups	(1 L) long grain rice
1 cup	(250 mL) seedless raisins
1½ cups	(375 mL) peas, blanched
1 cup	(250 mL) toasted slivered almonds

Heat the butter in a pot. Add the onions and celery; sauté until tender.

Add the salt and curry powder; sauté for 2 minutes.

Add the broth and bring to a boil. Add the rice and simmer, covered, until tender, about 20 minutes.

Drain, stir in raisins, peas and almonds.

Serve hot, or chill and serve as a cold rice salad.

Indian Curry Rice

Green Beans, Almonds, Mushrooms with Triple Rice

4 servings

3 cups	(*750 mL*) cut green beans
1 cup	(*250 mL*) cooked long grain rice, hot
1 cup	(*250 mL*) cooked brown rice, hot
½ cup	(*125 mL*) cooked wild rice, hot
¼ cup	(*60 mL*) butter
2 cups	(*500 mL*) button mushrooms
1 cup	(*250 mL*) toasted slivered almonds
1 tsp	(*5 mL*) thyme
1 tsp	(*5 mL*) oregano
½ tsp	(*3 mL*) pepper
1 tsp	(*5 mL*) salt

Blanch the green beans for 7 minutes.

Place the rice in a mixing bowl and keep hot.

Heat the butter in a skillet. Sauté the mushrooms and green beans until tender.

Stir into the rice along with the almonds and seasonings.

Serve hot.

Pepper Rice Salad

6 servings

6	green peppers
2 cups	(*500 mL*) baby shrimp
2 cups	(*500 mL*) cooked rice, cooled
¼ cup	(*60 mL*) finely diced onions
¼ cup	(*60 mL*) finely diced celery
4 oz	(*115 g*) bacon, cooked and crumbled
1 tsp	(*5 mL*) basil
1 tsp	(*5 mL*) salt
¼ tsp	(*1 mL*) pepper
1 cup	(*250 mL*) mayonnaise
6	large shrimp, peeled, deveined, cooked and chilled
6	cherry tomatoes

Slice the tops from the green peppers. Remove the seeds and ribs inside peppers. Dice the tops.

Mix shrimp, rice, vegetables, bacon and seasonings together in a mixing bowl with the mayonnaise.

Stuff into the green peppers.

Garnish with shrimp and cherry tomatoes.

Rice, Okra and Ham Casserole

8 servings

1 lb	(*450 g*) okra
8 cups	(*2 L*) chicken broth
3 cups	(*750 mL*) long grain rice
1 tsp	(*5 mL*) salt
¼ tsp	(*1 mL*) pepper
1 lb	(*450 g*) ham, diced
3 cups	(*750 mL*) Mornay Sauce (see *Sauces*)
2 cups	(*500 mL*) grated Havarti cheese

Dice the okra and blanch 3 minutes.

Heat the broth in a pot to boiling. Add the rice, cover and simmer for 20 minutes. Drain.

Preheat oven to 400°F (*200°C*).

In a mixing bowl, mix the rice, okra, seasonings, ham and Mornay Sauce together.

Pour into a lightly buttered casserole dish.

Sprinkle with cheese.

Bake in oven for 20 minutes.

Three Rice Almond Medley

6 servings

2 cups	(*500 mL*) cooked long grain rice, hot
2 cups	(*500 mL*) cooked brown rice, hot
1 cup	(*250 mL*) cooked wild rice, hot
2 tbsp	(*30 mL*) butter
4 oz	(*115 g*) mushrooms, sliced
½ tsp	(*3 mL*) basil
¼ tsp	(*1 mL*) pepper
1 tsp	(*5 mL*) salt
1 cup	(*250 mL*) toasted slivered almonds

Place rice into a mixing bowl. Keep hot.

Heat the butter in a skillet. Sauté the mushrooms until tender.

Sprinkle with seasonings. Stir into rice.

Sprinkle with almonds. Serve at once.

Three Rice Almond Medley

Risi e Bisi

6 servings

2 tsp	(*10 mL*) butter
4	slices bacon, diced
1	small onion, minced
1½ cups	(*375 mL*) long grain rice
3 cups	(*750 mL*) chicken stock (see *Soups*)
2 cups	(*500 mL*) peas, fresh or frozen
½ tsp	(*3 mL*) nutmeg
¼ cup	(*60 mL*) grated Parmesan cheese
3 tbsp	(*45 mL*) sherry

Heat butter in a skillet. Add bacon and onion. Sauté until tender. Add rice and cook, stirring for 1 minute.

Add the chicken stock and cook over low heat for 20 minutes, or until rice is tender. Stir in the peas, nutmeg, cheese and sherry.

Cook for 3 more minutes. Serve.

Rice Oh So Good!

8 servings

½ cup	(125 mL)	olive oil
2¼ lbs	(1 kg)	lamb, diced
1		onion, finely diced
4 oz	(115 g)	mushrooms, sliced
2		celery stalks, finely diced
1 cup	(250 mL)	diced apples
½ cup	(125 mL)	diced dried apricots
3 cups	(750 mL)	long grain rice
1 cup	(250 mL)	brown rice
½ cup	(125 mL)	sultana raisins
8 cups	(2 L)	chicken stock (see *Soups*)
2 tsp	(10 mL)	salt
1 tsp	(5 mL)	cinnamon
½ tsp	(3 mL)	ground cloves
¼ cup	(60 mL)	pine nuts

Preheat oven to 375°F (190°C).

In a large skillet, heat the oil. Sauté the lamb until browned. Remove and set aside.

Add the onion, mushrooms, celery, apples and apricots. Sauté until tender.

Place the rice in a large casserole dish. Top with lamb, sautéed fruit, vegetables and raisins.

Heat the chicken stock with the seasonings to boiling. Pour over rice. Sprinkle on the pine nuts.

Bake on lower rack of oven for 30 minutes. Remove, cover and rest for 5 minutes. Serve.

Cheese and Chive Rice

6 servings

6 cups	(1,5 L)	chicken broth
2 cups	(500 mL)	long grain rice
2 cups	(500 mL)	Mornay Sauce (see *Sauces*)
3 tbsp	(45 mL)	chopped chives
2 cups	(500 mL)	grated Cheddar cheese

Heat the broth to boiling. Add the rice. Cover and simmer 20 minutes. Drain.

Preheat oven to 350°F (180°C).

Place rice into a lightly buttered casserole dish. Pour sauce over rice.

Sprinkle with chives. Top with cheese.

Bake in oven 15 to 20 minutes or until golden brown.

Rice Pilaf

6-8 servings

8		slices bacon, cut into ½-in. (1 cm) pieces
1		onion, finely chopped
1		celery stalk, thinly sliced
1		carrot, finely chopped
1		green pepper, diced
¼ cup	(60 mL)	butter
3 cups	(750 mL)	cooked rice, hot

Sauté the bacon until tender but not crisp; drain well.

Sauté the vegetables in butter until tender.

Combine bacon, vegetables and rice; mix well and serve.

Broccoli Rice au Gratin

Broccoli Rice au Gratin

6 servings

2 cups	(*500 mL*) broccoli florets
1 cup	(*250 mL*) Mornay Sauce (see *Sauces*)
3 cups	(*750 mL*) cooked rice
¼ cup	(*60 mL*) grated mild Cheddar cheese
¼ cup	(*60 mL*) grated Havarti cheese
2 tbsp	(*30 mL*) grated Parmesan cheese
2 tbsp	(*30 mL*) fine dry breadcrumbs

Preheat oven to 300°F (*150°C*).

Cook the broccoli in boiling, salted water until almost tender, about 3 minutes. Drain.

Combine the Mornay Sauce, rice and cheeses; fold in the broccoli.

Spoon into a greased 8 x 8 in. (*20 x 22 cm*) baking pan.

Sprinkle with breadcrumbs and bake in oven 35 to 45 minutes.

Sauces

Some French chefs tend to judge a cook by his sauces, and it is true that sauces play a particularly important role in French cuisine.

But I think it's a good idea for every cook to have a repertory of basic sauces, which can be adapted to fill a variety of needs.

Sauces can be hot or cold, but there are definitely more hot sauces. The hot sauces are usually based on a basic brown sauce (the basis of Espagnole and tomato sauces, for example) or on a basic white sauce, which includes béchamel and velouté.

Basic brown sauce or **Espagnole sauce** is made from browned beef bones, brown stock, brown roux and vegetables and herbs.

It is simmered for a long period, then strained and degreased. You can use the recipe for Espagnole sauce in this chapter as the foundation for many other sauces.

Basic white sauce or **Béchamel** is made with a white roux and cream or milk, simmered gently to the desired consistency. It is used as the basis for **Supreme Sauce** (see recipe) and many other sauces.

In addition to these two, I suggest you master the recipes for **Tomato Sauce** and **Hollandaise Sauce.** Variations on these four themes will provide endless eating enjoyment.

Creole Sauce

Creole Sauce

3 cups (750 mL)

2	garlic cloves, minced
¼ cup	(*60 mL*) olive oil
1	medium onion, finely chopped
2	green peppers, finely chopped
1½ cups	(*375 mL*) finely chopped mushrooms
4	large tomatoes, seeded and diced
½ tsp	(*3 mL*) salt
pinch	pepper
3	drops hot pepper sauce
¼ cup	(*60 mL*) chopped green onions
2 tbsp	(*30 mL*) chopped parsley

In a saucepan, cook the garlic in oil 1 minute.

Add the onion, peppers and mushrooms; sauté until vegetables are tender.

Stir in the tomatoes and simmer until sauce is reduced and thickened.

Season with salt, pepper and hot pepper sauce.

Just before serving, stir in the green onions and parsley.

Champagne Sauce

1¾ cups (430 mL)

3 tbsp	(*45 mL*) butter
3 tbsp	(*45 mL*) flour
½ cup	(*125 mL*) chicken stock (see *Soups*)
½ cup	(*125 mL*) heavy cream
½ cup	(*125 mL*) champagne

Melt the butter in a saucepan. Add the flour and stir into a paste (roux).

Add chicken stock, cream and champagne. Whisk all the ingredients together.

Simmer for 10 minutes over medium heat.

White Wine Sauce 1

1¾ cups (430 mL)

3 tbsp	(*45 mL*) butter
3 tbsp	(*45 mL*) flour
½ cup	(*125 mL*) chicken stock (see *Soups*)
½ cup	(*125 mL*) heavy cream
½ cup	(*125 mL*) white wine

In a saucepan, heat the butter. Add the flour. Cook for 2 minutes.

Add the liquids and simmer until thick.

White Wine Sauce 2

2 cups (500 mL)

4 tsp	(*20 mL*) butter
4 tsp	(*20 mL*) flour
1½ cups	(*375 mL*) chicken stock (see *Soups*)
½ cup	(*125 mL*) white wine
1	egg yolk

In a saucepan, heat the butter. Add the flour and cook for 2 minutes.

Add the chicken stock and wine. Simmer for 5 minutes.

Remove from heat and whisk in the egg yolk.

Chicken Velouté

4 cups (1 L)

½ cup	(*125 mL*) butter
½ cup	(*125 mL*) flour
4 cups	(*1 L*) chicken stock (see *Soups*)

In a saucepan, melt the butter, add the flour and stir into a blond roux (paste).

Add the chicken stock and stir.

Simmer for 30 minutes.

Mushroom and Parmesan Cream Sauce

2½ cups (625 mL)

1½ cups	(*375 mL*) sliced mushrooms
4 tsp	(*20 mL*) butter
4 tsp	(*20 mL*) all-purpose flour
¾ cup	(*180 mL*) chicken stock (see *Soups*)
¾ cup	(*180 mL*) heavy cream
2 tbsp	(*30 mL*) grated Parmesan cheese
	salt and pepper

Sauté the mushrooms in butter over high heat until tender.

Sprinkle with flour and cook, stirring, for 2 minutes.

Gradually stir in stock and cream; heat just to simmering.

Stir in Parmesan; season to taste.

Mushroom and Parmesan Cream Sauce

Supreme Sauce

1 cup (250 mL)

1 cup	(*250 mL*) Chicken Velouté
1 cup	(*250 mL*) heavy cream
2 tbsp	(*30 mL*) cold butter

Over high heat, reduce chicken velouté to ½ cup (*125 mL*).

Whisk in the cream and continue reducing until the sauce is thickened and reduced to about 1 cup (*250 mL*).

Cut the butter into cubes and whisk in, a few cubes at a time, over medium heat.

Espagnole Sauce

6 cups (1,5 L)

4½ lbs	(*2 kg*) beef or veal bones
1	onion, diced
4	carrots, diced
3	celery stalks, diced
3	bay leaves
3	garlic cloves
2·tsp	(*10 mL*) salt
½ cup	(*125 mL*) flour
12 cups	(*3 L*) water
1	bouquet garni
1 cup	(*250 mL*) tomato purée
¾ cup	(*180 mL*) chopped leeks
3	parsley sprigs

Preheat oven to 450°F (*230°C*).

Put bones, onion, carrots, celery, bay leaves, garlic and salt in a roasting pan.

Bake 45 to 50 minutes until bones are nicely browned, take care not to let them burn.

Sprinkle with flour and bake another 15 minutes.

Transfer ingredients to a stock pot. Swirl roasting pan with a little water. Pour drippings into stock pot.

Add all the remaining ingredients. Bring to a boil.

Reduce heat and simmer 3 to 4 hours or until half reduced.

Skim off all scum that rises to the top. Strain the sauce to remove bones, etc.

Then strain a second time through a cheesecloth.

Use as required.

Demi-Glace

1¾ cups (430 mL)

3 cups	(*750 mL*) Espagnole Sauce
1¼ cups	(*310 mL*) brown beef stock (see *Soups*)
¼ cup	(*60 mL*) sherry

Combine the Espagnole Sauce and beef stock.

Simmer until sauce is reduced in volume by two thirds.

Add sherry and use as required.

Chasseur Sauce

2 cups (500 mL)

2 tbsp	(*30 mL*) butter
4 oz	(*115 g*) mushrooms, sliced
1 tbsp	(*15 mL*) minced shallots
½ tsp	(*3 mL*) salt
¼ cup	(*60 mL*) white wine
1 cup	(*250 mL*) demi-glace
½ cup	(*125 mL*) tomato sauce

Heat the butter in a saucepan; sauté the mushrooms, shallots and salt until most of the liquid has evaporated.

Add the wine, demi-glace and tomato sauce.

Simmer for 20 minutes, stirring occasionally. Use as required.

Red Wine or Madeira Mushroom Sauce

2½ cups (625 mL)

2 cups	(*500 mL*) Espagnole Sauce (see *Sauces*)
1 cup	(*250 mL*) red wine or Madeira
1½ cups	(*375 mL*) sliced mushrooms
1 tbsp	(*15 mL*) butter
2 tsp	(*10 mL*) all-purpose flour

Boil the Espagnole Sauce until reduced by half.

Stir in red wine or Madeira and simmer 5 minutes.

Sauté the mushrooms in butter over high heat.

Stir in flour; mix well. Stir mushroom mixture into sauce; simmer 5 minutes.

Red Wine or Madeira Mushroom Sauce

Italienne Sauce

3 cups (750 mL)

8	slices bacon, diced
1	small onion, finely diced
4 oz	(*115 g*) mushrooms, sliced
2	celery stalks, finely diced
1	green pepper, finely diced
3 cups	(*750 mL*) tomato sauce (see *Sauces*)
¼ cup	(*60 mL*) sherry

Sauté the bacon in a saucepan.

Add the onion, mushrooms, celery and green pepper.

Cook until tender. Drain off grease.

Add tomato sauce and sherry.

Simmer 10 minutes and use as required.

Béchamel Sauce

1¼ cups (310 mL)

2 tbsp	(30 mL)	butter
2 tbsp	(30 mL)	flour
1 cup	(250 mL)	milk
¼ tsp	(1 mL)	salt
¼ tsp	(1 mL)	white pepper
pinch		nutmeg

Melt the butter in a saucepan.

Add flour and stir into a paste (roux).

Add the milk and stir; simmer until thickened.

Add the seasonings and simmer 2 more minutes.

1

Melt the butter in a saucepan and add the flour.

2

Stir into a paste (roux).

3

Add the milk and stir, simmering until thickened.

4

Add the seasonings and simmer 2 more minutes.

Mornay Sauce

1¼ cups (310 mL)

2 tbsp	*(30 mL)*	butter
2 tbsp	*(30 mL)*	flour
½ cup	*(125 mL)*	chicken stock (see *Soups*)
½ cup	*(125 mL)*	heavy cream
¼ tsp	*(1 mL)*	salt
¼ tsp	*(1 mL)*	pepper
¼ cup	*(60 mL)*	grated Parmesan cheese

In a saucepan, melt the butter, add the flour and stir into a paste (roux).

Add the chicken stock, cream and seasonings.

Simmer, while stirring, until thickened.

Add cheese and simmer 2 more minutes.

Teriyaki Sauce

Teriyaki Sauce

2 cups (500 mL)

⅓ cup	*(80 mL)*	brown sugar
1 tsp	*(5 mL)*	ground ginger
1 cup	*(250 mL)*	beef broth
⅓ cup	*(80 mL)*	soya sauce
2 tbsp	*(30 mL)*	cornstarch
¼ cup	*(60 mL)*	white wine

Dissolve the sugar and ginger in the broth and soya sauce.

Bring to a boil.

Blend the cornstarch in the wine.

Add to the broth.

Simmer until thickened.

BBQ Sauce

3 cups (750 mL)

1 cup	(*250 mL*) chopped onions
⅓ cup	(*80 mL*) oil
2 cups	(*500 mL*) tomato sauce
⅔ cup	(*160 mL*) water
⅓ cup	(*80 mL*) lemon juice
⅓ cup	(*80 mL*) brown sugar
4 tsp	(*20 mL*) Worcestershire sauce
4 tsp	(*20 mL*) prepared mustard
1 tbsp	(*15 mL*) salt
½ tsp	(*3 mL*) hot pepper sauce

Mix and combine all the ingredients.

Simmer slowly for 15 minutes.

Remove from heat.

Wine BBQ Sauce

1½ cups (375 mL)

2 tbsp	(*30 mL*) chopped onion
1 tbsp	(*15 mL*) butter
¼ cup	(*60 mL*) white wine
¼ cup	(*60 mL*) ketchup
pinch	black pepper
½ tsp	(*3 mL*) oregano
½ tsp	(*3 mL*) cumin
2 tbsp	(*30 mL*) brown sugar
10 oz	(*284 mL*) can chopped tomatoes
pinch	salt
1 tbsp	(*15 mL*) cornstarch
3 tbsp	(*45 mL*) water

Sauté the onion in the butter until tender.

Add the wine, ketchup, pepper, oregano, cumin, brown sugar and tomatoes.

Bring sauce to a slow boil. Simmer 20 minutes and add salt.

Blend the cornstarch with the water, add to sauce and cook to desired consistency, stirring constantly.

Curry Sauce

1½ cups (375 mL)

2 tbsp	(*30 mL*) butter
2 tbsp	(*30 mL*) flour
2 tsp	(*10 mL*) curry powder
⅔ cup	(*160 mL*) chicken stock (see *Soups*)
½ cup	(*125 mL*) heavy cream

In a saucepan, heat the butter. Add the flour and curry powder.

Blend into a smooth paste (roux). Cook 2 minutes.

Add the stock and reduce heat to simmer.

Simmer for 3 minutes.

Add cream and simmer for 2 more minutes. Use as required.

BBQ Sauce and Wine BBQ Sauce

Hollandaise Sauce

¾ cup (180 mL)

½ cup	(*125 mL*) butter
2	egg yolks, beaten
2 tsp	(*10 mL*) lemon juice
pinch	cayene pepper

Melt the butter to very hot.

Place the egg yolks in a double boiler over low heat.

Add the lemon juice slowly. Be sure it is thoroughly incorporated.

Remove from heat. Slowly whisk in the hot butter.

Add the cayenne pepper and use sauce at once.

 Place the egg yolks in a double boiler over low heat and slowly add the lemon juice.

Slowly whisk in the melted butter.

 Add the cayenne pepper.

 Sauce is ready to use.

Simple Pesto, Béarnaise Sauce and Hollandaise Sauce

Simple Pesto

2 cups (500 mL)

1½ cups	(*375 mL*) fresh basil leaves
6	garlic cloves
⅓ cup	(*80 mL*) toasted pine nuts
⅔ cup	(*160 mL*) grated Parmesan cheese
1 tsp	(*5 mL*) salt
½ tsp	(*3 mL*) pepper
¾ cup	(*180 mL*) olive oil

Combine all the ingredients in a food processor.

Blend until well incorporated.

Use by tossing into hot cooked pasta.

Béarnaise Sauce

¾ cup (180 mL)

3 tbsp	(*45 mL*) white wine
1 tbsp	(*15 mL*) dried tarragon leaves
½ tsp	(*3 mL*) lemon juice
½ cup	(*125 mL*) butter
3	egg yolks

Combine wine, tarragon and lemon juice in a small saucepan.

Over high heat, reduce to 2 tbsp (*30 mL*).

In another small saucepan, melt butter and heat almost to boiling.

In a blender or food processor, process egg yolks until blended.

With machine running, add butter in a slow, thin stream.

With machine off, add reduced wine mixture.

Process just until blended.

Honey-Mustard Sauce

1⅓ cups (330 mL)

⅔ cup	(160 mL) mayonnaise (see Dressings)
⅓ cup	(80 mL) honey
⅓ cup	(80 mL) Dijon mustard

Blend all ingredients together. Chill.

Creamy Horseradish

1¾ cups (430 mL)

½ cup	(125 mL) sour cream
1 cup	(250 mL) cream cheese
¼ cup	(60 mL) grated horseradish

Thoroughly blend all ingredients together.
Chill before using.

Herb Sauce

½ cup (125 mL)

½ cup	(125 mL) mayonnaise (see Dressings)
1 tsp	(5 mL) dried basil leaves
1 tsp	(5 mL) dried chervil (optional)
1 tsp	(5 mL) chopped chives
1 tsp	(5 mL) chopped parsley

Whisk ingredients until smooth.

Creamy Chili Sauce

¾ cup (180 mL)

¼ cup	(60 mL) chili sauce (see Vegetables)
½ cup	(125 mL) French dressing (see Dressings)
1 tsp	(5 mL) paprika
1 tsp	(5 mL) seasoned salt
½ tsp	(3 mL) chili powder
1 tsp	(5 mL) lemon juice
1 tsp	(5 mL) Worcestershire sauce

Whisk ingredients until smooth.

Orange Liqueur Sauce

¾ cup (180 mL)

½ cup	(125 mL) marmalade preserves
¼ cup	(60 mL) orange liqueur or brandy
2 tbsp	(30 mL) water

Blend all ingredients together.
Bring to a boil, reduce heat and simmer for 5 minutes, stirring until thick.

Honey-Garlic Sauce

1 cup (250 mL)

| 1 cup | (250 mL) liquid honey |
| 1 tbsp | (15 mL) garlic, powder or minced |

Heat the honey in a saucepan or in the microwave. Blend in the garlic.

Herb Sauce, Orange Liqueur Sauce, Honey-Garlic Sauce and Creamy Chili Sauce

Tomato Sauce

2½- 3 cups (625 - 750 mL)

¼ cup	(60 mL) butter
2	carrots, diced
2	celery stalks, diced
2	garlic cloves, minced
1	onion, diced
3	bay leaves
1 tsp	(5 mL) thyme
1 tsp	(5 mL) oregano
1 tsp	(5 mL) basil
1 tbsp	(15 mL) salt
1 tsp	(5 mL) pepper
3 lbs	(1,4 kg) tomatoes, peeled, seeded and chopped

Heat the butter and sauté the carrots, celery, garlic and onion until tender.

Add the seasonings and tomatoes. Simmer for 2 hours.

Strain the sauce. Return to heat and simmer until desired thickness.

Tomato Sauce

Cherbourg Sauce

3½ cups (875 mL)

6 tbsp	(90 mL) butter
3 tbsp	(45 mL) flour
1 cup	(250 mL) chicken stock
1 cup	(250 mL) light cream
1½ cups	(375 mL) cooked crayfish tails or cooked shrimp meat
¼ tsp	(1 mL) salt
pinch	white pepper
pinch	paprika

Heat half the butter in a saucepan. Add the flour and cook for 2 minutes. Do not brown.

Add both the chicken stock and cream. Reduce heat and simmer gently for 15 minutes or until sauce tickens.

Purée the remaining butter with ½ cup (125 mL) of crayfish tails. Remove sauce from heat. Whisk in the purée. Add the remaining seafood and seasonings. Serve with seafood, fish, chicken or over noodles.

Cajun Spice Sauce

2¼ cups (560 mL)

2 tbsp	(*30 mL*) oil
2 tbsp	(*30 mL*) minced onion
2 tbsp	(*30 mL*) minced green pepper
2	garlic cloves, minced
1 cup	(*250 mL*) ketchup
1 cup	(*250 mL*) tomato purée
½ cup	(*125 mL*) water
1 tbsp	(*15 mL*) Worcestershire sauce
½ tsp	(*3 mL*) Tabasco sauce
1 tsp	(*5 mL*) paprika
½ tsp	(*3 mL*) oregano
½ tsp	(*3 mL*) thyme
1 tsp	(*5 mL*) salt

In a saucepan, heat the oil. Sauté the onion, green pepper and garlic until tender.

Add all remaining ingredients. Bring to a boil.

Reduce to a simmer. Simmer for 20 minutes.

Raspberry Coulis

Raspberry Coulis

3 cups (750 mL)

2¼ lbs	(*1 kg*) raspberries
1 tbsp	(*15 mL*) cornstarch
3 tbsp	(*45 mL*) sherry
4 tbsp	(*60 mL*) fine sugar

Purée raspberries in a food processor. Strain. Discard pulp and seeds.

Using 3 cups (*750 mL*) of raspberry juice, mix the cornstarch, sherry and sugar together.

Heat slowly until sauce thickens.

Use as required.

Cheese

There are hundreds of varieties of cheese in the world — more than 400 made in France alone ! So there is no excuse to limit yourself to the same old standby cheeses. But don't overlook the domestic cheeses. Some of them are incredibly good and they can be much less expensive than the imported varieties.

Cheese can be a real adventure, and one of the most interesting ways to indulge is to plan a cheese tasting or wine and cheese party. Plan on 6 ounces (*170 g*) of cheese per person.

Cheese is also a superb cooking ingredient. This chapter will give you an idea of the many wonderful ways cheese can be used, in everything from soups to desserts.

When you cook with cheese, remember that too high heat will result in a stringy and possibly tough product.

Cheese Storage

All cheeses should be stored at a temperature of between 36°F and 40°F (*2°C and 4°C*). Soft cream type cheeses will keep up to 14 days in the refrigerator, if tightly wrapped. Mozzarella is one cheese that is definitely best when it's young, so buy only what you need.

Hard cheeses will keep up to 90 days, if tightly wrapped. The appearance of surface mold is not harmful; simply trim it off.

It is better not to freeze cheese, but if you must, cut it into ½ lb (*225 g*) blocks and wrap it tightly. Use it within 90 days, and defrost it in the refrigerator.

Try to avoid freezing homemade cheesecake, as well. It tends to crumble.

Cheddar Scones

12 servings

2 cups	(*500 mL*) all-purpose flour
¼ cup	(*60 mL*) baking powder
½ tsp	(*3 mL*) granulated sugar
¼ tsp	(*1 mL*) salt
¼ cup	(*60 mL*) lard
⅔ cup	(*180 mL*) milk
2 cups	(*500 mL*) finely diced medium Cheddar cheese
1	egg

Preheat oven to 400°F (*200°C*).

Combine flour, baking powder, sugar and salt.

Cut in lard until mixture resembles coarse crumbs.

Add milk all at once; stir with a fork to make a soft dough.

Turn dough onto a lightly floured board and gently knead in the cheese.

Roll out to about 1-in. (*2,5 cm*) thickness and cut into 12 squares.

Place on an ungreased baking sheet.

Beat egg; brush over dough.

Bake in oven for 15 minutes or until lightly browned.

Cheese Twists

Cheese Twists

8 servings

14 oz	(*398 g*) pkg. frozen puff pastry, thawed
1	egg, beaten
¼ cup	(*60 mL*) grated Romano cheese

Preheat oven to 450°F (*230°C*).

Roll pastry to a thickness of ¼ in. (*0,5 cm*) on a lightly floured surface.

Brush with beaten egg and sprinkle with cheese.

Cut the pastry crosswise into strips ½-in. (*1 cm*) wide. Cut to desired lengths.

Twist strips several times and place on an ungreased baking sheet, pressing down the ends to prevent the pastry from unrolling.

Bake in oven 8 to 10 minutes or until golden.

Potato and Cheese Soup

4-6 servings

1 cup	(*250 mL*) coarsely grated potatoes
2½ cups	(*625 mL*) chicken stock (see *Soups*)
1 cup	(*250 mL*) heavy cream
1 cup	(*250 mL*) grated Brick cheese
1½ tbsp	(*22 mL*) butter
2 tbsp	(*30 mL*) all-purpose flour
	salt and pepper
¼ cup	(*60 mL*) chopped green onions
4	slices bacon, cooked and crumbled

Simmer potatoes in stock until tender. Do not drain. Beat until smooth. Stir in cream and cheese.

Melt butter in a small saucepan; stir in flour until smooth.

Add mixture to soup, whisking to blend. Season.

Simmer 4 to 5 minutes or until slightly thickened.

Serve garnished with onions and bacon.

Manicotti Crêpes

6 servings

1	250 g pkg. cream cheese, at room temperature
½ cup	(*125 mL*) dry curd cottage cheese
½ cup	(*125 mL*) coarsely grated medium Cheddar cheese
½ cup	(*125 mL*) coarsely grated Havarti cheese
1½ tbsp	(*22 mL*) softened butter
1	egg
3 tbsp	(*45 mL*) chopped parsley
3 tbsp	(*45 mL*) chopped green onions
½ tsp	(*3 mL*) salt
12	8-in. (*20 cm*) crêpes (see *Breads*)
2 cups	(*500 mL*) tomato sauce (see *Sauces*)
½ cup	(*125 mL*) grated Romano cheese

Preheat oven to 350°F (*180°C*).

Combine cheeses, butter and egg; beat until well blended.

Stir in parsley, onions and salt.

Spoon 3 to 4 tbsp (*45 to 60 mL*) of mixture onto each crêpe; roll and place in an ovenproof 13 x 9-in. (*32 x 22 cm*) serving dish.

Pour tomato sauce over the crêpes and sprinkle with Romano cheese.

Bake in oven 25 to 30 minutes.

Cheese Potato Pancakes

6-8 servings

1	250 g pkg. cream cheese, at room temperature
3 tbsp	(*45 mL*) all-purpose flour
2	eggs
¼ tsp	(*1 mL*) salt
3 cups	(*750 mL*) grated raw potatoes
2 cups	(*500 mL*) sour cream, divided
1 cup	(*250 mL*) diced Havarti cheese
¼ cup	(*60 mL*) margarine
1 lb	(*450 g*) bacon, cooked and crumbled

Combine cream cheese and flour; beat until well blended. Add eggs and salt; beat until smooth.

Place grated potatoes in a blender or food processor with steel blade; process until smooth.

Beat potato purée into cream cheese mixture. Stir in 1 cup (*250 mL*) sour cream and diced cheese.

Drop mixture by spoonfuls onto a medium hot griddle or pan brushed with margarine.

Turn when golden and continue cooking until second side is golden.

Add additional margarine when necessary.

Serve hot, topped with remaining sour cream and sprinkled with bacon.

Creamy Cheese Fondue

4 servings

¾ cup	*(180 mL)* grated Havarti cheese
¾ cup	*(180 mL)* grated old Cheddar cheese
¾ cup	*(180 mL)* grated Swiss cheese
1 tbsp	*(15 mL)* cornstarch
1 tsp	*(5 mL)* paprika
1½ cups	*(375 mL)* dry white wine
¼ cup	*(60 mL)* brandy
	salt and pepper
	French bread, cut into bite-size cubes
	bite-size pieces of cauliflower, broccoli, zucchini, red pepper or mushrooms

Combine cheeses, cornstarch and paprika; toss to blend.

Pour wine into a fondue pot and bring to a boil over medium heat.

Stir in cheese mixture a little at a time, letting each portion melt before adding more.

Cook, stirring constantly, until very hot and smooth. Stir in brandy. Season to taste.

Set fondue pot over a warmer.

Arrange bread cubes and assorted vegetables on a platter to accompany fondue.

1

Pour wine into fondue pot and bring to boil over medium heat. Stir in cheese mixture a little at a time.

2

Let each portion melt before adding more.

3

Pour in brandy, stirring constantly until very hot and smooth.

4

Set fondue pot over warmer and serve with bread and vegetables.

Cubed Cheese Fondue

8 servings

2¼ lbs	(*1 kg*) Havarti cheese, cut into bite-size pieces
1 cup	(*250 mL*) all-purpose flour
3	eggs, well beaten
2 cups	(*500 mL*) fine dry breadcrumbs
1 tbsp	(*15 mL*) seasoned salt
pinch	dried basil leaves
pinch	dried oregano leaves
2 - 3 cups	(*500 - 750 mL*) vegetable oil

Dip each cheese cube into the flour, then the eggs, then a mixture of the breadcrumbs, salt and herbs, being sure that the cheese is completely covered at each stage.

Allow to stand at room temperature for 30 minutes.

Heat the oil to very hot in the fondue pot.

Skewer each piece of cheese and brown in the oil. Serve with an assortment of sauces.

Cubes of beef, chicken and seafood can also be cooked in this manner.

Welsh Rarebit

6 servings

¼ cup	(*60 mL*) butter
¼ cup	(*60 mL*) all-purpose flour
1 cup	(*250 mL*) heavy cream
¼ tsp	(*1 mL*) dry mustard
¼ tsp	(*1 mL*) Worcestershire sauce
½ cup	(*125 mL*) beer (Old Vienna)
2 cups	(*500 mL*) grated old Cheddar cheese
	salt and pepper
6	slices toast

Melt the butter, sprinkle with flour; stir until well blended.

Add cream and simmer, stirring, until thickened.

Stir in mustard, Worcestershire sauce and beer.

Gradually sprinkle in the cheese, stirring constantly. Season with salt and pepper.

When all of cheese has melted, pour over toast and serve.

Indian Rarebit

6 servings

2 cups	(*500 mL*) milk, divided
1 tbsp	(*15 mL*) cornstarch
2½ cups	(*625 mL*) grated Gruyère or Swiss cheese
¼ tsp	(*1 mL*) curry powder
2	shallots, minced (optional)
2	green onions, finely chopped
1 tbsp	(*15 mL*) chutney sauce
6	slices toast
1 tbsp	(*15 mL*) sliced chives

Heat 1½ cups (*375 mL*) milk in a saucepan until simmering.

Stir cornstarch into remaining ½ cup (*125 mL*) milk until smooth. Pour into hot milk and simmer, stirring, until slightly thickened.

Stir in cheese, curry powder, shallots, green onions and chutney; simmer 2 to 3 minutes until well blended.

Pour over toast, sprinkle with chives and serve.

Note of caution : metal skewers when heated in oil get very hot. If placed directly into the mouth from the fondue pot, they can cause a serious burn.

Indian Rarebit

Bob's Lasagne

8 servings

6	lasagne noodles
2¼ lbs	(*1 kg*) lean ground beef
2 cups	(*500 mL*) tomato sauce (see *Sauces*)
1½ cups	(*375 mL*) dry curd cottage cheese
¾ cup	(*180 mL*) sour cream
1½ cups	(*375 mL*) grated Brick cheese
1½ cups	(*375 mL*) grated mozzarella cheese

Preheat oven to 425°F (*220°C*).

Cook lasagne noodles according to package directions; drain.

Cook ground beef until no pink remains; drain. Stir ground beef into tomato sauce.

Spread a thin layer of meat sauce in a 13 x 9-in. (*32 x 22 cm*) pan.

Cover with 3 lasagne noodles, half of the meat sauce and half the cottage cheese.

Repeat the layers of remaining noodles, meat sauce and cottage cheese.

Spread with sour cream, sprinkle with cheeses, and bake in oven 35 to 40 minutes or until cheese is golden brown.

Pizza

6 servings

3 tbsp	(*45 mL*) vegetable oil
2	garlic cloves, minced
1	small onion, finely chopped
1	celery stalk, finely chopped
½	green pepper, finely chopped
6	medium tomatoes, peeled, seeded and diced
¼ tsp	(*1 mL*) dried oregano leaves
¼ tsp	(*1 mL*) dried thyme leaves
¼ tsp	(*1 mL*) dried basil leaves
½ tsp	(*3 mL*) salt
¼ tsp	(*1 mL*) pepper
1 tbsp	(*15 mL*) Worcestershire sauce
1 tbsp	(*15 mL*) red wine (optional)
⅓ cup	(*80 mL*) tomato paste
½	recipe pizza dough (see *Breads*)

Low moisture toppings : pepperoni, ham, crab, onions, taco hamburger mix

Cheese : grated mozzarella, Brick, Swiss, Monterey Jack, or a combination of these

High moisture toppings : tomatoes, green peppers, mushrooms, pineapple, shrimp

Sauce : Sauté the vegetables in oil over medium heat until tender.

Stir in the seasonings, wine and tomato paste. Simmer 10 minutes.

Assembly : Preheat oven to 450°F (*230°C*).

Spread a thin layer of sauce evenly over rolled out pizza dough.

Sprinkle your choice of low moisture toppings over sauce. Sprinkle with grated cheese.

Arrange your choice of high moisture toppings on top of cheese.

Bake in oven 15 to 20 minutes or until crust is golden brown and cheese is bubbly.

Oysters Florentine

6-8 servings

10 oz	(*284 g*) spinach, coarsely chopped
¼ cup	(*60 mL*) butter
2 tbsp	(*30 mL*) lemon juice
1 tbsp	(*15 mL*) Worcestershire sauce
32	oysters
1 cup	(*250 mL*) Mornay Sauce (see *Sauces*)
½ cup	(*125 mL*) grated old Cheddar cheese
½ cup	(*125 mL*) grated Swiss cheese
½ cup	(*125 mL*) crumbled blue cheese

Sauté the spinach in butter over high heat, stirring until tender, about 2 to 3 minutes. Stir in the lemon juice and Worcestershire sauce.

Shuck oysters; drain. Discard flat upper shell. Over each oyster in shell, spoon a little spinach mixture and a little Mornay sauce.

Sprinkle with combined grated cheeses and place under heated broiler about 3 minutes, or until cheese melts. Serve hot.

Oysters Florentine

Swiss and Ham Log

1 large loaf

4 cups	(*1 L*) all-purpose flour
1 tsp	(*5 mL*) salt
1	envelope (*8 g*) instant yeast
1¼ cups	(*310 mL*) milk
3 tbsp	(*45 mL*) butter
1 lb	(*450 g*) thinly sliced ham
4 cups	(*1 L*) coarsely grated Swiss cheese
1	egg
2 tbsp	(*30 mL*) milk

Set aside 1 cup (*250 mL*) flour. Mix remaining flour, salt, and yeast in a large bowl. Scald milk and butter. Stir into flour mixture.

Mix in enough reserved flour to make a soft dough. Knead on a lightly floured surface until smooth and no longer sticky, about 10 minutes.

Place dough in a greased bowl, turning dough to grease all over. Cover and let rise until doubled, about 30 minutes.

Punch down and roll dough into a rectangle ⅛ in. (*0,3 cm*) thick. Cover with ham slices and sprinkle with cheese. Roll the dough tightly and place on a greased baking sheet, seam side down. Tuck ends underneath. Cover and let rise until doubled.

Preheat oven to 350°F (*180°C*).

Combine egg and milk; stir until well blended. Brush over loaf and bake in oven 40 to 45 minutes or until crust is golden brown. Cool on a rack.

Pyrohy

4-6 dozen

Dough

4 cups	(1 L) all-purpose flour
½ tsp	(3 mL) salt
1	egg, well beaten
1 cup	(250 mL) warm water

Filling

10	potatoes, boiled and mashed
2 cups	(500 mL) grated process cheese
¼ cup	(60 mL) sour cream
4	slices bacon, cooked and crumbled
6	green onions, sliced
¼ cup	(60 mL) sliced mushrooms, sautéed in butter

Topping

¼ cup	(60 mL) butter
2	large Spanish onions, diced
2 cups	(500 mL) sour cream
1 cup	(250 mL) cooked, crumbled bacon

Dough : Mix flour and salt in a deep bowl. Add egg and enough water to make a soft dough.

Knead on a floured board just until smooth (too much kneading will toughen the dough).

Place in a greased bowl, turning dough to grease all over. Cover and let stand 10 to 15 minutes.

Filling : Combine all ingredients; mix well.

Roll out dough on a lightly floured surface. Cut into 3-in. (7,5 cm) squares.

Place a spoonful of filling into the center of each square and fold into triangles; pinch edges to seal.

Drop pyrohy, a few at a time, into a large pot of salted water. Stir gently with a wooden spoon to prevent sticking.

Continue boiling until each puffs and floats. Remove with a slotted spoon; drain well.

Topping : Sauté onions in butter over low heat until onions are tender.

Toss drained pyrohy in butter and onions mixture.

Serve with bowls of sour cream and crumbled bacon.

Buffet Vegetables au Gratin

15-18 servings

1	small head cauliflower
1	bunch broccoli
½ lb	(225 g) button mushrooms
1	onion, sliced
3	small zucchini, sliced
3	carrots, sliced
3	celery stalks, sliced
2	green peppers, sliced
2	red peppers, sliced
2	yellow peppers, sliced
½ lb	(225 g) snow peas
2 cups	(500 mL) fine dry breadcrumbs
4 cups	(1 L) Mornay Sauce (see *Sauces*)
1 cup	(250 mL) grated Swiss cheese
1 cup	(250 mL) grated medium Cheddar cheese
1 cup	(250 mL) grated Havarti cheese

Preheat oven to 375°F (190°C).

Cut the cauliflower and broccoli in bite-size pieces. Combine all the vegetables.

Sprinkle the breadcrumbs evenly into the bottom of a greased 13 x 9-in. (32 x 22 cm) baking dish.

Add the mixed vegetables; top with Mornay Sauce.

Sprinkle with the cheese and bake, uncovered, in oven 45 minutes or until vegetables are tender.

Stuffed Green Peppers

Stuffed Green Peppers

6 servings

6	large green peppers
1 lb	(450 g) lean ground beef
1	small onion, finely chopped
1	celery stalk, finely chopped
2	medium carrots, finely chopped
1 tbsp	(15 mL) chili powder
1 tsp	(5 mL) paprika
1/2 tsp	(3 mL) dried oregano leaves
1/2 tsp	(3 mL) dried basil leaves
1/2 tsp	(3 mL) dried thyme leaves
1 tsp	(5 mL) salt
1 cup	(250 mL) tomato sauce (see *Sauces*)
1 cup	(250 mL) cooked rice
1 cup	(250 mL) grated Edam cheese

Preheat oven to 350°F (180°C).

Cut the tops off the peppers and remove seeds. Blanch the peppers in boiling water for 5 minutes; drain.

Sauté the beef in a non-stick pan until no pink remains. Stir in the vegetables, seasonings and half the tomato sauce; bring to a boil. Stir in rice.

Stuff mixture into peppers and place them upright in an ungreased baking dish.

Pour remaining sauce over peppers, cover and bake in oven 45 minutes.

Remove cover and continue baking for 15 minutes.

Sprinkle with cheese, let stand until melted and serve.

Coconut Cheesecake

6-8 servings

2	250 g pkg. cream cheese, at room temperature
¾ cup	(*180 mL*) granulated sugar, divided
2 tbsp	(*30 mL*) all-purpose flour
¾ cup	(*180 mL*) whipping cream
1 tbsp	(*15 mL*) coconut cream (optional)
¼ cup	(*60 mL*) coconut rum or dark rum
4	eggs, separated
½ cup	(*125 mL*) flaked coconut
1	unbaked 9-in. (*22 cm*) pastry shell

Preheat oven to 325°F (*160°C*).

Beat the cream cheese and ½ cup (*125 mL*) sugar until smooth. Beat in the flour, whipping cream, coconut cream and rum.

Add the egg yolks, one at a time, beating well after each addition. Stir in the coconut.

Beat the egg whites until foamy. Gradually add the remaining ¼ cup (*60 mL*) sugar and continue beating until stiff peaks form; fold into the cheese mixture.

Pour into pastry shell and bake in oven 60 minutes. Turn oven off and prop door open slightly.

After 30 minutes, transfer to rack to cool. Chill at least 4 hours.

Apple and Cheddar Pie

6 servings

Pastry

2 cups	(*500 mL*) all-purpose flour
½ tsp	(*3 mL*) salt
¼ cup	(*60 mL*) cold butter
¼ cup	(*60 mL*) cold lard
1	egg
¼ cup	(*60 mL*) cold water

Filling

4	large Granny Smith apples, peeled, cored and sliced
½ cup	(*125 mL*) raisins
⅓ cup	(*80 mL*) pecan pieces
1 cup	(*250 mL*) coarsely grated medium Cheddar cheese
½ cup	(*125 mL*) granulated sugar
1 tsp	(*5 mL*) cinnamon

Preheat oven to 400°F (*200°C*).

Pastry : Combine flour and salt. Cut in butter and lard until mixture resembles coarse crumbs. Beat together egg and water until blended.

Stirring with a fork, add just enough liquid, 1 tbsp (*15 mL*) at a time, to make dough hold together. Press into a ball and roll immediately or wrap in plastic wrap and refrigerate. (Let refrigerated pastry soften a bit a room temperature before rolling).

Roll about ⅔ of the pastry and fit into a 9-in. (22 cm) pie plate.

Filling : Combine apples, raisins, pecans and cheese in a large bowl.

Stir together sugar and cinnamon; sprinkle over apple mixture and toss just until blended.

Spoon filling into prepared crust. Roll remaining pastry and place over filling. Trim top crust, leaving a 1-in. (*2,5 cm*) overhang.

Tuck top edge of pastry under edge of bottom crust, then press edges together firmly with a fork or flute with fingers to seal tightly.

Make small slashes in top to vent steam.

Bake in oven about 40 minutes or until apples are tender and pastry is golden.

Garlic Cheese Bread

2 loaves

1 cup	*(250 mL)*	milk
2 tbsp	*(30 mL)*	sugar
2 tsp	*(10 mL)*	salt
1 tbsp	*(15 mL)*	butter
1 tsp	*(5 mL)*	sugar
1 cup	*(250 mL)*	warm water
1		pkg. active dry yeast
5 cups	*(1,2 L)*	flour
1 tbsp	*(15 mL)*	minced garlic
1 cup	*(250 mL)*	grated old Cheddar cheese
1 cup	*(250 mL)*	grated Monterey Jack cheese

In saucepan, combine milk, 2 tbsp (*30 mL*) sugar, salt and butter. Heat until butter melts. Cool to lukewarm.

In large mixing bowl, dissolve 1 tsp (*5 mL*) sugar in warm water; sprinkle yeast over and let stand for 10 minutes or until foamy. Add milk mixture, 1 cup (*250 mL*) flour, garlic and cheeses to yeast mixture; beat until well blended, about 3 minutes. Gradually stir in enough of remaining flour to make a soft dough.

Knead dough on a lightly floured surface until smooth and no longer sticky, about 10 minutes. Place dough in a greased bowl, turning dough to grease all over. Cover and let rise until doubled, about 1 hour.

Preheat oven to 350°F (*180°C*).

Punch down dough, shape into 2 loaves, and place in two 8 x 4-in. (*20 x 10 cm*) greased

Garlic Cheese Bread

loaf pans. Let rise until doubled.

Bake in oven 45 minutes or until crusts are golden brown and loaves sound hollow when tapped on bottom. Remove from pans and cool on racks.

Cœur à la Crème

6-8 servings

2		250 g pkg. cream cheese, at room temperature
2 tbsp	*(30 mL)*	softened butter
1½ cups	*(375 mL)*	dry cottage cheese
½ cup	*(125 mL)*	heavy cream
⅓ cup	*(80 mL)*	icing sugar
4 cups	*(1 L)*	fresh strawberries

In blender or food processor with steel blade, combine cream cheese, butter, cottage cheese, cream and icing sugar; process until smooth.

Pour mixture into 4-cup (*1 L*) heart-shaped mold lined with a double thickness of slightly dampened cheesecloth. Place the mold on a plate to catch the drippings. Refrigerate the mold 24 to 48 hours until the cheese is firmly set. Unmold heart on a serving plate and arrange strawberries around it.

Sandwiches

John Montagu, the 4th Earl of Sandwich, is credited with the invention of the sandwich, apparently as a result of his reluctance to leave the gambling table while he was having a run of luck.

But although he may have given the sandwich its name, it seems likely that people have been eating some variation of the sandwich since bread was invented.

Every cuisine in the world, it seems, has its own variation — whether it's called pizza, a donair, or an egg roll.

This chapter has recipes for sandwiches made with regular bread, as well as suggestions for fillings to be packed into pita bread, tucked into tortillas and taco shells and spread between thick slabs of homemade nut bread.

What you won't find here are recipes for dainty little tea sandwiches to serve to the girls or round out a plate of canapés.

Instead, I have concentrated on entrée-style sandwiches that can make a fine lunch or dinner all on their own. Some of them are so unusual that you'll want to serve them on special occasions to impress your friends.

A sandwich can be as good as the occasion, so make every sandwich great.

Bacon, Basil Tomato Sandwich

Bacon, Basil Tomato Sandwich

4 servings

12	tomato slices
1 tsp	(*5 mL*) salt
1 tsp	(*5 mL*) basil
½ tsp	(*3 mL*) pepper
8	slices bacon
4	Kaiser buns
4	slices Cheddar

Sprinkle the tomato slices with the seasonings.

Fry the bacon. Discard the fat.

Slice the buns in half. On the heel of each bun, place 3 tomato slices.

Top with 2 slices cooked bacon and 1 slice of cheese. Place on pastry sheet and put under broiler until cheese melts.

Top with crown of bun. Serve with potato salad.

Chicken Cashew Pitas

4 servings

3 cups	(*750 mL*) cooked diced chicken
1 cup	(*250 mL*) cashew nuts
1 cup	(*250 mL*) mayonnaise
2 tbsp	(*30 mL*) minced onion
2 tbsp	(*30 mL*) minced green pepper
2 tbsp	(*30 mL*) minced pimiento
4	pita breads
1½ cups	(*375 mL*) alfalfa sprouts

Blend together the chicken, cashews, mayonnaise, onion, green pepper and pimientos.

Slit open the pitas. Stuff with filling and alfalfa sprouts.

Chicken Buns

6 servings

6	crusty dinner rolls
2 tbsp	(*30 mL*) melted butter
2 cups	(*500 mL*) chicken meat, boned and cooked
¼ cup	(*60 mL*) finely diced onion
¼ cup	(*60 mL*) finely diced celery
¼ cup	(*60 mL*) finely diced green pepper
½ cup	(*125 mL*) mayonnaise
¼ tsp	(*1 mL*) salt
pinch	pepper
pinch	paprika
1 cup	(*250 mL*) grated Cheddar cheese
1 cup	(*250 mL*) grated Swiss cheese

Cut off the top crusts from rolls. Scoop out the centers. Brush with the butter and toast under a broiler.

Combine the chicken, vegetables, mayonnaise and seasonings.

Stuff into the buns. Sprinkle with the cheese.

Place under the broiler for 2 more minutes.

Replace top crusts. Serve at once.

Barbecued Chicken Buns

6 servings

1 tbsp	(*15 mL*) oil
½ cup	(*125 mL*) minced onions
¾ cup	(*180 mL*) water
¼ cup	(*60 mL*) tomato sauce
¼ cup	(*60 mL*) ketchup
½ tsp	(*3 mL*) salt
½ tsp	(*3 mL*) paprika
½ tsp	(*3 mL*) oregano
½ tsp	(*3 mL*) thyme
½ tsp	(*3 mL*) pepper
½ tsp	(*3 mL*) chili powder
1 lb	(*450 g*) chicken, cooked and diced
6	Kaiser buns

Heat the oil in the skillet. Add the onion and sauté until tender.

Add the water, tomato sauce, ketchup and seasonings. Simmer for 20 minutes.

Add the chicken and simmer for 5 minutes.

Slice the rolls. Stuff with chicken. Serve.

Barbecued Beefwiches

6 servings

1 tbsp	(*15 mL*) oil
½ cup	(*125 mL*) finely diced onions
¾ cup	(*180 mL*) water
1 tbsp	(*15 mL*) Worcestershire sauce
¼ cup	(*60 mL*) tomato sauce
¼ cup	(*60 mL*) ketchup
½ tsp	(*3 mL*) salt
¼ tsp	(*1 mL*) pepper
¼ tsp	(*1 mL*) chili powder
¼ tsp	(*1 mL*) paprika
1 lb	(*450 g*) beef, shaved and cooked
6	large Kaiser buns

Heat the oil in a skillet. Sauté the onions until tender.

Add the water, Worcestershire sauce, tomato sauce, ketchup and seasonings.

Reduce heat and simmer for 20 minutes, or until very thick.

Add the beef and continue to simmer for 5 minutes.

Slice the buns in half. Fill with beef and sauce.

Replace the top or crown of the buns. Serve very hot.

1

In a skillet, sauté the onions in the oil until tender.

2

Add water, Worcestershire sauce, tomato sauce, ketchup and seasonings. Reduce heat and simmer 20 minutes.

3

Add beef and continue to simmer 5 minutes.

4

Slice buns in half and fill with beef and sauce.

Chicken Tube

6 servings

2 cups	(*500 mL*) cream cheese
1	egg
1 tsp	(*5 mL*) paprika
1 tsp	(*5 mL*) basil
¼ tsp	(*1 mL*) pepper
¼ tsp	(*1 mL*) salt
3 cups	(*750 mL*) finely diced chicken
1 cup	(*250 mL*) pine nuts
1	French baguette

Preheat oven to 350°F (*180°C*).

Cream the cheese, egg and seasonings together. Fold in the chicken and pine nuts.

Slice the ends from the French bread and scoop out the bread.

Do not break the crust. Fill the hollow with the filling. Wrap very tightly in foil.

Bake in oven for 20 minutes. Remove and slice. Serve with a spinach salad.

Chicken Oscar

4 servings

1 tbsp	(*15 mL*) butter
4	chicken breasts, 3 oz (*90 g*) each
4	thick slices dark rye bread
½ lb	(*225 g*) crab meat
12	asparagus spears, blanched
1 cup	(*500 mL*) Béarnaise Sauce (see *Sauces*)

Heat the butter in a skillet. Sauté the chicken breasts 2½ minutes each side.

Place each breast on a bread slice. Top with crab and asparagus.

Pour ¼ cup (*60 mL*) of sauce over each. Broil in oven for 1 minute.

Chicken Melt

4 servings

2	Kaiser buns
4	chicken breasts, 3 oz (*90 g*) each
1 cup	(*250 mL*) diced bacon
¼ cup	(*60 mL*) finely diced onions
¼ cup	(*60 mL*) finely diced celery
¼ cup	(*60 mL*) finely diced green pepper
½ cup	(*125 mL*) chopped tomatoes
4	slices Cheddar cheese

Slice the buns in half.

Broil the chicken in oven 2 to 3 minutes each side.

Sauté the bacon until crisp. Drain excess grease. Add the vegetables and cook until tender.

Place one chicken breast on each half of roll. Spread with sautéed mixture.

Top with cheese. Broil for 2 minutes in the oven. Serve at once.

Apple Sandwich

6 servings

3 cups	(*750 mL*) apples, peeled and diced
3 tbsp	(*45 mL*) honey
½ cup	(*125 mL*) mayonnaise
½ tsp	(*3 mL*) ground cinnamon
1	loaf Apple Raisin Nut Bread (see *Breads*)
1½ cups	(*375 mL*) grated medium Cheddar

Mix the apples, honey, mayonnaise and cinnamon together.

Slice bread. Top each slice with an even amount of mixture. Place on a pastry sheet.

Sprinkle with cheese.

Place under broiler until cheese melts. Serve at once.

Crab and Avocado

Crab and Avocado

6 servings

1 cup	(*250 mL*) mayonnaise
¼ cup	(*60 mL*) confectioners' sugar
1 lb	(*450 g*) crab meat
2	avocados, diced
1 cup	(*250 mL*) red seedless grapes
½ cup	(*125 mL*) walnut pieces
1	loaf banana bread

Mix the mayonnaise with the sugar.

Blend the crab meat, avocados, grapes and walnuts.

Blend in the mayonnaise. Cut the banana bread into thick slices.

Top with crab mix. Serve.

Croque Monsieur

4 servings

12 oz	(*340 g*) shaved ham
4	slices Gruyère cheese, 2 oz (*60 g*) each
8	slices bread, crusts trimmed
⅓ cup	(*80 mL*) butter

Preheat oven to 425°F (*220°C*).

Place 3 oz (*90 g*) of ham and 1 slice of cheese between two slices of bread. Butter the outside of the sandwich.

Bake in oven for 5 minutes or until golden brown.

Cut in quarters and serve with potato salad.

Crab Monte Cristo

4 servings

8	slices white bread
2 cups	(*500 mL*) crab meat
1 tbsp	(*15 mL*) minced onion
1 tbsp	(*15 mL*) minced celery
½ cup	(*125 mL*) mayonnaise
¼ tsp	(*1 mL*) paprika
¼ tsp	(*1 mL*) pepper
¼ tsp	(*1 mL*) salt
4	slices Swiss cheese
2	eggs
⅓ cup	(*80 mL*) milk
3 tbsp	(*45 mL*) butter

Trim the bread crusts. Blend the crab meat, onion, celery, mayonnaise and seasonings together.

Divide the filling equally over four slices of bread.

Top with a slice of cheese and the second slice of bread.

Mix the eggs in the milk.

Heat the butter in a large skillet.

Dip the sandwiches in the egg/milk mixture.

Fry in the butter to golden brown. Serve at once.

Creole Shrimp Po-Boy

1 serving

1	10-in. (*25 cm*) French baguette
1 tbsp	(*15 mL*) butter
4 oz	(*115 g*) shrimp, shelled and deveined
¼ tsp	(*1 mL*) salt
pinch	cayenne pepper
pinch	paprika
pinch	garlic powder
pinch	thyme
pinch	oregano
pinch	pepper
¼ cup	(*60 mL*) grated cheese (any type)
½ cup	(*125 mL*) shredded lettuce

Cut baguette in half lengthwise.

In a skillet, heat the butter. Sauté the shrimp until pink. Sprinkle with seasonings.

Place mixture on bottom half of baguette. Sprinkle with cheese.

Broil for 2 minutes. Top with lettuce.

Cover with top of baguette.

Creole Shrimp Po-Boy

Garlic Tomato Sauté

2-4 servings

1	12-in. (*30 cm*) French baguette
½ cup	(*125 mL*) finely diced onions
½ cup	(*125 mL*) finely diced green pepper
2 cups	(*500 mL*) tomatoes, chopped and drained
¼ cup	(*60 mL*) garlic butter
2 cups	(*500 mL*) grated Cheddar cheese

Slice the loaf in half lengthwise.

In a skillet, gently sauté the onions, green pepper and tomatoes in the garlic butter.

Spread mixture on top of French baguette halves. Sprinkle with cheese.

Broil 2 minutes. Serve hot.

Garlic Tomato Sauté

Curried Chicken Pitas

4 servings

1 cup	(*250 mL*) cooked boneless chicken
1	onion, finely diced
½	green pepper, finely diced
½ cup	(*125 mL*) pine nuts
½ cup	(*125 mL*) mayonnaise
1 tsp	(*5 mL*) curry powder
4	pita breads
1 cup	(*250 mL*) alfalfa sprouts
8	cherry tomatoes

Dice the chicken. Mix the chicken with the onion, green pepper, pine nuts, mayonnaise and curry powder.

Slit pitas open. Stuff with chicken mixture.

Top with alfalfa sprouts. Garnish with tomatoes.

Hawaiian Chicken Roll

Hawaiian Chicken Roll

4 servings

1 tbsp	(15 mL) brown sugar
1/4 tsp	(1 mL) ground ginger
1 tbsp	(15 mL) soya sauce
4	chicken breasts, 3 oz (90 g) each
4	pineapple rings
4	Kaiser buns
2 tbsp	(30 mL) Dijon mustard
4	slices Swiss cheese

Mix the sugar, ginger and soya sauce together.

Broil the chicken breasts and pineapple rings. Brush with sauce. Broil 2 1/2 to 3 minutes each side.

Slice buns in half. Spread with mustard.

Place a chicken breast on the bottom of each bun.

Top with a pineapple slice and then a cheese slice. Place under oven broiler to melt cheese.

Place top half of bun on sandwiches and serve.

Indian Sandwich

4 servings

4 oz	(115 g) cream cheese
¼ cup	(60 mL) diced mango
1 tsp	(5 mL) curry powder
6.5 oz	(184 g) can salmon, drained
2	bagels
4	orange slices, ¼-in. (0,5 cm) thick

Preheat oven to 400°F (200°C).

Blend the cream cheese into the diced mango. Mix in the curry powder. Blend together with the salmon.

Cut each bagel in half.

Divide salmon evenly and spread on the bagels; cover with 1 orange slice.

Place on a pastry sheet. Bake in oven for 6 minutes.

Indian Sandwich

Lobster Melt

4 servings

½ lb	(225 g) lobster meat, coarsely diced
¼ cup	(60 mL) mayonnaise
2 tsp	(10 mL) lemon juice
1 tsp	(5 mL) mild horseradish
2	Kaiser buns
8	tomato slices
2 cups	(500 mL) grated Cheddar cheese

Blend the lobster meat with the mayonnaise, lemon juice and horseradish.

Slice the buns in half. Top each half with equal amounts of mixture.

Place two tomato slices on each. Sprinkle with cheese and broil two minutes.

Serve with lobster bisque.

Milwaukee Sandwich

4 servings

8	slices bread, buttered
1 lb	(*450 g*) chicken meat, sliced and cooked
6 oz	(*170 g*) Roquefort cheese, crumbled
1 tsp	(*5 mL*) paprika

Between two bread slices, with buttered side on outside, place 4 oz (*115 g*) of chicken and 1½ oz (*42 g*) of cheese. Sprinkle with paprika.

Sauté over medium heat until golden brown.

Serve hot.

Milwaukee Sandwich

Saag Paratha

4 servings

4	pita breads
3 tbsp	(*45 mL*) butter
2 cups	(*500 mL*) chicken, boned, diced and cooked
10 oz	(*284 g*) spinach, chopped
2 tsp	(*10 mL*) curry powder
½ tsp	(*3 mL*) salt
1 cup	(*250 mL*) diced feta cheese

Cut the pitas in half.

Heat the butter in a skillet. Add the chicken and spinach; sauté 2 minutes. Sprinkle with curry powder and salt.

Add the feta and sauté 1 more minute. Stuff mixture into pitas.

Serve with cold rice salad or Mulligatawny Soup (see *Soups*).

Shrimp Croissant

1 serving

½ cup	(125 mL)	baby shrimp
1 tbsp	(15 mL)	minced onion
1 tbsp	(15 mL)	minced green pepper
1 tbsp	(15 mL)	minced celery
4 tsp	(20 mL)	mayonnaise
1		croissant
¼ cup	(60 mL)	alfalfa sprouts
1		lettuce leaf
2		cherry tomatoes

Blend together the shrimp, onion, green pepper, celery with the mayonnaise.

Slice the croissant in half. Fill with shrimp mixture.

Garnish with alfalfa, lettuce and cherry tomatoes.

Smoked Salmon Slice

1 serving

1		hard-boiled egg, chopped
1 tsp	(5 mL)	minced onion
1 tsp	(5 mL)	minced celery
pinch		salt
pinch		pepper
1 tbsp	(15 mL)	mayonnaise
1		dark rye bread slice, buttered
3 oz	(90 g)	smoked salmon
3		onion rings
1 tbsp	(15 mL)	red caviar
½ tsp	(3 mL)	minced chives

Blend the egg with the onion, celery, seasonings and mayonnaise. Spread onto bread.

Lay the salmon across the filling. Garnish with onion rings.

Sprinkle with caviar and chives.

Sloppy Joes

8 servings

4 tsp	(20 mL)	oil
1		onion, minced
1		green pepper, minced
2		garlic cloves, minced
4 oz	(115 g)	mushrooms, sliced
1½ lbs	(675 g)	lean ground beef
2 tsp	(10 mL)	salt
1 tsp	(5 mL)	pepper
½ tsp	(3 mL)	cayenne pepper
2 tsp	(10 mL)	chili powder
1 tsp	(5 mL)	basil
1 tbsp	(15 mL)	Worcestershire sauce
3 tbsp	(45 mL)	flour
½ cup	(125 mL)	crushed tomatoes
⅓ cup	(80 mL)	water
2 tbsp	(30 mL)	tomato paste
8		Kaiser buns, toasted
2 cups	(500 mL)	grated medium Cheddar

Heat the oil. Sauté the onion, green pepper, garlic and mushrooms. Add the beef and cook thoroughly. Drain excess fat.

Add all the seasonings and sprinkle in the flour. Simmer for 3 minutes.

Add the tomatoes, water and tomato paste. Simmer for 15 minutes or until very thick.

Spoon mixture on the heel half of the buns, top with cheese and cover with crown of buns. Serve.

Wiener Schnitzel Sandwich

4 servings

1	egg
¼ cup	(60 mL) milk
4	veal pieces, 2 oz (60 g) each, pounded flat
¼ cup	(60 mL) flour
½ cup	(125 mL) seasoned breadcrumbs
2 tbsp	(30 mL) butter
3 tbsp	(45 mL) applesauce
3 tbsp	(45 mL) mayonnaise
4	Kaiser buns
4	lettuce leaves

Mix the egg in the milk. Dust the veal with flour. Dip in milk mixture. Dredge in breadcrumbs.

Heat the butter in a large skillet and sauté the breaded veal 2½ minutes each side.

Blend the applesauce with the mayonnaise.

Cut the buns in half. Spread with apple mayonnaise.

Place one lettuce leaf and one piece of veal per bun.

Close and serve.

Wiener Schnitzel Sandwich

Tacos

8 servings

1 lb	(450 g) lean ground beef
2	garlic cloves, minced
1	small onion, minced
1 tsp	(5 mL) Worcestershire sauce
1 tsp	(5 mL) salt
2 tsp	(10 mL) chili powder
¼ tsp	(1 mL) cayenne pepper
½ cup	(125 mL) oil
8	tortilla shells
1 cup	(250 mL) Enchilada Sauce (see *Enchiladas*)
¼	head lettuce, shredded
2	tomatoes, diced
2 cups	(500 mL) sharp Cheddar cheese, crumbled

Sauté the beef with the garlic and onion. Drain excess fat.

Add Worcestershire sauce and seasonings. Combine.

Heat oil and fry tortilla shells. As they are cooking, fold them over to form a pocket.

Remove from oil and drain well. Fill tortilla shells with meat mixture.

Top with 1 tbsp (15 mL) sauce, lettuce, tomato and cheese.

The Classic Club

1 serving

2	slices bacon
3	slices bread
1 tsp	(5 mL) mayonnaise
4	tomato slices
2	lettuce leaves
1	3 oz (90 g) chicken breast, broiled and sliced

Fry the bacon. Toast the bread. Butter two slices and spread the mayonnaise on the third.

On one slice of bread, place the tomatoes, bacon and 1 lettuce leaf. Top with a second slice of bread.

Place the other lettuce leaf and the chicken breast on this slice.

Place the final slice of bread on top. Cut into fours. Serve with chips.

Timothy's Crazy Mixed Up Super Loaf

4 servings

4	12-in. (30 cm) French baguettes
¼ cup	(60 mL) Dijon mustard
1	onion, sliced
1	green pepper, sliced
4 oz	(115 g) mushrooms, sliced
2 tbsp	(30 mL) butter
4	smoked sausages, 2 oz (60 g) each
1 lb	(450 g) cooked roast beef, thinly sliced
4 oz	(115 g) grated medium Cheddar
4 oz	(115 g) grated Havarti cheese

Slice the bread in half lengthwise. Spread with mustard.

Sauté the onion, green pepper and mushrooms in the butter until tender. Place on loaf halves.

Slice the smoked sausages lengthwise. Quickly fry in the skillet.

Place on top of vegetables. Top with roast beef and cheeses.

Broil for two minutes under a broiler in the oven. Serve at once.

Tortillas

12-16 tortillas

2 cups	(500 mL)	cornmeal
1 cup	(250 mL)	flour
1 tsp	(5 mL)	salt
1 tsp	(5 mL)	butter
⅓ cup	(80 mL)	water
1 tbsp	(15 mL)	oil

Sift together the dry ingredients. Cut in the butter.

Add just enough water to knead into a stiff ball.

Let dough stand for 30 minutes.

Preheat oven to 350°F (180°C).

Divide dough into even pieces. Shape into balls.

Roll out dough into thin rounds.

Lightly grease rounds and bake both sides in oven until dry, but still pliable.

1

Prepare dough and knead into a stiff ball; let stand 30 minutes.

2

Shape dough into balls and roll out into thin rounds.

3

Lightly grease rounds.

4

Bake in oven until dry yet pliable.

Tropical Treat

8 servings

1	papaya
1	mango
2 tbsp	*(30 mL)* honey
½ cup	*(125 mL)* mayonnaise
1 cup	*(250 mL)* baby shrimp
8	slices banana bread
1 cup	*(250 mL)* grated Monterey Jack cheese

Peel and dice the papaya and mango.

Mix with the honey and mayonnaise. Add the shrimp. Blend.

Top each slice of banana bread with mixture. Place on pastry sheet.

Sprinkle with cheese. Broil just until cheese melts.

Whaler Sandwich

6 servings

6	Kaiser buns
2 tbsp	*(30 mL)* butter
2	eggs
½ cup	*(125 mL)* milk
6	cod tails, 3 oz *(90 g)* each
1 cup	*(250 mL)* flour
2 cups	*(500 mL)* fine seasoned breadcrumbs
4 cups	*(1 L)* oil
⅔ cup	*(180 mL)* tartare sauce (see *Sauces*)

Slice the buns and butter them. Mix the eggs in the milk.

Dust the cod with flour. Dip into egg mixture. Dredge with breadcrumbs.

Heat oil. Fry cod for 3 minutes or until golden brown.

Spread 2 tbsp *(30 mL)* of tartare sauce on each bun.

Place a fried cod tail on top. Serve with clam chowder.

Tuna Melt

4 servings

4	croissants
2 cups	*(500 mL)* tuna, drained and flaked
¼ cup	*(60 mL)* minced onions
¼ cup	*(60 mL)* minced celery
½ cup	*(125 mL)* mayonnaise
1 tbsp	*(15 mL)* Dijon mustard
1 cup	*(250 mL)* grated Cheddar cheese
1 cup	*(250 mL)* grated Swiss cheese

Slice the croissants in half.

Blend the tuna with the onions, celery, mayonnaise and mustard.

Spread mixture on croissants. Sprinkle with cheeses and broil for two minutes.

Serve with a rich cream soup.

Tuna Melt

Super Chef's Sandwich

4 servings

8	slices light rye bread
12 oz	(*340 g*) thinly sliced turkey
6 oz	(*170 g*) thinly sliced or shaved ham
12	slices cooked bacon
12	slices tomato
4	slices Swiss cheese
4	slices old Cheddar cheese
	softened butter

Between each two slices of bread, place 3 oz (*85 g*) turkey, 1½ oz (*42 g*) ham, 3 slices bacon, 3 tomato slices, 1 slice of Swiss cheese and 1 slice of Cheddar cheese.

Butter the outside of each of the sandwiches and grill until golden on both sides.

Serve with Onion Soup au Gratin.

Super Chef's Sandwich

Monte Cristo Sandwich

4 servings

8	slices white bread, crusts removed
8 oz	(*225 g*) thinly sliced or shaved turkey
8 oz	(*225 g*) thinly sliced or shaved ham
8 slices	Swiss cheese
4	eggs
¼ cup	(*60 mL*) milk
	margarine

Between each two slices of bread, place 2 oz (*56 g*) turkey, 2 oz (*56 g*) ham and 2 slices of cheese.

In a large flat dish, beat together eggs and milk with a fork. Dip both sides of sandwiches in egg mixture.

In frying pan, melt margarine over medium heat. Grill sandwiches until golden on both sides.

Repeat with remaining sandwiches, adding margarine as required.

Serve hot with a medley of fresh fruit.

Reuben Sandwich with Mustard Sauce

4 servings

Sandwich

8	slices dark rye bread
¾ lb	(*340 g*) thinly sliced cooked corned beef
¾ cup	(*180 mL*) drained sauerkraut
8	slices Swiss cheese

Mustard Sauce

¼ cup	(*60 mL*) mayonnaise
2 tbsp	(*30 mL*) Dijon mustard
1 tbsp	(*15 mL*) prepared horseradish

Between each two slices of bread, place about 3 oz (*85 g*) corned beef, 3 tbsp (*45 mL*) sauerkraut and 2 slices cheese.

Butter the outside of each of the sandwiches and grill until golden on both sides.

Serve with mustard sauce and fries.

To prepare mustard sauce, combine all ingredients and mix thoroughly.

Reuben Sandwich with Mustard Sauce

Some Kind of Different

4 servings

2	mangos
8	thin slices prosciutto
4	slices Zucchini Nut Bread (see *Breads*)
8	slices Monterey Jack cheese

Peel and slice the mangos in 4.

Wrap each mango with a slice of prosciutto. Place 2 mango wraps on a slice of bread.

Top each with a slice of cheese. Place on a pastry sheet.

Broil just until cheese melts. Serve at once.

Philadelphia Steak and Cheese Sandwich

4 servings

2	large onions, sliced
1	green pepper, sliced
	butter
1 cup	(*250 mL*) sliced mushrooms
1 lb	(*450 g*) very thinly sliced sirloin
8	processed cheese slices
4	8-in. (*20 cm*) buns

Sauté onions and green pepper in butter over medium heat until tender; place in oven to keep warm.

Sauté mushrooms in additional butter over high heat; add to onion mixture in oven.

In additional butter, over high heat, sauté the sirloin slices until cooked to desired doneness.

Slice buns in half lengthwise. Place 4 oz (*115 g*) meat on bottom half of each bun, top with one quarter of the vegetable mixture and two cheese slices.

Place under heated broiler just until cheese melts. Toast tops of buns and place on each sandwich.

Deviled Ham Spread

3 cups (750 mL)

1	250 g pkg. cream cheese
¼ cup	(*60 mL*) mayonnaise
¼ tsp	(*1 mL*) Tabasco sauce
2 tbsp	(*30 mL*) prepared mustard
1 tsp	(*5 mL*) minced onion
10 oz	(*280 g*) ham, minced
½ tsp	(*3 mL*) chili powder
½ tsp	(*3 mL*) paprika

Cream together the cheese and mayonnaise.

Add the remaining ingredients. Blend thoroughly.

Use either as a dip or sandwich spread. Great for vegetables.

Shrimp Crab Spread

3 cups (750 mL)

8 oz	250 g pkg. cream cheese
½ cup	(*125 mL*) sour cream
4 oz	(*115 g*) crab meat, cooked and chopped
4 oz	(*115 g*) shrimp meat, cooked and chopped
1 tbsp	(*15 mL*) minced onion
1 tsp	(*5 mL*) paprika
½ tsp	(*3 mL*) pepper
½ tsp	(*3 mL*) salt
3 tbsp	(*45 mL*) chili sauce

Cream the cheese together with the sour cream.

Blend in the seafood, onion and seasonings.

Add the chili sauce and combine well.

Fiji Island Sandwich

Fiji Island Sandwich

8 servings

1 cup	(*250 mL*) shredded coconut
¼ cup	(*60 mL*) coconut cream
14 oz	(*398 mL*) can pineapple tidbits, drained
1 cup	(*250 mL*) mayonnaise
1 lb	(*450 g*) crab meat, shredded
10 oz	(*284 mL*) can mandarin oranges, drained
2	bananas, sliced
1	Banana Nut Loaf (see *Breads*) cut into 8 thick slices
1 cup	(*250 mL*) grated Swiss cheese
1 cup	(*250 mL*) grated mild Cheddar cheese

Combine coconut, coconut cream and pineapple tidbits. Stir in mayonnaise until well blended.

Gently stir in crab meat, orange sections and banana slices.

Spoon a generous portion of crab mixture onto each slice of banana bread, sprinkle with grated cheeses and place under heated broiler just until cheese melts.

Serve with Romaine Salad with Oranges or Broccoli and Cheddar Soup.

Breads

No doubt you've heard the saying that "Man cannot live by bread alone."

True as that may be, it's also true that meals would be a lot more boring without the infinite variety of breads and other baked goods available to us.

In the chapter, I have given you a limited but all-purpose selection of some of the best bread and muffin recipes. You'll find breads for everyday use, including whole wheat bread and dinner rolls. But you'll also find some special breads to give added flair to special meals.

You'll find some unusual muffins for Sunday morning brunching, and some fruity nut breads for munching at tea time or anytime.

I've even included a few special breads to add authenticity to Tex-Mex or Cajun meals.

Bread Baking Hints

1) When baking recipes call for eggs or milk, let them come to room temperature first.

2) If the top of your baking starts to turn too brown before the insides are cooked, place a tent of foil over the top and continue baking.

3) Measure your ingredients carefully. Baking is not the time for experimentation, unless you really know what you are doing.

4) Use all-purpose flour unless the recipe specifies something else.

5) Remember that yeast is a living product. Feeding it a little sugar will help it grow faster, but hot water above 130°F (55°C) will kill it.

Bacon Muffins

Bacon Muffins

12 muffins

1 lb	(*450 g*) bacon
1½ cups	(*375 mL*) flour
1 tbsp	(*15 mL*) baking powder
½ cup	(*125 mL*) butter
1	egg, beaten
½ cup	(*125 mL*) heavy cream
1 cup	(*250 mL*) grated sharp Cheddar
3	green onions, sliced
1 tbsp	(*15 mL*) caraway seeds

Preheat oven to 400°F (*200°C*).

Fry the bacon. Drain excess fat, reserving 1 tbsp (*15 mL*). Dice or crumble the bacon.

In a bowl, sift together the flour and baking powder.

Cut in the butter. Stir in the egg and cream.

Add the bacon, cheese and green onions.

Grease 12 muffin tins with reserved bacon fat.

Drop batter into each cup, filling to ¾. Sprinkle with caraway seeds.

Bake in oven 15 to 20 minutes or until golden brown. Serve hot.

French Bread

2 loaves

2 tbsp	(*30 mL*) active dry yeast
2½ cups	(*625 mL*) warm water
7½ cups	(*1,9 L*) sifted flour
2 tsp	(*10 mL*) salt
1	egg white, lightly beaten
1 tbsp	(*15 mL*) cold water

In a mixing bowl, soften yeast in warm water. Let soak 10 minutes.

In another bowl, mix 2 cups (*500 mL*) flour with the salt. Add to the water; mix well. Add the remaining flour 1 cup (*250 mL*) at a time. Incorporate well after each addition. Machine knead 20 to 25 minutes, no less. Dough should be smooth and elastic.

Place in a lightly greased bowl. Cover and allow to rise double in size, 1¼ to 1½ hours.

Punch down, cover and allow to rise a second time 1 hour.

Place dough on a flour-dusted board. Divide in two. Roll out into large rectangles, 16 x 14 in. (*40 x 35 cm*). Then roll up very tightly like a jelly roll. Seal the ends. Place seam side down on a greased pastry sheet.

Mix the egg white with cold water. Brush on bread. Cover with a towel. Allow bread to double in size a third time.

Preheat oven to 375°F (*190°C*).

Place a shallow pan half-filled with water on bottom rack of oven.

Bake the bread on the center rack of the oven for 20 minutes.

Brush a second time with egg white then bake for 20 more minutes.

White Bread

3 loaves

1 cup	(*250 mL*) milk
⅓ cup	(*80 mL*) sugar
⅓ cup	(*80 mL*) butter
1 tbsp	(*15 mL*) salt
2 oz	(*60 g*) active dry yeast
12 cups	(*3 L*) all-purpose flour
3 cups	(*750 mL*) warm water
2	eggs

Heat the milk to lukewarm. Mix in the sugar, butter and salt.

Sprinkle in the yeast and set aside for 10 minutes.

Place flour in large bowl. Slowly mix in liquids. Add the eggs and mix; knead for 10 minutes or until a smooth ball forms.

Cover and allow to rise twice in size. Punch down, shape into loaves or divide into 3 equal portions.

Place in greased loaf pans. Allow to rise at least double in size.

Bake in a 350°F (*180°C*) oven 40 to 45 minutes.

Remove from pans and cool on a wire rack.

Oat Bran Bread

2 loaves

2 cups	(*500 mL*) scalded milk
¼ cup	(*60 mL*) brown sugar, firmly packed
1 tbsp	(*15 mL*) salt
2 tbsp	(*30 mL*) butter
2 cups	(*500 mL*) oat bran
1 tbsp	(*15 mL*) active dry yeast
½ cup	(*125 mL*) warm water
5 cups	(*1,2 L*) flour
1	egg white, lightly beaten
1 tbsp	(*15 mL*) cold water

Pour the scalded milk into a large bowl; mix in the brown sugar, salt, butter and oat bran. Cool.

In a small bowl, soften the yeast in the warm water for 10 minutes.

Combine the oat bran mixture, yeast and 2 cups (*500 mL*) of flour and blend into a smooth batter.

Continue to add flour 1 cup (*250 mL*) at a time, blending well. Knead 8 minutes. Place in a lightly greased bowl.

Cover and let rise for 1¼ - 1½ hours. Punch down and let rise a second time.

Preheat oven to 375°F (*190°C*).

Turn out dough onto a flour-dusted board. Divide in two; shape into loaves. Place into two 9-in. (*22 cm*) loaf pans and let rise for 1 hour.

Brush with egg white mixed with the cold water.

Bake in oven 35 to 40 minutes.

Old-Fashioned Dinner Rolls

Southern Corn Bread

1 loaf

2	eggs
2 cups	(*500 mL*) buttermilk
1 tsp	(*5 mL*) baking soda
2 cups	(*500 mL*) cornmeal
1 tsp	(*5 mL*) salt
1 tsp	(*5 mL*) sugar

Preheat oven to 450°F (*230°C*).

Grease a 9-in. (*22 cm*) pan.

Mix the eggs in the buttermilk.

In a bowl, sift together all dry ingredients.

Mix the milk mixture with the dry ingredients until smooth.

Place in pan and bake for 25 minutes.

Cut in squares and serve very hot.

Old-Fashioned Dinner Rolls

24 rolls

1 oz	(*30 g*) yeast
1 cup	(*250 mL*) warm water
3 tbsp	(*45 mL*) sugar
3 tbsp	(*45 mL*) butter
1 tsp	(*5 mL*) salt
1	egg
3 cups	(*750 mL*) flour

In a large bowl, dissolve the yeast in the water with the sugar. Set aside for 10 minutes.

Add the butter, salt and egg. Mix in flour. Knead into a soft smooth ball.

Cover and allow to rise until double in size. Punch down and shape into buns.

Place on pastry sheets and bake for 15 minutes, or until golden brown.

Banana Nut Loaf

2 loaves

4	eggs
1½ cups	(*375 mL*) granulated sugar
1 cup	(*250 mL*) melted butter
1 tsp	(*5 mL*) almond extract
4	very ripe, medium bananas, mashed
2½ cups	(*625 mL*) all-purpose flour
2½ tsp	(*12 mL*) baking powder
1 tsp	(*5 mL*) baking soda
1 tsp	(*5 mL*) salt
1 cup	(*250 mL*) shredded coconut
1 cup	(*250 mL*) coarsely chopped walnuts
1 cup	(*250 mL*) maraschino cherries, halved

Preheat oven to 350°F (*180°C*).

Beat eggs well. Gradually beat in sugar, melted butter and almond extract. Stir in mashed bananas.

In a large bowl, mix together flour, baking powder, baking soda and salt.

Add egg mixture, stirring just until blended. Fold in coconut, walnuts and cherries.

Pour batter into two greased 8 x 4 in. (*20 x 10 cm*) loaf pans and bake in oven for 1 hour or until a toothpick inserted in the center comes out clean.

Let cool in pans for 10 minutes, then turn out onto racks to cool completely.

1

Stir mashed bananas into egg mixture.

2

Add banana mixture to flour mixture, stirring just until blended.

3

Pour batter into greased loaf pans.

4

Turn out baked loaves onto racks to cool completely.

Pumpkin Bread

2 loaves

1 cup	(250 mL)	oil
1 cup	(250 mL)	honey
2 cups	(500 mL)	sugar
4		eggs, beaten
3½ cups	(875 mL)	flour
1 tsp	(5 mL)	baking powder
1 tsp	(5 mL)	salt
½ tsp	(3 mL)	ground cloves
½ tsp	(3 mL)	nutmeg
½ tsp	(3 mL)	allspice
2 tsp	(10 mL)	cinnamon
2 cups	(500 mL)	pumpkin purée
1½ cups	(375 mL)	walnut pieces

Preheat oven to 325°F (160°C).

Blend together the oil, honey, sugar and eggs.

Sift together all the dry ingredients. Mix with sweetened oil. Stir in the pumpkin. Blend thoroughly.

Add the walnuts. Pour batter into 2 well-greased 9-in. (22 cm) loaf pans.

Bake in oven for 1¼ hours. Remove and rest 10 minutes. Turn out on a cooling rack.

Peanut Butter Bread

Peanut Butter Bread

1 loaf

4 tbsp	(60 mL)	peanut butter
3 tbsp	(45 mL)	butter
2 tbsp	(30 mL)	sugar
1		egg
1 cup	(250 mL)	flour
½ tsp	(3 mL)	salt
1 tsp	(5 mL)	baking powder
½ cup	(125 mL)	milk

Preheat oven to 350°F (180°C).

Cream together the peanut butter, butter and sugar.

Add the egg. Blend in the flour, salt and baking powder.

Slowly blend in the milk.

Pour into a greased loaf pan.

Bake in oven 45 to 50 minutes. Turn out on a wire rack to cool.

Zucchini Nut Bread

2 loaves

½ cup	(*125 mL*) butter
½ cup	(*125 mL*) oil
1¾ cups	(*430 mL*) sugar
2	eggs
1 tsp	(*5 mL*) vanilla
½ cup	(*125 mL*) heavy cream
1½ cups	(*375 mL*) whole wheat flour
1 cup	(*250 mL*) all-purpose flour
½ tsp	(*3 mL*) baking powder
1 tsp	(*5 mL*) baking soda
½ tsp	(*3 mL*) cinnamon
½ tsp	(*3 mL*) ground cloves
½ tsp	(*3 mL*) nutmeg
2 cups	(*500 mL*) finely diced zucchini
1 cup	(*250 mL*) chopped walnuts

Preheat oven to 350°F (*180°C*).

Cream together butter, oil and sugar. Add the eggs, vanilla and cream.

Mix together all the dry ingredients. Add the zucchini and nuts.

Pour batter into two greased loaf pans.

Bake in oven 30 to 35 minutes.

Turn out on a wire rack and cool before serving.

Sweet-As-Honey Whole Wheat Bread

2 loaves

¼ cup	(*60 mL*) brown sugar, firmly packed
¼ cup	(*60 mL*) honey
1 tbsp	(*15 mL*) salt
2 tbsp	(*30 mL*) shortening
1½ cups	(*375 mL*) boiling water
1 tsp	(*5 mL*) sugar
¼ cup	(*60 mL*) warm water
1 tbsp	(*15 mL*) active dry yeast
6 cups	(*1,5 L*) whole wheat flour
¼ cup	(*60 mL*) melted butter

Combine the brown sugar, honey, salt and shortening in a mixing bowl.

Pour in the boiling water and stir until dissolved. Cool to lukewarm.

Dissolve 1 tsp (*5 mL*) sugar in the ¼ cup (*60 mL*) of water. Sprinkle in the yeast and allow to rise 10 minutes. Add to the sweetened water.

Slowly mix in the flour. Knead in mixer for 10 minutes.

Cover and allow to double in size 1½ to 2 hours. Punch down.

Place dough into two 9-in. (*22 cm*) well-greased loaf pans. Allow to rise again for 1 to 1½ hours.

Bake in a preheated 375°F (*190°C*) oven 25 to 30 minutes. Turn out on a cooling rack. Brush with melted butter.

Apple Bread

1 loaf

½ cup	(*125 mL*) shortening
1 cup	(*250 mL*) sugar
2	eggs
2 cups	(*500 mL*) flour
1 tsp	(*5 mL*) salt
1 tsp	(*5 mL*) baking soda
1 tsp	(*5 mL*) baking powder
1 tsp	(*5 mL*) vanilla extract
2 tbsp	(*30 mL*) heavy cream
2 cups	(*500 mL*) apples, peeled and diced

Preheat oven to 350°F (*180°C*).

Cream the shortening and sugar until very light.

Add the eggs and cream together.

Blend in the flour, salt, baking soda and baking powder in small amounts.

Add the vanilla and blend together. Add the apples. Pour batter into a greased loaf pan.

Bake in oven 55 to 60 minutes.

Turn out and cool on a wire rack.

Apple Raisin Nut Bread

Apple Raisin Nut Bread

	1 loaf
2 cups	*(500 mL)* sifted flour
1 tsp	*(5 mL)* baking soda
1 tsp	*(5 mL)* baking powder
½ tsp	*(3 mL)* salt
½ cup	*(125 mL)* butter
1 cup	*(250 mL)* sugar
2	eggs
2 tbsp	*(30 mL)* sour cream
1 tsp	*(5 mL)* vanilla
½ cup	*(125 mL)* chopped walnuts
1 cup	*(250 mL)* apples, peeled and diced
½ cup	*(125 mL)* sultana raisins

Preheat oven to 350°F (*180°C*).

Sift together flour, baking soda, baking powder and salt.

In another bowl, cream the butter with the sugar. Mix in the eggs one at a time.

Cream the sour cream and vanilla into the butter mixture.

Add the flour mixture and blend. Mix in the walnuts, apples and raisins.

Pour into a greased loaf pan and bake in oven 30 to 35 minutes.

Test for doneness.

Parker House Rolls

3-4 dozen

2 tbsp	(30 mL)	sugar
¼ cup	(60 mL)	warm water
1 tbsp	(15 mL)	yeast
2 cups	(500 mL)	milk
1 tsp	(5 mL)	salt
3 tbsp	(45 mL)	butter
6 ½ cups	(1,6 L)	flour
1		egg, beaten
¼ cup	(60 mL)	heavy cream

Mix 1 tsp (5 mL) of sugar in the water. Add yeast and let soften 10 minutes.

In a saucepan, combine the milk, remaining sugar, salt and butter. Scald, cool then transfer to a mixing bowl.

Stir in the yeast mixture and 3 cups (750 mL) of flour. Beat for 2 minutes.

Allow to rise 1 hour, then beat in the egg and remaining flour.

Knead in a mixer for 8 minutes. Cover and allow to rise.

On a flour-dusted board, roll out dough to ⅓ its thickness. Cut with 3 in. (7 cm) round cutters. Cut a slit in the center about ⅛ in. (0,3 cm) deep.

Fold over, sealing the edges. Place 1 in. (2,5 cm) apart on a pastry sheet.

Allow to rise to double in size. Brush with cream.

Bake in a preheated 425°F (220°C) oven 15 to 17 minutes, or until golden brown.

Apricot Bread

1 loaf

⅔ cup	(160 mL)	milk
4 tsp	(20 mL)	butter
4 tsp	(20 mL)	sugar
¾ tsp	(4 mL)	salt
2 tsp	(10 mL)	active dry yeast
4 tsp	(20 mL)	water
1		egg, beaten
3¼ cups	(810 mL)	flour

Scald the milk. Add the butter, sugar and salt. Dissolve and cool.

Soften the yeast in the water. Add to cooled milk. Add the egg.

Slowly add the flour. Knead 8 minutes in a mixer.

Allow to double in size. Punch down.

Allow to double in size. Punch down and roll to ¼-in. (0,5 cm) thickness.

Spread filling (see below). Roll up like a jelly roll. Seal the edges and ends.

Allow to rise again, covered, to double in size.

Bake in a 350°F (180°C) oven 25 to 30 minutes. Cool.

Filling

1 cup	(250 mL)	dried apricots
1 cup	(250 mL)	water
½ cup	(125 mL)	honey
¼ tsp	(1 mL)	cinnamon

Soak the apricots in the water for 1 hour.

Bring to a boil. Add the honey and cinnamon.

Mash with a fork. Reduce to a simmer.

Simmer to a thick pulp, until most of liquid has evaporated.

Sour Cream Spice Muffins

12 muffins

2 cups	(500 mL)	flour
2 tsp	(10 mL)	cinnamon
½ tsp	(3 mL)	allspice
½ tsp	(3 mL)	nutmeg
½ tsp	(3 mL)	salt
1 tsp	(5 mL)	baking soda
3		eggs
½ cup	(125 mL)	butter
2 cups	(500 mL)	brown sugar, firmly packed
1 cup	(250 mL)	sour cream

Preheat oven to 350°F (180°C).

Sift together the flour, spices, salt and baking soda. Cream together the eggs, butter and sugar.

Fold in the sour cream. Carefully beat in the dry mixture.

Grease 12 muffin tins. Fill tins ⅔ full.

Bake in oven 25 to 30 minutes.

Cool 5 minutes before serving.

Blueberry Muffins

Blueberry Muffins

12 muffins

1½ cups	(375 mL)	sifted flour
2 tsp	(10 mL)	baking powder
½ tsp	(3 mL)	salt
¾ cup	(180 mL)	sugar
¼ cup	(60 mL)	butter
⅔ cup	(160 mL)	milk
1 tsp	(5 mL)	white vanilla
1 cup	(250 mL)	blueberries*

Preheat oven to 350°F (180°C).

Sift together the dry ingredients.

Cut in the butter, add the milk and vanilla. Beat 3 minutes with mixer. Fold in the blueberries.

Lightly grease 12 muffin tins, or use muffin papers. Fill each ⅔ full.

Bake in oven 30 to 35 minutes or until golden brown.

*If using frozen, use in that state and reduce quantity to ½ cup (125 mL). Fresh is best.

Apple Spice Muffins

12 muffins

2 cups	(*500 mL*) flour	
1 tbsp	(*15 mL*) baking powder	
1 tsp	(*5 mL*) cinnamon	
¼ tsp	(*1 mL*) nutmeg	
¼ tsp	(*1 mL*) ground cloves	
¼ tsp	(*1 mL*) allspice	
⅔ cup	(*160 mL*) brown sugar, firmly packed	
1 cup	(*250 mL*) grapenuts cereal	
2	eggs	
⅔ cup	(*160 mL*) milk	
¼ cup	(*60 mL*) oil	
1 cup	(*250 mL*) apples, pared and diced	

Preheat oven to 350°F (*180°C*).

Sift together the flour, baking powder and spices.

Combine with the sugar and cereal.

Beat together the eggs, milk and oil. Combine with dry ingredients. Blend 2 minutes. Add the apples.

Lightly grease 12 muffin tins. Pour batter into tins to ¾ full.

Bake in oven 15 to 20 minutes.

Marmalade Muffins

12 muffins

½ cup	(*125 mL*) marmalade	
2 tbsp	(*30 mL*) lemon juice	
¾ cup	(*180 mL*) milk	
1 tsp	(*5 mL*) white vanilla	
¾ cup	(*180 mL*) sugar	
¼ cup	(*60 mL*) butter	
2	eggs	
2½ cups	(*625 mL*) flour	
1 tsp	(*5 mL*) baking powder	
1 tsp	(*5 mL*) baking soda	
1 tsp	(*5 mL*) salt	

Preheat oven to 350°F (*180°C*).

Mix together the marmalade, lemon juice, milk and vanilla.

In a big bowl, cream together the sugar and butter. Add the eggs.

In another bowl, sift together the flour, baking powder, baking soda and salt.

Fold into the creamed mixture, alternating with the marmalade mixture, ⅓ quantity at a time.

Grease 12 muffin tins. Pour in batter to ⅔ full.

Bake in oven 30 to 35 minutes. Test for doneness.

Let cool 5 minutes before unmolding.

Oat Bran Muffins

12 muffins

1 cup	(*250 mL*) flour	
1 tsp	(*5 mL*) baking powder	
1 tsp	(*5 mL*) baking soda	
½ tsp	(*3 mL*) salt	
1 cup	(*250 mL*) raisins	
1 cup	(*250 mL*) oat bran	
1 cup	(*250 mL*) heavy cream	
⅓ cup	(*80 mL*) oil	
3 tbsp	(*45 mL*) corn syrup	
1	egg	
¼ cup	(*60 mL*) brown sugar, firmly packed	
½ tsp	(*3 mL*) vanilla	

Preheat oven to 375°F (*190°C*).

In a mixing bowl, combine the flour, baking powder, baking soda, salt and raisins.

In small bowl, soak the oat bran in the cream for 5 minutes.

Add the oil, corn syrup, egg, sugar and vanilla. Pour into dry ingredients.

Beat for 2 minutes. Batter should be lumpy.

Grease 12 muffin tins. Pour batter into tins to ⅔ full.

Bake in oven 20 to 25 minutes.

Carrot Muffins

Carrot Muffins

3 dozen

2 cups	(*500 mL*) flour
¾ cup	(*180 mL*) sugar
1 tsp	(*5 mL*) baking powder
1 tsp	(*5 mL*) baking soda
½ tsp	(*3 mL*) salt
1 tsp	(*5 mL*) cinnamon
pinch	allspice
pinch	nutmeg
pinch	ground cloves
2	eggs

½ cup	(*125 mL*) oil
1 cup	(*250 mL*) grated carrots
1 cup	(*250 mL*) apples, peeled and finely diced
½ cup	(*125 mL*) nuts
½ cup	(*125 mL*) raisins

Preheat oven to 400°F (*200°C*).

Sift together the flour, sugar, baking powder, baking soda and spices.

Beat the eggs until frothy, add the oil, carrots, apples, nuts and raisins.

Fold into dry ingredients. Mix 2 minutes.

Grease 36 muffin tins. Pour batter into tins to ¾ full.

Bake in oven 20 to 25 minutes.

Let rest 5 minutes. Remove from pans.

Crêpe Batter

16-18 crêpes

1 cup	*(250 mL)*	flour
¼ tsp	*(1 mL)*	salt
2 tbsp	*(30 mL)*	oil
1 cup	*(250 mL)*	milk
¼ cup	*(60 mL)*	water or soda water
1		egg

Sift together the flour and salt.

Blend together the oil, milk and water.

Beat the egg and add it to the liquid. Blend in the dry ingredients.

Beat into a smooth thin batter.

To cook crêpes, spread about 3 tbsp (*45 mL*) crêpe batter in a lightly buttered skillet.

Cook about 1½ minutes, turn crêpes and cook 1 minute over medium heat.

Waffle Batter

16-18 waffles

2 cups	*(500 mL)*	flour
½ tsp	*(3 mL)*	salt
2 tbsp	*(30 mL)*	baking powder
1 tbsp	*(15 mL)*	sugar
1 cup	*(250 mL)*	milk
1 cup	*(250 mL)*	heavy cream
3		eggs
4 tsp	*(20 mL)*	melted butter

Sift together the flour, salt, baking powder and sugar.

In a mixing bowl, beat together the milk, cream, eggs and butter until frothy.

Slowly add the dry ingredients to make a thick batter.

Cook in a well-greased waffle iron.

Pancake Batter

12 pancakes

1½ cups	*(375 mL)*	flour
2½ tsp	*(13 mL)*	baking powder
¾ tsp	*(4 mL)*	salt
1		egg, beaten
1¼ cups	*(310 mL)*	milk
3 tbsp	*(45 mL)*	oil

Sift together the flour, baking powder and salt.

Blend together the egg, milk and oil. Slowly add the dry ingredients. Stir into a smooth batter.

Cook in a hot greased frying pan, turning over only once.

Stuffed Crêpes Suzettes

8 servings

16	8-in. (*20 cm*) crêpes

Filling

1	250 g pkg. cream cheese, at room temperature
¼ cup	(*60 mL*) heavy cream
1 cup	(*250 mL*) icing sugar
½ cup	(*125 mL*) chopped pecans (optional)

Sauce

½ cup	(*125 mL*) butter
½ cup	(*125 mL*) sugar
1 cup	(*250 mL*) orange juice
⅓ cup	(*80 mL*) Grand Marnier
4 tsp	(*20 mL*) cornstarch
4 tsp	(*20 mL*) lemon juice
10 oz	(*284 mL*) can mandarin oranges

Filling : Beat the cream cheese, cream and icing sugar until smooth. Stir in nuts. Spoon about 2 tbsp (*30 mL*) onto each crêpe and roll. Refrigerate filling if not using immediately.

Sauce : In a heavy saucepan, melt the butter. Stir in the sugar over low heat and cook, stirring, until sugar becomes golden brown. Add orange juice and Grand Marnier liqueur. Stir cornstarch into lemon juice and pour into sauce. Simmer, stirring, until mixture thickens. Place 2 crêpes on each plate. Top with a few oranges, and drizzle with hot sauce. Serve immediately.

1 Stir chopped pecans into cream cheese mixture.

2 Spoon about 2 tbsp (*30 mL*) of mixture onto each crêpe and roll.

3 Prepare sauce and let simmer, stirring until mixture thickens. Stir in oranges, reserving some for garnish.

4 Drizzle crêpes with hot sauce and garnish with remaining mandarin slices.

Pizza Dough

four 8-in. (20 cm) pizzas or two 14-in. (35 cm) pizzas

1 tsp	(*5 mL*) granulated sugar
1 cup	(*250 mL*) warm water
1	envelope active dry yeast or 1 tbsp (*15 mL*)
2 tbsp	(*30 mL*) butter, melted and cooled
3 cups	(*750 mL*) all-purpose flour
pinch	salt

In a large bowl, dissolve sugar in warm water.

Sprinkle with yeast and let stand 10 minutes or until foamy. Stir butter into yeast mixture.

Stir about half the flour and the pinch of salt into the yeast mixture. Gradually stir in enough of remaining flour to make a slightly sticky ball.

Knead dough on a lightly flour surface until smooth and elastic, about 5 minutes.

Place dough in a greased bowl and let rest 15 minutes.

Punch down dough; cut in half. Roll out each piece of dough into an 11-in. (*28 cm*) circle.

Place on a greased 14-in. (*35 cm*) pizza pan. Let rest 15 minutes.

With fingertips, press dough from center to edges until dough covers pan completely.

Dough is now ready for sauce and toppings.

Yorkshire Pudding

12 servings

3	eggs
1 cup	(*250 mL*) milk, scalded and cooled
1 cup	(*250 mL*) flour
½ tsp	(*3 mL*) salt
¼ tsp	(*1 mL*) pepper
¼ tsp	(*1 mL*) nutmeg
¼ cup	(*60 mL*) beef fat

Preheat oven to 450°F (*230°C*).

Whip the eggs with milk.

In another bowl, sift together the dry ingredients.

Add the milk mixture. Blend into a smooth batter.

Heat the beef fat. Pour into 12 muffin tins. Pour batter into tins to ½ full.

Bake in oven 30 minutes.

Serve with roast beef.

Brioche

16-20 buns

½ cup	(*125 mL*) milk, scalded and cooled
½ cup	(*125 mL*) butter
⅓ cup + 2 tsp	(*90 mL*) sugar
¼ cup	(*60 mL*) lukewarm water
2 tbsp	(*30 mL*) yeast
3¾ cups	(*930 mL*) flour
1	egg, separated
4	eggs, beaten

Cream together the butter and ⅓ cup (*80 mL*) sugar.

In a small bowl, place 1 tsp (*5 mL*) sugar in the water, add the yeast and let soften for 15 minutes.

Blend together the yeast, creamed mixture, flour, egg yolk and beaten eggs. Beat for 2 minutes.

Cover and let rise to twice its size in bulk. Punch down. Beat for 2 minutes.

Cover with greased foil wrap and refrigerate 8 hours or overnight.

Punch down and place on a floured board.

Divide and form into 16 to 20 even buns.

Place in well-greased muffin tins or brioche pan.

Cover and let rise to double size.

Preheat oven to 425°F (*220°C*).

Beat the egg white with 1 tsp (*15 mL*) sugar. Brush on brioche.

Bake in oven 15 to 20 minutes, or until golden brown.

Cinnamon Buns

Cinnamon Buns

12 large, 24 small buns

1 cup	(*250 mL*) sugar
¼ cup	(*60 mL*) warm water
2 tbsp	(*30 mL*) yeast
4	eggs, beaten
1¼ cups	(*310 mL*) milk, scalded and cooled
1 cup	(*250 mL*) melted butter
7 cups	(*1,7 L*) flour
2 tbsp	(*30 mL*) cinnamon
2 cups	(*500 mL*) chopped pecans
2 cups	(*500 mL*) raisins
2 cups	(*500 mL*) brown sugar

Dissolve 1 tsp (*5 mL*) of sugar in the water. Sprinkle in the yeast. Allow to rise 10 minutes.

In a large bowl, cream together the eggs, milk, remaining sugar and half the butter.

Blend in the flour, 1 cup (*250 mL*) at a time, blending well after each addition.

Add the yeast and blend well. Knead 8 minutes in a mixer.

Cover. Allow to rise to double in size.

Preheat oven to 325°F (*160°C*).

Roll out dough to ⅛-in. (*0,3 cm*) thickness.

Brush with remaining butter. Sprinkle with cinnamon. Sprinkle with pecans, raisins and brown sugar.

Roll up tightly like a jelly roll. Slice into 1¼ in. (*3 cm*) rolls.

Place on a greased pastry sheet, 2 in. (*5 cm*) apart. Allow to double in size.

Bake in oven 25 to 30 minutes, or until golden brown.

Desserts

Almost everyone has some kind of sweet tooth, although some of us are addicted to chocolate, others to ice cream, and many have a passion for anything that involves fruit.

Fortunately, this chapter has a dessert to thrill every sweet tooth of your acquaintance. Many of them are my own "old favorites," and I think they might become "new favorites" to young people who have never tasted them.

For example, I've included a recipe for "Simplest Rice Pudding" which has been part of my repertoire ever since I worked as a chef at a small hotel in Jasper, Alberta. Our patrons ate at least five gallons of rice pudding a day.

I have also included a number of recipes for ices, sherbets, and ice creams, because I like the way they can provide a light and refreshing end to a heavier meal.

And I've included some easy candy recipes. I think if you try making candy at home instead of buying it, you'll have more fun, and the recipients will get more appreciation out of them.

But you will notice that a good number of the recipes in this chapter are based on chocolate.

Perhaps that can be explained by the fact that I grew up in Niagara Falls, Canada. Niagara Falls happened to be the place were Reese's peanut butter cups were created, but it was also the home of a wonderful exhibit about chocolate-making put on by the famous Hershey chocolate company.

I spent many hours mesmerized by that display, and have been fascinated by chocolate ever since. I'm certainly not alone in that attitude. First used by the Aztecs, chocolate was introduced to Europe by the Spanish conquistadors. In its history, it has been known not just as a food, but as a stimulant, aphrodisiac, currency and sacred substance.

The Dutch refined the cacao beans into a powder and discovered the wonders of cocoa butter, which was soon made into the revered chocolate bar. It was back in North America where chocolate finally came into its own as the foundation for numerous fortunes — the Hersheys, Cadburys, Mars and Frys.

I hope you'll try some of these chocolate recipes and become part of a great tradition.

Pies, Cakes and Cookies

Nothing is quite as rewarding as the smiles and praise you receive when you present your friends or family with a home-baked pie or cake. It makes your work in the kitchen truly a "labor of love."

Unfortunately, many home cooks today seem to have lost the art of baking for their loved ones, which is a shame. I hope you will abandon any reservations you may have about baking and try some of the recipes in this section.

Just remember that the art of baking is a precise one, so you have to follow some simple rules.

1) Always read your recipe through before you begin.

2) Prepare and grease all your pans in advance. Get out all your ingredients and have them at room temperature.

3) Preheat your oven in plenty of time. You should check your oven every year to make sure it is baking at the selected temperature.

4) Follow mixing instructions exactly. Sift all dry ingredients together to make sure they are well mixed.

5) Whip egg whites to stiff peaks before folding them into batters. Do no overmix.

6) Overmixing is the major reason for tough pie crusts. When you cut the butter or shortening into the flour, cut only until a very coarse meal texture. This will produce a far flakier crust. To add to the flakiness, mix an egg or a little vinegar into your dough.

Cooking with Fruit

Fresh fruit provides incomparable flavor, but must be handled carefully.

To prevent fruit from turning brown (caused when the enzymes oxidize tannins in the fruit), brush the fruit with something acidic, such as lemon juice. Or add an antioxidant, such as sugar or salt.

Chocolate Mocha Mint Bombe

8 servings

2 tbsp	(*30 mL*) unflavored gelatine
3 cups	(*750 mL*) hot coffee
4 oz	(*115 g*) unsweetened chocolate
¾ cup	(*180 mL*) sugar
pinch	salt
½ tsp	(*3 mL*) mint extract
2 cups	(*500 mL*) whipping cream

Soften the gelatine in the hot coffee. Melt the chocolate in a double boiler.

Add the coffee, sugar, salt and extract. Refrigerate to cool but not set.

Whip the cream until stiff peaks form. Fold into cooled chocolate mixture.

Pour into an 8-cup (*2 L*) mold.

Refrigerate for 3 hours.

Unmold and serve with Chocolate Fudge Sauce.

Chocolate Mint Patties

24-30 patties

¼ cup	(60 mL) butter
1 lb	(*450 g*) confectioners' sugar
3 tbsp	(*45 mL*) whipping cream
1 tsp	(*5 mL*) mint extract
6 oz	(*170 g*) semi-sweet chocolate
2 tbsp	(*30 mL*) melted butter

In a mixing bowl, cream the butter, add half the sugar, the cream and the extract.

Beat until very smooth. Slowly incorporate the remaining sugar.

Working quickly, shape into ½-in (*1 cm*) balls and flatten.

Mold into even round patties. Stick a toothpick into the side of each patty. Dry 1 hour.

In a double boiler, melt the chocolate. Add the melted butter and stir.

Dip each patty into the chocolate. Place on a pastry sheet lined with wax paper.

Refrigerate until ready to use.

Chocolate Fondue

1½ cups (375 mL)

8 oz	(*225 g*) semi-sweet chocolate
½ cup	(*125 mL*) whipping cream
3 tbsp	(*45 mL*) fresh orange juice
1 tsp	(*5 mL*) grated orange rind

In a double boiler, melt the chocolate. Add the cream, juice and orange rind.

Stir until thoroughly incorporated.

Pour into a fondue pot set over a candle. Serve.

Use strawberries, bananas, oranges, peaches, kiwi, marshmallows, etc. for dipping.

Chocolate Fondue

Irish Cream Chocolate Bavarian

6-8 servings

4 tsp	*(20 mL)* unflavored gelatine
½ cup	*(125 mL)* cold water
4 oz	*(115 g)* semi-sweet chocolate
2 cups	*(500 mL)* boiling water
½ cup	*(125 mL)* sugar
⅓ cup	*(80 mL)* Irish cream liqueur
¾ cup	*(180 mL)* heavy cream

Soften the gelatine in the cold water.

In a double boiler, melt the chocolate.

Add the gelatine, boiling water, sugar and Irish cream. Set aside to cool, do not allow to set.

Whip the cream. Fold into the cooled chocolate mixture. Pour into a mold. Set for 3 to 4 hours.

Unmold and garnish with whipped cream, chocolate curls or fresh fruit. Serve.

 Melt the chocolate in a double boiler. Add the dissolved gelatine, boiling water, sugar and Irish cream.

 Whip the cream and fold into the cooled chocolate mixture.

 Pour into a mold and let set 3 to 4 hours.

Unmold and garnish.

Chocolate Peach Dream Custard

6 servings

⅔ cup	(160 mL) peach liquid (canned)
⅓ cup	(80 mL) cocoa powder
¼ cup	(60 mL) butter
¼ cup	(60 mL) sugar
1	egg
½ tsp	(3 mL) vanilla

1 cup	(250 mL) flour
1 tsp	(5 mL) baking powder
1 cup	(250 mL) canned sliced peaches

Boil ½ cup (125 mL) of peach liquid, add the cocoa powder and blend well. Cool.

Cream together the butter, sugar and remaining peach liquid. Add the egg and vanilla and beat well.

Sift together the flour and baking powder.

Add slowly to the cream mixture. Add the cocoa mixture and sliced peaches.

Scoop into 6 lightly greased custard cups.

Heat a skillet with ⅓ cup (80 mL) water. Place the custard cups in the water.

Cover and cook for 20 minutes. Turn out onto serving plates.

Serve with Chocolate Fudge Sauce.

Chocolate Peach Dream Custard

Chocolate Orange Cake

8-10 servings

4 oz	(*115 g*) semi-sweet chocolate
1 tbsp	(*15 mL*) cocoa powder
2 tbsp	(*30 mL*) baking powder
2 cups	(*500 mL*) sifted pastry flour
½ cup	(*125 mL*) butter
1 cup	(*250 mL*) sugar
⅔ cup	(*160 mL*) orange juice
3	egg whites, whipped stiff

Preheat oven to 350°F (*180°C*).

In a double boiler, melt the chocolate.

In a bowl, sift together the cocoa powder, baking powder and flour.

In another bowl, cream the butter with the sugar until very light.

Add the dry ingredients and the orange juice, alternating ⅓ of each at a time.

Blend in the melted chocolate. Fold in the egg whites. Lightly grease and flour two 9-in. (*22 cm*) cake pans.

Bake in oven 20 to 25 minutes. Cool 5 minutes. Turn out on racks.

Frost or ice with chocolate icing.

Chocolate Mousse

Chocolate Mousse

4 servings

1⅓ cups	(*330 mL*) semi-sweet chocolate
⅓ cup	(*80 mL*) black coffee
1 tbsp	(*15 mL*) butter
2 tbsp	(*30 mL*) Triple Sec liqueur
4	eggs
1¼ cups	(*310 mL*) whipping cream

Melt the chocolate in a double boiler. Add the coffee. Remove from heat, stir in the butter and Triple Sec.

Separate the eggs. Add the yolks one at a time, blending them into the warm chocolate.

Whip the egg whites until stiff and fold into the chocolate mixture.

Pour into dessert glasses.

Whip the cream and pipe on top of each serving.

Chocolate Nut Clusters

24-30 clusters

1 lb	(450 g) sweet chocolate
2 oz	(60 g) melted butter
½ cup	(125 mL) cashew pieces
½ cup	(125 mL) walnut pieces
½ cup	(125 mL) pecan pieces
½ cup	(125 mL) unsalted peanuts

In a double boiler, melt the chocolate.

Add the butter and stir until melted. Stir in the nuts.

Combine well. Drop spoonfuls onto pastry sheets lined with wax paper.

Refrigerate until hardened.

Chocolate Orange Strawberries

Chocolate Orange Strawberries

20 pieces

3 oz	(90 g) semi-sweet chocolate
1 tbsp	(15 mL) melted butter
2 tsp	(10 mL) Triple Sec liqueur
20	medium strawberries with stems

In a double boiler, melt the chocolate.

Remove from heat. Stir in the butter and Triple Sec.

Wash and pat dry the strawberries.

Dip into the chocolate to ¾ of the berry. Place on a cookie sheet covered with wax paper.

Refrigerate. Berries must be used same day.

Chocolate Pralines

12-16 pieces

1½ cups	(*375 mL*) dark brown sugar, firmly packed
¾ cup	(*180 mL*) heavy cream
¼ cup	(*60 mL*) butter
4 oz	(*115 g*) semi-sweet chocolate
1 cup	(*250 mL*) pecan pieces

In a heavy saucepan, combine the sugar and cream.

Stirring constantly, heat to 240°F (*115°C*) on a candy thermometer.

Remove from heat, stir in the butter and chocolate. Cool to 110°F (*43°C*).

Stir in the pecans.

Drop spoonfuls of mixture onto a lightly greased pastry sheet.

Allow to cool and harden.

Chocolate Pound Cake

8-10 servings

½ cup	(*125 mL*) butter
1 cup	(*250 mL*) shortening
2 cups	(*500 mL*) sugar
6	eggs
1 tbsp	(*15 mL*) vanilla
1 tbsp	(*15 mL*) orange juice
1 tbsp	(*15 mL*) lemon juice
2 cups	(*500 mL*) flour
1 cup	(*250 mL*) apricot jam
10 oz	(*280 g*) semi-sweet chocolate
2 tbsp	(*30 mL*) melted butter

Preheat oven to 325°F (*160°C*).

Cream the butter, shortening and sugar until light and fluffy.

Beat in eggs, one at a time. Add vanilla, juices and flour.

Combine only until incorporated.

Pour into a lightly greased 11 x 7-in. (*28 x 18 cm*) loaf pan.

Bake in oven 55 to 60 minutes. Remove; cool 5 minutes.

Unmold. Place on a cooling rack.

Heat the jam in a small saucepan. Purée into a smooth paste.

Melt the chocolate and melted butter together in a double boiler.

Brush the cooled cake with the jam. Pour the chocolate over the cake.

Refrigerate until hardened.

Chocolate Pie

8 servings

1½ cups	(*375 mL*) chocolate wafers, crushed fine
¼ cup	(*60 mL*) sugar
6 tbsp	(*90 mL*) melted butter
5 oz	(*150 g*) semi-sweet chocolate
¼ cup	(*60 mL*) heavy cream
4	eggs, separated and at room temperature
1 tsp	(*5 mL*) vanilla extract

Preheat oven to 350°F (*180°C*).

Mix the wafers with 2 tbsp (*30 mL*) sugar and the melted butter.

Press into a 9-in. (*22-cm*) pie plate. Bake in the center rack of oven for 6 minutes. Remove and cool.

In a double boiler, melt the chocolate with the cream.

Add the remaining sugar and stir until smooth. Let cool.

Once cooled, fold in 1 egg yolk at a time, incorporating thoroughly before adding the next. Add the vanilla.

Whip the egg whites until stiff. Gently fold the chocolate mixture into the egg whites.

Pour into cooled pie shell. Refrigerate for 4 hours.

Chocolate Pie

The Simplest Rice Pudding

6 servings

1½ cups	(375 mL) sugar
2 cups	(500 mL) milk
1 tsp	(5 mL) vanilla
2 cups	(500 mL) heavy cream
1½ cups	(375 mL) rice (not converted)
1 cup	(250 mL) raisins
2 tsp	(10 mL) cinnamon

Dissolve the sugar in the milk. Add the vanilla and cream. Bring to a boil.

Add the rice. Cook, covered, for about 40 minutes, over low heat.

Stir in the raisins. Pour into a shallow pan.

Sprinkle with cinnamon. Chill.

The Simplest Rice Pudding

Jennifer's Chocolate Bars

12-16 bars

1 cup	(250 mL) pitted dates
½ cup	(125 mL) currants
½ cup	(125 mL) unsalted peanuts
1 cup	(250 mL) crunchy-style peanut butter
½ cup	(125 mL) sweetened condensed milk
¼ cup	(60 mL) icing sugar
8 oz	(225 g) semi-sweet chocolate
2 tbsp	(30 mL) melted butter

Chop the dates and currants. Combine with peanuts, peanut butter, milk and icing sugar. Shape into little cigar shapes.

In a double boiler, melt the chocolate with the butter. Dip peanut bars into chocolate.

Place on a pastry sheet lined with wax paper. Chill.

Chocolate Iced Soufflé

6 servings

3 tbsp	(*45 mL*) sugar
2 tbsp	(*30 mL*) unflavored gelatine
4 oz	(*115 g*) semi-sweet chocolate
¼ tsp	(*1 mL*) salt
6	egg whites
2 cups	(*500 mL*) whipping cream
	chocolate curls

In a saucepan, mix the sugar with the gelatine. Add the chocolate and melt over very low heat.

Stir until sugar has dissolved. Add the salt and blend. Cool.

Whip the egg whites stiff. Whip the whipping cream stiff. Fold egg whites into whipping cream.

Fold in chocolate mixture. Pour into an 8-cup (*2 L*) soufflé dish with a 6-in. (*15 cm*) foil collar.

Freeze 6 hours or overnight. Remove collar.

Garnish with chocolate curls.

Chocolate Zabaglione

Chocolate Zabaglione

4 servings

6	egg yolks
½ cup	(*125 mL*) sugar
2 oz	(*60 g*) semi-sweet chocolate
⅓ cup	(*80 mL*) sherry
3 tbsp	(*45 mL*) heavy cream

In a double boiler over low heat, beat the egg yolks with the sugar until foamy.

Melt the chocolate in a second double boiler. Add the sherry and the cream.

Slowly pour the chocolate mixture into the eggs.

Whisk continuously until the mixture thickens. Pour into dessert glasses.

Serve hot with fresh fruit.

Nanaimo Bars

12-16 bars

Layer # 1

½ cup	(*125 mL*) butter
¼ cup	(*60 mL*) sugar
¼ cup	(*60 mL*) cocoa powder
1	egg, beaten
1½ cups	(*375 mL*) graham cracker crumbs
1 cup	(*250 mL*) coconut
½ cup	(*125 mL*) walnuts

In a double boiler, melt the butter, sugar and cocoa powder. Fold in the egg. Stir until thickened, then remove at once from heat. Fold in the remaining ingredients. Press into a 9 x 9 in. (*22 X 22 cm*) pan.

Layer # 2

½ cup	(*125 mL*) butter
3 tbsp	(*45 mL*) heavy cream
2 tbsp	(*30 mL*) vanilla pudding mix
2 cups	(*500 mL*) icing sugar

Cream together the butter, cream and pudding mix. Fold in the sugar. Beat until very light. Pour on top of the cookie crust.

Layer # 3

1 cup	(*250 mL*) semi-sweet chocolate
1 tbsp	(*15 mL*) butter

In a double boiler, melt the chocolate. Fold in the butter. Cool. Pour onto second layer. Refrigerate for 2 hours. Cut and serve.

1 Prepare first layer, the cookie crust, and press into a pan.

2 Pour pudding layer on top of cookie crust.

3 Melt chocolate in double boiler, cool and spread on top of second layer.

4 Refrigerate for 2 hours, then cut and serve.

Chocolate Bavarian Cream

8 servings

3 oz	*(90 g)* semi-sweet chocolate
1¼ cups	*(310 mL)* half & half cream
2	eggs, separated
4 tsp	*(20 mL)* unflavored gelatine
2 tbsp	*(30 mL)* sugar
1 cup	*(250 mL)* whipping cream

In a double boiler, melt the chocolate. In a small bowl, mix the half & half with the egg yolks. Add melted chocolate.

In a saucepan, stir the gelatine into the sugar. Stir until mixture begins to thicken slightly. Stir in chocolate mixture. Refrigerate until cold but not set.

Whip the egg whites stiff. Whip the whipping cream stiff. Fold egg whites into whipped cream. Gently fold in chocolate mixture. Pour into a 6-cup *(1,5 L)* mold. Refrigerate 3 hours. Unmold. Serve with Chocolate Fudge Sauce.

Chocolate Fudge Sauce

1 cup (250 mL)

½ cup	*(125 mL)* sugar
1½ tbsp	*(22 mL)* cocoa powder
⅓ cup	*(80 mL)* water
1 tbsp	*(15 mL)* butter

Chocolate Fudge Sauce

½ tsp	*(3 mL)* vanilla extract

Blend the sugar, cocoa powder and water together. Heat to a soft ball stage 250°F *(120°C)* on a candy thermometer.

Stir in the butter and vanilla. Serve with your choice of dessert.

Chocolate Butter Cream Icing

2½ cups (625 mL)

3 oz	*(90 g)* unsweetened chocolate
¼ cup	*(60 mL)* butter
2 cups	*(500 mL)* icing sugar
½ tsp	*(3 mL)* vanilla

Melt the chocolate in a double boiler.

Cream together the butter and 1 cup *(250 mL)* sugar.

Add the vanilla and the melted chocolate. Blend in the remaining sugar.

If icing is too thick, thin with a little milk to desired consistency.

Serve with your choice of dessert.

Apple Pecan Pudding

8 servings

1 cup	(250 mL)	flour
1 tsp	(5 mL)	baking powder
1 tsp	(5 mL)	cinnamon
¼ tsp	(1 mL)	allspice
¼ tsp	(1 mL)	mace
¼ tsp	(1 mL)	salt
¼ cup	(60 mL)	softened butter
1 cup	(250 mL)	sugar
1		egg
2 cups	(500 mL)	apples, pared and diced
½ cup	(125 mL)	pecan pieces

Preheat oven to 350°F (180°C).

Sift together the flour, baking powder, cinnamon, allspice, mace and salt.

In a large bowl, cream the butter with the sugar.

Add the egg. Slowly blend in the flour. Stir in apples and pecans.

Pour into a lightly greased 9-in. (22 cm) cake pan.

Bake in oven 40 to 45 minutes.

Serve with a hot Raspberry Coulis (see *Sauces*).

Apple Fritters

8 servings

1 cup	(250 mL)	flour
2 tsp	(10 mL)	baking powder
1 tsp	(5 mL)	salt
¼ cup	(60 mL)	sugar
¼ tsp	(1 mL)	cinnamon
½ cup	(125 mL)	milk
1		egg
2 tsp	(10 mL)	vanilla extract
1 tbsp	(15 mL)	melted butter
1 cup	(250 mL)	diced apples
4 cups	(1 L)	oil
¼ cup	(60 mL)	cinnamon sugar*

Sift together the flour, baking powder, salt, sugar and cinnamon.

Combine together the milk, egg, vanilla and butter. Blend into the flour mixture. Mix in the apples.

Heat the oil to 375°F (190°C). Drop spoonfuls of fritter batter into oil.

Fry to golden brown on all sides. Place on draining tray. Sprinkle with cinnamon sugar while hot.

To make cinnamon sugar, mix ¼ cup (60 mL) sugar with 2 tsp (10 mL) cinnamon.

Apple Flan

8 servings

1 cup	(250 mL)	sifted flour
½ cup	(125 mL)	softened butter
1 tbsp	(15 mL)	sugar
½ tsp	(3 mL)	grated lemon rind
pinch		salt
1		egg yolk
1 tbsp	(15 mL)	ice water
1 cup	(250 mL)	sugar
1 tsp	(5 mL)	cinnamon
4 cups	(1 L)	apples, peeled and sliced
½ cup	(125 mL)	melted butter

Sift flour into mixing bowl. Cut in the softened butter. Add 1 tbsp (15 mL) sugar, lemon rind, salt and egg yolk.

Mix the ingredients into a paste, using only as much water as needed.

Work dough into a ball. Wrap dough and chill one hour.

Roll out dough onto a floured surface. Roll out about 2 in. (5 cm) larger than a flan pan.

Put dough in pan. Press into the sides and bottom. Refrigerate 2 hours before using.

Preheat oven to 400°F (200°C).

Mix 1 cup (250 mL) sugar with the cinnamon. Sprinkle on apples. Pour melted butter over and mix.

Place apples in prepared flan dish. Bake in oven 40 minutes.

Apple Pizza Pie

Apple Pizza Pie

8 servings

½	recipe pizza dough (see *Breads*)
6 cups	(*1,5 L*) sliced apples
2 tbsp	(*30 mL*) lemon juice
½ cup	(*125 mL*) brown sugar
1¼ tsp	(*6 mL*) cinnamon
¼ cup	(*60 mL*) butter
½ cup	(*125 mL*) breadcrumbs
1 cup	(*250 mL*) grated Cheddar cheese
1 cup	(*250 mL*) grated mozzarella cheese

Preheat oven to 450°F (*230°C*).

Make the pizza dough according to recipe directions.

Sprinkle the apples with the lemon juice.

Roll out the dough into a 15-in. (*37 cm*) circle and place on a greased pastry sheet, or on a pizza pan.

Place the apples on the dough. Sprinkle with sugar and cinnamon.

Cut the butter into the breadcrumbs. Sprinkle onto the apples.

Sprinkle with cheeses.

Bake in oven 20 minutes, or until golden brown. Serve hot.

Banana Fritters

8 servings

2	eggs
3 tbsp	(*45 mL*) sugar
½ tsp	(*3 mL*) baking powder
¾ cup	(*180 mL*) flour
4	ripe bananas, mashed
2 cups	(*500 mL*) oil
1 tsp	(*5 mL*) cinnamon
3 tbsp	(*45 mL*) sugar

Beat the eggs.

Sift together 3 tbsp (*45 mL*) sugar, baking powder and flour. Blend into the eggs. Stir in the bananas. Mix thoroughly.

Heat the oil to 350°F (*180°C*). Drop spoonfuls of batter into oil. Cook until golden brown.

Mix the cinnamon with 3 tbsp (*45 mL*) sugar and sprinkle on fritters.

Peach and Pear Salad

6 servings

6	clingstone peaches
6	red Bartlett pears
2 tbsp	(*30 mL*) lemon juice
¾ cup	(*180 mL*) sugar
2 cups	(*500 mL*) water
½ tsp	(*3 mL*) cinnamon
½ cup	(*125 mL*) red currant jelly
6	romaine lettuce leaves

Peel and slice the peaches. Core and slice the pears. Place peaches and pears in a bowl. Sprinkle with lemon juice. Chill.

In a saucepan, dissolve the sugar in water, add the cinnamon and jelly. Bring to a boil, reduce heat and simmer until reduced to ⅓. Cool.

Pour sauce over fruit. Arrange fruit on lettuce leaves and serve.

Cherries Jubilee

6 servings

2	10 oz (*284 mL*) cans cherries
¼ cup	(*60 mL*) cherry brandy
2 tbsp	(*30 mL*) cornstarch
	vanilla ice cream

Drain the cherries. Reserve the liquid. Heat the cherries in a saucepan. Flame with the cherry brandy.

Mix the cornstarch in 1½ cups (*375 mL*) of the reserved liquid. Add to cherries. Simmer until thickened.

Divide into 6 portions and spoon the cherries and juice over 1 scoop of ice cream for each serving. Serve at once.

Cherries Jubilee and Peach and Pear Salad

Dried Apple Rings

2 tsp	(10 mL) salt	
8 cups	(2 L) water	
2 tbsp	(30 mL) lemon juice	
12	apples	

Mix the salt into the water and lemon juice.

Pare and core the apples. Cut in ring slices.

Place into water as soon as you cut the rings to prevent oxidation (discoloration).

Remove and dry rings. Arrange on trays in single layers.

Place in a 120°F (50°C) oven for 5 1/2 to 6 hours.

Pack in a wax paper-lined container. Store in a dry place.

Note : Follow the same procedure for pears.

To rehydrate, soak 24 to 36 hours in sugar water. Heat gently to a boil, then reduce heat and simmer until tender.

Christmas Plum Pudding

8 servings

1 cup	(250 mL) sifted flour	
1 tsp	(5 mL) baking powder	
1/2 tsp	(3 mL) salt	
1/4 tsp	(1 mL) nutmeg	
1/4 tsp	(1 mL) allspice	
1/2 tsp	(3 mL) cinnamon	
1/2 cup	(125 mL) butter	
1 1/2 cups	(375 mL) brown sugar, firmly packed	
2	eggs	
1 tsp	(5 mL) rum flavoring	
1 cup	(250 mL) mixed candied fruit	
1 cup	(250 mL) apples, pared, cored and diced	
1 cup	(250 mL) seedless raisins	
1 cup	(250 mL) toasted slivered almonds	
1 cup	(250 mL) fine breadcrumbs	

Sift together the flour, baking powder, salt and spices. Set aside.

In a big bowl, cream together the butter and sugar until light. Add the eggs one at a time, creaming after each addition.

Add the rum flavoring. Stir in the candied fruit, apples, raisins and almonds. Blend in the flour mixture, then the breadcrumbs.

Pour into a well-greased 6-cup (1,5 L) bowl or mold.

Cover with greased wax paper. Fold around the edge of the mold and tie in place with a string.

Place bowl into a water bath of boiling water. Steam for 3 hours.

Serve hot with rum or butterscotch sauce.

Apricot Cherry Preserves

8 cups (2 L)

1/4 lb	(115 g) dried apricots	
4 cups	(1 L) Bing cherries, halved and pitted	
3 1/2 cups	(875 mL) sugar	
1 tsp	(5 mL) grated lemon rind	
2 cups	(500 mL) water	

Chop the apricots. Mix with the cherries. Sprinkle with sugar, lemon rind and add the water.

Place in a large saucepan. Bring slowly to a boil. Boil 20 minutes.

Pour into sterilized jars. Seal.

Strawberries Romanoff

Strawberries Romanoff

6 servings

¼ cup	(60 mL) orange brandy
¼ cup	(60 mL) orange juice
2 tbsp	(30 mL) Triple Sec liqueur
1 lb	(450 g) strawberries, washed
½ cup	(125 mL) whipping cream
4 tsp	(20 mL) icing sugar

In a small mixing bowl, combine the brandy, juice and Triple Sec.

Halve the strawberries. Place in liquid. Soak for 2 hours.

Whip the cream with the icing sugar.

Place strawberries in dessert glasses. Top with whipped cream.

Pears Dianna

10 servings

4 cups	(*1 L*) water
1½ cups	(*375 mL*) granulated sugar
2 tsp	(*10 mL*) vanilla
10	pears, peeled

Sauce Dianna

½ cup	(*125 mL*) sugar
5 oz	(*142 g*) semi-sweet chocolate
¼ cup	(*60 mL*) crumbled blue cheese
1	125 g pkg. cream cheese, at room temperature
3 tbsp	(*45 mL*) Irish cream liqueur
	vanilla ice cream

Combine water, sugar and vanilla in a large saucepan; heat to simmering. Peel pears, core with a melon baller and cut a small slice off the bottom. Place pears in the simmering liquid in a single layer, adding more water to cover the pears. With the liquid barely simmering, cook the pears until just tender when pierced with a knife, about 20 minutes. Drain pears, reserving 1 cup (*250 mL*) liquid.

Sauce : Combine reserved pear liquid, sugar and chocolate over low heat. When chocolate is melted and mixture is smooth and very hot, stir in cheeses and liqueur. Whisk until well blended; cool. Place each pear on an individual plate with a small scoop of ice cream. Drizzle with sauce.

1

Peel pears and cut a small slice off the bottom.

2

Core pears with a melon baller.

3

Place pears in simmering liquid in a single layer, adding more water, if necessary, to cover pears.

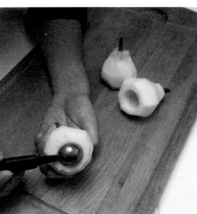

4

To prepare sauce, let chocolate mixture melt until smooth and very hot, and then stir in cheeses and liqueur.

Pears Dianna

Pepper Strawberries

6 servings

3 tbsp	(*45 mL*) butter
3 tbsp	(*45 mL*) brown sugar
4 cups	(*1 L*) fresh strawberries, sliced
¼ cup	(*60 mL*) strawberry schnapps
½ tsp	(*3 mL*) fresh cracked pepper
4 cups	(*1 L*) vanilla ice cream

In a skillet, heat the butter and caramelize the sugar in the butter, being careful not to let it burn.

Add the strawberries and heat.

Add the schnapps and flame. Sprinkle with fresh pepper.

Spoon over ice cream. Serve at once.

Melon Ball Salad

Melon Ball Salad

6-8 servings

1	cantaloupe
1	honeydew melon
1	crenshaw melon
1 cup	(*250 mL*) port wine
1 tbsp	(*15 mL*) milled black pepper

Cut and seed melons. Using a melon baller, scoop out little balls.

Pour wine over melon balls.

Mill the pepper onto melon. Mix.

Chill for several hours. Serve.

Cherry Banana Flip

6 servings

3 oz	(*90 g*) cherry gelatine
2 cups	(*500 mL*) boiling water
2 cups	(*500 mL*) canned cherries, drained
3	bananas, mashed
¼ cup	(*60 mL*) confectioners' sugar
1½ cups	(*375 mL*) whipping cream, whipped

Mix the gelatine in the water. Chill until half set.

Stir in the cherries and bananas. Chill until set.

Blend the sugar into the whipped cream.

Fold into the set gelatine. Serve.

Cointreau Peaches

Cointreau Peaches

4 servings

4	peaches
¼ cup	(*60 mL*) lemon juice
¼ cup	(*60 mL*) sugar
¾ cup	(*180 mL*) water
8	cloves
1	cinnamon stick
¼ cup	(*60 mL*) Cointreau liqueur

Preheat oven to 250°F (*120°C*).

Place peaches in large bowl and pour boiling water over them. Let stand 2 minutes. Peel.

Sprinkle or brush with the lemon juice.

Dissolve the sugar in the water. Add the cloves, cinnamon stick and Cointreau. Bring to a boil.

Place peaches in a casserole. Pour liquid over peaches. Bake for 20 minutes in oven.

Remove and serve or remove cinnamon and cloves and chill before serving.

Cherry Jam, Peach Jam and Grape Jelly

Peach Jam

8 cups (2 L)

16	peaches
2 tbsp	(*30 mL*) lemon juice
5 cups	(*1,2 L*) sugar

Boil peaches a few at a time for 1 minute. Remove skin and chop. Sprinkle with lemon juice. Mix cut-up peaches with sugar. Bring to a boil and mash. Skim off foam. Simmer for 25 minutes.

Pour into sterilized jars. Seal.

Cherry Jam

8 cups (2 L)

6 cups	(*1,5 L*) cherries, pitted and halved
3 cups	(*750 mL*) fine sugar
1 tbsp	(*15 mL*) lemon juice

In a large pot, mash the cherries.

Add the sugar and lemon juice. Bring to a boil. Simmer 30 minutes.

Pour into sterilized jars. Seal.

Grape Jelly

8 cups (2 L)

12 cups	(*3 L*) grapes, (red, blue, green)
¾ cup	(*180 mL*) water
2 cups	(*500 mL*) fine sugar

In a large pot, place grapes and water. Bring to a boil. Mash while cooking. Refrigerate overnight. Strain through a sieve then through a cheesecloth. Mix 8 cups (*2 L*) of the juice with the sugar. Bring to a boil and simmer for 40 minutes. Pour into sterilized jars. Seal.

Peach and Tangerine Marmalade

8 cups (2 L)

12	peaches
½ cup	(125 mL) lemon juice
6	tangerines
3½ cups	(875 mL) sugar

Peel and stone the peaches. Cut into slices. Marinate in lemon juice.

Peel the tangerines. Remove the white membrane. Cut the rind in julienne strips.

Mash the tangerines into a pulp. Mix with the peaches.

Add the sugar. Place in a saucepan; heat slowly to a boil. Simmer 20 minutes.

Remove and stir.

Pour into sterilized jars. Seal.

Peach and Tangerine Marmalade

Strawberry Jam

8 cups (2 L)

4 cups	(1 L) fine sugar
8 cups	(2 L) strawberries, washed and hulled
2 tbsp	(30 mL) lemon juice

In a large pot, mix together sugar, strawberries and lemon juice. Mash with a potato masher.

Place on heat and bring to a boil.

Skim any foam as it rises to the top (foam contains the impurities).

Bring to a boil and simmer 30 to 35 minutes.

Pour into sterilized jars. Remove any drippings. Seal.

Candy Apples

8 servings

2 cups	*(500 mL)* sugar
⅔ cup	*(160 mL)* water
¼ cup	*(60 mL)* butter
3 tbsp	*(45 mL)* corn syrup
¼ tsp	*(1 mL)* red food coloring
8	apples

Place the sugar and water in a large saucepan. Heat until dissolved.

Add the butter, corn syrup and food coloring. Bring to 300°F *(148°C)* on a candy thermometer.

Place saucepan into another pan of boiling water (ie. a double boiler).

Skewer the apples. Dip apples in the candy.

Place on a pastry sheet lined with wax paper. Let harden.

Candy Apples

Apple Crisp

6 servings

6	large apples, sliced
1 tbsp	*(15 mL)* lemon juice
½ cup	*(125 mL)* sugar
½ cup	*(125 mL)* graham cracker crumbs
½ cup	*(125 mL)* cashew pieces
1 tsp	*(5 mL)* cinnamon
2 tbsp	*(30 mL)* butter
⅓ cup	*(80 mL)* heavy cream

Preheat oven to 350°F *(180°C)*.

Slice the apples and sprinkle with lemon juice to prevent oxidation (browning).

Place in a 9-in. *(23 cm)* pie plate.

Combine the sugar, graham crackers, nuts and cinnamon.

Sprinkle over apples. Dot with butter. Bake in oven 25 to 30 minutes.

Serve hot with 1 tbsp *(15 mL)* of cream over each serving.

Crème Brûlée

Crème Brûlée

6-8 servings

8	egg yolks
¼ cup	(*60 mL*) sugar
4 tsp	(*20 mL*) cornstarch
4 cups	(*1 L*) heavy cream
½ tsp	(*3 mL*) cinnamon
1 tsp	(*5 mL*) vanilla
1 tsp	(*5 mL*) grated lemon rind
2 cups	(*500 mL*) brown sugar, firmly packed

Cream the egg yolks with the sugar and cornstarch in a saucepan over low heat.

Slowly stir in the cream. Add the cinnamon, vanilla and lemon rind. Simmer 10 minutes, stirring constantly.

Pour into molds; cool. Refrigerate to set.

Caramelize the brown sugar.

Unmold custard onto serving plates.

Pour hot sugar over and serve at once.

Caramel Custard

6 servings

1 cup	(*250 mL*) milk
1 cup	(*250 mL*) heavy cream
¼ cup	(*60 mL*) sugar
¼ cup	(*60 mL*) honey
4	egg yolks
¾ tsp	(*4 mL*) vanilla
pinch	salt

Preheat oven to 350°F (*180°C*).

In a double boiler, scald the milk and cream.

In a large saucepan, caramelize* the sugar and honey together.

Add the scalded cream to the sugar. Simmer until the caramel is incorporated.

In a mixing bowl, whip the egg yolks. Slowly stir in the cream mixture, a little at a time. Add the vanilla and salt.

Pour mixture into molds. Place molds in a water bath. Cover molds with tin foil.

Bake in oven for 1 hour.

Unmold and serve.

*Caramelize means to melt sugar until golden brown, just before the burning point.

Chocolate Nut Fudge

12-16 squares

8 oz	(*225 g*) unsweetened chocolate
3 cups	(*750 mL*) sugar
¾ cup	(*180 mL*) sweetened condensed milk
½ cup	(*125 mL*) corn syrup
3 tbsp	(*45 mL*) cocoa powder
¼ cup	(*60 mL*) butter
1 cup	(*250 mL*) walnut pieces

In a double boiler, melt the chocolate.

In a heavy saucepan, mix the sugar, milk, corn syrup and cocoa.

Heat to 238°F (*114°C*) on a candy thermometer. Cook for 5 minutes.

Remove from heat and cool to 110°F (*43°C*).

Stir in the melted chocolate, butter and nuts.

Pour into a lightly buttered 8-in. (*20 cm*) square cake pan.

Cool completely. Cut into squares.

Grandma K's Potato Candy

4 dozen

1 cup	(*250 mL*) mashed potatoes, lukewarm, unseasoned
½ tsp	(*3 mL*) salt
1 tbsp	(*15 mL*) vanilla
8 cups	(*2 L*) confectioners' sugar

Combine the potatoes, salt and vanilla.

Sift in the sugar 1 cup (*250 mL*) at a time. Beat well after each addition.

Knead well. Shape into small balls.

You may want to dip balls in melted chocolate.

Chocolate Nut Fudge and Grandma K's Potato Candy

Tropical Dream

8 servings

1 tbsp	(*15 mL*) unflavored gelatine
⅓ cup	(*80 mL*) cold water
1 cup	(*250 mL*) mango pulp*
1 cup	(*250 mL*) papaya pulp*
½ cup	(*125 mL*) sugar
2 tbsp	(*30 mL*) lemon juice
1 cup	(*250 mL*) whipping cream

Soften the gelatine in the cold water.

Press the mango and papaya through a sieve or food mill. Stir in the sugar and lemon juice.

Heat the gelatine water in a saucepan. Add the fruit.

Bring to a boil, simmer 2 minutes and remove from heat. Cool, but do not let set.

Whip the cream. Fold into fruit mixture.

Pour into 8 dessert cups or glasses. Chill 3 hours.

Serve with whipped cream or fruit garnish.

Chocolate Almond Cookies

12-18 cookies

⅔ cup	(*160 mL*) sugar
¾ cup	(*180 mL*) blanched almonds, ground fine
¼ cup	(*60 mL*) flour
1	egg, lightly beaten
2	egg whites
4 tbsp	(*60 mL*) melted butter
½ tsp	(*3 mL*) white vanilla
1 tbsp	(*15 mL*) water
4 oz	(*115 g*) semi-sweet chocolate

Preheat oven to 450°F (*230°C*).

Blend the sugar, almonds and flour together.

Add the whole egg, egg whites and blend thoroughly. Stir in the butter, vanilla and water.

Butter a cookie sheet. Using a spoon, drop 6 cookies 3½ to 4 in. (*8 to 10 cm*) apart.

Bake for about 5 minutes or until cookies are brown around the edges.

While hot, roll cookies into cigar shapes. Cool.

Melt chocolate in a double boiler. Dip one end of cookie in chocolate. Refrigerate to cool.

Vanilla Custard

8 servings

2 tbsp	(*30 mL*) flour
¾ cup	(*180 mL*) sugar
4	eggs
4 cups	(*1 L*) scalded milk
2 tsp	(*10 mL*) white vanilla extract

Sift the flour with the sugar.

In a double boiler, cream the eggs and add the sugar.

Pour the hot milk slowly into eggs. Add vanilla. To prevent curdling, do not boil.

Serve hot or cold, with fruit or use in trifle.

You may substitute other fruit such as kiwis, passion fruit, bananas, star fruit, etc.

Streusel

8 servings

1 cup	(*250 mL*)	flour
½ cup	(*125 mL*)	brown sugar
2 tsp	(*10 mL*)	cinnamon
½ cup	(*125 mL*)	butter
2¼ lbs	(*1 kg*)	apples, pared, cored and sliced
¼ cup	(*60 mL*)	sugar
½ cup	(*125 mL*)	raisins
½ cup	(*125 mL*)	toasted slivered almonds
½ cup	(*125 mL*)	apricot preserves

Preheat oven to 400°F (*200°C*).

Sift together the flour, brown sugar and cinnamon into a mixing bowl.

Cut in the butter. Mix into coarse pieces.

Lightly grease a 8 x 4-in. (*20 x 10 cm*) cake pan.

Blend together the apples, sugar, raisins and almonds.

Place in an even layer in the pan. Dot with apricot preserves.

Sprinkle the flour mixture on top. Do not pack.

Bake 40 to 45 minutes, or until golden brown.

Serve hot with hot custard.

Streusel

Choux Pastry

24 puffs or 12 éclairs

1 cup	(*250 mL*)	water
¼ cup	(*60 mL*)	butter
¼ tsp	(*1 mL*)	salt
1 cup	(*250 mL*)	sifted flour
4		eggs

Heat the water to boiling. Add the butter and salt. Stir in the flour.

Cook to the consistency of mashed potatoes.

Add one egg at a time, beating well after each addition. Use as required.

Cream Puffs

24 puffs

1	recipe choux pastry
1	recipe vanilla custard, cooked
½ cup	(*125 mL*) icing sugar

Preheat oven to 400°F (*200°C*).

On a lightly greased pastry sheet, drop 1 tbsp (*15 mL*) of choux pastry 2 in. (*5 cm*) apart.

Bake in oven 20 to 25 minutes, or until golden brown. Cool.

Cut puffs in half. Fill with custard. Dust with icing sugar.

Cream Puffs

Cinnamon Caramels

about 24 candies

1⅓ cups	(*330 mL*)	honey
½ cup	(*125 mL*)	butter
1½ cups	(*375 mL*)	heavy cream
½ tsp	(*3 mL*)	ground cinnamon

Combine all the ingredients in a saucepan.

Heat to 244°F (*117°C*) on a candy thermometer. Cook 2 minutes.

Pour into an 8-in. (*20 cm*) lightly buttered cake pan. Cool.

Cut into desired size pieces. Wrap in plastic wrap.

Chocolate Éclairs

12 éclairs

1	recipe choux pastry
6 oz	(*170 g*) semi-sweet chocolate
2 tbsp	(*30 mL*) melted butter
3 cups	(*750 mL*) whipping cream, whipped

Preheat oven to 400°F (*200°C*).

Using a pastry bag, pipe the choux pastry in 1 x 3 in. (*2,5 x 7 cm*) strips, on a lightly greased pastry sheet.

Bake 20 to 25 minutes, or until golden brown. Cool.

In a double boiler, melt the chocolate and add the butter.

Cut the éclairs in half lengthwise.

Fill bottom halves with whipped cream.

Dip top halves in melted chocolate and reassemble.

Cut the baked éclairs in half lengthwise.

Fill bottoms with whipped cream.

Dip the tops in melted chocolate.

Reassemble tops and bottoms.

Banana Coconut Ice Cream

6 cups (1,5 L)

4 cups	(1 L) half & half cream
¾ cup	(180 mL) sugar
4	ripe bananas
½ cup	(125 mL) flaked coconut

Heat the cream with sugar in a double boiler. Cool. Mash bananas and mix with the coconut. Add to the cooled cream.

Freeze according to directions of ice cream maker.

Coffee Ice Cream

4 cups (1 L)

4 cups	(1 L) half & half cream
3 tbsp	(45 mL) instant coffee crystals
1 cup	(250 mL) sugar
1 tbsp	(15 mL) vanilla extract

In a double boiler, scald the cream. Add the coffee, sugar and vanilla. Cool.

Freeze according to directions of ice cream maker.

A Taste of the Tropics Ice Cream

A Taste of the Tropics Ice Cream

6 cups (1,5 L)

2	mangos
1	large papaya
4	passion fruit
¼ cup	(60 mL) water
4 cups	(1 L) half & half cream
1 cup	(250 mL) sugar
2 tbsp	(30 mL) lemon juice

Peel the mangos and slice. Scoop out papaya flesh and mix with mangos.

Scoop out passion fruit pulp (seeds included), and mix with other fruits.

Place fruit in saucepan, add water and cook until most of the moisture has evaporated.

Add cream and sugar.

Heat to scalding. Cool then add lemon juice.

Freeze according to directions of ice cream maker.

Chocolate Ice Cream

6 cups (1,5 L)

1 cup	(*250 mL*) sugar
pinch	salt
1 tbsp	(*15 mL*) cocoa powder
¼ cup	(*60 mL*) water
2 oz	(*60 g*) unsweetened chocolate
4 cups	(*1 L*) half & half cream
1 tsp	(*5 mL*) vanilla extract

Dissolve the sugar, salt and cocoa powder in the water. Add the chocolate and melt in a double boiler. Slowly add the half & half and heat. Remove from heat and cool. Add vanilla and freeze according to directions of ice cream maker.

Rocky Road Ice Cream

6 cups (1,5 L)

1	recipe chocolate ice cream
⅓ cup	(*80 mL*) chopped walnuts
⅓ cup	(*80 mL*) chocolate chips
⅓ cup	(*80 mL*) miniature marshmallows

When chocolate ice cream is half frozen in ice cream maker, fold in the walnuts, chocolate chips and marshmallows, then finish freezing.

Rocky Road Ice Cream

Vanilla Ice Cream

4 cups (1 L)

2 cups	(*500 mL*) light cream or half & half
½ cup	(*125 mL*) fine sugar
pinch	salt
4	egg yolks
2 tsp	(*10 mL*) vanilla
1 cup	(*250 mL*) whipping cream

Combine the light cream, sugar, salt, egg yolks and vanilla.

Cook in a double boiler 25 to 30 minutes, or until very thick. Cool.

Stir in the whipping cream and freeze according to directions of ice cream maker.

Lemon Ice

2 cups (500 mL)

6 tbsp	(*90 mL*) sugar
1 cup	(*250 mL*) water
½ cup	(*125 mL*) lemon juice

Combine all the ingredients.

Bring to a boil; boil 5 minutes.

Cool and freeze in ice cream maker according to manufacturer's directions.

If you don't have an ice cream maker, place mixture in a shallow pan; place pan in freezer.

Stir once or twice during freezing.

When frozen to a slush, place in a mixing bowl and mix until mushy.

Return to freezer to finish freezing.

Grape Ice

2 cups (500 mL)

½ cup	(*125 mL*) grape juice concentrate
1 cup	(*250 mL*) water

Mix the grape juice concentrate with the water.

Freeze in ice cream maker according to manufacturer's directions or see Lemon Ice.

Pineapple Ice

3½ cups (875 mL)

¼ cup	(*60 mL*) sugar
1 cup	(*250 mL*) water
2 cups	(*500 mL*) pineapple juice

Boil sugar in water 5 minutes.

Add pineapple juice and boil 5 minutes. Cool.

Freeze in ice cream maker according to manufacturer's directions or see Lemon Ice.

Lime Sherbet

3½ cups (875 mL)

½ cup	(*125 mL*) lime juice
½ cup	(*125 mL*) sugar
2 cups	(*500 mL*) milk

Mix the lime juice with the sugar and boil 2 minutes. Cool.

Add the milk.

Freeze according to directions of ice cream maker.

Tangerine Raspberry Sherbet

6 cups (1,5 L)

1½ cups	(*375 mL*) tangerine juice
1½ cups	(*375 mL*) raspberry juice
2 cups	(*500 mL*) sugar
2 cups	(*500 mL*) milk

Boil the juices with the sugar for 7 minutes. Cool.

Add milk and freeze according to directions of ice cream maker.

Lemon Ice, Grape Ice and Pineapple Ice

Almond Torte

two 9-in. (22 cm) tortes

Pastry

2 cups	(500 mL)	pastry flour
2 tsp	(10 mL)	baking powder
1/4 tsp	(1 mL)	salt
1/2 cup	(125 mL)	sugar
1 cup	(250 mL)	butter
1		egg
1 tsp	(5 mL)	grated lemon rind

Filling

4 cups	(1 L)	finely ground almonds
4 cups	(1 L)	confectioners' sugar
2		egg whites
1/2 cup	(125 mL)	Amaretto liqueur
2/3 cup	(160 mL)	raspberry preserves

Pastry : Sift together the dry ingredients into a mixing bowl. Cut in the butter and mix into a coarse meal.

Whip the egg together with the lemon rind. Stir into pastry.

Divide into two equal portions. Roll out on a lightly flour-dusted surface into two 12-in. (30 cm) rounds.

Place into two 9-in. (23 cm) pie plates. Crimp the edges. Chill until ready for use.

Preheat oven to 350°F (180°C).

Filling : Blend together the almonds, sugar, egg whites and liqueur.

Spread the raspberry preserves on the bottom of each shell. Spoon the almond filling on top. Foil wrap the edges.

Bake in oven 55 to 60 minutes, or until nicely browned. Chill before serving.

Peach Meringue Shell

6 servings

4 cups	(1 L)	sliced fresh peaches
2 1/2 cups	(625 mL)	fine sugar
6		egg whites
1/2 tsp	(3 mL)	cream of tartar
1 tsp	(5 mL)	white vanilla
1 tsp	(5 mL)	cornstarch

Preheat oven to 225°F (105°C).

Sprinkle peaches with 1/2 cup (125 mL) of sugar. Set aside.

Whip the egg whites with the cream of tartar until very stiff.

Gradually beat in the remaining sugar.

Add the vanilla. Spoon meringue into 9-in. (23 cm) pie plate (making sure to push it up the sides).

Bake the pie shell in oven 15 to 20 minutes. Allow to cool and harden.

Drain the liquid from the peaches.

Pour peaches into meringue shell. Whip the cornstarch into peach liquid.

Heat in a small saucepan to thicken.

Pour over peaches and serve.

Blueberry Cheese Pie

8 servings

6 oz	(170 g)	cream cheese
2		eggs
2 tbsp	(30 mL)	heavy cream
1 tsp	(5 mL)	grated lemon rind
4 cups	(1 L)	blueberries, fresh or frozen
1		pie crust (see *Old-Fashioned Apple Pie*)
1 tbsp	(15 mL)	lemon juice
1/4 cup	(60 mL)	apple juice
1 cup	(250 mL)	sugar
2 tbsp	(30 mL)	cornstarch

Preheat oven to 350°F (180°C).

Soften the cream cheese. Beat the eggs. Beat in the cream cheese.

Add the cream.

Fold in lemon rind and 2 cups (500 mL) of blueberries. Pour into pie shell.

Bake in oven 30 minutes. Remove.

In a saucepan, add the 2 cups (500 mL) of blueberries, lemon juice, apple juice, sugar and cornstarch. Blend thoroughly.

Heat over low heat until mixture thickens.

Pour on top of pie. Chill 3 hours.

Old-Fashioned Apple Pie

8 servings

Crust

¼ cup	(60 mL)	water
1		egg
1 tsp	(5 mL)	vinegar
2 cups	(500 mL)	flour
¼ cup	(60 mL)	cold butter
¼ cup	(60 mL)	cold shortening (lard)
½ tsp	(3 mL)	salt

Filling

5		apples, pared, cored and sliced
½ cup	(125 mL)	sugar
¼ tsp	(1 mL)	allspice
¼ tsp	(1 mL)	cinnamon
1 tbsp	(15 mL)	butter

Preheat oven to 400°F (200°C).

Blend the water, egg and vinegar together. Place the flour in a mixing bowl. Cut in the butter and shortening. Add the salt. Blend in the liquid. Mix to a coarse meal texture. Divide into two. Place dough on a lightly floured surface. Roll into 12-in. (30 cm) rounds. Place one round into a 9-in. (23 cm) pie plate.

Mix together apples, sugar and spices. Spoon into pie shell. Dot with butter. Place second dough round over filling. Tuck top edge of pastry under bottom edge. Crimp to seal. Make several slits with small knife in upper crust. Bake in oven 40 minutes, or until pastry is golden brown.

Banana Cream Pie

2 pies

2		pie crusts (see *Old-Fashioned Apple Pie*)
3 cups	(750 mL)	milk
⅔ cup	(160 mL)	sugar
3		egg yolks
1 tbsp	(15 mL)	flour
1 tbsp	(15 mL)	butter
1 tbsp	(15 mL)	cornstarch
6 cups	(1,5 L)	sliced bananas
2 tsp	(10 mL)	banana extract
1 cup	(250 mL)	whipping cream

Preheat oven to 400°F (200°C).

Line two 9-in. (23 cm) pie plates with pie crusts. Prick bottom and sides with fork. Bake in oven 8 to 10 minutes.

Heat the milk and sugar together. Whip in the egg yolks.

Blend in the flour, butter and cornstarch. Add to milk and heat slowly until thickened.

Add the bananas and extract. Pour mixture into pie shells. Chill.

Whip the cream and pipe rosettes on the pies.

Banana Cream Pie

Christmas Cake

12-16 servings

1 lb	(*450 g*) maraschino cherries, halved
1 lb	(*450 g*) candied pineapple
1 lb	(*450 g*) mixed candied fruit
1 lb	(*450 g*) seedless raisins
1 lb	(*450 g*) pecan pieces
4 cups	(*1 L*) flour
1½ tsp	(*8 mL*) salt
½ tsp	(*3 mL*) baking powder
2 tsp	(*10 mL*) cinnamon
½ tsp	(*3 mL*) allspice
½ tsp	(*3 mL*) nutmeg
1 cup	(*250 mL*) butter
2 cups	(*500 mL*) brown sugar, firmly packed
6	eggs
½ cup	(*125 mL*) molasses
4 tsp	(*20 mL*) rum flavoring
4 tsp	(*20 mL*) orange flavoring
1 cup	(*250 mL*) liquid honey or rum

Preheat oven to 300°F (*150°C*).

Mix together the fruit and nuts.

In a bowl, sift together the flour, salt, baking powder and spices.

Remove 2 cups (*500 mL*) flour and set aside. Then mix the remaining flour into fruit mixture.

Cream the butter with the sugar. Add the eggs one at a time, creaming after each addition. Blend in the molasses and flavorings.

Slowly add the reserved flour.

Lightly butter a tube pan or large loaf pan.

Pour in half the batter. Top with half the floured fruit. Add half the remaining batter, then the remaining fruit. Finish pouring the batter over the fruit.

Bake in oven 3½ hours.

Remove and cool 10 minutes before unmolding.

While still hot, brush with honey or rum. Continue to brush until all liquid is used.

Pound Cake

8 servings

1 cup	(*250 mL*) shortening
½ cup	(*125 mL*) butter
3 cups	(*750 mL*) sugar
6	eggs
3 cups	(*750 mL*) flour
½ tsp	(*3 mL*) cinnamon
½ tsp	(*3 mL*) baking powder
½ tsp	(*3 mL*) salt
1 cup	(*250 mL*) light cream
2 tsp	(*10 mL*) vanilla extract

Preheat oven to 325°F (*160°C*).

Cream together the shortening, butter and sugar.

Add the eggs one at a time; whip after each addition.

Sift together the flour, cinnamon, baking powder and salt.

Fold into mixture ⅓ at a time, alternating with ⅓ of cream.

Add vanilla and stir.

Pour into a greased loaf pan and bake in oven 1¼ hours.

Test for doneness.

Christmas Cake

Baklava

12 servings

10	sheets phyllo pastry
¾ cup	(*180 mL*) melted butter
1½ cups	(*375 mL*) slivered almonds
1 cup	(*250 mL*) honey
2 cups	(*500 mL*) water
2 cups	(*500 mL*) sugar
2 tsp	(*10 mL*) cinnamon

Preheat oven to 350°F (*180°C*).

Lay one sheet of phyllo on a greased pan.

Brush with butter. Top with ¼ cup (*60 mL*) almonds.

Repeat process seven times.

Place the remaining phyllo on top after each sheet has been brushed with butter.

Bake in oven for 65 minutes.

Combine the honey, water, sugar and cinnamon. Stir until sugar is dissolved.

Bring to a boil over medium heat. Boil for 3 minutes.

Pour over pastry. Cut and let syrup soak into pastry.

Baklava

Peanut Brittle

3½- 4 lbs (1,5 - 1,8 kg)

3 cups	(*750 mL*) sugar
1 cup	(*250 mL*) corn syrup
1 tbsp	(*15 mL*) butter
½ cup	(*125 mL*) water
1 tsp	(*5 mL*) salt
5 cups	(*1,2 L*) unsalted peanuts
3 tbsp	(*45 mL*) baking soda

Mix the sugar, corn syrup, butter, water and salt in a saucepan.

Bring to 250°F (*121°C*) on a candy thermometer.

Add the peanuts and cook to 300°F (*149°C*).

Add the baking soda and stir thoroughly.

Pour mixture into a greased pan, and spread ¼ in. (*0,5 cm*) thick. Cool.

Break into pieces.

Brownies

Brownies

36 squares

¾ lb	*(340 g)*	semi-sweet chocolate
¼ cup	*(60 mL)*	honey
½ cup	*(125 mL)*	butter
1 cup	*(250 mL)*	sugar
2		eggs
1 tsp	*(5 mL)*	vanilla
½ cup + 1 tbsp	*(140 mL)*	flour
¼ tsp	*(1 mL)*	baking powder
pinch		salt
3 tbsp	*(45 mL)*	heavy cream
¼ cup	*(60 mL)*	walnut pieces

Preheat oven to 350°F (*180°C*).

In a double boiler, melt half the chocolate and stir in the honey.

Cream together half the butter with ¼ cup (*60 mL*) of sugar until light and fluffy. Add the eggs one at a time. Add ½ tsp (*3 mL*) of vanilla. Stir in the melted chocolate.

Sift together the flour, baking powder and salt. Add to the creamed mixture.

Pour into a lightly buttered 9-in. (*23 cm*) square cake pan.

Bake in oven 20 to 25 minutes. Cool.

In a saucepan, blend the remaining sugar and butter with the cream. Bring to a boil.

Add the remaining chocolate, walnuts and vanilla. Stir until chocolate melts.

Pour over brownies. Cut into squares.

Poured Chocolate Icing

2½ cups (625 mL)

½ cup	*(125 mL)*	light corn syrup
6 tbsp	*(90 mL)*	water
5 tbsp	*(75 mL)*	butter
1		300 g pkg. chocolate chips

Combine the corn syrup, water and butter in saucepan.

Bring to a rapid boil, stirring until butter is melted.

Remove from heat, add chocolate chips and cool to room temperature.

Pour over cake.

New York-Style Cheesecake

12-14 servings

Crust

3½ cups	(*875 mL*) graham cracker crumbs
1 tbsp	(*15 mL*) cinnamon
¼ cup	(*60 mL*) melted butter

Filling

5	250 g pkg. cream cheese, at room temperature
2 cups	(*500 mL*) sugar
1½ cups	(*375 mL*) heavy cream
2 tbsp	(*30 mL*) lemon juice
1 tbsp	(*15 mL*) vanilla
4	eggs, at room temperature
1½ cups	(*375 mL*) sour cream

Crust : Combine crust ingredients. Press into bottom and sides of 10-in. (*25 cm*) springform pan. Chill.

Preheat oven to 325°F (*160°C*).

Filling : Beat cream cheese and sugar until smooth. Add cream, lemon juice and vanilla; beat until well blended. Add the eggs, one at a time, beating well after each addition. Stir in sour cream.

Pour mixture into prepared shell and bake in oven until center is just set, about 90 minutes. Turn off oven and prop door open slightly.

After about 30 minutes, transfer to a rack to cool. Chill overnight. Serve with fresh fruit or a fruit sauce.

Combine crust ingredients and press into bottom and sides of a springform pan.

To make filling, beat cream cheese and sugar until smooth. Add cream, lemon juice and vanilla; blend well.

Add the eggs, one at a time, beating well after each addition.

Pour mixture into prepared shell and bake.

New York-Style Cheesecake

Chocolate Mocha Mint Cheesecake

Chocolate Mocha Mint Cheesecake

12-14 servings

Crust

3 cups	(*750 mL*) finely crushed chocolate wafer crumbs
1 tsp	(*5 mL*) unsweetened cocoa powder
3 tbsp	(*45 mL*) melted butter

Filling

1¼ cups	(*310 mL*) chocolate mint chips
5	250 g pkg. cream cheese, at room temperature
1½ cups	(*375 mL*) granulated sugar
⅓ cup	(*80 mL*) strong coffee
1 cup	(*250 mL*) whipping cream
4	eggs
1 cup	(*250 mL*) sour cream

Preheat oven to 350°F (*180°C*).

Crust : Combine crushed wafers, cocoa and butter.

Press into the bottom and sides of a greased 10-in. (*25 cm*) springform pan; set aside.

Filling : Melt the chocolate chips; set aside.

Beat the cream cheese and sugar until smooth. Gradually beat in coffee and cream.

Add the eggs, one at a time, beating well after each addition.

Stir in the sour cream and melted chocolate.

Pour mixture into prepared pan and bake in oven 75 minutes.

Turn oven off and prop door open slightly.

After about 30 minutes, transfer to a cooling rack. Chill overnight.

Black Forest Cake

10-12 servings

1¾ cups	(430 mL) pastry flour
½ cup	(125 mL) cocoa powder
1 tsp	(5 mL) baking soda
½ tsp	(3 mL) salt
¼ tsp	(1 mL) baking powder
½ cup	(125 mL) butter
1¼ cups	(310 mL) sugar
2	eggs
¼ cup	(60 mL) kirsch or cherry brandy
¾ cup	(180 mL) warm water
3 cups	(750 mL) whipping cream
3 cups	(750 mL) Bing cherries
2 cups	(500 mL) chocolate shavings

Black Forest Cake

Preheat oven to 350°F (180°C).

Sift together the flour, cocoa, baking soda, salt and baking powder.

Cream the butter with the sugar until very light. Add the eggs one at a time.

Mix the kirsch with water. Fold into the cream mixture alternating ⅓ portions with flour mixture.

Lightly butter and flour-dust two 9-in. (23 cm) round cake pans. Pour batter evenly into each.

Bake in oven 25 to 30 minutes. Remove and cool for 10 minutes. Chill.

Whip the cream. Place the cherries on top of one cake.

Top cherries with a little whipped cream.

Cut second cake into two layers. Place one layer on top. Spread with a little whipped cream.

Place the second half of cake on top. Decorate with remaining whipped cream and chocolate shavings.

NOTE : You may want to sweeten the cream by adding 1 cup (250 mL) of confectioners' sugar after it's whipped.

German Chocolate Turtle Cake

8-10 servings

Cake

¼ tsp	(*1 mL*) salt
1 tsp	(*5 mL*) baking soda
2½ cups	(*625 mL*) pastry flour
8 oz	(*225 g*) German chocolate
½ cup	(*125 mL*) boiling water
1 cup	(*250 mL*) butter
2 cups	(*500 mL*) sugar
4	egg yolks
1 tsp	(*5 mL*) vanilla
1 cup	(*250 mL*) heavy cream
4	egg whites

Preheat oven to 350°F (*180°C*).

Sift together the salt, baking soda and flour. Melt the chocolate in the boiling water.

Cream the butter and sugar until very light. Add the egg yolks one at a time.

Blend in the melted chocolate and vanilla. Add the flour and cream, ⅓ portions at a time.

Whip the egg whites until stiff. Fold gently into the batter.

Lightly butter three 8-in. (*20 cm*) round cake pans.

Bake in oven 35 to 40 minutes.

Cool 10 minutes before unmolding.

Filling

1¼ cups	(*310 mL*) brown sugar
½ cup	(*125 mL*) sugar
1⅓ cups	(*330 mL*) corn syrup
⅓ cup	(*80 mL*) butter
1 cup	(*250 mL*) condensed milk
½ tsp	(*3 mL*) vanilla
2 cups	(*500 mL*) walnut pieces

Combine the sugars and corn syrup together. Heat in a heavy saucepan.

Boil to 245°F (*118°C*) on a candy thermometer.

Add the butter, milk, vanilla and walnuts.

Return to 245°F (*118°C*).

Pour filling onto each cake layer top. Stack layers together.

Frosting

8 oz	(*225 g*) semi-sweet chocolate
½ cup	(*125 mL*) butter

In a double boiler, melt the chocolate.

Add the butter. Pour over cake and chill.

Serve cake once frosting is set.

Oatmeal Cookies

4 dozen

2 cups	(*500 mL*) flour
1 tsp	(*5 mL*) baking powder
1 tsp	(*5 mL*) baking soda
1 tsp	(*5 mL*) salt
1 cup	(*250 mL*) shortening
1 cup	(*250 mL*) brown sugar, firmly packed
1 cup	(*250 mL*) sugar
2	eggs
1 tsp	(*5 mL*) vanilla
2½ cups	(*625 mL*) quick-cooking oats

Preheat oven to 350°F (*180°C*).

Sift together the flour, baking powder, baking soda and salt. Set aside.

Cream together shortening and sugars until light and fluffy.

Add eggs one at a time, mixing well. Blend in vanilla.

Gradually add dry ingredients to creamed mixture. Stir in oats.

Shape into balls and place on a greased cookie sheet, 2 in. (*5 cm*) apart.

Bake 10 to 12 minutes.

Old-Fashioned Butter Drop Cookies

2 dozen

1¾ cups	(*430 mL*) flour
½ tsp	(*3 mL*) baking powder
½ tsp	(*3 mL*) baking soda
½ cup	(*125 mL*) butter
1 cup	(*250 mL*) sugar
1	egg
1 tsp	(*5 mL*) vanilla
¼ cup	(*60 mL*) milk

Preheat oven to 375°F (*190°C*).

Sift together the flour, baking powder and baking soda. Set side.

Cream together the butter and sugar until very light.

Add egg and blend well; mix in vanilla.

Gradually add dry mixture to creamed mixture. Slowly blend in milk.

Drop cookies on a greased cookie sheet, placing each 2 in. (*5 cm*) apart.

Bake 8 to 10 minutes.

Old-Fashioned Butter Drop Cookies

Ice Box Cookies

2 dozen

½ cup	(*125 mL*) butter
⅔ cup	(*160 mL*) sugar
1	egg
2 cups	(*500 mL*) flour
⅓ tsp	(*2 mL*) baking soda
½ tsp	(*3 mL*) cinnamon
½ tsp	(*3 mL*) nutmeg
pinch	salt

Preheat oven to 350°F (*180°C*).

Cream the butter with the sugar. Add the egg. Add the remaining ingredients.

Incorporate well and shape into a roll; wrap in wax paper.

Chill 4 to 6 hours or freeze. Unwrap and cut into 24 pieces.

Bake on a lightly buttered pastry sheet for 15 minutes.

Beverages

The art of making a good drink is really an art, but not necessarily a complicated one. You've probably ended up with a bad drink in a restaurant from time to time, and that's no doubt because the bartender neglected to measure the ingredients exactly. Always measure and mix carefully, and your results will be perfect.

This chapter has recipes for the most popular alcoholic and non-alcoholic drinks. Enjoy, but in moderation.

Serving and Cooking With Wine

1) Cook with the same type of wine as will be served with the meal.

2) Beware of wines labelled cooking wines. They contain a high percentage of salt and therefore impart a salt taste instead of the desired flavor.

3) Do not substitute grape juice for wine in recipes. Even though the alcohol burns off, wine has a different flavor.

4) Do not serve wines with tart or vinegary dishes, such as salad.

5) Beverages with a high alcohol content are useful for flambéing food, but exercise care. Never pour directly from the bottle, and ignite with the pan tilted away from you and your guests.

Pairing Wine With Food

	White	Rosé	Red	Sparkling	Sherry
Hors d'œuvres	dry medium sweet	dry medium	medium	medium	dry sweet Port Madeira
Patés terrines	dry medium	dry medium	very dry (with fish) dry medium		
Soups	dry medium sweet		medium		dry medium sweet Port Madeira
Fish and Shellfish	dry medium	dry medium	dry	dry medium	
Poultry	dry medium sweet	dry medium	very dry dry medium	dry medium	
Game	dry		very dry dry medium		
Beef	dry medium	dry medium	very dry dry medium		
Lamb			very dry dry medium		
Veal	dry medium		very dry dry		
Pork	dry medium	dry medium	very dry dry medium		
Dessert	medium sweet	sweet		medium sweet	medium sweet Madeira

Café Mocha and California Almond Coffee

Café Mocha

6 servings

1 cup	(250 mL) semi-sweet chocolate shavings
1¼ cups	(310 mL) heavy cream
3 cups	(750 mL) fresh hot coffee
⅓ cup	(80 mL) honey
2 tsp	(10 mL) vanilla
1½ cups	(375 mL) whipping cream, whipped

Melt the chocolate in a double boiler. Add the heavy cream, coffee, honey and vanilla. Heat for 5 minutes.

Pour into 6 mugs. Top each with whipped cream.

Café Vandermint

1 serving

4 oz	(115 mL) coffee
¼ oz	(7 mL) Crème de Cacao liqueur
1¼ oz	(35 mL) Vandermint liqueur
¼ cup	(60 mL) heavy cream
1 tbsp	(15 mL) sweet chocolate shavings

Pour the coffee and liqueurs into a coffee mug. Top with whipped cream and chocolate shavings.

California Almond Coffee

2 servings

¼ tsp	(1 mL) almond extract
1½ cups	(375 mL) hot coffee
2	scoops chocolate ice cream

Blend the extract in the coffee. Pour into 2 mugs. Top with a scoop of ice cream. Serve.

Café Brûlot

4 servings

1	lemon
1	orange
20	cloves
4	cinnamon sticks
3 oz	(*90 mL*) brandy
3 oz	(*90 mL*) Grand Marnier
4 cups	(*1 L*) strong coffee, freshly brewed

Grate the lemon rind. Peel the orange in one long spiral.

Mix the cloves, lemon rind and cinnamon sticks in a chafing dish. Place over a low flame.

Warm a ladle over the flame. Pour the brandy and Grand Marnier into the warm ladle.

Attach the rind of the orange to a fork. Hold the rind over the chafing dish.

Slowly pour the liqueurs over the rind while flaming.

Add the coffee and simmer slowly for 5 minutes.

Strain, pour into demi-tasse cups and serve.

Blueberry Tea

Herb Tea

1 serving

6 oz	(*180 mL*) cold water
1¼ tsp	(*6 mL*) herb tea, choose from : anise, basil, cinnamon clover, cloves, dandelion, elderberry, fennel, ginger, ginseng, lavender, lemon, licorice, marjoram, mint, nutmeg, raspberry, rose, rosemary, sarsaparilla, sassafras, strawberry, wintergreen

Boil water in a kettle just until it reaches boiling point.

Place tea in a preheated teapot.

Pour in boiling water. Steep tea 3 to 5 minutes. Strain through a very fine tea sieve. Serve.

Blueberry Tea

1 serving

6 oz	(*180 mL*) freshly brewed hot tea
1 oz	(*30 mL*) Amaretto liqueur
1 oz	(*30 mL*) blueberry liqueur

Pour the hot tea over the liqueurs in a brandy snifter. Serve at once.

French Chocolate

4 servings

1½ oz	(43 g)	semi-sweet chocolate
3 tbsp	(45 mL)	corn syrup
2 tbsp	(30 mL)	water
¼ tsp	(1 mL)	vanilla
1 cup	(250 mL)	light cream
2 cups	(500 mL)	milk

In a double boiler, melt the chocolate. Add the corn syrup, water and vanilla.

In a saucepan, heat the cream and milk. Whip in the chocolate mixture. Serve hot.

Chocolate Peppermint Shake

4 servings

½ cup	(125 mL)	sugar
2 cups	(500 mL)	milk
1 tbsp	(15 mL)	cocoa powder
1 tsp	(5 mL)	peppermint extract
2 cups	(500 mL)	chocolate ice cream

Mix the sugar completely in the milk. Blend in the cocoa powder and peppermint.

Whip in the ice cream and serve very cold.

Lemon Iced Tea

6-8 servings

6 cups	(1,5 L)	water
1 tsp	(5 mL)	ground cloves
1 tsp	(5 mL)	cinnamon
3 tbsp	(45 mL)	black tea
4 tbsp	(60 mL)	lemon juice
½ cup	(125 mL)	sugar

Boil the water and add all the remaining ingredients.

Boil for 3 minutes. Strain through a fine sieve. Chill. Serve over ice.

Grape Crush Soda

1 serving

⅓ cup	(80 mL)	sweet grape juice concentrate
⅔ cup	(160 mL)	club soda

Pour the grape juice over 2 oz (60 mL) of crushed ice in a 10 oz (280 mL) tumbler.

Pour the soda over the juice. Serve.

Hawaiian Sip

1 serving

½ cup	(125 mL)	mango juice
¼ cup	(60 mL)	orange juice
¼ cup	(60 mL)	pineapple juice
1		fresh pineapple slice
1 tsp	(5 mL)	grenadine

Pour the juices over 2 oz (60 mL) of crushed ice in a 10 oz (280 mL) tumbler.

Pour the grenadine over juices. Garnish with pineapple slice.

Something Else Punch

10-12 servings

4 cups	(1 L)	soda water
2 cups	(500 mL)	orange juice
2 cups	(500 mL)	pineapple juice
2 cups	(500 mL)	cranberry juice
2 cups	(500 mL)	white grape juice

Mix all the ingredients together.

Serve over crushed ice in tall glasses.

Grape Crush Soda, Lemon Iced Tea and Something Else Punch

Black Russian

1 serving

¾ oz	*(20 mL)* vodka	
¾ oz	*(20 mL)* Kahlua liqueur	
1	maraschino cherry	

Pour liquors over ice in an old-fashioned glass. Garnish with cherry.

California Sunshine

1 serving

3 oz	*(90 mL)* fresh orange juice	
3 oz	*(90 mL)* rosé wine	
1 oz	*(30 mL)* peach schnapps	

Pour juice, wine and schnapps into a cocktail shaker with crushed ice.

Shake and strain into a fluted champagne glass.

Cuba Libre

1 serving

1¼ oz	*(35 mL)* dark rum	
4 oz	*(115 mL)* cola	
1	lime wedge	

Pour the rum and cola into a highball glass filled with ice. Squeeze the lime and place it into the drink.

Manhattan

1 serving

1¼ oz	*(35 mL)* Canadian rye whiskey	
½ oz	*(15 mL)* sweet vermouth	
½ oz	*(15 mL)* dry vermouth	
1	maraschino cherry	

Pour rye and vermouths over ice in an old-fashioned glass.

Garnish with cherry.

Licorice Stick

1 serving

¾ oz	*(20 mL)* Pernod	
¾ oz	*(20 mL)* anisette	
2 oz	*(60 mL)* light cream	
1	egg white	

Blend the ingredients together with crushed ice in a blender for 1 minute.

Strain into a wine glass.

Harvey Wallbanger

1 serving

1¼ oz	*(35 mL)* vodka	
3 oz	*(90 mL)* orange juice	
½ oz	*(15 mL)* Galliano	

In a tall glass half-filled with ice, pour the vodka and juice.

Top with Galliano.

Kir Royale

1 serving

6 oz	(*180 mL*)	champagne
½ oz	(*15 mL*)	blackberry liqueur
½ oz	(*15 mL*)	cassis

In a champagne glass, pour the champagne, blackberry liqueur and cassis.

Stir and serve.

Gin Fizz

1 serving

½ tsp	(*3 mL*)	sugar
1 oz	(*30 mL*)	lemon juice
1 oz	(*30 mL*)	lime juice
1¼ oz	(*35 mL*)	gin
2 oz	(*60 mL*)	soda

Dissolve the sugar in the fruit juices.

Pour gin and juices into a cocktail shaker with crushed ice. Stir.

Strain into a cocktail glass. Top with soda. Serve.

Daiquiri

1 serving

½ tsp	(*3 mL*)	sugar
1 oz	(*30 mL*)	lemon juice
1 oz	(*30 mL*)	lime juice
1¼ oz	(*35 mL*)	rum
1		maraschino cherry

Dissolve the sugar in the juices.

Pour juices and rum into a cocktail shaker.

Shake and strain into a cocktail glass.

Garnish with cherry.

Kir Royale and Gin Fizz

Bloody Mary

1 serving

1	slice lime
½ tsp	(*3 mL*) celery salt
1¼ oz	(*35 mL*) vodka
3 oz	(*90 mL*) tomato juice
¼ tsp	(*1 mL*) Worcestershire sauce
dash	Tabasco sauce
pinch	salt
pinch	pepper
1	celery stick

Rim a highball glass first with the lime slice, then dip in the celery salt. Fill with ice.

Pour in the vodka and juice. Add the sauces, salt and pepper. Stir. Garnish with celery stick.

Sangria

6-8 servings

4 cups	(*1 L*) red wine
½	lemon
6	peaches, peeled and sliced
1	orange, halved
½	lime
2 cups	(*500 mL*) sweet sherry

Combine all the ingredients in a pitcher. Chill 4 hours.
Serve very cold over ice.

Planters Punch

1 serving

1¼ oz	(*35 mL*)	Myers' rum
1 oz	(*30 mL*)	orange juice
1 oz	(*30 mL*)	pineapple juice
½ oz	(*15 mL*)	lime juice
½ tsp	(*3 mL*)	grenadine
1		orange slice
1		maraschino cherry

Pour the rum and juices into a tall glass half-filled with crushed ice. Float the grenadine on top.

Garnish with orange slice and cherry.

Zombie

1 serving

¾ oz	(*20 mL*)	light rum
¾ oz	(*20 mL*)	Myers' rum
¾ oz	(*20 mL*)	dark rum
1 oz	(*30 mL*)	lemon juice
1 oz	(*30 mL*)	orange juice
1 oz	(*30 mL*)	lime juice
½ tsp	(*3 mL*)	grenadine
½ oz	(*15 mL*)	cherry brandy
1		maraschino cherry

Pour the rums and juices over crushed ice in a zombie glass.
Float the grenadine and brandy on top. Garnish with cherry.

Tequila Sunrise

1 serving

1¼ oz	(*35 mL*)	tequila
2 oz	(*60 mL*)	orange juice
1 oz	(*30 mL*)	lemon juice
½ tsp	(*3 mL*)	grenadine
½ oz	(*15 mL*)	crème de cassis

In a collins glass, place 2 oz (*60 mL*) of crushed ice.

Pour the tequila, orange juice and lemon juice over the ice. Top with grenadine and crème de cassis.

Slings

1 serving

1¼ oz	(*35 mL*)	liquor*
1 oz	(*30 mL*)	lime juice
1 oz	(*30 mL*)	lemon juice
2 oz	(*60 mL*)	orange juice
½ oz	(*15 mL*)	cherry brandy
½ tsp	(*3 mL*)	grenadine

Blend liquor and juices into a tall glass half-filled with crushed ice.

Float brandy and grenadine on top.

*There are three main slings. Singapore, Bombay and Shanghai. The mix is the same; the liquors are different.
Singapore - gin
Bombay - rum
Shanghai - rye*

Sling, Planters Punch and Sangria

Microwave

All microwave ovens come with their own instructions, and these should be followed as if they were law! Safety is of utmost importance, so when in doubt, always check your manual.

Always use microwave-safe cookware when cooking in your microwave oven. Most cookware sold today is labelled as microwave-safe if is suitable for such use. However, if you are not sure about the suitability of a particular piece of cookware, use the following test. Put the container in the microwave. Fill a glass measuring cup half full with water, and set it in the container. Turn the microwave on at HIGH for 30 seconds. Touch the container. If it is still cool to the touch, it is safe to use in your microwave oven. Only the water and the measuring cup should be warm. Never use metal in your microwave unless the instructions specifically state how to do so safely. The same goes for aluminum foil. Metal and foil should never touch the door or walls of the oven.

The wattage of microwave ovens ranges from 350-750 watts. Note that the recipes in this chapter are timed for a 600 watt oven.

Microwaving Vegetables

	Quantity	Temp	Minutes	Note
Artichoke	1	HIGH	4-4½	fresh with water
Asparagus	1 lb (450 g)	MEDIUM	16	fresh ,cut ,with water
Asparagus	½ lb (225 g)	HIGH	8	frozen, with water
Beans	1 lb (450 g)	HIGH	11	fresh (includes lima)
Beans	1 lb (450 g)	HIGH	15	frozen (includes lima)
Beets	1 lb (450 g)	HIGH	15	fresh, with water
Broccoli	1 lb (450 g)	HIGH	8	fresh, with water
Broccoli	10 oz (300 g)	HIGH	10	frozen, with water
Brussels sprouts	½ lb (225 g)	HIGH	5	fresh, water
Cabbage	1 lb (450 g)	HIGH	6	fresh, ½ head
Carrots	4	HIGH	7	fresh, whole, diced, sliced
Carrots	10 oz (300 g)	HIGH	8	frozen, with water
Cauliflower	1	HIGH	7	whole, fresh
Corn cobs	6	HIGH	7	fresh, with water
Corn cobs	4	HIGH	11	frozen, no water
Corn kernels	10 oz (300 g)	HIGH	6	frozen, with water
Eggplant	1	HIGH	6	fresh or 4 cups (1L), diced
Mushrooms	1 lb (450 g)	HIGH	7	fresh, with butter
Onions	1 lb (450 g)	HIGH	7	fresh, with butter
Parsnips	1 lb (450 g)	HIGH	7	fresh, with water
Peas	2 lbs (900 g)	HIGH	7	fresh, with water
Peas	10 oz (300 g)	HIGH	7	frozen, no water
Potatoes	1	HIGH	3½	baked; add 3 min for each extra
Squash	1 lb (450 g)	HIGH	8	fresh, halved, buttered
Zucchini	1 lb (450 g)	HIGH	8	fresh, halved, buttered

Microwaving Meat

	Quantity	Temp	Minutes
Hamburgers	4 per lb (*450 g*)	HIGH	6
Hamburgers, frozen	4 per lb (*450 g*)	HIGH	10
Stewing beef*	1½-2 lbs (*675 - 900 g*)	HIGH	20
		LOW	60
Chuck steak**	1½-2 lbs (*675 - 900 g*)	MEDIUM	70-80
Chuck roast	3-5 lbs (*1,3 - 2,2 kg*)	MEDIUM	27 per lb (*450 g*)
Tip roast	3 lb (*1,3 kg*)	MEDIUM	24 per lb (*450 g*)
Rib roast		MEDIUM	16 per lb (*450 g*)
Rib eye		MEDIUM	18 per lb (*450 g*)

* Stewing beef is cooked in 2 stages, the first at HIGH, the second stage at LOW.

** All roasts must be cooked in a cooking bag or covered. All above roasting times are for roasts cooked to medium doneness. Reduce time by 2 minutes per lb (*450 g*) for rare, and increase by 2 minutes per lb (*450 g*) for well done. Use of a temperature probe is recommended. Let stand 15 minutes before carving

Poultry

	Temp	Time
Chicken in 9 pieces*	HIGH	17 min
Chicken in quarters	HIGH	13 min
Chicken in halves	HIGH	15 min
Whole chicken	MED-HIGH	8 min per lb (*450 g*)
Whole turkey**	MEDIUM	12 min per lb (*450 g*)

* When cooking chicken pieces, rearrange them twice during the cooking period.

** Turkey must be cooked in a roasting bag. Increase time 8 minutes per lb (*450 g*) if roasting without a bag.

Pork

	Temp	Time
Loin roast	MEDIUM	18 min per lb (*450 g*)
Rib roast	MEDIUM	18 min per lb (*450 g*)
Cooked ham	MEDIUM	11 min per lb (*450 g*)
Raw ham	MEDIUM	17 min per lb (*450 g*)

Note: The times given for loin and rib roasts are for roasts 3 lbs (*1,3 kg*) and over, cooked in a roasting bag. Add 1 minute per lb (*450 g*) without the bag. Let stand 15 minutes before carving.

Shellfish

	Quantity	Temp	Time
Clams, mussels	6	HIGH	4 min
Crab legs	1 lb (*450 g*)	HIGH	6 min
Lobster tails	1 lb (*450 g*)	HIGH	6 min
Whole lobster	2 lbs (*900 g*)	HIGH	12 min
Scallops	1 lb (*450 g*)	HIGH	6 min
Shrimp, shelled	1 lb (*450 g*)	HIGH	5 min

Note: The shells of clams and mussels will open when they are cooked.

If you double the amount of crab legs, increase the time by 50%.

Lobster tails should be cooked in 1 lb (*450 g*) batches only.

When cooking whole lobster, add ½ cup (*125 mL*) liquid.

Beef Rib Roast

8 servings

2 tbsp	(30 mL) soya sauce
2 tbsp	(30 mL) Worcestershire sauce
1 tsp	(5 mL) dry mustard
¼ cup	(60 mL) sherry
½ cup	(125 mL) beef broth
¼ tsp	(1 mL) pepper
¼ tsp	(1 mL) paprika
½ tsp	(3 mL) salt
5 lb	(2,2 kg) prime rib roast

Browning Sauce : Blend together the soya sauce, Worcestershire sauce, mustard, sherry, broth and seasonings.

Pour into a saucepan. Gently reduce to ⅓ of the volume over low heat on stove.

Tie the roast with string. Place roast on a trivet. Place in 12 x 8 x 2-in. (30 x 20 x 5 cm) microwave-safe casserole.

Brush with sauce. Cover with wax paper. Microwave for 1¼ hours at MEDIUM, brushing with sauce every 15 minutes. Let stand for 10 minutes.

Roast will be medium. For rare, decrease cooking time by 15 minutes. For well-done, increase cooking time by 12 minutes. Standing times remain the same.

If using a temperature probe, insert in center of roast and set time temperature to 120°F (49°C) for rare, 135°F (57°C) for medium and 155°F (68°C) for well-done.

Beef Bordelaise

6 servings

2¼ lb	(1 kg) round steak, cut in 1-in. (2,5 cm) slices
2 tbsp	(30 mL) butter
4 oz	(115 g) button mushrooms
2 tbsp	(30 mL) beef marrow, finely chopped
¼ cup	(60 mL) chopped shallots
2 tbsp	(30 mL) cornstarch
½ cup	(125 mL) Bordeaux wine
2 cups	(500 mL) Espagnole Sauce (see *Sauces*)
1 tbsp	(15 mL) chopped parsley

In a 12-cup (3 L) casserole dish, place the beef, butter, mushrooms, marrow and shallots.

Mix the cornstarch into the wine. Blend into Espagnole Sauce. Pour over beef.

Cover and microwave 25 minutes at MEDIUM, stirring every 5 minutes. Reduce to DEFROST and microwave 10 minutes.

Let stand 5 minutes. Sprinkle with parsley.

Beef and Broccoli

4 servings

4 tbsp	(60 mL) soya sauce
½ cup	(125 mL) sherry
2 tbsp	(30 mL) brown sugar
½ tsp	(3 mL) ginger
1 tsp	(5 mL) cornstarch
½ lb	(225 g) raw beef, thinly sliced
½ lb	(225 g) broccoli florets

Blend together the soya sauce, sherry, sugar, ginger and cornstarch.

Arrange beef and broccoli in an 8-cup (2 L) casserole dish. Pour sauce over and cover.

Microwave 4 minutes at HIGH. Stir and microwave 4 more minutes.

Let stand, covered, for 5 minutes.

Lamb Chops à l'Orange

Veal Cutlets

6 servings

2 cups	(*500 mL*) fine breadcrumbs
¼ cup	(*60 mL*) chopped bacon
1 tsp	(*5 mL*) grated orange rind
2 tbsp	(*30 mL*) chopped parsley
1 tsp	(*5 mL*) chervil
½ tsp	(*3 mL*) salt
¼ tsp	(*1 mL*) pepper
1	egg
6	veal cutlets, 4 oz (*115 g*) each
⅓ cup	(*80 mL*) butter
¼ cup	(*60 mL*) flour
1	onion, minced
2 cups	(*500 mL*) chicken broth
1 tsp	(*5 mL*) paprika

Blend the breadcrumbs, bacon, orange rind, seasonings and egg together.

Spread over veal cutlets and roll. Secure with toothpicks.

Heat a browning dish at HIGH for 8 minutes. Place butter on browning dish.

Brown the veal in the butter, 1 minute at HIGH. Turn and repeat. Remove rolls.

Add the flour. Cook for 1 minute at MEDIUM.

Stir in the onion, broth and paprika. Return rolls to dish.

Microwave 40 minutes at MEDIUM.

Lamb Chops à l'Orange

4 servings

1 tbsp	(*15 mL*) grated orange rind
⅔ cup	(*160 mL*) chicken broth
½ cup	(*125 mL*) orange juice
⅓ cup	(*80 mL*) orange brandy
1 tbsp	(*15 mL*) cornstarch
1 tbsp	(*15 mL*) sugar
2 tbsp	(*30 mL*) vinegar
8	lamb chops, 1 in. (*2,5 cm*) thick

Blend together the orange rind, broth, juice, brandy and cornstarch.

Dissolve sugar in the vinegar. Pour into 8-cup (*2 L*) casserole dish. Microwave on HIGH 4 minutes, or until caramelized. Pour in the liquid mixture. Arrange chops in the liquid.

Microwave, covered, 40 to 45 minutes at MEDIUM. Let stand for 5 minutes.

Cornish Hens with Hunter Sauce

4 servings

2	Cornish game hens
2 tbsp	(*30 mL*) butter
¼ tsp	(*1 mL*) salt
¼ tsp	(*1 mL*) pepper
¼ tsp	(*1 mL*) paprika
¼ tsp	(*1 mL*) chervil

Sauce

¼ cup	(*60 mL*) butter
¼ cup	(*60 mL*) minced onions
1 cup	(*250 mL*) sliced mushrooms
2 tbsp	(*30 mL*) flour
¼ cup	(*60 mL*) sherry
1 cup	(*250 mL*) beef stock
1 cup	(*250 mL*) tomatoes, seeded and chopped
½ tsp	(*3 mL*) paprika
½ tsp	(*3 mL*) chervil
½ tsp	(*3 mL*) salt
¼ tsp	(*1 mL*) pepper

Split the hens in half. Place in a 12 x 8 x 2-in. (*30 x 20 x 5 cm*) microwave-safe dish.

Brush with butter and seasonings. Cover with wax paper.

Microwave at MEDIUM 20 minutes. Let stand while sauce cooks.

Sauce : Heat the butter in an 8-cup (*2 L*) casserole dish. Add the onions and mushrooms.

Stir and microwave 3 minutes at HIGH. Stir in flour; microwave 1 minute at MEDIUM.

Stir in the sherry, stock, tomatoes and seasonings.

Microwave 6 minutes at MEDIUM. Stir every minute.

New York Chicken Wings

2-3 servings

2¼ lbs	(*1 kg*) chicken wings, tips removed
¼ cup	(*60 mL*) oil
1 tsp	(*5 mL*) hot pepper sauce
1 cup	(*250 mL*) Cajun Spice Sauce (see *Sauces*)

Arrange wings in a 12 x 8 x 2-in. (*30 x 20 x 5 cm*) microwave-safe dish.

Brush with oil. Cover with wax paper. Microwave 5 minutes at HIGH.

Mix the hot sauce with the spice sauce. Brush onto wings.

Cover with wax paper. Microwave 5 more minutes at HIGH. Serve.

Roast Chicken with Honey-Garlic Sauce

4 servings

2¼ lb	(*1 kg*) fryer chicken
1 tbsp	(*15 mL*) melted butter
1 tsp	(*5 mL*) salt
½ tsp	(*3 mL*) paprika
¼ tsp	(*1 mL*) pepper
1 cup	(*250 mL*) Honey-Garlic Sauce (see *Sauces*)

Place the chicken in a 12 x 8 x 2-in. (*30 x 20 x 5 cm*) microwave-safe dish.

Brush with melted butter. Sprinkle with seasonings. Cover with wax paper. Insert probe thermometer in the thigh.

Microwave 1¼ hours at MEDIUM-HIGH, or until probe reaches 190°F (*88°C*).

Check for doneness. Drain juice. Reserve if you wish.

Brush with Honey-Garlic Sauce several times while chicken stands for 10 minutes.

Chicken Supreme with Cherries

Chicken Supreme with Cherries

6 servings

6	chicken breasts, 6 oz (*170 g*) each
2 cups	(*500 mL*) chicken stock
2 tbsp	(*30 mL*) sugar
⅓ cup	(*80 mL*) sherry
1½ cups	(*375 mL*) canned cherries, pitted, reserve the liquid
¼ cup	(*60 mL*) orange juice
¼ cup	(*60 mL*) red currant preserves
pinch	cinnamon
1½ tbsp	(*22 mL*) cornstarch
2 tsp	(*10 mL*) grated orange rind

Arrange chicken breasts in a 12-cup (*3 L*) casserole dish. Pour the chicken stock over the breasts.

Cover and microwave for 10 minutes at MEDIUM-HIGH. Drain stock.

In a mixing bowl, dissolve the sugar in the sherry.

Add 1 cup (*250 mL*) of cherry liquid, orange juice, preserves, cinnamon and cornstarch. Blend well. Pour over chicken.

Add cherries and orange rind.

Microwave at MEDIUM-HIGH for 8 minutes. Let stand for 5 minutes.

Ham Casserole

4 servings

1 tbsp	*(15 mL)*	butter
¼ cup	*(60 mL)*	diced onions
¼ cup	*(60 mL)*	diced celery
3 cups	*(750 mL)*	diced ham
3		eggs, beaten
1 cup	*(250 mL)*	milk
¾ cup	*(180 mL)*	crushed soda crackers
2 cups	*(500 mL)*	grated Cheddar cheese
½ tsp	*(3 mL)*	pepper
½ tsp	*(3 mL)*	paprika
½ tsp	*(3 mL)*	basil
½ tsp	*(3 mL)*	salt

In a 12-cup *(3 L)* casserole dish, add the butter, onions and celery. Microwave 1 minute at HIGH.

Sprinkle in the ham.

Blend together the eggs, milk, crackers, cheese and seasonings. Pour over ham.

Cover and microwave 15 to 16 minutes at MEDIUM-HIGH. Let stand for 5 minutes.

Pork Roast

8 servings

5 lb	*(2,2 kg)*	pork rib roast
1 tbsp	*(15 mL)*	dry mustard
1 tsp	*(5 mL)*	salt
½ tsp	*(3 mL)*	pepper
1 tsp	*(5 mL)*	rosemary
1 tsp	*(5 mL)*	savory
2 tbsp	*(30 mL)*	soya sauce
1 tbsp	*(15 mL)*	water
1 tsp	*(5 mL)*	Worcestershire sauce
3 tbsp	*(45 mL)*	honey

Trim the roast of excess fat. Rub in the mustard and sprinkle with the seasonings.

Place roast in a microwave cooking bag or in a microwave-safe roast dish with ½ cup *(125 mL)* water and cover with wax paper.

If using a temperature probe, insert in the center of roast. Microwave 1½ hours at MEDIUM.

Mix the soya sauce, water, Worcestershire and honey together. Brush onto roast during standing time of 20 minutes.

Sweet-and-Sour Pork

6 servings

2¼ lbs	*(1 kg)*	boneless pork, diced in 1-in. *(2,5 cm)* cubes
1		onion, sliced
¼ cup	*(60 mL)*	soya sauce
1 tbsp	*(15 mL)*	Worcestershire sauce
2 cups	*(500 mL)*	pineapple chunks, with juice
½ tsp	*(3 mL)*	salt
½ tsp	*(3 mL)*	ginger
½ cup	*(125 mL)*	brown sugar
¼ cup	*(60 mL)*	vinegar
¼ cup	*(60 mL)*	cornstarch
¾ cup	*(180 mL)*	water chestnuts, drained and diced
1		green pepper, sliced
6 cups	*(1,5 L)*	cooked rice, hot

In a 12-cup *(3 L)* casserole dish, place the pork, onion, soya sauce, Worcestershire sauce and pineapple juice; reserve ¼ cup *(60 mL)* of juice.

Sprinkle with salt and ginger; stir well. Cover and microwave 30 minutes at MEDIUM. Stir after 15 minutes.

In a mixing bowl, mix the brown sugar, vinegar, cornstarch, pineapple and water chestnuts. Pour into pork.

Cover and microwave 15 minutes at MEDIUM-HIGH. Halfway through the final cooking, stir in the green pepper. Let stand 8 minutes. Serve over hot cooked rice.

Pork and Snow Peas Amandine

4 servings

1 lb	(*450 g*) lean pork, thinly sliced
3 tbsp	(*45 mL*) oil
2 cups	(*500 mL*) snow peas
2 cups	(*500 mL*) plain yogurt
¼ cup	(*60 mL*) sherry
1 tbsp	(*15 mL*) curry powder
1 cup	(*250 mL*) toasted slivered almonds
4 cups	(*1 L*) cooked rice, hot

Place the pork in an 8-cup (*2 L*) casserole dish. Pour the oil over meat. Cover and microwave 5 minutes at MEDIUM.

Add the snow peas and microwave 2 minutes at MEDIUM-HIGH.

In a small mixing bowl, blend together the yogurt, sherry, curry powder and almonds.

Pour over pork. Cover and microwave 3 minutes at HIGH.

Let stand 5 minutes. Pour over rice.

Pork and Snow Peas Amandine

Barbecued Cajun Ribs

2 servings

2¼ lbs	(*1 kg*) back ribs
1 tsp	(*5 mL*) salt
½ tsp	(*3 mL*) pepper
1½ cups	(*375 mL*) Cajun Spice Sauce (see *Sauces*)

Place the ribs in an 8-cup (*2 L*) casserole dish. Season with salt and pepper.

Cover and microwave 22 to 25 minutes at HIGH. Drain excess grease.

Pour sauce over ribs. Microwave, covered, an additional 8 to 10 minutes at MEDIUM.

Jambalaya

6 servings

½ cup	(*125 mL*) oil
4	garlic cloves, minced
1	onion, diced
2	celery stalks, diced
1	green pepper, diced
1 cup	(*250 mL*) raw rice
1 lb	(*450 g*) hot Italian sausage, diced
1 cup	(*250 mL*) cooked diced chicken
1 cup	(*250 mL*) shrimp, peeled and deveined
3 cups	(*750 mL*) chicken broth
1 cup	(*250 mL*) chopped tomatoes
½ cup	(*125 mL*) chopped green onions
½ tsp	(*3 mL*) cayenne pepper
¼ tsp	(*1 mL*) pepper
¼ tsp	(*1 mL*) thyme
¼ tsp	(*1 mL*) oregano
¼ tsp	(*1 mL*) basil
1 tsp	(*5 mL*) salt
¼ tsp	(*1 mL*) paprika
3 tbsp	(*45 mL*) chopped parsley

In a 12-cup (*3 L*) casserole dish, heat the oil 30 seconds at HIGH.

Add the garlic, onion, celery and green pepper. Microwave 6 minutes at MEDIUM.

Add rice and stir. Microwave 4 minutes at MEDIUM.

Add the sausage, chicken and shrimp.

Pour over the broth, tomatoes and green onions. Stir in the seasonings.

Cover and microwave 30 minutes at MEDIUM.

Stuffed Sole Mornay

6 servings

1	onion, chopped
¼ cup	(*60 mL*) chopped celery
½ cup	(*125 mL*) melted butter
1	egg
pinch	thyme
pinch	basil
pinch	chervil
¼ tsp	(*1 mL*) paprika
¼ tsp	(*1 mL*) pepper
½ tsp	(*3 mL*) salt
2 cups	(*500 mL*) fine breadcrumbs
6	sole filets, 6 oz (*170 g*) each
2 cups	(*500 mL*) Mornay Sauce (see *Sauces*)

In a 4-cup (*1 L*) casserole dish, microwave the onions and celery in the butter 1 minute at HIGH, uncovered.

Blend the egg together with the seasonings. Add to the vegetables and stir in the breadcrumbs.

Place the filling on the sole filets and roll up.

Place the fish seam side down in a 12-cup (*3 L*) casserole dish.

Pour the Mornay Sauce over the fish. Cover. Microwave 12 to 15 minutes at MEDIUM.

Rotate ¼ turn every five minutes. Let stand 4 to 5 minutes.

Curried Shrimp

6 servings

⅓ cup	(*80 mL*) oil
1	onion, diced
1	green pepper, diced
2	celery stalks, finely diced
1	garlic clove, minced
2 cups	(*500 mL*) chopped tomatoes
⅓ cup	(*80 mL*) tomato paste
1 cup	(*250 mL*) chicken stock
½ tsp	(*3 mL*) salt
2 tbsp	(*30 mL*) curry powder
2¼ lbs	(*1 kg*) shrimp, peeled and deveined

In a 12-cup (*3 L*) casserole, microwave the oil for 30 seconds at HIGH. Stir in the onion, green pepper, celery and garlic. Microwave 5 minutes at MEDIUM.

Stir in the tomatoes, tomato paste, chicken stock and salt. Microwave 2 minutes at MEDIUM.

Add curry powder and shrimp. Stir and cover. Microwave 5 minutes at MEDIUM.

Let stand 3 minutes. Serve.

Curried Shrimp

Warm Scallop Salad

4 servings

1 cup	(*250 mL*) scallops, cut in half
1 tbsp	(*15 mL*) melted butter
¼ cup	(*60 mL*) white vermouth
2 tbsp	(*30 mL*) olive oil
¼ tsp	(*1 mL*) minced garlic
pinch	salt and pepper
4 cups	(*1 L*) spinach, stemmed and washed

In a small microwave-safe dish, combine the scallops and the butter; microwave, covered, 1 minute at HIGH.

Add the remaining ingredients, except spinach, and microwave, covered, 2 minutes at MEDIUM-HIGH.

Let stand 2 minutes. Divide the spinach into 4 portions and pour mixture on top. Serve at once.

Denver Omelet

Denver Omelet

2 servings

3 tbsp	(*45 mL*) butter
¼ cup	(*60 mL*) minced ham
2 tbsp	(*30 mL*) diced green onion
3 tbsp	(*45 mL*) diced green pepper
3	eggs, separated
½ cup	(*125 mL*) mayonnaise
2 tbsp	(*30 mL*) water
½ cup	(*125 mL*) grated Cheddar cheese

In a small bowl, place 1 tbsp (*15 mL*) butter, ham, onion and green pepper. Microwave 1½ minutes at HIGH. Drain butter.

Whip the egg whites until soft peaks form.

Blend together thoroughly the egg yolks, mayonnaise and water. Gently fold into the egg whites.

In a 9-in. (*22 cm*) microwave pie plate, melt 2 tbsp (*30 mL*) butter 30 seconds at HIGH. Swirl to coat plate.

Fold egg mixture over butter. Microwave 6 to 8 minutes at MEDIUM.

Top with filling and sprinkle with cheese.

Microwave 2 minutes at MEDIUM.

Quickly fold in half with a spatula. Place on serving plates.

Bacon, Cheddar and Onion Quiche

6 servings

½	recipe pie dough (see *Apple Crumb Pie*)
4	eggs
½ cup	(*125 mL*) grated medium Cheddar
4 oz	(*115 g*) bacon, diced and cooked
3	green onions, minced
½ cup	(*125 mL*) heavy cream
pinch	paprika
¼ tsp	(*1 mL*) salt

Form pie crust around a microwave-safe pie plate. Brush with 1 beaten egg. Microwave 4½ minutes at HIGH.

Sprinkle half the cheese over shell. Top with half the bacon and half the green onions.

Beat the eggs with the cream. Season.

Pour eggs into a casserole and microwave 7 to 8 minutes at MEDIUM-HIGH. Stir every minute.

Pour into the pie shell. Sprinkle with remaining cheese, bacon and green onions.

Microwave 6 to 7 minutes at MEDIUM-HIGH. Let stand 5 minutes before serving.

Breakfast Cheese and Shrimp

4 servings

4	eggs
½ cup	(*125 mL*) heavy cream
pinch	pepper
pinch	paprika
¼ tsp	(*1 mL*) salt
1 cup	(*250 mL*) baby shrimp
½ cup	(*125 mL*) tomato sauce
½ cup	(*125 mL*) grated Havarti cheese
6	toast points*

Blend together the eggs, cream and seasonings. Pour into 6-cup (*1,5 L*) casserole dish. Microwave, covered with some plastic wrap, 4 minutes at HIGH.

Uncover, stir and top with shrimp, sauce and cheese. Microwave 5 minutes at MEDIUM-HIGH.

Surround with toast points. Let stand 2 minutes.

*To make toast points, remove crusts from bread slices, toast and cut corner to corner.

Breakfast Cheese and Shrimp

Zucchini Bake

4 servings

1	medium zucchini, diced
2 cups	(*500 mL*) chopped tomatoes, drained
¼ tsp	(*1 mL*) chervil
¼ tsp	(*1 mL*) basil
¼ tsp	(*1 mL*) oregano
¼ tsp	(*1 mL*) thyme
½ tsp	(*3 mL*) pepper
1 tsp	(*5 mL*) salt
1 cup	(*250 mL*) sour cream
1½ cups	(*375 mL*) grated medium Cheddar

In a 12-cup (*3 L*) casserole dish, layer the zucchini and tomatoes.

Sprinkle with the seasonings. Spread with sour cream.

Sprinkle with cheese. Cover and microwave 10 minutes at HIGH. Let stand 2 minutes.

Cauliflower with Orange Butter Sauce

4 servings

1	head cauliflower, in florets
½ cup	(*125 mL*) water
⅓ cup	(*80 mL*) orange juice
2 tbsp	(*30 mL*) dry vermouth
¼ cup	(*60 mL*) unsalted butter
	zest of 2 oranges
pinch	nutmeg

Place cauliflower in an 8-cup (*2 L*) casserole dish. Pour the water into the dish.

Cover and microwave 15 minutes at MEDIUM-HIGH. Turn vegetable over after 7 minutes.

While cauliflower is cooking, place orange juice and vermouth in a saucepan.

Reduce on range top to ⅓. Whip in the butter. Do not reheat. Add the zest and nutmeg.

Drain cauliflower. Place on serving platter.

Pour sauce over. Serve.

Asparagus Casserole

4 servings

1 lb	(*450 g*) asparagus
4	hard-boiled eggs, sliced
1 cup	(*250 mL*) soda crackers, crushed fine
1 cup	(*250 mL*) grated Cheddar cheese
¼ tsp	(*1 mL*) pepper
¼ tsp	(*1 mL*) salt
1 cup	(*250 mL*) heavy cream
1 cup	(*250 mL*) toasted slivered almonds

In a 12-cup (*3 L*) casserole dish, layer the asparagus and eggs. Sprinkle with the crackers and cheese.

Season and pour cream over cheese. Cover.

Microwave 15 minutes at MEDIUM.

Uncover, let stand 4 minutes and sprinkle with almonds.

Zucchini Bake and Asparagus Casserole

Scalloped Potatoes

4 servings

1½ cups	(375 mL)	light cream
3 tbsp	(45 mL)	chopped parsley
1 tsp	(5 mL)	salt
½ tsp	(3 mL)	pepper
6 cups	(1,5 L)	potatoes, thinly sliced
1		onion, finely diced
2 cups	(500 mL)	grated Havarti cheese
¼ cup	(60 mL)	butter

Blend together the cream, parsley, salt and pepper.

Layer the potatoes and onion in a 12-cup (3 L) casserole dish.

Sprinkle with cheese. Pour over the cream. Dot with butter.

Cover and microwave 15 minutes at HIGH.

Uncover and microwave 4 minutes at HIGH. Let stand 3 minutes.

Tarragon Mushrooms

4 servings

1 lb	(450 g)	mushrooms
3 tbsp	(45 mL)	butter
3 tbsp	(45 mL)	oil
3		garlic cloves, minced
2 tsp	(10 mL)	dry tarragon

Wash the mushrooms and cut in half.

In an 8-cup (2 L) casserole dish, microwave the butter, oil and garlic together 1 minute at MEDIUM-HIGH.

Stir in the mushrooms. Microwave 5 minutes at MEDIUM-HIGH.

Stir each minute. Sprinkle with tarragon. Serve.

Spanish Rice

4 servings

¼ cup	(60 mL)	butter
1		onion, finely diced
1		green pepper, finely diced
1 cup	(250 mL)	raw rice
1 tsp	(5 mL)	salt
½ tsp	(3 mL)	paprika
½ tsp	(3 mL)	chili powder
¼ tsp	(1 mL)	pepper
2		tomatoes, chopped
2 cups	(500 mL)	chicken broth

Heat the butter in a 4-cup (1 L) casserole dish 30 seconds at HIGH.

Add the onion and green pepper. Microwave 4 minutes at MEDIUM.

Add the rice, seasonings, tomatoes and broth. Stir, cover and microwave 15 minutes at HIGH. Fluff with a fork.

Almond Rice Pilaf

4 servings

¼ cup	(*60 mL*) butter
1	onion, finely diced
¼ cup	(*60 mL*) finely diced green pepper
1	garlic clove, minced
¼ cup	(*60 mL*) finely diced pimiento
½ cup	(*125 mL*) sliced mushrooms
1½ cups	(*375 mL*) long grain rice, raw
3 cups	(*750 mL*) chicken broth, hot
1 cup	(*250 mL*) toasted slivered almonds

In an 8-cup (*2 L*) casserole dish, place the butter, onion, green pepper, garlic, pimiento, mushrooms and rice.

Stir, cover and microwave 5 minutes at MEDIUM. Stir once, and add the chicken broth.

Cover and microwave 14 minutes at MEDIUM. Stir once during cooking.

Remove cover and sprinkle with almonds. Stir and let stand 5 minutes.

1

In a casserole dish, place butter, onion, green pepper, garlic, pimiento, mushrooms and rice. Stir, cover and microwave 5 minutes at MEDIUM.

2

Stir once, add the chicken broth, cover and microwave 14 minutes at MEDIUM.

3

Stir once during cooking.

4

Remove cover, sprinkle with almonds, stir and let stand 5 minutes.

Carrot Cake

6 servings

1 cup	*(250 mL)*	flour
½ tsp	*(3 mL)*	salt
1 tsp	*(5 mL)*	cinnamon
¼ tsp	*(1 mL)*	allspice
¼ tsp	*(1 mL)*	nutmeg
1 tsp	*(5 mL)*	baking powder
¼ cup	*(60 mL)*	oil
¼ cup	*(60 mL)*	butter
½ cup	*(125 mL)*	sugar
2		eggs
2		medium carrots, grated
1		apple, grated
½ cup	*(125 mL)*	raisins
½ cup	*(125 mL)*	chopped walnuts

Sift the flour, salt, spices and baking powder together.

Cream the oil, butter and sugar together.

Add the eggs one at a time. Fold in the flour mixture.

Blend in the carrots, apples, raisins and nuts.

Spread in a 10 x 6-in. *(25 x 15 cm)* glass baking dish.

Microwave 7 minutes at LOW, then 4 minutes at HIGH. Check for doneness. (A toothpick inserted will come out clean).

Pierce cake throughout with fork.

Turn cake out at one onto a cooling rack. Frost.

Frosting

¼ cup	*(60 mL)*	butter
½ cup	*(125 mL)*	cream cheese
1 tsp	*(5 mL)*	vanilla
1 tbsp	*(15 mL)*	grated orange rind
2 cups	*(500 mL)*	confectioners' sugar
2 tbsp	*(30 mL)*	orange juice

Cream the butter and cheese together.

Add the vanilla and orange rind.

Whip in the sugar and juice.

Spread over cake.

Apple Crumb Pie

6 servings

Crust

1½ cups	*(375 mL)*	graham cracker crumbs
¼ cup	*(60 mL)*	melted butter
¼ cup	*(60 mL)*	sugar
1 tsp	*(5 mL)*	cinnamon

Combine the ingredients. Press into a 9-in. *(22 cm)* glass pie plate.

Filling

1 cup	*(250 mL)*	sugar
½ tsp	*(3 mL)*	cinnamon
½ tsp	*(3 mL)*	nutmeg
5		large apples, pared, cored and sliced
½ cup	*(125 mL)*	raisins
½ cup	*(125 mL)*	pecan pieces

Blend the sugar with the spices. Sprinkle onto the sliced apples. Stir in the raisins and pecans. Fill pie shell.

Topping

½ cup	*(125 mL)*	butter
1 cup	*(250 mL)*	flour
¾ cup	*(180 mL)*	brown sugar

Cut the butter into the flour. Blend in the sugar. Sprinkle on top of pie.

Microwave 8 to 10 minutes at HIGH.

Rotate ¼ turn every 2 minutes during cooking, then let rest 4 minutes.

Rocky Road Pie

6 servings

Crust

1¼ cups	(*310 mL*) graham cracker crumbs
¼ cup	(*60 mL*) melted butter
¼ cup	(*60 mL*) sugar

Combine all the ingredients. Press into a 9-in. (*22 cm*) glass pie plate. Microwave 1½ minutes at HIGH. Chill.

Filling

2 tsp	(*10 mL*) unflavored gelatine
½ cup	(*125 mL*) heavy cream
8 oz	(*225 g*) semi-sweet chocolate
1½ cups	(*375 mL*) whipping cream
½ cup	(*125 mL*) toasted almond pieces
2 cups	(*500 mL*) miniature marshmallows

Soften gelatine in the cream. Pour the cream and 6 oz (*170 g*) of chocolate into an 8-cup (*2 L*) casserole dish. Microwave 4 minutes at HIGH. Stir every minute.

Chill until thick but not hard.

Chop the remaining chocolate into pieces.

Whip the whipping cream stiff and fold into melted chocolate.

Stir in almonds, marshmallows and chocolate pieces.

Fold into the pie shell. Chill for 1 hour. Serve.

Rocky Road Pie

Grasshopper Pie

6 servings

Crust

1½ cups	(*375 mL*) chocolate wafer crumbs
¼ cup	(*60 mL*) melted butter
¼ cup	(*60 mL*) sugar

Combine all the ingredients thoroughly. Press into a 9-in. (*22 cm*) glass pie plate.

Filling

¾ cup	(*180 mL*) milk
3 cups	(*750 mL*) miniature marshmallows
1 tsp	(*5 mL*) mint extract
8	drops green food coloring
1 cup	(*250 mL*) chocolate shavings

In an 8-cup (*2 L*) microwave-safe bowl, combine the milk and marshmallows. Microwave 2 minutes at HIGH.

Stir in the extract and food coloring. Fold into the pie shell.

Chill 3 to 4 hours. Garnish with chocolate shavings.

Blueberry Muffins

12 muffins

1¼ cups	(310 mL) flour
1 tbsp	(15 mL) baking powder
¼ tsp	(1 mL) salt
3 tbsp	(45 mL) butter
¾ cup	(180 mL) sugar
2	eggs
½ cup	(125 mL) milk
1 tsp	(5 mL) vanilla
1 cup	(250 mL) blueberries (well drained if frozen)

Sift together the flour, baking powder and salt.

Cream together the butter and sugar.

Add the eggs one at a time, creaming after each addition.

Fold in the flour, alternating with the milk, mixing ⅓ of quantity each time.

Add the vanilla. Stir in the blueberries.

Pour into microwave muffin trays.

Microwave at HIGH, 3½ to 4 minutes for 6 and double the time for 12.

Banana Muffins

12 muffins

1¼ cups	(310 mL) flour
1 tbsp	(15 mL) baking powder
pinch	salt
1 cup	(250 mL) sugar
⅓ cup	(80 mL) butter
2	eggs
3 tbsp	(45 mL) sour cream
¾ cup	(180 mL) mashed bananas

Sift together the flour, baking powder and salt.

Cream the sugar with the butter until fluffy.

Add the eggs one at a time. Blend in the sour cream and bananas. Stir in the flour.

Fill microwave muffin tins ¾ full. Microwave 3½ minutes at MEDIUM.

Test for doneness. (A toothpick inserted in the center will come out clean).

While still hot, sprinkle muffins with cinnamon sugar.*

NOTE : Time is for 6 muffins at a time. Double time if microwaving both batches together on a microwave shelf.

* To make cinnamon sugar, mix ½ cup (125 mL) sugar with 2 tsp (10 mL) cinnamon.

Butterscotch Nut Pudding

4 servings

2 tbsp	(30 mL) unflavored gelatine
2 cups	(500 mL) light cream
½ cup	(125 mL) sugar
4	egg yolks
¾ cup	(180 mL) butterscotch chips
1 cup	(250 mL) whipping cream, whipped
¾ cup	(180 mL) walnut pieces

Soften the gelatine in the light cream. Whip in the sugar, egg yolks and butterscotch chips.

Microwave 4½ minutes at HIGH. Stir every 1½ minutes.

Chill until cool and thick but not set.

Fold in whipped cream and nuts. Chill 1 hour.

Chocolate Mint Candy Pudding

Chocolate Mint Candy Pudding

6 servings

2 tbsp	*(30 mL)* unflavored gelatine
2 cups	*(500 mL)* milk
½ cup	*(125 mL)* sugar
pinch	salt
5	egg yolks
½ cup	*(125 mL)* chocolate chips
½ cup	*(125 mL)* mint candy canes, crushed (or striped mints)
1 cup	*(250 mL)* whipping cream, whipped

Soften the gelatine in the milk. Whip in the sugar, salt and egg yolks.

Pour into an 8-cup *(2 L)* microwave-safe dish.

Microwave 4½ minutes at HIGH. Stir every 1½ minutes.

Chill until cool and thick but not set.

Fold in the chocolate chips, candy and whipped cream. Chill for 1 hour.

Index

Almonds

Almond Cheese Slices 10
Almond Potato Fritters 242
Almond Rice Pilaf* 435
Almond Torte 398
Almonds, Peas and Pork 135
Bass Amandine 170
Chocolate Almond Cookies 390
Green Beans, Almonds, Mushrooms with Triple Rice 290
Green Beans Amandine 226
Lamb Chops in Almond Mushroom Cream 152
Nelusko (Cream of Chicken Almond Soup) 41
Pork and Snow Peas Amandine* 427
Three Rice Almond Medley 291

Apples

Apple and Cheddar Pie 320
Apple and Chicken Liver Terrine 28
Apple Bread 350
Apple Butter 257
Apple Crisp 386
Apple Crumb Pie* 436
Apple Duckling 118
Apple Flan 374
Apple Fritters 374
Apple Pecan Pudding 374
Apple Pizza Pie 375
Apple Raisin Nut Bread 351
Apple Sandwich 327
Apple Spice Muffins 354
Appled Brussels Sprouts 230
Apples Stuffed with Smoked Salmon 160
Baked Carrots and Apples 232
Candy Apples 386
Dried Apple Rings 378
Old-Fashioned Apple Pie 399
Pork aux Pommes 134
Pork Steak with Pepper Apple Sauce 129
Pork Tenderloin Stuffed with Prunes and Apples 127
Spiced Crab Apples 257

Streusel 391
Vermicelli with Apples 282

Apricots

Apricot Bread 352
Apricot Cherry Preserves 378
Apricot Soufflé with Hot Brandy Sauce 78
Apricot-Glazed Ham 139
Pork Tenderloin with Apricots 126

Artichokes

Artichokes au Gratin 224
Seashell Artichoke Salad 281

Asparagus

Asparagus Casserole 224
Asparagus Casserole* 432
Asparagus Shrimp Béarnaise 224

Avocado

Avocado Dip 21
Crab and Avocado 327
Guacamole 211

Bacon

Bacon 'n Egg Crêpes 75
Bacon, Basil Tomato Sandwich 323
Bacon, Cheddar and Onion Quiche* 431
Bacon Muffins 345

Bananas

Banana Coconut Ice Cream 394
Banana Cream Pie 399
Banana Fritters 376
Banana Muffins* 438
Banana Nut Loaf 348
Bananas Foster 196
Blueberry and Banana Soup 34
Cherry Banana Flip 383

Beans

Barbecued Baked Beans 226
Black Bean Soup 192
Five Bean Salad 59
Green Beans, Almonds, Mushrooms with Triple Rice 290
French Beans Lyonnaise 227
Green Beans Amandine 226
Green Beans Provençale 226
Red Beans and Rice 193

Beef

Barbecued Beefwiches 325
Beef and Broccoli* 422
Beef and Cheese Goulash 89
Beef and Mushrooms with Old Cheddar 90
Beef Bordelaise 88
Beef Bordelaise* 422
Beef Bourguignon 90
Beef Rib Roast* 422
Beef Stroganoff 90
Boiled Beef 86
Borscht 218
Cheese Burger Insane 95
Chef K's Fire Chili 87
Cocktail Meatballs 16
Cornish Pasty 12
Daube de Bœuf Provençale 197
Deli Corned Beef 86
Enchiladas 210
English Steak and Kidney Pie 88
Filet de Boeuf Wellington 84
Filet Oscar 82
Filet Oscar Crêpes 92
Flank Steak Florentine 83
Gnocchi with Sour Cream and Beef 204
Goulash 202
Ground Sirloin Wellington 95
Gulyassuppe 204
Herb and Spice Steaks 81
Hungarian Goulash 202
Hungarian Paprikache 204
Italian Meatballs for Spaghetti 208
Java Beef 96
Meatball Soup 94
Meat Loaf with Mushroom Sauce 97
Old-Fashioned Beef Stew 87
Old-Fashioned Beef Vegetable Soup 44
Old-Fashioned Chili 'n Cheese 96
Pepper Steak 89
Philadelphia Steak and Cheese Sandwich 342
Pot-au-Feu 86
Rib Roast of Beef 85
Rigatoni with Beef, Tomatoes and Mushrooms 274

Rouladen 198
Sauerbraten 198
Shepherd's Pie 94
Sloppy Joes 334
Steak au Poivre 81
Steak Diane 82
Steak Tartare 93
Stuffed Green Peppers 319
Swedish Meatballs 217
Swiss Steak 83
Tacos 336
Texan Short Ribs 92
Timothy's Crazy Mixed Up Super Loaf 336
Tournedos Rossini 82

Beets

Borscht 218
Pickled Beets 254

Blueberries

Blueberry and Banana Soup 34
Blueberry Cheese Pie 398
Blueberry Muffins 353
Blueberry Muffins* 438
Shrimp in Blueberry Sauce 18

Breads

Apple Bread 350
Apple Raisin Nut Bread 351
Apricot Bread 352
Banana Nut Loaf 348
Brioche 358
Cinnamon Buns 359
French Bread 346
Garlic Cheese Bread 321
Oat Bran Bread 346
Old-Fashioned Dinner Rolls 347
Parker House Rolls 352
Peanut Butter Bread 349
Pumpkin Bread 349
Southern Corn Bread 347
Sweet-As-Honey Whole Wheat Bread 350
White Bread 346
Yorkshire Pudding 358
Zucchini Nut Bread 350

Broccoli

Beef and Broccoli* 422
Broccoli and Cauliflower in Orange Almond Sauce 228
Broccoli and Cheddar Soup 46
Broccoli Cake 227

microwave recipe

Broccoli in Puff Pastry 223

Broccoli Rice au Gratin 293

Broccoli Surprise 228

Potato Broccoli Casserole 243

Brussels Sprouts

Appled Brussels Sprouts 230

Brussels Sprouts Bonne Femme 229

Brussels Sprouts Paprika 229

Buffalo

Braised Buffalo Steak with Mushrooms 154

Buffalo Burgers 154

Buffalo Filets in Peppercorn Sauce 154

Cabbage

Cabbage Rolls 137

Caraway Red Cabbage 238

Holubsti (Cabbage Rolls) 220

Roast Pork Loin and Red Cabbage 199

Cakes

Black Forest Cake 407

Brownies 403

Carrot Cake* 436

Chocolate Mocha Mint Cheesecake 406

Chocolate Orange Cake 366

Chocolate Pound Cake 368

Christmas Cake 400

Christmas Plum Pudding 378

Coconut Cheesecake 320

German Chocolate Turtle Cake 408

New York-Style Cheesecake 404

Pound Cake 400

Sachertorte 198

Candies

Candy Apples 386

Chocolate Mint Patties 362

Chocolate Nut Clusters 367

Chocolate Nut Fudge 388

Chocolate Pralines 368

Cinnamon Caramels 392

Grandma K's Potato Candy 388

Jennifer's Chocolate Bars 370

Peanut Brittle 402

Cannelloni

Cannelloni 264

Carrots

Baked Carrots and Apples 232

Carrot Cake* 436

Carrot Muffins 355

Cashew Carrots 233

Cream of Carrot and Pumpkin 46

Honeyed Carrot Salad 56

Julienned Carrots with Cheddar Sauce 232

Just Peachy Carrots 232

Cauliflower

Broccoli and Cauliflower in Orange Almond Sauce 228

Cauliflower with Orange Butter Sauce* 432

Cauliflower with Shrimp Sauce 230

Cheese

Almond Cheese Slices 10

Apple and Cheddar Pie 320

Bacon, Cheddar and Onion Quiche* 431

Beef and Cheese Goulash 89

Beef and Mushrooms with Old Cheddar 90

Blueberry Cheese Pie 398

Blue Cheese Dressing 65

Breakfast Cheese and Shrimp* 431

Broccoli and Cheddar Soup 46

Cheddar Scones 311

Cheese and Chive Rice 292

Cheese Burger Insane 95

Cheese Lasagne Verdi 266

Cheese Potato Pancakes 312

Cheese Rice with Fruit and Nuts 285

Cheese Soufflé 78

Cheese Twists 311

Cheese Vegetable Pâté 27

Chicken Tomato Rice with Old Cheddar 287

Chive Cheese Soup 43

Chocolate Mocha Mint Cheesecake 406

Coconut Cheesecake 320

Coeur à la Crème 321

Creamy Cheese Fondue 313

Cubed Cheese Fondue 314

Fusilli with Cheese and Tomatoes 264

Garlic Cheese Bread 321

Ham and Cheese Boat 9

Ham and Cheese Wontons 13

Herb and Cheese Lamb Cutlets 151

Indian Rarebit 314

Julienned Carrots with Cheddar Sauce 232

Macaroni with Gruyère and Parmesan 266

Mushroom and Parmesan Cream Sauce 297

New York-Style Cheesecake 404

Old-Fashioned Chili 'n Cheese 96

Old-Fashioned Macaroni and Cheese 270

Pasta Topped with Cheese-Stuffed Tomatoes 260

Penne with Four Cheeses 272

Pepper and Cream Cheese Soup 40

Philadelphia Steak and Cheese Sandwich 342

Potato and Cheese Soup 312

Pyrohy 318

Ricotta Ravioli 275

Smoked Cheese Potato Salad 52

Swiss and Ham Log 317

Twice Baked Blue Cheese Potatoes 253

Welsh Rarebit 314

Cherries

Apricot Cherry Preserves 378

Cherries Jubilee 376

Cherry Banana Flip 383

Cherry Jam 384

Chicken Supreme with Cherries* 425

Chicken

Apple and Chicken Liver Terrine 28

Arroz con Pollo 216

Baked Chicken Kasha 221

Barbecued Chicken Buns 324

Chicken à la King 111

Chicken à la Nantua 106

Chicken and Shrimp Gumbo 191

Chicken Buns 324

Chicken Cacciatore 207

Chicken Cashew Pitas 324

Chicken Chili 113

Chicken Cordon Bleu 110

Chicken Curry 115

Chicken Divan 114

Chicken Florentine and Rice 45

Chicken Florentine Rice 288

Chicken Kiev 219

Chicken Melba 109

Chicken Melt 326

Chicken Newburg 111

Chicken Normandy 197

Chicken Oscar 326

Chicken Paprika 104

Chicken Parmigiana 207

Chicken Rombough 108

Chicken Sauté Chasseur 102

Chicken Sauté Cumberland 108

Chicken Sauternes Veronique 103

Chicken Supreme with Cherries* 425

Chicken Supremes en Papillote 107

Chicken Tetrazzini 208

Chicken Tomato Rice with Old Cheddar 287

Chicken Tube 326

Chicken Velouté 296

Chicken Washington 108

Chicken with Espagnole Sauce 102

Cock-a-Leekie Soup 38

Coq au Vin 105

Corn and Chicken Chowder 42

Cream of Chicken and Mushrooms 38

Creamed Mace Chicken 114

Curried Chicken Pitas 330

Curry Chicken Wontons 13

Fettuccine with Smoked Chicken 263

Ginger Garlic Chicken Wings 110

* microwave recipe

Greek Pilaf of Chicken 201
Guadalajara Special 210
Hawaiian Chicken Roll 331
Hot Chicken & Tomato Salad 50
Lemon Chicken 107
Milwaukee Sandwich 333
Moo Goo Gai Pan 111
My Mulligatawny 40
Nelusko (Cream of Chicken Almond Soup) 41
New York Chicken Wings* 424
Old-Fashioned Chicken and Rice 36
Pamela's Favorite Chicken and Rice 112
Peach and Mango Chicken 99
Pistachio and Chicken Terrine 26
Polynesian Chicken 104
Roast Chicken with Honey-Garlic Sauce* 424
Rosemary Roast Chicken 99
Saag Paratha 333
Sautéed Chicken Niçoise 100
Sautéed Chicken Petit-Duc 100
Smoked Chicken Véronique 57
Southern Fried Chicken Marylands 102
Spring Chicken Bonne Femme 100
Swiss Chicken 106
The Classic Club 336
Three Pepper Chicken Breasts 106

Chili
Chef K's Fire Chili 87
Chicken Chili 113
Chili Sauce 256
Creamy Chili Sauce 306
Old-Fashioned Chili 'n Cheese 96

Chocolate
Brownies 403
Chocolate Almond Cookies 390
Chocolate Bavarian Cream 373
Chocolate Butter Cream Icing 373

Chocolate Éclairs 393
Chocolate Fondue 362
Chocolate Fudge Sauce 373
Chocolate Ice Cream 395
Chocolate Iced Soufflé 371
Chocolate Mint Candy Pudding* 439
Chocolate Mint Patties 362
Chocolate Mocha Mint Bombe 362
Chocolate Mocha Mint Cheesecake 406
Chocolate Mousse 366
Chocolate Nut Clusters 367
Chocolate Nut Fudge 388
Chocolate Orange Cake 366
Chocolate Orange Strawberries 367
Chocolate Peach Dream Custard 365
Chocolate Peppermint Shake 414
Chocolate Pie 368
Chocolate Pound Cake 368
Chocolate Pralines 368
Chocolate Soufflé 79
Chocolate Zabaglione 371
French Chocolate 414
German Chocolate Turtle Cake 408
Grasshopper Pie* 437
Irish Cream Chocolate Bavarian 364
Jennifer's Chocolate Bars 370
Poured Chocolate Icing 403

Clams
Clams Casino 16
New England Clam Chowder 42

Cod
Cod Soufflé 172
English-Style Fish 172
Whaler Sandwich 338

Coffee
Café Brûlot 413
Café Mocha 412
Café Vandermint 412
California Almond Coffee 412
Coffee Ice Cream 394

Cookies
Chocolate Almond Cookies 390
Ice Box Cookies 409
Oatmeal Cookies 408
Old-Fashioned Butter Drop Cookies 409
Nanaimo Bars 372

Coquilles St. Jacques
Coquilles St. Jacques à l'Indienne 178
Coquilles St. Jacques Florentine 178
Coquilles St. Jacques Meunière 180

Corn
Corn and Chicken Chowder 42
Corn Puffs 230
Southern Corn Bread 347

Cornish Hens
Cornish Hens Rochambeau 196
Cornish Hens with Hunter Sauce* 424
Roast Stuffed Cornish Hens 115
Rock Cornish Game Hens with Prune Stuffing 114

Crab
Baked Crab au Gratin 183
Baked Red Snapper with Crab Stuffing 170
Crab and Avocado 327
Crab and Spinach Soufflé 238
Crab Louis 183
Crab Monte Cristo 328
Crustless Crab Quiche 74
Fiji Island Sandwich 343
Guadalajara Special 210
Lobster Crab Casserole 188
Paella 216
Salmon with Crab and Béarnaise Sauce 160
Shrimp Crab Spread 342
Shrimp & Crab Tomato Vinaigrette 58
Sylvia's Jumbo Crab Claws 182

Crêpes
Bacon 'n Egg Crêpes 75
Crêpe Batter 356
Filet Oscar Crêpes 92
Manicotti Crêpes 312
Stuffed Crêpes Suzettes 357

Cucumbers
Bread and Butter Pickles 254
Dill Pickles 254
Swedish Cucumber Sour Cream Salad 56
Sweet Relish 256

Dressings and Dips
Avocado Dip 21
Blue Cheese Dressing 65
Creamy Basil Dressing 64
Curry Dip 21
French Dressing 61
French Onion Dip 22
Fresh Tomato Dressing 62
Garlic & Herb Dressing 61
Green Goddess Salad Dressing 62
Guacamole 211
Honey Lemon Dressing 64
Italian Salad Dressing 62
Mayonnaise 61
Mexicali Salad Dip 22
Piquant Dressing 64
Poppy Seed Dressing 65
Ranch Dressing 64
Roquefort Dip 21
Russian Dressing 62
1000 Island Dressing 65
Vegetable Dip 22

Drinks
Black Russian 416
Bloody Mary 418
California Sunshine 416
Cuba Libre 416
Daiquiri 417
Gin Fizz 417
Grape Crush Soda 414
Harvey Wallbanger 416
Hawaiian Sip 414
Kir Royale 417
Licorice Stick 416
Manhattan 416
Planters Punch 418
Sangria 418
Slings 418
Something Else Punch 414
Tequila Sunrise 418
Zombie 418

Duck
Apple Duckling 118
Orange-Flavored Duck Terrine 26
Roast Duck Bigarade 116
Roast Duckling Grand Marnier 116

italic microwave recipe

Roast Duckling
Montmorency 117

Eggplant

Eggplant and Shrimp au
Gratin 235

Moussaka 200

Ratatouille 234

Eggs

Bacon 'n Egg Crêpes 75

Breakfast Cheese and
Shrimp* 431

Chilled Eggs Carême 68

Crustless Crab Quiche 74

Denver Omelet* 430

Egg Drop Soup 46

Eggs à la Suisse 72

Eggs Hussarde 69

Eggs Maharaja 71

Eggs Nantua 71

Eggs Parmentier 70

Indian Omelette 206

Kedgeree 206

Lobster Eggs 70

Mexican Eggs 72

Molded Shrimp Eggs 67

Pastry Egg Breakfast 67

Perch Filets with Eggs
and Brown Butter 173

Pickled Eggs 68

Poached Eggs Oscar 70

Quiche Lorraine 72

Shirred Eggs à la Reine
76

Shirred Eggs Florentine
76

Shirred Eggs Puerto Rico
76

Shrimp Egg Foo Yong
214

Spanish Omelette 76

Tea Eggs 20

Twenty-Four Hour
Omelette 72

Endives

Baked Endives in Tomato
Cream 235

Escargots

Escargots 18

Escargots à la
Bourguignonne 188

Prosciutto Escargots 17

Fettuccine

Fettuccine My Way 262

Fettuccine Niagara 262

Fettuccine Primavera
259

Fettuccine with Scallops
and Sherry 263

Fettuccine with Smoked
Chicken 263

Fish (see also individual
types)

Apples Stuffed with
Smoked Salmon 160

Baked Orange Roughy
166

Baked Red Snapper with
Crab Stuffing 170

Baked Stuffed Salmon
160

Bass Amandine 170

Bouillabaisse 39

Broiled Orange Roughy
Parmesan 166

Cod Soufflé 172

Dill Swordfish 168

English-Style Fish 172

Fennel Orange Roughy
166

Filet of Sole Florentine
163

Filet of Sole Nantua 164

Filet of Sole Olga 162

Filet of Sole with
Mushrooms 164

Fish Stock 32

Gravlax 217

Grilled Swordfish with
Walnut Sauce 168

Halibut with Rémoulade
Sauce 171

Kedgeree 206

Linguine with Prosciutto
and Smoked Salmon
269

Monkfish en Brochette
170

Penne with Smoked
Salmon and Snow
Peas 272

Peppered Orange
Roughy and Lime
Butter 167

Perch Filets with Eggs
and Brown Butter 173

Perch Filets with Shrimp
Sauce 173

Pike Baked in Cream 172

Poached Salmon with
Blue Cheese Sauce
161

Russian Salmon
Kulebyaka 218

Salmagundi 40

Salmon Filets with
Raspberry, Kiwi and
Green Peppercorn
Sauce 159

Salmon Salad Mold 59

Salmon with Crab and
Béarnaise Sauce 160

Salmon with Orange and
Pecans 161

Sandacz Na Winie 215

Shrimp and Salmon
Mousse 25

Smoked Salmon Slice 334

Smoked Salmon Timbali
with Lobster Cream 28

Sole Meunière 162

Sole Normandy 164

Sole Walewaska 162

Stuffed Sole Mornay* 428

Trout Jodee 169

Tuna Melt 338

Whaler Sandwich 338

Whitefish Rolls 169

Frog Legs

Deep-Fried Frog Legs 15

Frog Legs Creole 195

Fruits (see also individual
types)

Cheese Rice with Fruit
and Nuts 285

Fruit Varenyky 220

Spiced Lime Fruit Salad
53

Fruit Salads

Melon Ball Salad 382

Peach and Pear Salad
376

Spiced Lime Fruit Salad
53

Fusilli

Fusilli with Cheese and
Tomatoes 264

Fusilli, Prosciutto and
Mustard Sauce 265

Gnocchi

Gnocchi 264

Gnocchi with Sour Cream
and Beef 204

Grapes

Grape Jelly 384

Guinea Fowl

Guinea Fowl
Champagne 120

Guinea Fowl with Ceps
120

Ham

Apricot-Glazed Ham 139

Clove-Studded Black
Forest Ham 138

Croque Monsieur 328

Deviled Ham Spread 342

Jambon au Gratin 139

Ham and Cheese Boat 9

Ham and Cheese
Wontons 13

Ham Casserole* 426

Rice, Okra and Ham
Casserole 290

Swiss and Ham Log 317

Ice Cream

A Taste of the Tropics Ice
Cream 394

Banana Coconut Ice
Cream 394

Chocolate Ice Cream 395

Coffee Ice Cream 394

Rocky Road Ice Cream
395

Vanilla Ice Cream 395

Ices and Sherbets

Grape Ice 396

Lemon Ice 396

Lime Sherbet 396

Pineapple Ice 396

Tangerine Raspberry
Sherbet 396

Jams and Preserves

Apricot and Cherry
Preserves 378

Cherry Jam 384

Grape Jelly 384

Peach and Tangerine
Marmalade 385

Peach Jam 384

Strawberry Jam 385

Kohlrabi

Kohlrabi in Sour Cream
236

Lamb

Carré d'Agneau 149

Curried Lamb 205

Greek-Style Leg of Lamb
200

Herb and Cheese Lamb
Cutlets 151

Irish Stew 211

Lamb Brochettes 200

Lamb Chops à l'Orange*
423

Lamb Chops in Almond
Mushroom Cream 152

Lamb Chops Provençale
152

Lamb Loaf with Chasseur
Sauce 150

Moussaka 200

New Zealand Roast
Lamb 150

Roast Lamb Rack 150

Shish Kebab Flambé 150

Lasagne

Bob's Lasagne 316

* microwave recipe

Cheese Lasagne Verdi 266

Lasagne Seafood Rolls 266

My Lasagne 267

Leeks

Cock-a-Leekie Soup 38

Linguine

Linguine and Crayfish Diable 269

Linguine Fisherman-Style 270

Linguine with Prosciutto and Smoked Salmon 269

Lobster

Harry Hatch's Lobster Bisque 42

Lobster Crab Casserole 188

Lobster Eggs 70

Lobster Henri Duvernois 185

Lobster Medallions in Pernod Cream 184

Lobster Melt 332

Lobster Mornay 184

Lobster Thermidor 184

Smoked Salmon Timbali with Lobster Cream 28

Macaroni

Macaroni with Gruyère and Parmesan 266

Old-Fashioned Macaroni and Cheese 270

Pasta Stuffed Peppers 268

Mangos

A Taste of the Tropics Ice Cream 394

Mangos in Prosciutto 9

Peach and Mango Chicken 99

Some Kind of Different 341

Tropical Dream 390

Tropical Treat 338

Manicotti

Manicotti Crêpes 312

Meatballs

Cocktail Meatballs 16

Italian Meatballs for Spaghetti 208

Meatball Soup 94

Swedish Meatballs 217

Veal Meatballs 148

Moose

Moose Roast 155

Muffins

Apple Spice Muffins 354

Bacon Muffins 345

Banana Muffins 438

Blueberry Muffins 353

Blueberry Muffins* 438

Carrot Muffins 355

Marmalade Muffins 354

Oat Bran Muffins 354

Sour Cream Spice Muffins 353

Mushrooms

Beef and Mushrooms with Old Cheddar 90

Braised Buffalo Steak with Mushrooms 154

Cream of Chicken and Mushrooms 38

Filet of Sole with Mushrooms 164

Green Beans, Almonds, Mushrooms with Triple Rice 290

Herb-Marinated Baby Mushrooms 51

Lamb Chops in Almond Mushroom Cream 152

Meat Loaf with Mushroom Sauce 97

Mushroom and Parmesan Cream Sauce 297

Pickled Mushrooms 255

Pork Chops Baked in Mushroom Cream 124

Pork Steak with Mushroom Sauce 128

Pork Tenderloin and Mushrooms Lucullus 134

Red Wine or Madeira Mushroom Sauce 299

Rigatoni with Beef, Tomatoes and Mushrooms 274

Stir-Fried Mushrooms and Peas 237

Stuffed Mushroom Caps 15

Tarragon Mushrooms* 434

Veal Medallions with Oyster Mushrooms and Brandy Sauce 141

Mussels

Steamed Mussels Mike Smith 20

Onions

Bacon, Cheddar and Onion Quiche* 431

Onion Rings 236

Onion Soup au Gratin 37

Orange Roughy

Baked Orange Roughy 166

Broiled Orange Roughy Parmesan 166

Fennel Orange Roughy 166

Peppered Orange Roughy and Lime Butter 167

Oranges

Orange Liqueur Sauce 306

Orange Rice 287

Orange Thyme Pork Chops 124

Orange-Flavored Duck Terrine 26

Romaine Salad with Oranges 61

Salmon with Orange and Pecans 161

Oysters

Angels on Horseback 10

John Hoyle's Fresh Oysters 188

Oyster Remique 19

Oyster Stew 36

Oysters Bienville 189

Oysters Florentine 317

Oysters Rockefeller 14

Rabbit and Oyster Casserole 156

Pancakes (see also *Crêpes*)

Cheese Potato Pancakes 312

Chive Potato Pancakes 249

Pancake Batter 356

Pasta
(see also *individual types*)

Basic Pasta Dough 260

Panzerotti 270

Pasta Ragu 260

Pasta Seafood Salad 55

Pasta Stuffed Peppers 268

Pasta Topped with Cheese-Stuffed Tomatoes 260

Sweet and Sour Pasta Salad 54

Pastry

Baklava 402

Chocolate Éclairs 393

Choux Pastry 392

Cream Puffs 392

Streusel 391

Pâtés (see also *Terrines*)

Cheese Vegetable Pâté 27

Cognac Black Peppercorn Pâté 29

Pâté de Champagne 26

Shrimp and Salmon Mousse 25

Smoked Salmon Timbali with Lobster Cream 28

Peaches

Chocolate Peach Dream Custard 365

Cointreau Peaches 383

Just Peachy Carrots 232

Peach and Mango Chicken 99

Peach and Pear Salad 376

Peach and Tangerine Marmalade 385

Peach Meringue Shell 398

Peach Jam 384

Peanuts

Peanut Brittle 402

Peanut Butter Bread 349

Pears

Jennifer's Pear Salad 54

Peach and Pear Salad 376

Pears Dianna 379

Peas

Almonds, Peas and Pork 135

Creamed Potatoes with Peas 244

Garden Pea Soup 33

Gourmet Peas 236

Minted Peas 238

Penne with Smoked Salmon and Snow Peas 272

Pork and Snow Peas Amandine* 427

Purée Mongole 33

Stir-Fried Mushrooms and Peas 237

Penne

Feta Penne with Veal Tomato Sauce 271

Pasta Topped with Cheese-Stuffed Tomatoes 260

Penne with Four Cheeses 272

Penne with Smoked Salmon and Snow Peas 272

Pheasant and Penne 272

*microwave recipe

444

Peppers
Pasta Stuffed Peppers 268
Pepper and Cream Cheese Soup 40
Pepper Rice Salad 290
Pepper Steak 89
Stuffed Green Peppers 319

Perch
Perch Filets with Eggs and Brown Butter 173
Perch Filets with Shrimp Sauce 173
Sandacz Na Winie 215

Pheasant
Pheasant and Penne 272
Pheasant Casserole 121
Sautéed Pheasant with Clementine Sauce 121

Pickles
Bread and Butter Pickles 254
Dill Pickles 254
Pickled Beets 254
Pickled Mushrooms 255
Sweet Relish 256

Pies
Almond Torte 398
Apple and Cheddar Pie 320
Apple Crisp 386
Apple Crumb Pie* 436
Apple Flan 374
Apple Pizza Pie 375
Banana Cream Pie 399
Blueberry Cheese Pie 398
Chocolate Pie 368
Grasshopper Pie* 437
Peach Meringue Shell 398
Old-Fashioned Apple Pie 399
Rocky Road Pie* 437

Pineapple
Fiji Island Sandwich 343
Pineapple Ice 396
Pineapple Sausage Tidbits 10

Pizza
Mini Pizzas 17
Pizza 316
Pizza Dough 358

Pork
Almonds, Peas and Pork 135
Barbecued Back Ribs 136

Breaded Pork Chops with Raisin Sauce 124
Breakfast Sausage Patties 136
Cabbage Rolls 137
Chinese Sweet-and-Sour Pork 134
Crown Roast of Pork 126
Honey Ginger Ribs 136
Italian Pork Tenderloin 131
Orange Thyme Pork Chops 124
Pork and Snow Peas Amandine* 427
Pork aux Pommes 134
Pork Chops Baked in Mushroom Cream 124
Pork Cutlets Robert 130
Pork Dijonnaise 123
Pork Roast* 426
Pork Schnitzel Milanese 129
Pork Steak with Mushroom Sauce 128
Pork Steak with Pepper Apple Sauce 129
Pork Tenderloin and Mushrooms Lucullus 134
Pork Tenderloin Diane 132
Pork Tenderloin in Sour Cream Sauce 132
Pork Tenderloin Stroganoff 132
Pork Tenderloin Stuffed with Prunes and Apples 127
Pork Tenderloin with Apricots 126
Roast Loin of Pork Provençale 128
Roast Pork Loin and Red Cabbage 199
Stuffed Pork Chops 125
Stuffed Pork Cutlets 130
Sweet-and-Sour Pork* 426

Potatoes
Almond Potato Fritters 242
Chantilly Potatoes 244
Cheese Potato Pancakes 312
Chive Potato Pancakes 249
Creamed Potatoes with Peas 244
Golden Mashed Potatoes 252
Grandma K's Potato Candy 388

Hungarian Paprika Potatoes 203
Lyonnaise Potatoes 250
Maitre d'Hôtel Potatoes 244
Marjoram Potatoes 250
Mojo Potatoes 246
Pamela's Sweet Potato Marshmallow Croquettes 250
Parisienne Potatoes 242
Potato and Cheese Soup 312
Potato Broccoli Casserole 243
Potato Croquettes 248
Potato Nests 249
Potato Tomato Bake 252
Potatoes Anna 252
Potatoes in Wine and Cream 246
Scalloped Potatoes* 434
Scalloped Potatoes au Gratin 250
Smoked Cheese Potato Salad 52
Soufflé Potatoes 246
Timothy's Tummy Tickler 251
Twice Baked Blue Cheese Potatoes 253
Twice Baked Herb Potatoes 253

Prosciutto
Fusilli, Prosciutto and Mustard Sauce 265
Linguine with Prosciutto and Smoked Salmon 269
Mangos in Prosciutto 9
Prosciutto Escargots 17
Some Kind of Different 341
Spaghetti, Prosciutto and Gorgonzola 276

Puddings and Custards
Apple Pecan Pudding 374
Butterscotch Nut Pudding* 438
Caramel Custard 388
Chocolate Mint Candy Pudding* 439
Chocolate Peach Dream Custard 365
Chocolate Zabaglione 371
Crème Brûlée 387
The Simplest Rice Pudding 370
Tropical Dream 390

Vanilla Custard 390

Pumpkin
Cream of Carrot and Pumpkin 46
Pumpkin Bread 349

Quails
Sautéed Quails Provençale 118
Roast Quails Cumberland 118

Quiches
Bacon, Cheddar and Onion Quiche* 431
Crustless Crab Quiche 74
Quiche Lorraine 72

Rabbit
Paprika Rabbit with Caraway Noodles 157
Rabbit and Oyster Casserole 156
Rabbit Provençale 156
Rabbit with Plums 156

Raspberries
Cranberry and Raspberry Soup 47
Raspberry Coulis 309
Salmon Filets with Raspberry, Kiwi and Green Peppercorn Sauce 159
Tangerine Raspberry Sherbet 396

Ravioli
Breaded Ravioli 283
Ricotta Ravioli 275

Ribs
Barbecued Back Ribs 136
Barbecued Cajun Ribs* 427
Bayou Short Ribs 192
Honey Ginger Ribs 136
Texan Short Ribs 92

Rice
Almond Rice Pilaf* 435
Arroz con Pollo 216
Broccoli Rice au Gratin 293
Cajun Dirty Rice 288
Cheese and Chive Rice 292
Cheese Rice with Fruit and Nuts 285
Chicken Florentine and Rice 45
Chicken Florentine Rice 288
Chicken Tomato Rice with Old Cheddar 287
Cream of Tomato Rice 31

Greek Pilaf of Chicken 201

Green Beans, Almonds, Mushrooms with Triple Rice 290

Indian Curry Rice 288

Kedgeree 206

Old-Fashioned Chicken and Rice 36

Orange Rice 287

Paella 216

Pamela's Favorite Chicken and Rice 112

Pepper Rice Salad 290

Red Beans and Rice 193

Rice Oh So Good! 292

Rice, Okra and Ham Casserole 290

Rice Pilaf 292

Rice-Stuffed Tomatoes 286

Risi e Bisi 291

Spanish Rice* 434

Sushi Rice 212

The Simplest Rice Pudding 370

Three Rice Almond Medley 291

Rigatoni

Rigatoni alla Vodka 274

Rigatoni with Beef, Tomatoes and Mushrooms 274

Rotini

Rotini Bolognese 274

Salads

Caesar Salad 58

Curried Seafood Salad 52

Dandelion Salad 52

Five Bean Salad 59

Greek Salad 201

Hearts of Palm Salad 57

Honeyed Carrot Salad 56

Hot Chicken & Tomato Salad 50

Jennifer's Pear Salad 54

Melon Ball Salad 382

Monte Cristo Salad 56

Pasta Seafood Salad 55

Peach and Pear Salad 376

Pepper Rice Salad 290

Romaine Salad with Oranges 61

Salade Niçoise 50

Salmon Salad Mold 59

Seashell Artichoke Salad 281

Seashell Seafood Salad 281

Smoked Cheese Potato Salad 52

Spiced Lime Fruit Salad 53

Spinach Scallop Salad 58

Swedish Cucumber Sour Cream Salad 56

Sweet and Sour Pasta Salad 54

Sweet and Sour Shredded Vegetable Salad 51

Tortellini Salad 279

Warm Scallop Salad* 429

Warm Spinach Salad 60

Salmon

Apples Stuffed with Smoked Salmon 160

Baked Stuffed Salmon 160

Gravlax 217

Kedgeree 206

Linguine with Prosciutto and Smoked Salmon 269

Penne with Smoked Salmon and Snow Peas 272

Poached Salmon with Blue Cheese Sauce 161

Russian Salmon Kulebyaka 218

Salmon Filets with Raspberry, Kiwi and Green Peppercorn Sauce 159

Salmon Salad Mold 59

Salmon with Crab and Béarnaise Sauce 160

Salmon with Orange and Pecans 161

Shrimp and Salmon Mousse 25

Smoked Salmon Slice 334

Smoked Salmon Timbali with Lobster Cream 28

Sandwiches

Apple Sandwich 327

Bacon, Basil Tomato Sandwich 323

Barbecued Beefwiches 325

Barbecued Chicken Buns 324

Chicken Buns 324

Chicken Cashew Pitas 324

Chicken Melt 326

Chicken Oscar 326

Chicken Tube 326

Crab Monte Cristo 328

Creole Shrimp Po-Boy 328

Croque Monsieur 328

Curried Chicken Pitas 330

Fiji Island Sandwich 343

Garlic Tomato Sauté 330

Hawaiian Chicken Roll 331

Indian Sandwich 332

Lobster Melt 332

Milwaukee Sandwich 333

Monte Cristo Sandwich 340

Philadelphia Steak and Cheese Sandwich 342

Reuben Sandwich with Mustard Sauce 341

Saag Paratha 333

Shrimp Croissant 334

Sloppy Joes 334

Smoked Salmon Slice 334

Super Chef's Sandwich 340

The Classic Club 336

Timothy's Crazy Mixed Up Super Loaf 336

Tortillas 337

Tuna Melt 338

Whaler Sandwich 338

Wiener Schnitzel Sandwich 335

Sauces

BBQ Sauce 302

Béarnaise Sauce 305

Béchamel Sauce 300

Cajun Spice Sauce 309

Champagne Sauce 296

Chasseur Sauce 298

Cherbourg Sauce 308

Chicken Velouté 296

Chili Sauce 256

Chocolate Fudge Sauce 373

Creamy Chili Sauce 306

Creamy Horseradish 306

Creole Sauce 295

Curry Sauce 302

Demi-Glace 298

Espagnole Sauce 298

Herb Sauce 306

Hollandaise Sauce 304

Honey-Garlic Sauce 306

Honey-Mustard Sauce 306

Italienne Sauce 299

Mornay Sauce 301

Mushroom and Parmesan Cream Sauce 297

Orange Liqueur Sauce 306

Raspberry Coulis 309

Red Wine or Madeira Mushroom Sauce 299

Simple Pesto 305

Supreme Sauce 297

Teriyaki Sauce 301

Tomato Sauce 308

White Wine Sauce 1 296

White Wine Sauce 2 296

Wine BBQ Sauce 302

Sausage

Breakfast Sausage Patties 136

Jambalaya* 428

Pineapple Sausage Tidbits 10

Polish Sausage in Pastry 215

Timothy's Crazy Mixed Up Super Loaf 336

Scallops

Coquilles St. Jacques à l'Indienne 178

Coquilles St. Jacques Florentine 178

Coquilles St. Jacques Meunière 180

Fettuccine with Scallops and Sherry 263

Kentucky Scallops 181

Marsala and Scallop Soup 41

Paprika Scallops 180

Scallops au Gratin 181

Spinach Scallop Salad 58

Warm Scallop Salad* 429

Seafood (see also individual types)

Curried Seafood Salad 52

Lasagne Seafood Rolls 266

Paella 216

Pamela's Seafood Sloppy Joes 186

Pasta Seafood Salad 55

Seafood Crêpes Mornay 186

Seafood Kabobs 18

Seashell Seafood Salad 281

Tortellini Seafood Soup 280

Shakes

French Chocolate 414

Chocolate Peppermint
  Shake 414

Shrimp
Asparagus Shrimp
  Béarnaise 224
B.B.Q. Shrimp 176
Breakfast Cheese and
  Shrimp* 431
Cauliflower with Shrimp
  Sauce 230
Chicken and Shrimp
  Gumbo 191
Chilled Shrimp with
  Mustard Mayonnaise
  14
Creole Shrimp Po-Boy
  328
Curried Shrimp* 429
Curried Tortellini and
  Prawns 280
Eggplant and Shrimp au
  Gratin 235
Guadalajara Special 210
Herb and Spice Shrimp
  14
Jambalaya* 428
Jumbo Fantail Shrimp
  176
Jumbo Stuffed Shrimp
  177
Molded Shrimp Eggs 67
Paella 216
Perch Filets with Shrimp
  Sauce 173
Shrimp à l'Étouffée 175
Shrimp Aïoli 174
Shrimp and Salmon
  Mousse 25
Shrimp Crab Spread 342
Shrimp Creole 196
Shrimp Creole au Gratin
  178
Shrimp Croissant 334
Shrimp Egg Foo Yong
  214
Shrimp in Blueberry
  Sauce 18
Shrimp Jambalaya 194
Shrimp & Crab Tomato
  Vinaigrette 58
Tempura Shrimp 176
Three-Pepper Prawns 174
Tropical Treat 338
Veal Medallions in
  Shrimp Sauce 142

Sole
Filet of Sole Florentine
  163
Filet of Sole Nantua 164
Filet of Sole Olga 162

Filet of Sole with
  Mushrooms 164
Sole Meunière 162
Sole Normandy 164
Sole Walewaska 162
Stuffed Sole Mornay* 428

Soufflés
Apricot Soufflé with Hot
  Brandy Sauce 78
Cheese Soufflé 78
Chocolate Iced Soufflé
  371
Chocolate Soufflé 79
Cod Soufflé 172
Crab and Spinach
  Soufflé 238

Soups
Black Bean Soup 192
Blackberry Soup 47
Blueberry and Banana
  Soup 34
Bouillabaisse 39
Broccoli and Cheddar
  Soup 46
Chicken Florentine and
  Rice 45
Chive Cheese Soup 43
Cock-a-Leekie Soup 38
Consommé 44
Corn and Chicken
  Chowder 42
Cranberry and Raspberry
  Soup 47
Cream of Carrot and
  Pumpkin 46
Cream of Chicken and
  Mushrooms 38
Cream of Tomato Rice 31
Egg Drop Soup 46
Garden Pea Soup 33
Gazpacho 34
Gulyassuppe 204
Harry Hatch's Lobster
  Bisque 42
Marsala and Scallop
  Soup 41
Meatball Soup 94
My Mulligatawny 40
Nelusko (Cream of
  Chicken Almond
  Soup) 41
New England Clam
  Chowder 42
New Orleans
  Bouillabaisse 194
Old-Fashioned Beef
  Vegetable Soup 44
Old-Fashioned Chicken
  and Rice 36
Onion Soup au Gratin 37

Oyster Stew 36
Pepper and Cream
  Cheese Soup 40
Potato and Cheese Soup
  312
Purée Mongole 33
Salmagundi 40
Tomato Soup 36
Tortellini Seafood Soup
  280
Vichyssoise 34

Spaghetti
Italian Meatballs for
  Spaghetti 208
Spaghetti Carbonara 276
Spaghetti Marsala 275
Spaghetti, Prosciutto and
  Gorgonzola 276
Spaghetti with Pickerel
  and Herbs 276

Spinach
Crab and Spinach
  Soufflé 238
Spinach Scallop Salad 58
Warm Spinach Salad 60

Squash
Cinnamon Spaghetti
  Squash 240

Steaks
Braised Buffalo Steak with
  Mushrooms 154
English Steak and Kidney
  Pie 88
Flank Steak Florentine 83
Herb and Spice Steaks 81
Pepper Steak 89
Philadelphia Steak and
  Cheese Sandwich 342
Pork Steak with
  Mushroom Sauce 128
Pork Steak with Pepper
  Apple Sauce 129
Steak au Poivre 81
Steak Diane 82
Steak Tartare 93
Swiss Steak 83
Venison Steaks 153

Stocks
Beef or Chicken Stock 32
Court Bouillon 32
Fish Stock 32
Vegetable Stock 32

Strawberries
Chocolate Orange
  Strawberries 367
Coeur à la Crème 321
Pepper Strawberries 382
Strawberries Romanoff
  379

Strawberry Jam 385

Sushi
Sushi 1 212
Sushi 2 212
Sushi 3 212
Sushi Rice 212

Swordfish
Dill Swordfish 168
Grilled Swordfish with
  Walnut Sauce 168

Tea
Blueberry Tea 413
Herb Tea 413
Lemon Iced Tea 414

Terrines (see also *Pâtés*)
Apple and Chicken Liver
  Terrine 28
Orange-Flavored Duck
  Terrine 26
Pistachio and Chicken
  Terrine 26

Tomatoes
Bacon, Basil Tomato
  Sandwich 323
Baked Endives in Tomato
  Cream 235
Chicken Tomato Rice
  with Old Cheddar 287
Cream of Tomato Rice 31
Fusilli with Cheese and
  Tomatoes 264
Garlic Tomato Sauté 330
Hot Chicken & Tomato
  Salad 50
Pasta Topped with
  Cheese-Stuffed
  Tomatoes 260
Potato Tomato Bake 252
Rice-Stuffed Tomatoes
  286
Rigatoni with Beef,
  Tomatoes and
  Mushrooms 274
Tomato Ketchup 256
Tomato Sauce 308
Tomato Soup 36
Tomatoes Provençale
  241

Tortellini
Curried Tortellini and
  Prawns 280
Tortellini 277
Tortellini au Gratin 279
Tortellini Marinara 278
Tortellini Salad 279
Tortellini Seafood Soup
  280

Trout
Trout Jodee 169

microwave recipe

Tuna
Tuna Melt   338

Turkey
Monte Cristo Sandwich   340
Thanksgiving Turkey   116

Veal
Blanquette de Veau   147
Escalope of Veal Cordon Bleu   142
Feta Penne with Veal Tomato Sauce   271
Rouladen   198
Swedish Meatballs   271
Veal à la Carte   144
Veal Chops in Papillote   144
Veal Croquettes   148
Veal Cutlets*   423

Veal Helena   144
Veal John B. Hoyle   143
Veal Meatballs   148
Veal Medallions in Shrimp Sauce   142
Veal Medallions with Oyster Mushrooms and Brandy Sauce   141
Veal Parmigiana   208
Veal Piccata   142
Veal Pizzaïola   146
Veal Scaloppine Velez   143
Veau Sauvage   146
Wiener Schnitzel Sandwich   335

Vegetables
(see also individual types)
Buffet Vegetables au Gratin   318

Cheese Vegetable Pâté   27
Jambalaya*   428
Old-Fashioned Beef Vegetable Soup   44
Ratatouille   234
Sweet and Sour Shredded Vegetable Salad   51
Vegetable Dip   22
Vegetable Stock   32

Venison
Venison Baden Baden   153
Venison Steaks   153

Vermicelli
Vermicelli Edmonton-Style   282
Vermicelli Pesto   282

Vermicelli with Apples   282

Waffles
Waffle Batter   356

Wontons
Curry Chicken Wontons   13
Ham and Cheese Wontons   13

Zucchini
Ratatouille   234
Zucchini Bake*   432
Zucchini Nut Bread   350
Zucchini Provençale   240

* microwave recipe

Microwave Index

A
Almond Rice Pilaf   435
Apple Crumb Pie   436
Asparagus Casserole   432

B
Bacon, Cheddar and Onion Quiche   431
Banana Muffins   438
Barbecued Cajun Ribs   427
Beef and Broccoli   422
Beef Bordelaise   422
Beef Rib Roast   422
Blueberry Muffins   438
Breakfast Cheese and Shrimp   431
Butterscotch Nut Pudding   438

C
Carrot Cake   436
Cauliflower with Orange Butter Sauce   432
Chicken Supreme with Cherries   425
Chocolate Mint Candy Pudding   439
Cornish Hens with Hunter Sauce   424
Curried Shrimp   429

D
Denver Omelet   430

G
Grasshopper Pie   437

H
Ham Casserole   426

J
Jambalaya   428

L
Lamb Chops à l'Orange   423

N
New York Chicken Wings   424

P
Pork and Snow Peas Amandine   427
Pork Roast   426

R
Roast Chicken with Honey-Garlic Sauce   424
Rocky Road Pie   437

S
Scalloped Potatoes   434
Spanish Rice   434
Stuffed Sole Mornay   428
Sweet-and-Sour Pork   426

T
Tarragon Mushrooms   434

V
Veal Cutlets   423

W
Warm Scallop Salad   429

Z
Zucchini Bake   432